W9-BXA-178

ROUSSEAU
Dreamer of Democracy

James Miller

YALE UNIVERSITY PRESS
NEW HAVEN AND LONDON

Membership card of
the Club révolutionnaire des amis de Jean-Jacques
and *Rousseau Méditant son Emile*
reproduced by courtesy of
the Musée Jean-Jacques Rousseau, Geneva.

Published with assistance from
the Louis Stern Memorial Fund.

Designed by Christopher Harris
and set in Linotron Fournier type
by Graphic Composition, Inc.
Printed in the United States of America
by BookCrafters, Inc., Chelsea, Michigan.

Library of Congress Cataloging in Publication Data

Miller, Jim, 1947–
Rousseau : dreamer of democracy.

Includes index.
1. Rousseau, Jean Jacques, 1712–1778—Political science. I. Title.
JC179.R9M54   1984   320'.01   83-27396
ISBN 0-300-03044-4

The paper in this book meets the guidelines
for permanence and durability of the
Committee on Production Guidelines for
Book Longevity of the Council on
Library Resources.

2   4   6   8   10   9   7   5   3   1

For Alexander and Sarah

Contents

vii

Acknowledgments

This study has its roots in a course given in 1966 at Pomona College by Lee McDonald, a wonderful teacher. When I finally got to teach a course on Rousseau myself, I learned much from my students at the University of Texas at Austin, particularly Susan Hinely, James Greene, and Kathleen Kelleher. A first draft of this book was made possible by a grant from the National Endowment for the Humanities.

Several colleagues offered comments on the manuscript at various stages: Jack Zammito, Mark Hulliung, James Schmidt, George Armstrong Kelly, Malcolm MacDonald, William Galston, Greil Marcus, and Jean Strouse. My father, James E. Miller, Jr., reviewed several drafts of chapter one. Maureen MacGrogan, my editor at Yale, read even more drafts of the whole manuscript—luckily for me, she has the training of a philosopher and the patience of a saint. Thanks are due to Charles Wirz of the Société Jean-Jacques Rousseau of Geneva for his help in locating the prints reproduced here. Finally, special thanks are due my dear friends Bruce Miroff, Stan Spyros Draenos, and Langdon Winner, whose detailed comments and generosity of spirit helped me to persevere.

J.M.
West Roxbury, Massachusetts
November 1983

Note on Texts and Translations

All citations from Rousseau are my own translations from the French. Where possible, I have used the text of the still unfinished Pléiade edition of the *Complete Works*. I have also included references to standard English translations.

There is one special class of terms that the reader should be aware of. Words like *Citoyen* and *Bourgeois* were legal categories in the Geneva of Rousseau's day. He was proud to be called a "Citoyen et Bourgeois" of Geneva, although the conjunction in that honored title of two terms that Karl Marx treated as antitheses ought to give the modern reader pause. A Genevan dictionary of 1679 defines a *bourgeois* as a "town-dweller. . . . Among working men, this word indicates the man in charge. . . . *(Familiar)*: *Cela est du dernier bourgeois* [the ultimate in bourgeois], meaning crude, ungallant." As an adjective, the familiar meanings of *bourgeois* may be even more surprising: "Lacking in Court graces, not altogether polite, over-familiar, insufficiently respectful." (See Pierre Goubert, *The Ancien Régime*, trans. Cox [New York, 1973], pp. 232–60.) There is something of Rousseau's demeanor and theory in that definition all right, but not quite what we might have expected.

In my own text, I have distinguished between the legal and more colloquial application of terms like citizen and bourgeois by capitalizing them in the former case but not in the latter. Rousseau himself, as it happens, plays on the ambiguity, insisting on the propriety of Genevan legal usage and then applying it generally as a theoretical norm. (See his comments in the *Social Contract*, bk. I, ch. 6; *P* III, pp. 361–62n.; *SC*, p. 54n.) In my translations also I have generally observed Rousseau's practice in capitalizing other terms, since this archaic mark of emphasis sometimes adds nuance.

To limit the proliferation of endnotes, I have placed them toward the end of paragraphs. All notes list the sources of quotations in the order in which they appear in the paragraph. Throughout, I have preferred short titles to op. cit.

Chronology

1712 Geneva's republican oligarchy revokes limited concessions to popular sovereignty passed during civil unrest of 1707.
Jean-Jacques Rousseau born in Geneva, June 28.

1728 Rousseau runs away and converts to Catholicism, thus forfeiting Genevan citizenship.

1734 Civil strife in Geneva is rekindled by new pamphlets demanding popular sovereignty.

1737 While visiting Geneva to claim his inheritance, Rousseau sees civil war erupt on August 21.

1741 Living in France, Rousseau writes his "Epistle to M. Bordes," his earliest written reference to his "helvetic muse."

1743 Appalled by the decadence he finds in the republic of Venice while serving as secretary to the French Ambassador, Rousseau forms a sustaining interest in political theory.

1749 An epiphany on the road to Vincennes convinces Rousseau that "man is naturally good" and that it is bad institutions which corrupt him; Rousseau resolves to reform himself and to explore his new ideas in writing.

1750 Rousseau's first use of the epithet "Citizen of Geneva."
Rousseau's *Discourse on the Sciences and Arts* published, bringing him fame and notoriety.

1754 Rousseau returns to Geneva, is readmitted to the church of Calvin, becomes a bona fide Citizen of Geneva, but decides to continue residing in France.

1755 Rousseau's second discourse, *On the Origin and Foundation of Inequality*, is published with a dedication praising Geneva for its "democratic government."

1758 In his open *Letter to M. d'Alembert on the Theater*, Rousseau warns Geneva to "avoid becoming corrupt."

1761 Rousseau publishes his novel *La Nouvelle Héloïse*, which becomes one of the century's best-selling books.

1762 Rousseau publishes *Emile*, his treatise on education, and the *Social Contract*, his treatise on politics; both books are censored in France, and the author driven into exile.
The government of Geneva bans *Emile* and the *Social Contract*, declaring both books subversive and the author *persona non grata*.

1763 Exiled in Neuchâtel, Rousseau renounces his Genevan Citizenship.

1764 In his polemical *Letters from the Mountain*, Rousseau urges Geneva to defend its legitimate "democratic constitution" from usurpation by a corrupt ruling class.

1765 Civil unrest returns to Geneva, in part fomented by debate over Rousseau's new book.

1768 Continuing civil strife in Geneva is averted by the compromise "Edict of 1768."

1778 Rousseau dies July 2.

1781 The publication of Rousseau's *Confessions* inspires a popular cult in France among readers devoted to the author.

1782 Revolution in Geneva, sparked by renewed demands for popular sovereignty.

1789 The French Revolution begins.

1790 Rousseau's bust is installed in the French National Assembly.

1792 Claiming the authority of Rousseau, Maximilien Robespierre urges democratic reforms to the French Constitution.

1793 The "sans-culottes" of Paris press demands for a revolutionary direct democracy; resisting these demands, Robespierre declares that "virtue" must be defended through "terror."

1794 Robespierre is guillotined; the sans-culottes suppressed.
France officially installs Rousseau in the Pantheon.

ROUSSEAU
Dreamer of Democracy

INTRODUCTION

The Great Democrat of the Eighteenth Century?

İN THE early days of the French Revolution, it is said that Jean Paul Marat held crowds in Paris spellbound by standing on a street corner and reading aloud Rousseau's *Social Contract*. A more unlikely crowd pleaser is difficult to imagine. Yet this was not an isolated incident. Shortly after the "second" Revolution of August 10, 1792, when the Tuileries were stormed and the King imprisoned, the assembly of the *Postes* section of Paris rechristened itself *La Section du Contrat Social*. In frimaire of year II, when this section held a festival to enshrine new busts of Marat and Rousseau, the crowd sang songs from Rousseau's opera *Le Devin du village*. A medallion commissioned by the section in year III depicts on one side "the cinders of J-J Rousseau deposited in an urn at the National Garden," and on the other the author looking pensive, modestly garbed in Armenian gown and squirrel fur cap, "composing his Social Contract." Such homage to Rousseau was frequent in Paris. When an aristocrat sought an old address on a boulevard recently renamed "Rousseau," the residents rudely told the disoriented visitor that they knew of no such place. Nor has the popularity of Rousseau among revolutionaries abated much over the past two hundred years. Fidel Castro packed more than a carbine and *Capital* into the Sierra Maestra; for he claims that he also "fought Battista with a copy of the *Social Contract* in his pocket."[1]

Such tales, apocryphal or not, were once thought definitive. It was widely assumed that Rousseau, of all the Enlightenment philosophers, had most profoundly influenced the French revolutionaries; that Rousseau, of them all, had most clearly justified democracy; that Rousseau had most vividly expressed a revolutionary desire. According to Michelet's classic account, by the time Voltaire and Rousseau "had formed their ideas, the Revolution was accomplished in the high realm of the mind." Acton's famous lectures are even more emphatic. Rousseau was "the author of the strongest political theory that had appeared amongst men." By applying "the ideas of pure democracy to the government of nations," he had given "the first signal of a universal subversion." His principles were so radically democratic that they were "as fatal to the Republic as to the Monarchy."

A half-century later, George Sabine, in his standard history of political theory, flatly asserted that "the great democrat of the eighteenth century was Rousseau."[2]

More recently, though, doubts about "the great democrat" have been raised. Some historians are skeptical about Rousseau's influence during the French Revolution, while other critics have wondered whether Rousseau saw himself in any meaningful sense as a democrat at all—let alone a revolutionary. Bertrand de Jouvenel finds in the *Social Contract* "not a hopeful prescription for a Republic to come, but a clinical analysis of political deterioration." Jean Starobinski believes that Rousseau was willing to settle for an illusory equality and a purely subjective feeling of freedom, while preserving domestic relations of domination and counseling the use of covert authority to manipulate others secretly. Judith Shklar, who agrees that Rousseau held some curious attitudes toward authority, distinguishes two incommensurable utopias in his work: the spartan city and the patriarchal household, neither of them particularly evocative of democracy. Finally, Alfred Cobban has argued that since Rousseau himself cannot be read accurately as an advocate of revolution or even liberal reform, it is scarcely plausible to credit or blame him for the French Revolution. Cobban's position has been supported by Joan McDonald, who cites evidence showing that relatively few people had read the *Social Contract* before 1789, and that those who actually understood the book were more often monarchists than democrats.[3]

We are confronted with two convergent but distinct lines of argument. One is primarily textual and points to Rousseau's pessimism, his passivity, his dreams of heroic authority figures, his distrust of change, his declared reservations about democracy: "A Government so perfect is not suited for men."[4] The other is historical and presents a plausible case that the impact of Rousseau's political ideas on the French Revolution was slight, despite tales like the one about Marat. The two arguments taken together amount to a devastating critique of the conventional wisdom; they affirm that whatever else he might have been, Rousseau was quite certainly *not* "the great democrat of the eighteenth century."

In this book, I will reconsider Rousseau's approach to democracy. At stake is the status of what once was commonly perceived as a dangerously radical theory of politics. Were the French revolutionaries deluded about Rousseau's relevance to their situation? I think not. For Rousseau was in fact a thinker with revolutionary things to say—particularly about democracy.

To be sure, much in the contemporary readings is compelling enough to preclude any simple reaffirmation of Rousseau the democrat. The critics are right: there *is* a problem here, and a rather complicated one at that. It will even turn out that some of the most troubling aspects of his approach to politics confirm insights offered by these critics. Yet I hope to show that Rousseau, in however problematic a fashion, did help awaken a new desire for democracy, at the same time that he defined and defended it in a new way; and moreover, that he was well aware of what he had done. If this much can be established, it will entail revising the iconoclastic conservativism of some recent interpretations. It will also restore Rousseau's work as a crucial document—arguably the decisive one—for anyone interested in modern democracy.

To assess Rousseau's political convictions, we must examine carefully the full range of his writings. In many respects, his thinking about democracy is most memorably conveyed not in the clinical language of the *Social Contract*, but rather in the poetic evocations of his dedication to Geneva of the *Second Discourse*, in his recollections of growing up in that city in the *Letter to d'Alembert*, and in the Alpine idyll of his novel *La Nouvelle Héloïse*—works of imagination that captured the fancy of his generation. By surveying his vivid scenes of Geneva, we can reconstruct a picture of Rousseau's ideal state. This picture embodies a detailed vision of civilized freedom that reconciles important aspects of two of his other social models, the spartan city and the patriarchal household. When seen in terms of this fanciful image, Rousseau's view of democracy appears in a clearer light. We can better understand how officials in Geneva could read the *Social Contract* as a seditious tract—and why the French revolutionaries seem to have attached so much importance to Rousseau's authority.

The organization of the book can be summarized briefly. The first half revolves around Rousseau's relationship to Geneva. Since this relationship involves the collision of one man's wishes with political realities, it is essential to examine Rousseau's assessment of the imagination and its capacities. Thus I have opened with a chapter on reverie that introduces a major theme: the central role played by imagination in Rousseau's transvaluation of democracy. To make plain what is fantasy in his vision of democracy, it is also essential to review the facts about his life and times, particularly his fate in the city of his birth. So I have composed a highly selective biography, focused on Rousseau's stormy love affair with Geneva. I have interwoven this narrative with four exegetical chapters, arranged to synchronize roughly with the chronology of Rousseau's life: first, a reconstruction of the democratic city evoked in Rousseau's Alpine reveries; second, an interpretation of the *Social Contract*, analyzing Rousseau's attitude in that book toward democracy and the city of Geneva; third, a summary of Rousseau's *Letters Written from the Mountain*, showing how his imaginative reconstruction of Genevan history in this work confirms his esteem for democracy; and, finally, an analysis of Rousseau's idea of democracy, and of why it represents something radically new in the history of political thought. By combining biography and exegesis in this way, a kind of montage is created, designed to show how Rousseau developed his strange new view of politics.

There follow two long chapters, one on the historical impact of Rousseau's democratic theory, the other on its philosophical cogency. In the first of these chapters, I retell the story of Rousseau's influence on the French Revolution and offer some conjectures about how it was effected, in the hope of clarifying "the central mystery"[5] of the Revolution: the origin of modern democracy. In the next chapter, by analyzing in some detail Rousseau's theory of free will, I explore the logic of his own central justification for democracy: freedom. Finally, in a brief epilogue, I summarize the fate of democracy after Rousseau, pointing out his enduring significance.

This book grew out of an interest in the history of modern democracy. In the course of my research, it became obvious that Rousseau's thought not only plays a pivotal role in this history, but also that the implications of this role have rarely been taken seriously enough.

It is often assumed that modern democracy appears as the progressive result of a gradual evolution, realizing the best in a great heritage of Western political thought. A suspiciously parochial tradition is then taken for granted. First practiced by the ancient Athenians, fruitfully justified in the republican theories of Aristotle and his successors, developed through the proud struggles between people and king in England, democracy finally bursts into full bloom through the English Civil War, the American Revolution, and the works of such modern luminaries as Locke, Rousseau, and Thomas Jefferson.

This account is misleading. Democracy before Rousseau's day was generally held to be a fool's paradise, if not worse. At the zenith of direct democracy in classical Athens, one critic called it a "patent absurdity"—and so it seemed for centuries afterward to political theorists from Plato to James Madison. Looking at the historical evidence critically, the most striking thing about democracy is the almost universal contempt in which the pure form was held for over two thousand years.

What needs to be explored, in other words, is not the gradual unfurling of the democratic ideal, but rather the relatively abrupt reversal in the fortunes of theories and parties of professed democratic inspiration. This reversal can be dated with some precision. It occurs not in the English Civil War or the American Revolution, but through the French Revolution. And its chief architect is not John Locke or Thomas Jefferson—it is Jean-Jacques Rousseau.[6]

By studying Rousseau carefully, we may therefore expect to discover some of the reasons for the rise of modern democracy, as well as some of the ingredients in its original appeal. His thinking marks a turning point. Through the French Revolution, democracy became an ideal of life and death importance to a broad mass of people captivated by the promise of an unprecedented human harmony. Reading Rousseau makes such hopes understandable. When he dreamt of a true democracy, the "Citizen of Geneva" envisioned something more than new laws or a new form of government. He imagined a new form of secular redemption— an end to alienation, an apotheosis of freedom. In discussions of Marxism and debates about participatory democracy, this dream still looms large. Exploring its sources is one way of breaking its spell and renewing a field of discourse that Rousseau, by the very clarity of his vision and the precision of his principles, helped both to constitute and to close.

I

The Rhetoric of Reverie

W E START where Rousseau himself started, in "the empire of imagination."
It is worth recalling Rousseau's account of the epiphany he experienced
on the road to Vincennes in the summer of 1749. He had set out to visit
Diderot, but the day was hot, the way long. To entertain himself, he had brought
along a copy of *le Mercure de France*. Upon seeing the question proposed by the
Academy of Dijon—"Has the restoration of the sciences and arts tended to
purify morals?"—Rousseau felt dizzy, faint, overcome. Gasping for breath, he
collapsed under a tree, weeping in agitation. "If anything ever resembled a sudden inspiration, it was the motion that was made in me as I read that; suddenly I
felt my mind dazzled by a thousand lights; crowds of lively ideas presented themselves at once, with a force and confusion that threw me into inexpressible turmoil; I felt my head seized with a vertigo like that of intoxication. . . . Oh, Sir, if
ever I could have written the quarter of what I saw and felt under that tree, with
what clarity would I have revealed all the contradictions of the social system,
with what force would I have exposed all the abuses of our institutions, with
what simplicity would I have demonstrated that man is naturally good and that
it is through these institutions alone that men become bad."[1]

Rousseau claimed that this one fleeting moment of ecstatic reverie laid the
basis for his entire lifework. "All my little passions were stifled by enthusiasm
for truth, freedom and virtue"—a trinity of values that would, in time, drive him
to formulate a critique of progress, an attack on inequality, a treatise on education, and, finally, his new doctrine of democracy. Yet at the start, he simply
grasped an image: "On the spot itself there was written only the personification
of Fabricius"—that unflinchingly noble Roman assigned the big question in
Rousseau's *First Discourse*: "Gods! What has become of those thatched roofs and
rustic hearths where moderation and virtue used to dwell?"[2]

Such vivid visions were not the work of any ordinary soul, as Rousseau was
the first to admit. "It is impossible for men, and difficult for nature herself, to
surpass the riches of my imagination." But what were these riches, how did he

mine them, and how should we evaluate them? What is the significance of Rousseau's epiphany on the road to Vincennes? What is the meaning and merit of images like Fabricius, and what is their relationship to those political ideas that, today, are more familiar? What are the perimeters and peculiar topography of this "land of chimeras"?[3] Since we will be dealing at length with one man's imagination, it will be good to know just what this one man believed he was doing with his wishful thinking, his ecstatic reveries—and, above all, his bewitching images of democracy in Geneva.

Images and Ideas

To appreciate the novelty—and complications—of Rousseau's appeal to imagery, it is useful to begin with the tradition that he inherited. When he speaks of "images" and "ideas," Rousseau generally observes a classical distinction: "idea" means a reasoned concept, a term of value in a logical argument. "Image," on the other hand, means a picture grasped by the senses, a visual impression—or, by analogy, any verbal figure or panorama that makes a similar impression. Rousseau describes the difference in these terms: "Before the age of reason, the child receives not ideas but images; and the difference between the two is that images are only absolute pictures of sensible objects, while ideas are notions of objects determined by relations. . . . When one imagines, one does nothing but see."[4] Rooted in the reception of visual impressions, the image first appears as a kind of pictograph stamped on a wax tablet, allowing the mind to become a storehouse of memory traces, each framing an "absolute picture"—a picture we can summon and represent, at will or by whim, whenever we imagine.

A similar understanding appears in Plato, a thinker Rousseau treated as a touchstone, even when he was silently struggling against him.[5] According to Plato, the crown of thought is the idea: an eternal, unchanging pattern, defining the species of individual objects that conform to it. While images are immediate and sensuous, participating, through perception, in the world of appearances surrounding us, ideas are invisible forms, confirmed only through the abstract medium of reasoning. From the standpoint of logic, images are like a ladder to be discarded once the mind is able to climb on its own, unaided by the senses. It was in this spirit that Plato censured the poet: his seductive imagery could lead the soul astray. Yet iconography—the art of communicating with images—remains an integral part of Plato's philosophy. For example, the image of the cave in the *Republic* dramatically illustrates the crux of Plato's doctrine; it helps the student grasp the notion of true knowledge, and it helps the philosopher, who is capable of such knowledge, remember the reasoning behind his own convictions.[6]

It is generally acknowledged that Rousseau, like Plato, was not averse to using images as a means of illustrating ideas. He, too, had recourse to images as an aid to memory, just as he felt the need to express a doctrine authoritatively without reasoning, "to persuade without convincing"—the same need that led Plato to use images to create myths for the masses of men he regarded as incapable of real knowledge.[7]

Yet there is something more in Rousseau. Sometimes he defends the autonomous value of imagery, the intrinsic worth of his own vivid reveries. Reluctantly, with great hesitation and many doubts, he inverts the Platonic evaluation of the relationship between image and idea. In so doing, he creates a counterweight to Plato's ideal republic—and opens the way for a radically new view of democracy.

Reverie

Rousseau was a man possessed by imagination. He was also a man intensely ambivalent about its power. Like his contemporaries, he considered the imagination to be our "talent of creating by imitating" those impressions relayed to the senses directly.[8] A source of new images rent from memories of old, imagination appears to offer a path beyond palpable experience—a way to depict an absent world, where familiar things may be represented in fresh forms.

This talent both repelled and attracted Rousseau. If we lacked the ability to imagine the feelings of another person—if our imagination, in pity, never took us "outside ourselves"—we could not be fully human. "He who imagines nothing is aware only of himself; he is isolated in the midst of humanity." Yet our ability to imagine fulfilling new desires, by extending "the measure of the possible" for us, might also destroy a happy balance between wants and the strength to satisfy them. "Whim (*fantasie*) succeeds need; thus prejudice and opinion take their first roots."[9]

Late in his life, looking back on a career filled with prodigious feats of fantasy, Rousseau tried to summarize his contradictory convictions. Yes, an "embittered heart" might fill the imagination "with a thousand deadly objects." "Jealousies, rivalries, offenses, vendettas, discontents"—a host of sorry matters could indeed poison our daydreams. But "whoever knows how to soar in the ethereal regions," leaving behind such petty terrestrial concerns, "can brave the blows of fate and the senseless judgment of men. . . . Such finally is the empire of imagination . . . that it engenders not only the virtues and vices, but also the goods and ills of human life; and it is principally the manner in which we devote ourselves to it that renders men good or evil, happy or unhappy here below."[10]

This passage is faithful to Rousseau's own experience. Instead of simply rejecting all the images that overtook him, he felt some to be of singular value. As a matter of biographical fact, he believed that his thinking was always intimately linked to the exercise of imagination: "I have sometimes thought quite deeply, but rarely with pleasure, almost always against my inclination and as if by force:

reverie relaxes and entertains me, reflection wearies and saddens me; to think was always for me an arduous vocation without charm. Sometimes my reveries end in meditation, but more often my meditations end in reverie, and during these deviations my soul strays and glides through the universe on the wings of imagination, amid ecstasies surpassing every other delight." [11]

Rêverie is a term that recurs throughout his writing, although he never explicitly defines it. Etymologically, *rêverie* derives from *rêver*, "to dream", a term that originally meant "to wander," like a vagabond, later coming to mean as well "to think profoundly." It is a word for wandering thoughts. As a form of contemplation, it is evocative of certain indolence and insularity, an intuitive way of thinking divorced from utilitarian interests, unconcerned with the commerce of everyday life. It follows no rules, allowing the mind the run of its own spontaneous motion, without diversion, obstacle, or conscious aim. Akin to meditation, yet undisciplined by reason, a kind of free association engendered by the free play of fantasy, reverie for Rousseau is a source of ideas as well as images, a questionable mode of thought that nonetheless opens up new perspectives, new ways of seeing the world: setting out on his wanderings, Rousseau "felt that a new paradise awaited me at the door; I thought only of going out to find it." [12] Reverie often takes the form of a gentle daydream. But it can also end in a moment teeming with insights, overwhelming with the force of revelation—as witness the extraordinary significance Rousseau attached to his epiphany on the road to Vincennes in 1749.

This was no isolated incident. As we shall see, his thinking about democracy grew out of reveries about his native city of Geneva. His memories of this place, richly embroidered by fantasy, crystallized into a picture of politics perfected. Out of this picture, Rousseau formed a new image of democracy—an image that illustrates the *Social Contract* and holds the key to what is revolutionary in his political thought.

"Oh," exclaims Rousseau at one point in his *Confessions*, "if one were able to keep a record of a feverish man's dreams, what grand and sublime things would sometimes be seen to result from his deliriums!" The problem, obviously, is to make one man's delirium seem grand and sublime to others. How to transcribe the sweep, the passionate certainty, of reveries like those Rousseau experienced about Geneva and on the road to Vincennes? Three avenues for expressing such insights lay open to him. He could describe as vividly as possible just what the experience was like; this he did primarily in his confessional works. By the adroit use of figures like that of Fabricius, by elaborating new images of familiar places like Geneva, and by conjuring up whole new fictional worlds, he could attempt to evoke a similar vision in others; this he did throughout his works, but most forthrightly in *La Nouvelle Héloïse*, his popular novel. Finally, he could apply reasoning to his reveries and let ideas supercede images; this he labored to do in his great theoretical treatises—for only a rigorous, logical argument can win over the skeptic, that "independent man" Rousseau imagines as his alter ego in the first draft of the *Social Contract*. [13]

The Limits of Reason—"At a Glance"

Rousseau wanted to be taken seriously as a thinker. He knew that most philosophers regarded the imagination and its products with suspicion. The modern authorities were even more censorious than Plato. Claiming that images did not pertain to the rational essence of thinking, Descartes dismissed them as mere "pictures in the corporeal imagination," belonging to the body, not the mind. For Hobbes, the imagination was "nothing but decaying sense." About the creative use of imagery, John Locke was equally adamant: "All the artificial and figurative applications of words eloquence hath invented, are for nothing else but to insinuate wrong ideas, move the passions, and thereby mislead the judgment; and so indeed are perfect cheats."[14]

For a serious thinker, the use of ideas is essential: to this extent, Rousseau retains his allegiance to the tradition of thought inaugurated by Plato and renewed by Descartes. Only by reasoning can a person define and clarify the "grand and sublime things" seen during his daydreams.

Yet Rousseau is also convinced that even the clearest ideas remain open to doubt. His ambivalent attitude to the classical tradition of philosophy—and the unusual weight he places on his own political imagery—springs not just from his personal taste for reverie, but also from an implicit, and distinctive, notion of the role played by imagination in attaining moral wisdom.

According to Rousseau, Plato's theory of knowledge—his belief in an unchanging realm of transcendent, intelligible being—cannot be sustained. "What do we see, what do we know, of that which exists?" The more one learns, "the more one finds reasons for doubt." There are no certain first principles on which knowledge may rest. "It is necessary to finish where Descartes began: *I think, therefore I am.*" In this situation, recourse to imagination is unavoidable. "Impenetrable mysteries surround us on all sides," declares the Savoyard Vicar, Rousseau's moral mentor in *Emile*. "For piercing them, we believe we have intelligence, but we have only imagination. Each blazes through this imaginary world a trail that he believes to be good; none can know whether his leads to the goal."[15]

One way to quell such doubts is to make plain the trails blazed by imagination: for it is the value we grant our fundamental intuitions that establishes the perspectives clarified by reasoning. In order to avert the suspicion of mere whimsy, Rousseau will thus follow a "simple method" whenever he addresses a new topic: "I will establish the state of the question anew, I will reveal my sentiment anew." It is in this spirit that Rousseau reports his epiphany on the road to Vincennes. "Vain and fallacious knowledge" must be measured against "the sovereign intelligence that sees at a glance the truth of all things"—the kind of intelligence exercised in reverie.[16]

Rousseau's phrasing here recalls Pascal. An intelligence that "sees at a glance," Pascal thought, evinced *l'esprit de finesse*. This "intuitive spirit" Pascal distinguished from the "logical spirit," or *l'esprit géometrique*. The great mathematician considered *l'esprit géometrique* by itself one-sided and insufficient. Formal reasoning needed to be oriented by an intuitive clarification of what the mind regularly did "tacitly, naturally and artlessly." At issue for *l'esprit de finesse* are principles "in common use and before the eyes of everyone. There is no need to turn our heads, or to strain ourselves; it is only a question of good sight, but it must be good. . . . The thing itself must be seen all at once, at a glance, and not as a result of progressive reasoning, at least up to a point." In its approach to this synoptic intuitiveness—what Pascal called *l'esprit de finesse* and Rousseau called *rêverie*— the mind acquires its specific gravity and elucidates the grounds of its own existence.[17] The beginning of wisdom is to appreciate—not disparage—the imagination.

The Value of Images

It was Rousseau's conviction that "science is not made for man in general." It has sometimes been assumed that by saying this, he meant to deprecate the capacity of ordinary men to reason rigorously. And so he did. But Rousseau also wished to emphasize that ordinary men had more important resources at their command. "Man is born to act and to think, not to reflect." Though few possess anything like the full rigor of Pascal's *esprit géometrique*, something like his *esprit de finesse* is within the grasp of everyone, for its principles are "before the eyes of everyone." These principles are all that the ordinary man needs in order to think and to act rightly; as we shall see, they are all that an ordinary man needs if he is to become a good citizen of a just state. In order to heed these principles, a man must be taught to think for himself. Like Rousseau's paradigmatic student, Emile, he must learn to trust his own intuitions and sentiments. Beyond that, he needs only to grasp a few key ideas, remember them with the help of images, and cultivate a taste for quiet meditation. Such a wise man, lucid in his insight, aware of his ignorance, would be neither bewitched by a mere show of scientific rigor nor incapable of appreciating its true worth: "If all men were like Socrates, then science would do them no harm. But neither would they have any need of it."[18]

Ideas remain important. But for a sound education, more is required. The mind needs something more vivid for recollection, the passions something more arresting for inspiration. "Always to reason is the mania of petty minds," writes Rousseau: "One of the errors of our age is to use reason in too naked a form, as if men were all mind. By neglecting the language of signs that speak to the imagination, they have lost the most energetic of languages." Thus the tutor determines to impress moral ideas on Emile "by moving his imagination." He "will animate the force of reasoning with images and figures." As Rousseau writes elsewhere, "clearly the most eloquent speeches are those containing the most imagery." The aim is apparent: to cultivate rather than condemn the capacities of the imagination. "Do not suffocate the imagination, guide it, lest it engender monsters."[19]

Because images have such power over the mind, novels and plays need to be judged by moral criteria. "To give to works of imagination the sole utility they can have, it is necessary to direct them," lest they degenerate into idle entertainment. "I consider all dramatic authors corrupters of the people," Rousseau says with preemptory decisiveness—only to add: "or whoever, letting himself be amused by images, is neither capable of considering them from their true point of view, nor of giving to these fables the correctives they need." Grasping the power of figures and considering images "from their true point of view," the novelist with moral concerns has aims higher than amusement. Instead of catering to an ill-formed popular taste and celebrating the conventional prejudices, his imagery—his personifications and narrative panoramas—ought to be used to "lead all back to nature; to give to men a love for a simple and egalitarian life; to cure them of the whims of opinion, restoring to them a taste for real pleasures; to make them love solitude and peace; to hold them at some distance from one another; and, in place of arousing them to crowd into towns, to incline them to spread themselves equally over the land, to vitalize it from all sides."[20]

The Virtue of Reverie

Yet Rousseau is being slightly disingenuous here. Insofar as he makes it sound as if the utility of images lies in their capacity to illustrate ideas, he is repeating a Platonic truism. Elsewhere, though, he recounts the genesis of his political ideas—and of his own novel, La Nouvelle Héloïse—in a fashion that makes clear the autonomous origin and truth value of imagery. For him, reverie precedes reasoning, and the images produced by imagination come before the clear and distinct ideas produced by reasoning. "Since objects in general make less of an impression on me than does the memory of them, and as all my ideas are in images, the first lines to be etched in my brain have remained there, and those imprinted in the sequel have combined with rather than effaced them."[21] His ideas—all of them—are in images. This is something new—for him, something embarrassingly at odds with the stern teachings of Plato and Descartes.

Yet so it was that he envisioned Fabricius during his vertigo on the road to Vincennes. So it was that his political ideas grew out of his memories of Geneva. And so it was that, while daydreaming on his solitary walks at the Hermitage in 1756, Rousseau found his spirit exalted by the magnificence of nature spread before him. Images of noble men and virtuous women arose within, forming "a genuinely new spectacle," a picture of perfect love. "I made a golden age at my whim," he confessed. "The impossibility of reaching real beings threw me into the land of chimeras, and seeing none that existed worthy of my delirium, I nurtured it in an ideal world which my creative imagination soon peopled with beings according to my own heart." Thus was born La Nouvelle Héloïse.[22]

In the seclusion of his country retreat, Rousseau was free to dream. In his reveries, he could develop "ways of seeing and feeling" other than those prompted by "the commerce of the world." A "small number of images always return," and the "more profound my reverie, the more vividly it paints them." Thus freed from "the cramped prison of personal interest" and "delivered from all the terrestrial passions which the tumult of social life engenders," the soul, in raising itself "on the wings of imagination," can "leap above this atmosphere" and banish afar "opinion, prejudices, all the artificial passions."[23]

In other words, the images produced by the imagination can express a purity missing from the world of everyday experience. By enabling the mind to transcend the imperfections of this world, reverie brings us closer to the innocence of an undefiled nature—and closer to what Rousseau felt were the figurative origins of all language—than the most subtle reasoning.[24]

We have arrived at the crux of Rousseau's implicit inversion of Platonism. For Rousseau in effect frees the image from its subordination to the idea, allying it instead with the free play of fantasy, the free association of reverie. Where Plato ostensibly establishes the perfect polity of the *Republic* through a rational dialectic, Rousseau, in constructing the society of *La Nouvelle Héloïse*—and in creating his own picture of a perfect republic—trusts to the resources of the imagination. Indicative of this subtle inversion is the opening sentence of "On Theatrical Imitation," his "Essay taken from the dialogues of Plato," written at roughly the same time as *La Nouvelle Héloïse*. "The more I think about the establishment of our imaginary republic," writes Rousseau, "the more it seems to me to have prescribed for us laws useful and appropriate to the nature of man." In its emphasis on *l'imaginaire*, this misrepresentation of Plato's dialectic offers a revealing symptom of Rousseau's real relationship to Plato. To be sure, the imaginary in Rousseau is subsequently expressed and defended through reasoned principles and maxims. Yet for Rousseau, unlike Plato, it is the "sacred fire" of reverie, the spontaneous upsurge of the imaginary in the individual's poetic experience, that initially clears the ground for reasoning, by moving the soul beyond quotidian concerns and securing for it a disinterested outlook on the whole.[25]

The Oracle of Geneva

The image in Rousseau thus becomes a potential badge of autonomous insight, unencumbered by inherited truisms. With the honest use of images as well as ideas, he even believes that it may be possible to establish a perfect standard by which others can measure the real world.[26]

The value of that standard Rousseau leaves for others to judge. By developing his images in conjunction with ideas, by composing reasoned principles and maxims—and by confessing the large role played by imagination in his own thinking—Rousseau enables others to decide whether his reveries are of any earthly use. As his insistence on tempering imagination with reason suggests, he never forgot the dangers—of frustration and delusion—built into the transcending power of reverie.

Even so, in the images of perfection produced by his reveries, Rousseau found a pedagogical tool of the first importance. Lacking a world hospitable to a healthy appetite for freedom and virtue, certain chimeras may be of use to the man who, by cultivating his own "intuitive spirit," wishes to preserve such ennobling desires.

Among the surviving notes for his projected "Political Institutions," we find Rousseau musing over the merits of Rome and Sparta as ancient models worthy of emulation. He also seems to have had in mind a passage from an essay by Montaigne, "Of Repentance." At one point in this essay, Montaigne rejects the idea, which he attributes to Pythagoras, that men can purify their souls by communing with divine icons: "I do not follow the belief of the sect of Pythagoras, that men can take on a new soul when they approach the simulacra of the Gods to receive their oracles."[27]

Rousseau ignores Montaigne's skepticism. In his own ruminations, he explores a different possibility suggested by Montaigne's account of the Pythagorean practice. Perhaps a kind of purification, repentance, and rebirth *are* possible—not by communing with "the simulacra of the Gods," but by communing with images of *human* perfection, such as those he believes offered by Rome and Sparta.

In his notes, Rousseau writes that "I am pleased to turn my eyes toward these venerable images of antiquity." (Where *images* stands in the sentence, he has crossed out *simulacres*, which in turn he had substituted for *majestueux monuments*.) Why do these particular graphic memorials to antiquity—these majestic simulacra—enchant him? Because, through these images, his intuitive understanding "sees men raised by sublime institutions to the highest degree of grandeur and virtue human wisdom can attain. In its turn, the soul soars, and courage is kindled in surveying [he has crossed out "in reading"] these respectable sights. In a way, one participates in the heroic actions of great men; it seems that a meditation on their grandeur communicates a part of it to us; and that one would be able to say of their personalities and their orations what Pythagoras said of the simulacra of the Gods: they give a new soul to those who draw near them to receive their oracles."[28]

Rousseau himself wished to give men a "new soul." He, too, bequeathed to posterity his own political oracles. We will find them in their purest form neither in the ideas of the *Social Contract* nor in the traditional figures of antiquity he so fondly resurrected, but rather in his own most personal reveries of a perfect freedom, in his graphic images of democracy in Geneva: the place where he was born, the homeland of his dreams.

(1712–1754)

The City and the Citizen of Geneva

GENEVA WAS an anomaly in eighteenth-century Europe. Bordered by Savoy and France, it was a Calvinist republic in the midst of Catholic kingdoms. In a continent dominated by giant nations, it was a small city-state, its borders confined, its population no more than 25,000. Even when compared with its Swiss neighbors, the cantons of Vaud and Valais, Geneva seemed unusual. For while they were rugged and rural, regions that survived on farming, Geneva, standing at the crossroads of the Alps, was cosmopolitan and commercial, a city rich in trade. A major center of banking, it was renowned for its literate population. It housed a major academy, several important book publishers, and a large number of prominent authors. The celebrated eighteenth-century naturalists Bonnet and De Luc lived there. So did Jean-Jacques Burlamaqui, the widely read professor of jurisprudence, much admired for his lucid style. Given the celebrity of its authors, publishers, and academy, it was no wonder that this city should attract the attention of knowledgeable outsiders like Voltaire, only mildly surprising when d'Alembert wrote a major essay on it for Diderot's *Encyclopedia*. For here, it seemed, was a city of sensible proportions and enlightened customs, "rich in its freedom and commerce," blessed with an abundance of material goods, an unusually well-educated population, and a remarkably prudent government.[1]

A Democracy?

According to d'Alembert, the government of Geneva enjoyed "all of the advantages and none of the difficulties of democracy." The "advantages" were presumably conferred by the General Council, an assembly of all citizens, which, in principle, possessed the power of legislation. Citizens were male heads of households long established in the city. Excluded where those "not yet twenty-five, bankrupt individuals, and those who have had some disgrace." Also excluded were "Natives" and "Inhabitants," relatively recent occupants and transient visitors denied the rights of full citizenship. In the Geneva of the mid-eighteenth century, that amounted to a lot of exclusions. According to d'Alembert, only about fifteen hundred men could vote in the General Council. But in the Europe of his day, the General Council must have nonetheless been a striking phenomenon. For in what monarchy could the citizens assemble in public to vote on their laws?

The appearance, however, was more impressive than the reality. For the "difficulties of democracy" were avoided by the concentration of effective power in the hands of four Syndics and a Small Council with twenty members. Although the Syndics were elected by the General Council, the Citizens had to choose them from a list of eight candidates supplied by the Small Council. The Small Council itself was selected by the wealthier citizens leagued in a Council of Two Hundred; new members of the Two Hundred were appointed, in turn, by the Small Council.

In truth, Geneva's government had "none of the difficulties of democracy" because it was not one. It was a functioning oligarchy. To quote d'Alembert, "Everything is under the direction of the Syndics, everything emanates from the Small Council for deliberation, and everything returns to it for execution."[2] By law, common Citizens could neither convene the General Council nor introduce legislation before it. Both powers were privileges of the Small Council.

Throughout the eighteenth century, Geneva was divided into two camps. On the one side stood the patrician ruling elite, beneficiaries of the trade in commodities and currency that passed through the favorably placed city. On the other side stood the bulk of the common Citizens and Bourgeois, most of them independent artisans, many of them watchmakers (a census in 1799 counted an astounding 6,000 people employed in the trade). What one historian has called "the golden age of Genevan capitalism" led to increasing polarization. When the rich got richer, they didn't hide their affluence, a display that offended many of the artisans, particularly those with a religious commitment to the discipline of labor. Theocracy was acquiring the vestments of plutocracy. Simple men of conscience were not pleased.[3]

Early in the eighteenth century, popular discontent had found a focus and a martyr. The hero was Pierre Fatio, a man whom the Small Council had appointed chairman of a committee to hear the grievances of the commoners. A citizen of impeccably patrician ancestry, Fatio was nonetheless impressed by the logic of popular demands for a larger share in political power. An eloquent orator and charismatic leader, Fatio had the talents to make these demands matter. The Small Council was duly appalled when it heard his committee's report in 1707. In this document, Fatio upheld the sovereignty of the people, the equality of all citizens, and the subordination of all magistrates to the body of the citizens. Even worse, to implement and protect these principles, he recommended that the constitution be revised, and that the General Council of all Citizens meet annually (instead of whenever the Syndics and Small Council chose) "to establish or to change the laws and edicts."[4]

At three General Council meetings in May of that year, the patrician party did battle with Fatio's faction over these proposed innovations. In an attempt to ram through a compromise, the Small Council submitted for consideration only their own proposal. This conceded the utility of regularly scheduled meetings of the General Council but set them only once every five years. Despite considerable popular support, Fatio's strength was not sufficient to force his original proposals before the General Council. In protest over how the whole affair had been handled, he and his supporters abstained on the final vote. Yet even in defeat, Fatio was hailed by many commoners as "our liberator." Shortly afterward, he was arrested, and eventually he was shot.

Bereft of leadership, the popular movement was momentarily crushed. At the first scheduled meeting of the General Council in 1712, the Small Council made certain that even the concession of periodic meetings was revoked. Yet the events of 1707 had raised the issue of popular sovereignty too vividly to be soon forgotten. Moreover, the fact that the opposition had been suppressed did not make it any less volatile. Many of the common Citizens were armed members of the civic militia. When the artisans moved their informal political clubs, or "circles," out of public view, they took with them their arms, organizing what amounted to a clandestine popular militia. From 1707 on, the patricians and the Citizens and Bourgeois were thus destined for conflict—a conflict to be fought over the terms of popular sovereignty, and a conflict with the potential of turning violent.

New strains appeared in 1734, when a pamphlet on behalf of the popular party was published, only to be condemned by the Small Council. According to the pamphlet's author, "Freedom is the right in a State which renders sovereign those who use it, which prevents anything being performed without the consent of those who possess this right. . . . A free people is then one which has the power to reject or to approve, to consent to or to oppose the changes that someone wants to lay down or to repeal, and this is a right that Nature has given to men, and which all prudent and wise peoples have conserved in order to oppose the tyranny of those to whom they have confided government and authority; a right for which they ought to sacrifice their goods and their lives."[5] According to this writer, the Small Council had usurped the sovereignty of the people. According to the Small Council, the writer of the pamphlet had raised the specter of sedition.

More trouble followed. A group of Citizens questioned the Small Council: "To what will our freedom be reduced, if we cannot prescribe it for ourselves, if we cannot change the Laws and the Government as soon as a great number among us indicate the desire?" Commissioners named by the Small Council replied: "Freedom . . . does not consist of license, nor of independence, nor in the confusion of changes and novelties. It consists in living as our fathers have lived, quietly and peacefully; entirely secure in our person, our goods, our possessions, our rights and privileges."[6]

Political pamphlets besieged the city. In "Conversation of a Citizen with a new bourgeois in catechism form," it was explained that in a democracy like Geneva's, the people ought to be sovereign; the Syndics had been elected, "not to govern as masters, but as officers subjected to the laws of the people." Patrician pamphlet writers countered such claims by arguing that "the current government is the gentlest and most equitable in the world." To change the government would be to risk disorder and chaos, for no good reason. Moreover, the people had contracted with the government—a reciprocal engagement enjoining the people to obey and the magistrates to rule, both according to the terms of the original contract.[7]

In an attempt to calm the mounting tension, an official government report was issued. It declared that the aim of government was to preserve order as well as freedom. To insure stability, "this fundamental constitution of the State can be dissolved neither by those who govern nor by those who are governed. It can be dissolved ... only by common accord, by the consent of both parties." In other words, the General Council had no unilateral power to rewrite the laws. Finally, to quell any lingering doubts about what form of government Geneva in fact had, the report decreed that it was "neither a pure democracy, nor a pure aristocracy, but an *aristo-democracy*."[8]

Matters could no longer be settled by decree. Wanting something more than disingenuous neologisms, the Citizens and Bourgeois of the popular party continued to press for more political power, sensing weakness on the part of the patricians. In the adamant words of a remonstration from 1736, "Our government is purely democratic." This petitioner explained that "in order to give a more precise and comprehensive idea of our Government, it is necessary to distinguish carefully the Right of Sovereignty with its Exercise; for a Sovereign, while conserving all its Rights, may nevertheless confide their exercise to whomever it pleases."[9]

Meanwhile, unrest was rife in several regiments of the civic militia. On August 21, 1737, a number of armed militia members took to the streets on behalf of the popular cause. This insurrection finally forced the patrician party to solicit aid from France, Berne, and Zurich. Intervening on behalf of the government, the three foreign powers subsequently helped arbitrate the dispute. The resulting Mediation of 1738 largely ratified the position of the ruling elite, adding the threat of renewed outside intervention if civil war again broke out. But several concessions were made to the Citizens and Bourgeois. One was to confirm a "right of representation" for all Citizens, enabling any group of them to protest abuses of government by petitioning the Small Council. Another was to call the General Council a "sovereign council" and to invest it nominally with "legislative, elective and confederative" powers. Yet by the terms of the Mediation, the General Council in fact still could not initiate new laws, could not negotiate with foreign powers, and could elect officials only from a list drawn up by the Small Council. Even the "representations" protected by law could always be rejected by the Small Council, which thus remained implicitly the sole arbiter of integrity in the government. And the chief effect of calling the General Council "sovereign" was to give the Citizens and Bourgeois a semantic weapon—one which they eagerly exploited at intervals over the following years.[10]

An Artisan's Education

This was the political climate surrounding the young Jean-Jacques Rousseau. Born in 1712, he grew up in the faubourg de Saint-Gervais, a quarter of Geneva largely populated by artisans and notorious as a center of popular agitation.

Politics, however, was but a backdrop to his early life. His childhood was not a particularly secure one. His mother, from the well-born family of Bernard, died a few days after his birth. His father Isaac, who aspired to upper-crust respectability, was a journeyman watchmaker with an irrepressible taste for sport and adventure, preferring the hunt and travel to the humdrum routines of family and work. By all accounts, he was a proud man, jealous of his freedom, firm in asserting his rights as a Citizen of Geneva. Like many watchmakers, he resented being ordered about and refused to be regarded as an ignorant commoner. He owned a small library and considered himself a man of independent judgment as well as independent means. Taking care to interest his youngest son in ennobling books, he supplied Jean-Jacques with Plutarch and Ovid as well as sentimental novels. Feeling himself at home in these imaginary worlds of heroes and lovers, Jean-Jacques proved himself an eager autodidact.[11]

As he later wrote, he "felt before thinking," and first became aware of his own feelings through the books that he read: "I do not know how I learned to read; I only remember my first readings and their effect upon me: it is the time from which I date the unbroken consciousness of myself." His imagination captured, he learned his lessons well. In the reveries excited by his reading, he conflated his father with the noble heroes of antiquity: "Continuously preoccupied with Rome and Athens; living, so to speak, among their great men, myself born a Citizen of a Republic, the son of a father whose love of his fatherland was his strongest passion, I was inflamed by his example; and supposed myself a Greek or Roman; I became the character whose life I was reading: the story of feats of perseverance and boldness was so striking to me that it made my eyes sparkling and my voice strong." Thus were the first images stamped on Rousseau's mind; through them he glimpsed the heroic actions of great men and felt for himself something of their spirit.[12]

His readings, however, were interrupted in 1722. One day in June of that year, his father was in a field hunting when he was confronted by the landlord, one M. Gautier, a captain in the service of Saxony with connections to the Small Council of Geneva. According to the report Gautier later filed with the Geneva police, Rousseau was asked to "take care not to damage our meadows," whereupon Isaac aimed his gun at the landlord and then went on his way. Four months later, Isaac and his nemesis chanced to meet again in the city. Rousseau, still testy about their previous encounter, suggested that they settle matters like gentlemen with a duel outside the city. Gautier, inflated with his own status, considered the idea preposterous. Intending apparently to belittle him, the landowner replied to the watchmaker that "with men of his sort," a sword "only served as a stick." Furious at having his honor and ability impugned, Isaac drew his sword and struck the nobleman on the cheek, shouting, "Listen to me, I'll give you something to remember. I am Rousseau! I am Rousseau!" When the landowner filed his complaint, Isaac, fearful of arrest, fled from Geneva, leaving the ten-year-old Jean-Jacques to be raised by a country clergyman.[13]

But Isaac was no more responsible as a father from afar. Three years later, he stopped sending money to the clergyman. Jean-Jacques was forced to become an apprentice, first to a lawyer, then to an engraver. The engraver treated him so brutally that he ran away frequently. Twice he found himself locked outside the city gates overnight. Twice he returned, to be punished. The third time was different.

One day in March of 1728, a mile and a half from the city, he heard the tattoo of drums announcing the close of the gates at nightfall. "I redouble my pace; I hear the drum beat, I run my hardest; I arrive breathless and bathed in sweat: my heart pounds; I see from afar the soldiers at their posts; running up, I cry in a choked voice. It is too late. Twenty paces before me, I see rising up the drawbridge. I tremble, seeing in the air its terrible horns, a sinister and fatal omen of the inevitable lot that at this moment began for me."[14] His fate was sealed, his mind made up: he would leave Geneva.

Turning away, he set out on his own, suddenly alone in the world. Behind him, he left a closed world that, as he grew older, came to contain nothing but memories made happy for him by imaginative renewal. Years later, writing his *Confessions*, he was certain that a destiny he considered wretched hinged on his departure from Geneva. If only he had stayed . . .

> I should have passed, in the bosom of my religion, my fatherland, my family and my friends, a peaceful and gentle life, such as my character required, in the regularity of a trade to my taste, and in a society according to my heart. I would have been a good Christian, a good citizen, a good father of a family, a good friend, a good worker, a good man in all things. I would have loved my state; I would have been honored perhaps, and then, after having passed a life simple and obscure, but also equable and sweet, I would have died peacefully in the bosom of my own. Soon forgotten, no doubt, I would have been mourned for at least as long as they remembered me. In place of this . . . what picture do I have to paint? Ah, let us not anticipate the miseries of my life![15]

And so Rousseau sought his fortunes in the world at large. When Geneva shut its gates before him, he was but sixteen, still in his minority; when shortly afterward, he allowed himself to be housed at a hospice and converted to Catholicism, he automatically forfeited all his rights by birth. He had never been an active Citizen.

Either/Or

Throughout his ensuing travels and troubles—from Chambéry to Lyon to Paris— Rousseau harbored his first memories, preserved his first desires. What he had abjured in fact, he came to repossess in fantasy. Even when he tried, he could not forget the lessons taught in the faubourg de Saint-Gervais.

Rousseau's early manhood was spent in the kingdom of Savoy, in Chambéry, a small village to the south of Geneva. According to the *Confessions*, he made periodic forays incognito back to the city of his birth. During these trips, he even made some new friends. Among them was Jacques Barrillot, a bookseller who would later publish the first editions of Montesquieu's *Spirit of the Laws* and Burlamaqui's *Principles of Natural Right*. When Barrillot passed through Chambéry in the winter of 1736, he brought with him advice as well as books, urging the exile to return to Geneva for a longer visit. According to Genevan law, Rousseau would become eligible to claim his portion of his mother's estate on June 28, 1737, when he became twenty-five years old. Barrillot suggested that the young man discreetly meet his father in Geneva and spend part of the summer there, clearing up the family's financial affairs.[16]

And so it happened. But the son was remarkably silent about his reunion with his father. In a letter written that summer, he seems absorbed in his own affairs, complaining about his health and finances, saddened that "I am not permitted to appear in the town. . . . The charm of being alone in a room every day has drawn out my melancholy into ceaseless trances."[17]

The two outcasts of the Rousseau family were only able to visit Geneva with impunity thanks to the troubles then preoccupying the government. Throughout that summer, tensions ran high between the Small Council and the popular party. Finally, on August 21, Jean-Jacques Rousseau watched in horror as the brief civil war of 1737 erupted around him. Repelled and yet swept up in the "hideous spectacle," he later wrote of "that first ferment of patriotism which Geneva in arms aroused in my heart."[18] It was not a sight he would soon forget.

Nor did he forget the earliest images of his childhood in Geneva. The strength of these first impressions is revealed by two letters Rousseau composed in verse, one to his friend Bordes, probably written in 1741, the other to another acquaintance, Parisot, written in 1742. The poem to Bordes was conceived at a time when Rousseau, then twenty-eight, was living in Lyon, an unusually enlightened urban center thriving on the manufacture and trade of silk goods. There he worked as a tutor, devoting his spare time to writing a treatise on music and composing operas and plays. But he felt dissatisfied. Taking pride in his native convictions, Rousseau felt himself a stranger on French soil. It was not a happy feeling.

He had decided to become an artist and wanted to be a success, someone with an audience. But by writing according to his "helvetic muse," he confided to Bordes, he would only be "preaching with difficulty sad truths, rousing against me revolted readers." He does not feel at one with their world. Scarcely knowing "the customs of France," he fears he will "offend arrogance," especially the arrogance of the rich, whose patronage he must seek, and yet "whose support I despise," particularly when "it requires groveling before them, applauding only them, rather than true merit." Such obsequiousness before vanity "revolts and irritates" the "proud republican" within Rousseau. Because he was raised to value freedom, he cannot quite become the courtier his present situation seems to require. That is the dilemma he must try to surmount.

But why occupy himself with "a vain chimera" drawn from his past? Why not admit that the prophets of progress are correct, and "that there is no wisdom where poverty prevails"? This is the resolution Rousseau presents to Bordes: in an attempt to reconcile his native sentiments with the world surrounding him, our aspiring writer will sing the praises of "innocent industry," that urban labor which "multiplies the comforts of life and, beneficial to all through its useful services, satisfies need by the route of luxury." He will write poetry for a people whose opulence has made them seem like "a mass of kings." [19]

Rousseau's resolution did not endure. In the poem to Parisot written two years later, he seems scarcely more resigned. Once again, he paints his past in the most rhapsodic terms, only to set it aside.

Growing up in a republic like Geneva, a young man is taught his right "to partake in supreme power," no matter the size of his estate. "As small as I was, a weak, obscure Citizen, I was nevertheless a member of the Sovereign." And that was no mean honor. To earn "so noble a benefit" required "the heart of a hero, the virtue of a sage." And it also required freedom, "this precious gift of the heavens," which, he had learned, "is only a fatal plague for vicious hearts." In the community he remembers, men "live without regret in humble obscurity, but at least within our soul we live in freedom." There, "Art is not a crutch. . . . To be just is the only politics."

But Rousseau still seeks recognition for his talents: the arts are to be *his* support. Writing these letters in verse, he fancies himself a poet. He is also an aspiring musician, a playwright, the author of scholarly works. He is about to move to Paris in an attempt to make his fortune with a new system of musical notation. Of what possible use can his "republican sentiments" be in this quest? For too long, "the brilliant chimera" of heroic virtue has "seduced" his mind: "Nothing ought to be exaggerated, not even virtue." He writes Parisot of his current conclusions:

> In society, it would not be good
> If there were less inequality among the classes.
> Shall I make of myself, in my vain obsession,
> A great declaimer, the new Don Quixote?
> Destiny on earth has ruled states
> And surely will not change them for me.

For his part, says Rousseau, all he wishes is "a good book, a friend, freedom, and peace." [20] Tilting at windmills he will leave to others—for the moment.

In these two letters, we can already see the force of Rousseau's memory, if only in the unwelcome doubt it kindles that he does not quite belong, at least within the French world of arts and sciences. Moreover, in his refusal to invoke Geneva by name and in his reference instead to his "helvetic muse," we can already see the resourcefulness of his imagination.

Of course, he remembered afternoons passed in the Swiss canton of Vaud, some forty miles across Lake Léman from Geneva, just as fondly as he remembered growing up in the city itself. As he later confessed, "When an ardent desire for that happy and gentle life which escapes me and for which I was born comes to inflame my imagination, it is always in the country of Vaud, near the lake, in the charming fields, that it fixes itself."[21] But Geneva in Rousseau's day was in fact no part of the loosely allied Swiss cantons; that came later, in 1815, when the city finally joined the strengthened federal entity we know today as Switzerland. Why then the reluctance to call Geneva by name, why instead the slightly misleading invocation of his "helvetic muse"?

Perhaps because Geneva to Frenchmen like Bordes and Parisot would only seem to be a city of affluent and cosmopolitan industry, as urban in its outlook as Lyon, a conflict-ridden society of artisans and aristocrats rather than the serenely self-governing community of hardy spirits conjured up by Rousseau's "helvetic muse."[22] By freely associating his Genevan upbringing with his Swiss idyll, on the other hand, Rousseau could conflate the virtues of the political education he received in the city with the happiness he attributed to a rustic tranquility. In these poems, he was already anxious to elaborate antinomies, to pit "republican sentiments" against that civilized prosperity he fitfully aspired to. Still uncertain of his choice, he allows his imagination to paint an either/or— an image of urbane French luxury beside one of austere Alpine virtue. The antithesis works best when its terms are purified of ambiguity.

"Citizen of Geneva"

It was with a similar rhetorical flourish that Rousseau ten years later separated himself from "the republic of letters." In the interval, he had been to Paris, to Venice, and back again. He had dabbled in diplomacy, freelanced as a composer, written plays, published a book on music, and earned the notice of Diderot, Condillac, and many of the other luminaries then making Paris the capital of the Enlightenment. He had struggled to win a name for himself. And though fame was not yet his, he was well positioned to make the next move.

Only recently had he resolved to make that move on his own terms. After his revelation on the road to Vincennes in 1749, he had decided to denounce the belief in progress. That in itself was not so unusual: in any age, one can find men uneasy at the changes they see around them. But within himself, Rousseau felt a new man. He was now convinced: he was simply not like his colleagues. He was preoccupied with "sad truths" that would revolt them, if only they knew.

His thoughts turned back to the *idées fixes* he had confessed to Parisot. By remembering the city of his birth, he renewed the unruly sentiments of his origin. Before him flared up old images of freedom and virtue, citizenship and sovereignty. This time, he surrendered to them, abandoning himself to his thoughts. Thus he found fortified a growing inner conviction: to live justly once more seemed to him "the only politics."

Once again, Rousseau summoned from his memory an either/or. By letting his imagination purify and embellish a real difference, he pictured an impassable chasm between himself and his contemporaries. They lived in two different worlds. But now his mind was made up. His republic was no salon, his audience no claque of patrons, his true peers no troupe of witty intellects. He imagined that his work belonged instead to a homeland of simple men and honest citizens. Within himself, he drew strength from his past. His friends and readers might live in Paris—but he was a Citizen of Geneva. Emboldened by the thought, he began to reform his appearance, discarding his fine shirts, gold lace, and white stockings, even selling his watch and saying to himself, "Thank Heaven, I shall no longer need to know what hour it is."[23] He became anxious to have others notice the change within.

His unilateral declaration of Genevan Citizenship is first revealed some three months after his shattering intuition on the road to Vincennes, at a time when he was still writing an answer to the question posed by the Academy at Dijon. The declaration occurs in a letter to Voltaire.

At the time, the celebrated high priest of the Enlightenment, then near the zenith of his influence, scarcely knew of Rousseau. It seems that the great man had recently been attacked in print by one "M. Rousseau." In his letter, our Rousseau is concerned both to defend his honor by asserting his innocence and to define his virtue by stressing his uniqueness. In the future, Voltaire will not be able to confuse Jean-Jacques Rousseau with anyone else.

"Rousseau of Geneva" is quite incapable of the insolence that the critic Rousseau exhibited—for our Rousseau is a modest as well as ardent republican: "I worship freedom, I detest domination and servitude equally, and I have no wish to impress anyone." He has even "given up letters and the whim of acquiring a reputation." And while a cynical observer might note that his literary lionization lay just around the corner, it is clear that he now imagines that he is different from other authors of the day. As if to underline that difference, the letter is signed "J.-J. Rousseau, Citizen of Geneva."[24]

Voltaire, quite unaware of the momentous symbolism at work, did not take the letter seriously. His adversary, he quipped back, "is certainly not a citizen of Geneva but, from what people say, a citizen of the quagmire at the foot of Parnassus."[25]

Rousseau was probably not amused. He rarely was. An addiction to the *bon mot* dishonors the seriousness a true republican will show in his concern to live justly—a glum doctrine, perhaps, but only one of the "sad truths" he had previously fended off. Now, though, he had decided to plumb his own intuitions. Avoiding frivolous exercises in style, he would sincerely address the truths he had been taught as a youth. Unfortunately, the savants of Paris treated the elements of his own education—the family and the fatherland—as if they were "words void of sense." The average luminary of the day was "neither parent, citizen or man." He was simply a self-styled "philosopher."[26]

Rousseau, by contrast, was no savant, and certainly no affable wit. He was a simple republican. By conveying this contrast without asserting it directly, his announced citizenship became a sign of difference: a badge of modesty and defiance simultaneously, it reflected an inner resolve he wished to exhibit indirectly.

He proudly displayed that badge on the title page of the first important essay he published, the "Discourse, which won the prize of the Academy of Dijon. In the year 1750. On this Question proposed by the same Academy: Whether the restoration of the Sciences and Arts has tended to purify mores." The original title page had but two other phrases: one, in Latin, from Ovid: *Barbarus hic ego sum quia non intelligor illis* ("Here I am the barbarian because no one understands me"); the other, in French, from Rousseau himself: *Par un Citoyen de Genève* ("By a Citizen of Geneva"). Apparently eschewing celebrity, the author remains anonymous on the title page. With the motto from Ovid, he expressed his alienation from the fine society of his French colleagues. And with his declaration of Citizenship, he points mutely to an alternative: a community of decent men, unconcerned with fame, because they, like the Rousseau re-formed in their image, seek only the truth, each according to his own light.[27]

Geneva. Rousseau now yearned for a true *patrie*, a homeland he could legitimately call his own. In this fatherland of free men, he trusted that he would find his merits appropriately honored; he imagined that he would enjoy a more secure sense of belonging. In 1751, he responded to a letter from one of his father's old friends in Geneva:

> You are by no means mistaken in believing that you have seen a heart penetrated by a singular manner of employing the word fatherland. I am infinitely grateful to you for this observation. . . . I received the light from an excellent Citizen; all the circumstances of my life have only served to make more energetic this ardent Love for the Fatherland that he inspired in me. It is by dint of living among slaves that I have completely felt the price of freedom. For you are lucky to live in the midst of your family and of your native lands, you dwell among men and obey only Laws, that is to say, reason!

While the memory of his childhood might console him, he must also have envied the lot of a real Citizen of Geneva—for Citizenship there was not really his to claim. When the first Genevan edition of his discourse was prepared in 1750, honesty compelled him to sign the title page simply *Par M. Rousseau, Genevois*: "By M. Rousseau, Genevan."[28]

Dedication

It seems plausible to assume that he desired to win back in fact what he had reclaimed in fantasy. Old friends still lived in or near Geneva. In 1751, in the midst of the uproar caused by the publication of his *First Discourse*, he had announced, for the first time explicitly, that Geneva offered an especially fruitful field for thinking about politics. Yet, if we are to believe Rousseau's account in

The Confessions, he rather casually drifted back to the city of his birth: "Gauffe-court, with whom I was then extremely intimate, finding himself obliged to go to Geneva on business, proposed that I should go with him; I agreed."[29]

It was the spring of 1754. Rousseau had just finished writing his second discourse, "On the Origin and Foundations of Inequality among Men," and had sent it off to the Academy at Dijon, which again had sponsored an essay contest. Without waiting for the prize to be announced, he had set to work preparing the essay for publication. Sometime that spring, he had decided to preface his new discourse with a dedication—a short essay in honor of Geneva.

Before leaving Paris, he had completed this eulogy in outline. Rousseau nonetheless seemed in no great hurry to reach Geneva. Instead, he chose to finish his dedication outside the city, in Chambéry, where he visited for several days en route. One biographer has speculated that Rousseau planned to use his text to curry favor with the authorities in Geneva, perhaps in the hope that a flattering portrait would expedite the restoration of his Citizenship. But this cannot be true, for the simple reason that the dedication was not published until months after Rousseau had regained his Citizenship and left Geneva, where he had shown the manuscript to virtually no one.[30]

There were other motives at play. In Chambéry, Rousseau kept a measured distance from Geneva—some forty-six miles, to be exact—while enjoying the company of old friends and the comfort of a rolling countryside, evoking fond memories of his younger years. Almost a decade had passed since his last visit to Geneva. His knowledge of the city's current state was spotty at best. He had few Genevan friends in Paris, and, of these, even fewer pretended to any awareness of political affairs in the homeland.[31] By completing his dedication in Chambéry, he safeguarded his ignorance. Going on strolls past familiar orchards and vineyards, he could freely indulge his "helvetic muse" and paint a picture of perfect civic virtue, a fitting antithesis to the Paris he had left behind. He would write of Geneva with imagination and heartfelt passion, rather than with bookish knowledge or even firsthand experience. What he praised as an ideal republic naturally bore scant resemblance to the real one on the shores of Lake Léman.

"Only the virtuous Citizen may give to his Fatherland honors which it may approve," declared Rousseau at the outset of his dedication. Since he did not yet meet this requirement, he asked to "be permitted here to follow the zeal that animates me, rather than the right that ought to authorize me." While suffering a "feeble and languishing career in other Climates," he had harbored a "tender and disinterested affection for my distant fellow citizens." Perhaps his pent-up zeal seemed excessive: "In this lively effusion of my Heart," he admitted that he might be "guilty of some indiscreet rapture." For that, he could only beg the pardon of Geneva's Citizens. Still, he hoped that they would recognize in his encomium to their homeland the "tender affection of a true patriot"—one who did not need the warrant of actual Citizenship to write, but one whose writings did honor to the ideal Citizens of an ideal state.[32]

2

The Image of Democracy

IT IS TIME to look more closely at the "lively effusions" prompted by Rousseau's "indiscreet rapture." What dubious offering does the wishful thinking of the patriot make to the city of his birth? What picture does he paint of Geneva and its institutions? To answer these questions, we must consider the city he shows us as an imaginary totality. For the moment, no attempt will be made to separate daydreams from realities, no emphasis placed on contrasts between urban Geneva and the rural Switzerland surrounding it. When writing according to his "helvetic muse," the Citizen of Geneva often enough conflated these matters. Though distinguishing them will become crucial for Rousseau as well as for us, we can dwell on such differences later.

Instead, by collating otherwise scattered themes, I will attempt to reanimate and give fresh force to the whole of Rousseau's Alpine fantasia. As if to recapture the forgotten program to a familiar piece of music, I will annotate recurrent motifs, organize them according to their structural coherence, describe the scenes they evoke. My primary guide in this task will be Rousseau's own dedication of his *Second Discourse* to Geneva, although supplementary material will be drawn from the passages on Switzerland and Geneva in the *Letter to d'Alembert* (1758), *La Nouvelle Héloïse* (1761), and a few other sources. The goal is to restore for the purposes of study the Alpine city of Rousseau's reveries: a model of harmony, a world of perfection—and, as we shall see, a strikingly new image of democracy.

The Natural Setting

Before us stands a city with "a charming site, a temperate climate, a fertile countryside, and the most delightful appearance that exists beneath Heaven." Bounded by mountains and a vast lake, it is "of a size limited by the extent of human faculties," an oasis of human industry in the midst of untamed nature.[1]

Sufficiently fertile to feed its own population but poor enough and remote enough to make conquest unappealing, the state is relatively immune to "the ambition of its neighbors." Unencumbered diplomatically, it requires for its defense only a modest civic militia: each citizen bears arms, though the city safely confines their display to yearly military festivals. While all men are thus called upon to maintain "that warlike ardor and that spirited courage which suit freedom so well and nourish the taste for it," no man need fall prey to the "most barbarous opinion which ever entered the human mind, namely, that bravery can take the place of all the duties of society."[2]

Here, then, is a city naturally well situated, happily encircled by a terrain that affords the security of peace, the satisfactions of plenty, and the pleasures of a sublime beauty. We may envision a town of modest dimensions, nestled in a verdant valley, framed by lofty peaks in the distance. A short walk beyond the city gates lie orchards and vineyards, fields and brooks, the rural homes where many of the citizens choose to live and work. Patchwork plots of farmland surround the city like a quilted comforter. Here, where the earth bears fruit thanks only to diligent labor, the face of nature is familiar and consoling, a source of quiet satisfactions.

Strolling in the solitude of a meadow, "the objects are smiling and agreeable, they excite recollection and reverie, here one feels oneself at large, beyond the melancholy walls of the town and the confines of prejudice." In the country, the distractions of everyday life are banished afar, and the mind can turn to other matters, aroused by the images of nature before it. "The woods, the brooks, the greenery, draw our heart away from the considerations of men; the birds flying here and there according to their caprice offer us in solitude the example of freedom.... The eyes, struck solely by the gentle images of nature, bring her closer to our heart."[3]

A longer trip, up the neighboring mountains, engenders by contrast an uncanny and exotic feeling. "Seeing about oneself nothing but entirely novel objects, strange birds, bizarre and unknown plants," a visitor atop the peaks has the pleasure "of observing, so to speak, another nature, of finding oneself in a new world." Here the air is clear, the atmosphere light. As lofty perspectives dwarf the familiar lands below, the traveler experiences "the magical, the supernatural, that ravishes the spirit and the senses."[4] While the valleys permit a contained if austere existence that attaches a man to what is nearest, the peaks above, in their awesome silence, awaken in the soul a feeling for what is transcendent.

The sublime Alpine setting has a moral significance. When the Savoyard Vicar in *Emile* decides to share his most deeply held convictions, he takes Rousseau "out of town on to a high hill." In the distance, the landscape is "crowned" by "the vast chain of the Alps." Looking out from this vantage point, "one could have said that nature spread before our eyes all her magnificence in order to furnish a text for our conversation." Experiencing such Alpine vistas, a man feels himself "lifted above human society." Leaving behind "all the base and terrestrial sentiments" as he approaches "the ethereal regions," a man's soul "acquires something of their inalterable purity." Contemplating the mountains, "one is serious ... but not melancholy, peaceful but not indolent, content to exist and to think."[5]

Thus do these Alpine residents come to explore their own most personal convictions about the meaning of life. But they are inspirited by more than the beauty of nature surrounding them. Their thinking and their conduct are also shaped by the institutions that meet their material and spiritual needs. The economy of the households, the rituals of the civic religion, the political clubs and civic festivals that structure time away from work, all combine to cultivate among the residents a feeling for freedom and fraternity, a taste for simplicity and self-sufficiency, a respect for good sense and the intuitive understanding common to all men.

The Household

To think about this city, we must imagine not merely a country (*pays*), but a fatherland (*patrie*): not merely a territory with inhabitants, but an association of families, its solidarity secured through "bonds of blood."[6] And at the core of this community, as its basic cell, we must imagine not isolated individuals, but patriarchal households; not men without ties, but families governed by fathers, each sustained by his labor on a plot of land he can call his own.

Here, within the family, the individual tastes "the patriarchal and rustic life, man's first life, the most peaceful, the most natural, and the sweetest life for anyone who does not have a corrupt heart." Here, too, the individual first develops his own identity and feels his ties to other men; his habits are forged, his good sense exercised; here his appetites are satisfied, the fruits of society first enjoyed.[7] For the family is the medium through which this culture instinctively invests its norms with the full force of filial affection.

As the first person to shape a child's feeling for himself and for others, the mother plays an especially important role. Early in life, she nurses the child and gives him his first experience of compassion. By the gentleness of her demeanor and the tenderness of her affection, she inspires a taste for modesty and an openness to sentiment. "Therefore always be what you are," Rousseau advises the women of his homeland, "The chaste guardians of mores and the gentle ties of peace; . . . continue to exploit on every occasion the rights of the Heart and of Nature for the profit of duty and virtue." The father's role, while more indirect, is no less essential. Rousseau recalls the "wise lessons" he learned simply watching his own father: "I see him still, living by the labor of his hands, and nourishing his soul on the most sublime Truths. I see Tacitus, Plutarch and Grotius, mingled with the instruments of his trade before him."[8]

During moments of relaxation from the trade a young man practices beside his father, learning has the appearance of occurring spontaneously. All the members of the household read "useful books and are tolerably well educated." Warmly enveloped within the family, each occupies the long days of winter not only in work, but also in acquiring useful knowledge. These Alpine men "reason sensibly about everything, and about many things with brilliance." The family forms a small commonwealth of autodidacts: "All know how to sketch, paint and calculate a bit; most play the flute, many know something of the principles of music and can sing true. These arts are not taught them by masters, but are passed down, as it were, by tradition."⁹

Within this cozy society, the "habit of living together" nourishes "the sweetest sentiments known to men: conjugal love and Paternal love." The family begins in the love a man feels for a woman. "Man and woman were formed for each other. God wants them to fulfill their destiny, and certainly the first and holiest of all the bonds of society is marriage." Love similarly structures the internal relations between parents and their progeny. The love they exchange among themselves rewards and restrains the father who governs the household and the mother who rears the children. If the family is "so to speak, the prototype of political societies," it is so only insofar as such larger associations ought also to unite feeling with understanding, anchoring their laws in sentiments of mutual affection.¹⁰

Yet the sentimental basis of the family does not render it an unfit topic of civic concern. On the contrary. Since, in an association of households, the first model of society is the family, it is only appropriate that the formation of families become a topic of common interest. Marriages are among the few "subjects of negotiation" between households. In order to lay a sound foundation for the community, the city gives to all families "common rules," providing "in a uniform manner for the authority of the father, the obedience of servants, and the education of infants."¹¹

Civic regulation of the family need not take the form of written law, however. For example, in Rousseau's city, "balls for young marriageable persons" will be held. At such balls, "inclination alone" is consulted, "no marriage ever being contracted for reasons of ambition, or prevented on grounds of interest and inequality." Yet, by having to show their inclinations before "the eyes of the public," the eligible youngsters at these balls will be encouraged to practice reserve and modesty. They will not deceive one another but will instead "show themselves off, with the charms and the faults which they might possess, to the people whose interest it is to know them well before being obliged to love them."¹² Thus can the free play of conjugal love be regulated discreetly by public scrutiny.

Because these Alpine denizens devote such attention to the family and make of it a condition of their association, the city of Rousseau's reverie embodies a form of life superior to the greatest of the ancient republics. For the ancients sometimes tried to stifle the sentiments a man spontaneously feels for his kin. Plutarch reports that Lycurgus, the heroic lawgiver at Sparta, believed that "children were not so much the property of their parents as of the whole commonwealth." Plato in the *Republic* is even more severe, entirely divorcing his ruling class of guardians from the family and eliminating any distinction in the education received by its sons and daughters.¹³

But Rousseau, like the healthy Alpine father he imagines, is unmoved by these attitudes of the ancients. Plato's ideas about the family are a subversion of the "sweetest sentiments of nature"—"as if a natural bond were not necessary to

form conventional ties; as if the love one has for those near were not the principle of the love one owes the state; as if it were not by means of that small *patrie*,
the family, that the heart is attached to the large one; as if it were not the good
son, the good husband, and the good father who make the good citizen!" Bonds
of love attach the soul securely to those virtues that constitute its perfection. The
wisdom of Rousseau's own republicans is to honor the force of this sentiment,
knowing that "it is difficult for an education in which the heart is involved to
remain forever lost." [14] The best fatherland, the best homeland, is one with real
fathers, real families, real homes.

On a trip into the mountains, Saint-Preux in *La Nouvelle Héloïse* encounters a
striking example of the harmony and freedom which typify the Alpine family.
Although he is a stranger, he is greeted as a brother. No insincere show of
cosmopolitanism, this greeting evinces a simple love of humanity, rooted in a
strongly held affection for those nearest. The table manners of this family are
also revealing: "Children who have reached the age of discretion (*âge de raison*)
are the equals of their parents; domestics sit at the table with their masters; the
same freedom reigns in the homes as in the republic, and the family is the image
of the State." [15]

The Swiss household of Wolmar, described by Saint-Preux later in *La Nouvelle
Héloïse*, offers a similar model of social order. "The simplicity and equality which
I see reign here have an appeal which touches me and shows me respect. I pass
serene days amid vivid reason and palpable virtue." In this domestic setting,
Wolmar teaches his children "the taste for labor, order, moderation, and all that
can make sweet and charming for sensible people the enjoyment of a modest
estate, as wisely conserved as it was honestly acquired." [16] Growing up in such a
climate, a child comes to inherit not only a parcel of material property, but also
the kind of sound habits that will make him a master of himself—a man of
independent judgment and means.

The function of the Alpine household is not solely to educate its progeny. For
each father, the family also defines a miniature commonwealth. Within its confines, the father can enjoy "the tranquility of a retreat" alongside "the sweetness
of society." [17] As the head of the household, he learns not only the art of justly
ruling others, but also the discipline of labor:

> These happy farmers, all in comfortable circumstances, free of . . . duties
> . . . and forced labor, cultivate with all possible care lands the produce of
> which is theirs, and employ the leisure that tillage leaves them to make
> countless artifacts with their hands and to put to use the inventive genius
> which nature gave them. In the winter especially, at a time when the deep
> snows prevent easy communication, each, warmly closed up with his big
> family in his pretty and clean wooden house, which he has himself built,
> busies himself with enjoyable labors which drive boredom from his sanctu-
> ary and add to his well-being. Never did carpenter, locksmith, glazier or
> turner enter this country. . . . Among the . . . pieces of furniture which make

up their household ... none is ever seen which was not made by the hand of the master. They ... invent ... all sorts of instruments ... ; many of these even get to Paris, among others those little wooden clocks that have been seen there during the last few years. They also make some of iron, and even make watches. And, what seems unbelievable, each joins in himself all the various crafts into which watchmaking is subdivided and makes all his tools himself.

In this world where division of labor is all but unknown, "each is everything for himself, no one is anything for another." [18]

The variety of work performed in each household and the type of material culture it supports have much to do with the sentiment of freedom that Rousseau attributes to this society of independent producers. "Each being adequate to his situation" and skilled at a variety of tasks, no one need rely unduly on others for help. [19] Each father wins a measure of self-sufficiency for his family.

By the use to which his work is put within the household, the Alpine artisan sees the worth of his efforts confirmed immediately. Because he need seek no further to profit from his own labor or to win the esteem of others, here he is "everything for himself," a man well aware of his own powers and talents. Through the satisfaction his work brings, the family craftsman comes to take pleasure in the patience and robustness required by manual labor, just as he feels a natural pride in producing "truly estimable goods." Laboring in such a context, a man overcomes vanity and idleness; in his own works, he discovers for himself "the first fruit of a well-ruled society." A real dignity surrounds this apparent necessity: "Of all the occupations which can provide subsistence to man, that which brings him closest to the state of Nature is manual labor: of all the conditions, the most independent of fortune and of men is that of the artisan." [20]

Yet among the forms of labor, there is one that Rousseau endows with supreme importance: farming. An association of families that can feed its members on the produce of its own land is significantly less dependent than a country that requires trade for survival: "Commerce produces wealth, but agriculture assures freedom." Nor is that all that agriculture assures. Farming is "the most honest, the most useful, and consequently the most noble" trade a man can practice. Tilling the soil attaches the farmer not only to the specific parcel of land he works, but also to the surrounding land worked by his fellows. From the thanksgiving he owes to the ground that nourishes them all springs naturally the sentiment of patriotism, a man's first feeling for what he has in common with his neighbors. [21]

Since a modicum of autarchy prevails within the perimeters of each family farm, envy is alleviated, mutual satisfaction promoted. Limiting the need for superfluous exchange limits the growth of superfluous desires. "Each, living on his own ground," succeeds "in extracting from it his necessities, in feeling himself at liberty there, in desiring nothing further." Because the "needs and interests" of the associated households rarely come into conflict, the fathers feel only "benevolence and friendship" for each other, rather than selfishness or distrust. A "laborious and independent life," where "each in his own house" practices "all the necessary arts," unites the families and gives them "two great means of defending" their homeland, "namely, concord in resoluteness, and courage in combat."[22]

But the happiest circumstance of all is when peace abroad and tranquility at home allow the fathers to withdraw into their families, governing serenely the domestic units dispersed evenly across the hills and valleys, "separated by distances as equal as the fortunes of their proprietors."[23] Then each family member finds the time not only to learn and to labor, but also to enter quietly into himself, there to sound the depths of his own thinking, to clarify for himself his own most personal convictions about the value and meaning of this life.

As the tutor exclaims to Emile, "Happy is the country . . . where one does not need to seek peace in a desert!" The visitor to Rousseau's city will find a "number of homes scattered out around the city. . . . Each [citizen], having spent the day at his business, leaves at the closing of the gates in the evening, and goes to his little retreat to breathe the purer air and enjoy the most charming countryside on earth." Here, occasions are lacking for invidious comparisons. In the haven of the household, the father instead "draws more from himself and puts more of his own in everything he does; because the human mind, less spread out, less drowned in vulgar opinions, elaborates itself and ferments better in tranquil solitude; because, in seeing less, more is imagined; finally, because less pressed for time, there is more leisure to extend and digest one's ideas."[24]

Religion

The households of this sturdy community are linked, not only by the land they work and the marriages they arrange, but also by the faith they share: for we confront a community united, in part, by its religious beliefs. On Sundays, all of the families in Rousseau's city attend church. The worship is conducted by pastors who preach a few simple doctrines and set an edifying example. Thoughtful and sincere, these "zealous trustees of the sacred dogmas" use their "lively and sweet eloquence" to kindle the imagination of their listeners, reinforcing their Biblical imagery and maxims by the goodness of their own conduct. By preaching the existence of a beneficent, powerful, and wise deity who provides for "the happiness of the just, the punishment of the wicked," and the sanctity of social bonds, the ministers convey to the associates a comforting and useful outlook on the meaning of life, one that alleviates sorrows by extending hope to all men equally, that helps a person to rise above any traces of petty selfishness and to discharge his duties to others. Unlike the chiefs of most other religions, these ministers indicate "some love for the terrestrial fatherland that nourishes them," even as they raise men's gaze toward "a more holy and a more sublime fatherland."[25]

Although solitary meditation naturally leads a man to think for himself and to discover in his conscience the "voice of the soul," the public profession of faith amplifies that voice and serves to remind each person publicly of the need to think for himself, in an awareness of the mysteries that surround him on all sides. The emphasis remains on individual conscience, not priestly authority. The enigma of transcendence requires thoughtful discussion, not glib formulas.[26]

The civic religion places its final trust in the layman: "Here, then, the individual mind is established as the unique interpreter of Scripture; here the authority of the Church is rejected; here each has set doctrine under his own jurisdiction."[27] The "sacred dogmas" are few in number, general in character, open-ended in significance. Rather than accepting decisions about matters of faith made for him, the individual is enjoined to make these decisions for himself. Once meditation on the meaning of life has become a settled taste, the public creed becomes less important than the natural religion each man has discovered for himself.[28]

"Seek the truth in yourself. . . . View the spectacle of nature; hear the inner voice"—these, as we have seen, are eminently practicable maxims for Rousseau's imaginary citizens. By meditating on the nature surrounding him, each one elucidates his own inner light, his own most deeply held convictions. Religious tolerance is required by the very uncertainty of this introspective quest. Since "human reason has no well-determined common measure," it would be "unjust for any man," even an authorized preacher, to "give his own" measure "as the rule for that of others."[29]

The spiritual culture of the civic religion and the material culture of the household complement each other. What the household accomplishes through its emphasis on independence, the city's religion confirms through its stress on introspection; corresponding to the mutual respect produced within the family is the humility engendered by the religion. Both institutions are at one in promoting autonomy as well as solidarity, self-respect as well as a regard for others.

Public Occasions

Other public pursuits reinforce similar ends. To the domestic pedagogy practiced in the family corresponds a civic education that commences as soon as a man steps out of the household and into public view. In Rousseau's city, "the sweet habit of seeing and knowing one another" insures that "love of the *Patrie*" is "love of the Citizens," rather than mere love of the land.[30] The cultivation of this affection occurs not only through the public religious ceremonies, but also through two important leisure activities: the "circles," where the men drink together and exchange opinions; and the festivals, where the entire community celebrates notable events. At these moments, the taste for community is forged unobtrusively, in the guise of friendly interaction and festive ritual.

The circles are informal voluntary associations of from twelve to fifteen men who rent "comfortable quarters which they provide with furniture and the necessary store at common expense." Every afternoon when work does not detain

him, a member meets with his chosen fellows and "gives himself without restraint to the amusements of his taste; they gamble, chat, read, drink and smoke.
Sometimes they dine there, but rarely, because the Genevan is a steady sort and
likes to live with his family. Also, they often go walking together, and the amusements they provide for themselves are exercises fit to cause and maintain a ro-
bust body."[31] While the men thus occupy their afternoons, the women stay at
home and entertain their friends in parallel societies that provide a relatively
harmless outlet for cardplaying and gossip.

In the fraternal company of the circles, Rousseau finds preserved "some image
of ancient mores among us." By constituting a distinctively modern space where
a political education can occur in public, the circles show a middle way "between
the public education of the Greek Republics and the domestic education of Monarchies, where all the subjects must remain isolated, and have nothing in common except obedience."[32]

Within their circles, the men are free to talk frankly about the affairs of the
patrie. In this setting, friends may dispense with the constricting etiquette governing social encounters between mere acquaintances. Discussion of "fatherland
and virtue" occurs in an atmosphere where "reasons take on more weight." Here
men "cannot get away with *bons mots* for answers"; their speech is "a bit rustic,"
but the directness of expression engenders in the mind "precision and vigor."
Conversations are not artificially isolated from everyday life but occur during
games and strolls that give the body exercise. Sedentary talk is replaced by
peripatetic discourse. "Many circles are held in the country, others go there.
There are gardens for walking, spacious courts for exercise, a big lake for swim-
ming, the whole country is open for the hunt."[33]

The exchange of opinion within these circles is remarkably uninhibited, behavior that is enhanced by the drinking that often accompanies the talk. Only in
countries with questionable manners are men fearful of the indiscretions occa-
sioned by the consumption of alcohol. "False men are sober." Whether at public
gatherings or at the family dinner table, where wine is also served, "great reserve . . . often enough indicates feigned mores and duplicitous souls. The frank
man fears less the fond babble and tender effusions that precede intoxication."[34]
In the relaxed and intimate setting of the circles, as at the family table, the
citizens show themselves to their fellows as they are, without false pretenses.

Because these circles are open to public scrutiny, their existence forestalls the
formation of secret cabals and factions that might imperil the *patrie*. "Of all the
kinds of links which can bring individuals together in a city like our own, the
circles form incontestably the most reasonable, the most decent, and the least
dangerous ones, because they neither wish nor are able to be hidden, because
they are public and permitted, because order and rule prevail in them," because,
finally, frankness in expressing opinions becomes a habitual disposition to the
citizen who attends them.[35]

That is why these "decent and innocent" associations are a valued bulwark of
Rousseau's city. For while the men of his imaginary society are the self-sufficient

and proud heads of independent households, they are not hermits. "They could not always live alone and separated," each warmly bundled up in his own hut with his own family. By participating in the circles, the conscience of the father is enlarged and refined through a healthy interaction with fellow fathers as independent and frank as himself. He comes to see them not simply as anonymous neighbors, but as thoughtful compatriots, free men as devoted to the *patrie* as himself. The circles, in sum, "combine everything which can contribute to making friends, citizens, and soldiers out of the same men, and, in consequence, everything which is most appropriate to a free people. . . . It is only the fiercest despotism which is alarmed at the sight of seven or eight men assembled, ever fearing that their conversation turns on their miseries."[36]

If the circles define a sphere of interaction confined to those men interested in public affairs, and if the civic religion unites the city on weekly occasions where a certain reserve and reticence are in order, the periodic festivals that enliven daily life reach outward to encompass the entire community in one intoxicating bacchanalian whirl, breaking down the boundaries that define the particularity of each individual. It is here that the truth of the whole is forged and reaffirmed. Wives and children, domestics and foreign residents, all flock together in a civic communion celebrating events and institutions that define their life in common. These moments of creative effervescence serve a function similar to that fulfilled by the tragic theater in ancient Greece: they unite a people in a joyful civic sacrament.[37]

There will be festivals to celebrate the wine harvest, the civic militia, the eligibility of youth for marriage.[38] The modesty and self-control otherwise exercised in Rousseau's city only sharpens "the sensuous delight" of the celebrants on these occasions: "To abstain in order to enjoy consummation, that is . . . the epicurism of reason." Sharing such pleasures makes them all the keener. "The only pure joy is public joy, and the true sentiments of nature reign only over the people."[39]

Through festive intercourse, the community regenerates itself and renews its living sense of plenitude. The sentiment of patriotic love is implanted anew in the hearts of each participant. "From the bosom of joy and pleasure would be born the preservation, the concord and the prosperity of the republic."[40]

"In the open air, under the sky," the population assembles to drink in the "sweet sentiment" of public joy. "The spectators themselves become an entertainment to themselves; make them actors themselves; do it so that each sees and loves himself in the others so that all will be better united." For one glorious instant, the festival rebaptizes society as one "big family." In the collective euphoria, individual reserve is swept aside, "all live on the most intimate terms." Within the festive spirit, "all the world is equal, no one is forgotten." "The sweet equality that reigns here re-establishes the order of nature, forms an instruction for some, a consolation for others, and a bond of amity for all." At the height of the celebration, differences momentarily melt, and the individual experiences the delicious sensation of abandoning himself to the collective spirit. In an ecstasy that takes him outside himself, he feels a part of a larger whole with a pleasurable intensity that is not soon forgotten: thus does his shared sense of self, his "*moi commun*," blossom in the common delirium. Besides, "to what peoples is it more fitting to assemble often and form among themselves sweet bonds of pleasure and joy than to those who have so many reasons to like one another and remain forever united?"[41]

Yet in every respect, the festival is an extraordinary occurrence. When it is over, the pleasure aroused by this civic communion gradually subsides, and the individual composes himself for the journey home. After lingering for a while to enjoy the fresh air as the crowd slowly thins, each husband rejoins his wife, each person finally "withdrawing peaceably with his family."[42] Back in their households, each in the family shares with the others memories of the delights they have all just experienced. The next morning, it is a freshly renewed community of households that sends its revivified members back into the fields and back into themselves, to resume the routine of hard work and the practice of independent thinking that constitute the wealth and virtue of Rousseau's Alpine society.

Mores and Manners

Each of the institutions we have thus far surveyed—the patriarchal household, the civic religion, the circles, and the festivals—makes some contribution to shaping the mores and manners that ennoble the residents of Rousseau's city. In their customary beliefs and behavior, "these singular men" show "an astonishing blend of delicacy (*finesse*) and simplicity."[43] On the one hand, they are modest, prudent, and friendly, with an enviable interest in thinking for themselves. On the other hand, they are industrious at work, courageous in battle, indifferent to fame and fortune, and frank, with no trace of false airs. Their independence spares them the insecurity created by envy, while their sense of mutual respect allows them the pleasure of feeling at home in the community. In this city of transparent relations, each man is everything for himself, in a community that is everything for him: here, alienation is unknown.[44]

Taken as a whole, all these traits help every man lead an autonomous life of virtue, happily lived in peace with his fellows. The man of virtue "has mastered his affections. For then he follows his reason, his conscience, he does his duty, he keeps himself in order and nothing can make him deviate from it."[45] This adherence to a chosen order is so strict that it appears as a kind of second nature, an inner sense of self daily renewed and reinforced by the shared routines of life, from farming to the festival.

When shaped by such conventions, behavior is harmoniously motivated. Nothing is at issue for the man who would be virtuous in this society "except to do wholeheartedly and with just confidence" what he "will always be bound to do" spontaneously, "through genuine interest, through duty, and with reason."[46] Rather than containing a constellation of conflicting impulses, the individual who enjoys self-mastery exhibits a love of self, a love of kin, a love of *patrie*, and a love of humanity—a strongly forged chain of affection that radiates out from that which is nearest to that which is most remote.

Rousseau's imaginary man thus combines the virtues of humanitarianism—gentleness, equanimity, moderation, charity, and leniency—with those of patriotism—courage, firmness, and a willpower capable of heroic feats.[47] Yet however habitual these dispositions may appear, our man of many virtues can always say, perhaps while contemplating his lot before the daunting peaks that frame his days, "I would not do it otherwise." No creature of blind instinct, he remains his own master, a thoughtfully free man in a society of peers. It is with this auspiciously formed human material that the lawmakers in Rousseau's city have to work.

The Laws

The laws are the crown of this community. A public expression of a spirit embedded in the mores and manners of each individual, they simultaneously define, hallow, and open to public inspection those rules constituting the form of life the people share. By making explicit what otherwise would remain tacit, the laws raise these rules to the level of self-conscious reflection: the change cannot help but influence the beliefs and practices of each individual. Yet the law equally presupposes a set of prior norms that *can* be made explicit. "If sometimes the laws influence mores, it is when the laws draw their force from them."[48]

Legislation in Rousseau's city brings to completion a process begun in the family and continued in the full range of civic institutions we have already observed. The meditation aroused by living amid a sublime nature, the discipline of varied labor, the sentiments engendered by working the land, the conscience reinforced by public professions of faith, the opinions about public affairs exchanged in the circles, the feeling of joy shared in periodic festivals: these are the primary ways in which the Alpine residents come to an intuitive understanding of their common needs and interests.[49] Lawmaking only renders transparent the norms that constitute these ways of life; for the laws simply underwrite the freedom, equality, and secure good order that are already every resident's birthright.

Still, the laws of Rousseau's city are no small achievement. They are remarkable for their popular provenance, their impersonal universality, and their great antiquity.

Perhaps the most unusual aspect of the laws is the direct role played by each citizen in approving them. Each gives his consent at regularly scheduled public assemblies, where the structure of the civic order may be debated. A citizen's voice is never delegated. Each always speaks for himself, since "who can know better than the citizens under what conditions it suits them to live together in the same society?"[50] Through these assemblies, legislation is open to popular deliberation and change.

In this city, no one can declare himself above the law. It applies equally and indifferently to every individual. As a result, the law embodies not the rule of a person or a privileged estate, but the rule of the community—a rule self-consciously affirmed by all the citizens meeting in orderly assembly.

Since the laws are venerated by the citizens, if only as the charter of their own freedom, changes in them are always contemplated with caution. When amendments seem necessary, they are undertaken with the greatest respect for what has been handed down. In their wisdom, the citizens agree that "in a state as small as the republic of Geneva, all innovations are dangerous, and they ought never to be made without urgent and grave motives."[51] Because the laws are regularly reviewed by all citizens in assembly, each experiences them as an expression of his own will; yet, because ancient laws also exhibit a reassuring durability, they are equally perceived as a natural foundation.

In a society like the one before us, where mores and manners are sound, the first duty of the laws is conservative. "It is easier to keep good mores than to put an end to bad ones," Rousseau advises the compatriots of his homeland. "All that human wisdom can do is forestall changes."[52] Good laws preserve sound primary institutions, regulating their pedagogical functions so that the moral and material culture of the community remains intact. They guarantee the authority of the father in the family, enjoin service in the civic militia, prescribe participation in the civic worship, provide for fitting entertainment at civic festivals.

In addition to ordering the institutions of domestic and civic education, the laws also regulate the rough equality of estates that already characterizes this Alpine society. By stipulating the size and distribution of land in the family—by protecting private property while confining it "within the narrowest possible limits"—legislation promotes adequacy rather than excess, equity rather than envy. A general modesty of fortunes insures that labor is a discipline tasted by all men, while a sufficiency of land for every household minimizes the need for trade, commerce, and money.

The means of winning recognition and discharging obligations can then remain a matter of living reciprocity. Merit can be honored by the visible esteem of others, rather than by an accumulation of easily hidden wealth. For similar reasons, care is taken to avoid legislating taxes. Where public works are considered necessary by the community, they are built by the citizens together. All remain accustomed to doing what needs to be done for themselves, rather than depending on the labor of others.[53]

"Your constitution is excellent," Rousseau tells his compatriots. "Your state is tranquil, you have neither wars nor conquerors to fear; . . . you are neither rich enough to enervate yourself by softness and lose in vain delights the taste for true happiness and solid virtues, nor poor enough to need more foreign help than your industry procures for you; and this precious freedom, which in large Nations is maintained by exorbitant Taxes, costs you almost nothing to preserve." Above all, this constitution is "dictated by a most sublime reason," for Rousseau's compatriots "have no other masters except the wise laws you have made, administered by upright Magistrates of your own choice."[54]

The Government

The governing magistrates of this city are charged with executing old laws and introducing new ones. Rousseau calls them "ministers of the Laws." The citizens together have seen fit to establish "respected tribunals" and have distinguished carefully "their various departments." Every year, these citizens assemble to "elect ... the most capable and most upright of their fellow Citizens to administer justice and govern the State." Thus are combined the benefits of wise leadership and civil equality. "Only confiding the administration to a small number" permits "the choice of thoughtful men," while "requiring the concurrence of all the members of the State in the supreme authority" places "all the people on a perfect level."[55]

Because there is a rough parity of fortunes in this association of families, and because occasions scarcely exist for an intimidating display of opulence, the false criteria of wealth and status do not enter into the elevation of citizens to high office. Instead, by entrusting public power to its most distinguished members, the association uses the common desire for distinction to harness self-interest. The most gifted citizens are singled out by their peers and receive their due through public esteem rather than pecuniary rewards. Here, "true talent" holds office.[56]

Since true talent is recognized, the elected magistrates will exercise great influence. The proposal of new laws is their prerogative. And the citizens, satisfied with their lot in life and happy to honor an authority well earned, are generally content "to give sanction to the laws and to decide in a body and upon the report of their chiefs the most important public affairs."[57]

Confidence in the government is also inspired by its very composition. Those who hold office are drawn annually from the body of common citizens and remain accountable to it. The government constitutes "so essential a part" of the larger "body politic" that "one cannot subsist without the other." During their term in office, the citizens who comprise the government, being "equal by birth in titles, privileges and authority," are all grouped together and called "patricians." Once out of office, though, they become again simple citizens, entitled to no more special respect than their distinctive merits would justify in any case.

"The equality of citizens" is thus so well established "that no one person can be preferred to any other as the most erudite or as the most crafty, but at the most as the best." Yet even electing magistrates according to this criterion—of who is "the best"—"is often dangerous," since any distinction that confers such power threatens to make men into "cheats and hypocrites." The love a leader feels for his people cannot be counted on to restrain him in the same way as the love a father feels for his children. Additional restraints are prudent. The city therefore assembles its citizens routinely, to review the behavior of its elected magistrates.[58]

"You will ask," anticipates Rousseau, "if it is by tilling a field that one acquires the talents needed for governing. I answer yes, in a government as simple and

upright as ours." In a city of such modest size, of course, even the most distinguished citizens rarely show genius. But too often "great talents are a substitute
for patriotic zeal." Men of genius are most necessary "to lead a people which
does not love its country (*pays*) and does not honor its leaders." Within a society
of free and equal peers, by contrast, skill at reasoning and cleverness at leading
are not as important as frankness, "love of the fatherland (*patrie*)," and a certain
regard for one's own intuitive understanding. "Good sense suffices to lead a
well-constituted state, and good sense is developed in the heart as much as in
the head."[59]

And who are these citizens of good sense? Rousseau, notoriously, does not
count women among them. To make the laws and govern his fatherland, Rousseau would include only persons who work the land and rule a family—that is,
patriarchs of independent means and judgment. Each such citizen is drawn from
a private domain where, as a boy, he received an education built on natural
sentiments, and where, as a man, he has exercised mastery for himself. In effect,
a citizen is entitled to become a magistrate only through the wisdom he has
already acquired by governing his own household.[60]

These common citizens are the foundation of the state—as Rousseau reminds
the magistrates of his city:

> If there is a rank in the world suited to make illustrious those who hold it,
> it is doubtless the one given by talents and virtue, the one of which you
> have made yourself worthy, and to which your fellow Citizens have raised
> you. Their own merit adds to yours still another luster; chosen by men
> capable of governing others, in order that they themselves be governed,
> you I find to be as much above other Magistrates as a free People, and
> especially the one which you have the honor to lead, is, by its lights and by
> its reason, above the populace of other States.[61]

Before the government stands "a free People": men of reason interested in the
good and the true, each according to his own light. Because these citizens are all
heads of independent households, they will be ill disposed to stand by idly and
permit any attempt to flout their hard-earned autonomy. In the laws they have
personally approved, each has found the charter of his own freedom in society.
The citizens in assembly remain the guardians of this government. They form
the vital heart of Rousseau's Alpine republic.

It is no wonder, then, that this state is properly called a democracy. Rousseau
himself desires a form of association where "the Sovereign and people could
have only one and the same interest. . . . Since that would not be possible unless
the People and the Sovereign were the same person, it follows that I would wish
to be born under a democratic government, wisely tempered."[62] And such is the
government he imagines his city to possess. A form of political life involving the
participation of all citizens, it is nonetheless notable for the good sense with
which the people exercise their legislative power, the veneration with which they
treat the ancient constitution, the discrimination with which they elect the truly

talented among them, the deference with which they honor magistrates of authentic wisdom and virtue. This is the kind of democracy Rousseau imagines in Geneva: this is the homeland of his dreams.

A New Image of Democracy

It is time to step back and see how far we have come. Democracy. It is but a name for the Alpine community before us. Probably we are not surprised by the picture: a directly self-governing city of rugged citizens united by simple interests, far removed from the tensions and complexities that in the modern democratic nation-state require a stern elite of experts in governing, at least according to the political science of our day.

But the familiarity of Rousseau's apparently anachronistic picture is deceptive. Since he wrote, it has become a commonplace to cite the old Swiss cantons as a colorful, albeit irrelevant, model of an ideal democracy. Yet Rousseau himself was instrumental in propagating the image of the free Swiss at a time when most cantons were in fact oligarchies.[63] Similarly, since his time, it has become a cliché of sorts to think of pure democracy in terms of an impossibly homogeneous community populated by sober rustics of rare virtue. Yet, for over two thousand years, that was not at all the picture most men had of democracy. If democracy in Rousseau evokes unity and happiness, freedom and secure good order, to most political theorists before him, it had spelled only disorder and decay, license and tyranny.

After all, the original prototype of democracy was not Geneva, but ancient Athens: the commercial capital of a large empire, a city, it was said, of ambitious demagogues and unruly plebeians, an undisciplined people responsible for losing the Peloponnesian War to Sparta, an ignorant mob responsible for persecuting Socrates and forcing the wise man to die. The ancient authorities are at one in condemning the extreme democracy and "licentious impunity" at Athens, particularly after the last noble authority, Pericles, had died: thus speak Thucydides and Aristotle, Cicero and Plutarch, all of them warning against the dangers of direct self-government.[64] Moreover, for two thousand years, the pictures of Athens that mattered most were those powerful portraits of injustice painted by Plato in the *Republic*. Long before Rousseau's Geneva, Plato's Athens was the preeminent image of democracy, an icon with all the authority of ancient wisdom behind it.

Plato linked democracy not with rural simplicity, but with urban chaos. Instead of displaying a veneration for ancient laws, Plato's democrats show a thoughtless fickleness, an insatiable "love of change." The democratic citizen "often engages in politics and, jumping up, says and does whatever chances to come to him; and if he ever admires any soldiers, he turns in that direction; and if it's moneymakers, in that one." Overtaken by an addiction to a limitless freedom, the democrat creates an anarchy so contagious that slaves become surly, and even asses are given the run of the streets, "bumping into whomever they

happen to meet." Small matter: by allowing himself to pursue whatever ephemeral pleasure strikes his fancy, the democratic man reduces himself to the level
of a lawless ass. They call it freedom, but it is really nothing but unbridled
instinct.[65]

Needless to say, such character traits do not make for a very dignified association. When "the many" are gathered together, whether in "assemblies, courts,
theaters, army camps, or any other common meeting of a multitude," they cause
"a great deal of uproar, blame some of the things said or done, and praise others,
both in excess, shouting and clapping; and, besides, the rocks and the very place
surrounding them, echo and redouble the uproar of blame and praise." A similar
scene is evoked in Plato's celebrated image of the ship of state. Here we face an
appalling picture of mutiny. After tying down the shipowner, a rowdy mob of
drunken sailors quarrel ceaselessly among themselves, hailing as a "skilled sailor"
whoever, with the assent of the crowd, grabs hold of the helm, while castigating
as a "stargazer" the true pilot, who pays attention not to the commotion on deck,
but to the auguries above, that heavenly order supplying the most appropriate
guide to the art of navigation.[66]

The influence of these images can still be felt today. They have something to
do with the self-evidence surrounding the idea, in modern political science as
well as in the republican tradition, that simple democracy inevitably degenerates
into mob rule. And such Platonic imagery recurs in the most unlikely of contexts. Thus, in Joseph Schumpeter's *Capitalism, Socialism and Democracy*—ostensibly an essay in hard-nosed "realism"—we discover that modern "radio audiences" and even "newspaper readers" are "terribly easy to work up into a
psychological crowd, and into a state of frenzy in which attempt at rational
argument only spurs the animal spirits."[67]

But if pure democracy for Plato and his numerous successors seems the very
picture of frenzied mob rule, Rousseau will have nothing to do with the image
of Athens that first leaves this impression. Of course, it is not impossible that in
a democracy the people would pass bad decrees and condemn innocent men. But
Rousseau cautions that this "will never happen unless the people is seduced by
particular interests, which some wily men, with their prestige and eloquence,
will know how to substitute for the interests of the people." In the Alpine democracy he imagines, however, where genuine self-government insures that the
common interest prevails, a wise man like Socrates would be elected by the
people to high office, not condemned. "Do not raise Athens as an objection,
then, because Athens was not in fact a democracy, but a highly tyrannical aristocracy, governed by learned men and orators": in that "country of Orators and
Philosophers," the demagogues and the sophists were just as responsible as the
common people they misled for the "dangerous innovations" that helped bring
defeat and discredit to Athens.[68]

Rather than argue with an entrenched image, Rousseau discards it, implying
that it is irrelevant. Instead of criticizing the ancient picture of democracy, he
creates an image of his own. Geneva, not Athens, exemplifies a true democracy.

And, in a striking departure from Plato's icon of Athens—and Schumpeter's picture of rabid newspaper readers—Rousseau's image of Geneva presents a tableau of serene order, a city where laws are venerated, not overturned. His democratic citizens, despite the Dionysian ecstasies of their festivals, will never be mistaken for a fickle mob: they are far too sober and self-disciplined for that. And it is doubtful whether Swiss asses are permitted the run of the streets.

Yet Rousseau's Alpine republic does not secure its unity and good order at the expense of individual freedom. As in the case of Plato's Athens, his Geneva is a city that values freedom. But its freedom, far from entailing license and anarchy, is associated with virtue, the peaceful submission to laws each citizen has participated in making for himself. The basis of this freedom is not limitless desire, but the stable autonomy each head of a household obtains, through the disciplines of independent production and independent thinking. In Geneva, citizens "long accustomed to a wise independence" are "not only free, but worthy of being so." [69] These are the democratic souls that populate Rousseau's self-governing city.

In his image of Geneva, we thus face something new: democrats shown as common men of virtue and wisdom, and democracy shown as a model of orderly justice as well as individual freedom.

Men and Citizens

This is one image of Rousseau's desire. In his dedication of the *Second Discourse* to Geneva, he hails it as the best city feasible, given "the nature of human things." Through its judicious combination of institutions designed to preserve a relative equality among families, and those intended to protect distinctive individuals with their own unequal properties, Geneva contributes "in the manner most approximate to natural law and most favorable to society, to the maintenance of public order and the happiness of individuals." How emphatically Rousseau approves of this society is made clear by the rhetorical device that structures the early paragraphs of the dedication: "If I had had to choose the place of my birth, I would have chosen. . . ." Geneva is not simply the *patrie* of Rousseau's birth. That is a contingent fact of his existence. More significantly, Geneva is his city of choice, an emblem of his self-conscious freedom, the essence of what human society might be—an eidetic intuition achieved by his inability, in the free play of his reveries, to "imagine that the nature of human things could admit of a better one." [70]

Of course, this is but one image of Rousseau's desire. There are several others, some of them portraying societies, some of them individuals, some of them apparently complementary, some of them *prima facie* incommensurable: the idyll of pure love that Saint-Preux pursues in *La Nouvelle Héloïse*; the well-ordered household of Wolmar in the same novel; the spartan regimen invoked periodically in the political writings; the heroic figure of the great Legislator; the natural man in *Emile*, carefully cultivated both to live for himself and to survive the vagaries of life in modern cities; the admirably oiled machine of state blueprinted in the *Social Contract*; the unselfconscious idle pleasure in merely existing indulged by the stoical hedonist in *Reveries of a Solitary Stroller*.

To some extent, though, we can imagine the resident of Rousseau's Alpine commonwealth satisfying all these desires. Although marriages are subjected to public scrutiny, they remain a matter of choice between consenting individuals; the basic cell of this society is the well-ordered household; the labor necessary to cultivate the land and the public policy regulating a rough equality of wealth insure a rather austere level of subsistence that might well be called spartan; the men educated naturally within the households of this society display such a well-rounded independence that they often evoke a flock of Emiles; the ancient yet wise laws of the city bear a certain resemblance to the machinery of state detailed in the *Social Contract*; and walks to the meadows and mountains let a man in reverie plumb the depths of his existence and soar on the wings of imagination. Geneva even has at least one great Legislator in its past: Calvin.[71]

Another way of appreciating the weight of Rousseau's image of Alpine democracy is to compare it with the picture painted in the first two discourses of the "golden age"—that happy time before "progress" turned society into a Hobbesian nightmare of bellicose selfishness. At this earlier period of social development, only the patriarchal household was established: each family was "a little Society all the better united because reciprocal affection and freedom were its only links." This "simple and solitary life," maintaining "a golden mean" between the indolence and isolation of primitive man and "the petulant activity of our vanity" in modern society, "must have been the happiest and most durable epoch." In those halcyon days "before Art had fashioned our manners and taught our passions to speak an affected language, our mores were rustic but natural, and differences of conduct announced at first glance those of character. . . . How sweet it would be to live among us if the external bearing were always the image of the inclinations of the heart."[72]

Yet so it is with the contemporary city Rousseau imagines: here also we find rustic and natural customs, as well as a healthy concordance between conduct and character. In the golden age of the *First Discourse*, "human nature, basically, was no better, but men found their security in the ease of comprehending each other." A similar security is enjoyed in Geneva, "where, all the individuals knowing one another, neither the obscure maneuvers of vice nor the modesty of virtue" can be "hidden from the gaze and judgment of the public."[73] In the Alpine society of Rousseau's reverie, there is no place, public or private, for the deceit and hypocrisy of a corrupt civil society. Instead, we find a network of spaces enabling a person to develop his own identity in private and to show himself transparently in public. The personally troubling and morally pernicious discrepancies—between the individual and his community, between the particular and the general, between seeming and being—here are dissolved, with all the force of an ontological rebirth, as if democracy could resurrect one of those innocent social beings that graced the golden age.

Ironically, if Rousseau's emphasis on the household links his Geneva with the golden age, it simultaneously distinguishes his Alpine society as a modern one, populated by distinct *individuals*. Here an "individual and domestic" education facilitates a sociable self-development in private, allowing every man to learn to rule himself in the affectionate setting of the family.[74] The character of this education is defined, in part, by the equal property of each father, who owns just enough land to support the independence of his household; by the dignity accorded the discipline of labor, which each father has to exercise on his own; and by the tolerance extended to questions of conscience, those mysteries about the meaning of life best settled by each person in solitary meditation. The laws governing Rousseau's association of families thus insure a large measure of individuation—that is, a self-defined sphere of beliefs and practices elaborated by each person on his own. Moreover, this measure of individuation is carefully preserved in public affairs. In the circles, each man is encouraged to express himself, in the confidence that his distinctive opinions and virtues will be appropriately recognized and rewarded. The freedom of the individual is finally honored in the civic assemblies, where each citizen is expected to share his *own* best thinking about matters of common concern. Whether we are looking at the material, spiritual, or political culture of this society, here "each is everything for himself, no one is anything for another"—not because the individual is antisocial, but rather because he perceives the community as an extension of himself.[75]

Yet if Rousseau's republic seems quite modern in its resurrection of a bygone golden age, it nevertheless shares certain features with ancient republican models that distinguish it from other sketches for a modern republic. Despite the attention paid to conscience, labor, and a domestic education of distinct individuals according to their natural sentiments, Rousseau's Geneva also shows a classical regard for virtue and, in the circles and festivals, a similarly classical respect for a civic education engendering some uncommon sentiments, including an intense solidarity and a passionate patriotism. The vivid evocation of these concerns helps to set apart Rousseau's Geneva, particularly from that other great model of a modern republic, Montesquieu's England. Though Montesquieu's image of England preserved enough elements of classical civic virtue to discredit the monarchies of the day, it also presents us with a large and complex commercial empire, a cosmopolitan and class-divided country, assured of its liberties only through a cleverly mixed constitution, combining a modicum of democracy and aristocracy to check the arbitrary powers of a monarch, while adroitly balancing the "separate views and interests" of the different estates of society.[76] England is a sprawling *pays*, not a compact *patrie*; for that reason alone, it cannot provide all its citizens with anything like a civic education in virtue, it cannot be anything like the Genevan democracy Rousseau imagines.

In a famous passage in *Emile*, Rousseau appears to go even further. He seems to argue that a civic education cannot occur at all in the modern world: "for where there is no longer a fatherland, there can no longer be citizens. These two words, *patrie* and *citoyen*, ought to be erased from modern languages." That seems to leave only "domestic or natural education" as a viable option for moderns. Moreover, Rousseau in *Emile* appears to say that they are incompatible in any case: "Forced to combat nature or social institutions, it is necessary to choose between making a man or a citizen; for one cannot simultaneously make both."

> Natural man is everything for himself: he is the numerical unity, the absolute whole who has relations only with himself or with those like himself. Civil man is only a fractional unity who depends on a denominator, his value is in relationship with the whole, which is the social body. Good social institutions are those which best know how to denature man, taking away his absolute existence in order to give him one that is relative, and transporting the *self* into the common unity (*transporter le moi dans l'unité commune*).[77]

Despite these remarks, Rousseau's Geneva is clearly one place where the antinomies posed at the outset of *Emile* are resolved. In the context of Rousseau's more traditional republican images—of Sparta and Rome—this, indeed, may be the most striking thing about it.[78] That the Alpine city of Rousseau's dreams is a *patrie* should require no further comment. That it contains citizens is obvious, both from the description we have given and from Rousseau's cherished title: Citizen of Geneva. That it contains men, he affirms equally emphatically: "In Geneva, one will find only men," not dissolute dandies, those urban creatures of etiquette, luxury, and ephemeral fashion. Geneva in effect looms as a privileged modern *patrie*, where a healthy natural education in the household is supplemented by a civic education in public. Before us stands "a free and simple country, where one finds ancient men in modern times."[79]

Rousseau's wishful thinking about Geneva thus implicitly resolves the question posed at the outset of *Emile*: "What will a man brought up uniquely for himself become for others?" The basic idea behind the resolution is spelled out laconically in the *Social Contract*: "Put each Citizen . . . in a position of perfect independence from all the others, and of excessive dependence on the City."[80] What "a man brought up uniquely for himself" will then "become for others" is a dedicated compatriot, whose duty to the *patrie* includes thinking for himself.

Rousseau's image of Alpine democracy assumes and protects the autonomy of the individual heads of each household. Yet, by making the lot in life enjoyed by each father virtually identical, the material culture of the *patrie* surmounts the possibility of conflict between individual interests and insures that each of these natural men has relations only "with those like himself," other free men who are his equals in more ways than one.[81] By establishing social institutions that attune the interests of each person to shared joys (as in the festivals) and to common concerns (as in the circles), the civil life of the *patrie* "transports the self" on pleasurable public occasions, in the process forging bonds of "common unity" through feelings of mutual enjoyment and reciprocal respect. Finally, by having the autonomous and independent heads of each household sanction in public the laws and customs that tie the households together, the democratic practice of self-government insures that every citizen comes to think of individual freedom as a common possession, and civic virtue as a personal disposition.

The human beings populating this *patrie* therefore remain men as well as citizens. They are independent and thoughtful, resourceful and wise, fit for a variety of tasks, tolerant of diversity, hospitable to strangers, with gentle manners and a sense of conscience—and they are proud patriots ready to die for their country, willing to devote themselves to public affairs, able to express love not only for themselves or for humanity in the abstract, but also for their families, their friends, their compatriots, their fatherland: for humanity in the concrete. In the civic festivals and whenever they vote in assembly, these human beings feel themselves but fractions of a larger whole. But at home and in solitude, each knows and feels himself to be a whole man, sufficient unto himself, an independent master beholden to no other. In the image of Alpine democracy, we have discovered a sure route of entry into the paradoxical unity of Rousseau's thinking.

As for the implausibilities and ellipses, the incongruities and clutter of memory, factual detail, and daydream that constitute this chimera and its domain of possibility, we cannot do better, I think, than to ponder the words that Italo Calvino composes for the visionary Venetian wanderer, Marco Polo, in his conversation with the aged Kublai Khan—as ruler of the vast Mogul Empire, the most powerful despot of his day. Their dialogue closes the philosophical fiction Calvino calls *Invisible Cities*:

> The Great Khan's atlas contains also the maps of the promised lands visited in thought but not yet discovered or founded: New Atlantis, Utopia, the City of the Sun, Oceana, Tamoé, New Harmony, New Lanark, Icaria.
>
> Kublai asked Marco: "You, who go about exploring and who see signs, can tell me toward which of these futures the favoring winds are driving us."
>
> "For these ports I could not draw a route on the map or set a date for the landing. At times all I need is a brief glimpse, an opening in the midst of an incongruous landscape, a glint of lights in the fog, the dialogue of two passersby meeting in the crowd, and I think that, setting out from there, I will put together, piece by piece, the perfect city, made of fragments mixed with the rest, of instants separated by intervals, of signals one sends out, not knowing who receives them. If I tell you that the city toward which my journey tends is discontinuous in space and time, now scattered, now more condensed, you must not believe the search for it can stop. Perhaps while we speak, it is rising, scattered, within the confines of your empire; you can hunt for it, but only in the way I have said."
>
> Already the Great Khan was leafing through his atlas, over the maps of the cities that menace in nightmares and maledictions: Enoch, Babylon, Yahooland, Butua, Brave New World.

He said: "It is all useless, if the last landing place can only be the infernal city, and it is there that, in ever-narrowing circles, the current is drawing us."

And Polo said: "The inferno of the living is not something that will be; if there is one, it is what is already here, the inferno where we live every day, that we form by being together. There are two ways to escape suffering it. The first is easy for many: accept the inferno and become such a part of it that you can no longer see it. The second is risky and demands constant vigilance and apprehension: seek and learn to recognize who and what, in the midst of the inferno, are not inferno, then make them endure, give them space."[82]

(1754–1762)

The Exile as Citizen

W HEN HE finally approached Geneva in June, 1754, Rousseau must have felt some of the emotions he imagines Saint-Preux experiencing on a similar return home. "The closer I came to Switzerland, the more excited I felt," writes the sentimental Swiss wanderer:

> The instant when, from the heights of the Jura, I discovered the Lake of Geneva, was an instant of ecstasy and delight. The sight of my country, of this country so cherished, where torrents of pleasure had flooded my heart; the air of the Alps so wholesome and pure; the gentle air of the fatherland, more pleasant than the perfumes of the Orient; that rich and fertile land, that unique countryside, the most beautiful ever to strike the human eye; that charming abode to which I had found nothing equal in my tour of the world; the aspect of a happy and free people; the mildness of the season, the serenity of the Climate; a thousand delicious memories which awakened all of the sentiments I had relished; all this threw me into raptures which I cannot describe and seemed to infuse me with the joy of my whole life at once.[1]

Homecoming

Geneva had never looked so good. He remembered the city of his father and had just written about the city of his dreams. Once he saw his celebrity among his compatriots, perhaps he recalled as well his adolescent forays incognito into what had once been a city all but forbidden to him. Relieved at his newfound recognition, still alive with the happiest memories of his childhood, he exalted his native surroundings.

In July, he wrote to Mme Dupin in Paris: "I cannot tell you, Madame, how much more beautiful Geneva appears to me, without anything changing; it must be that the change is in my manner of seeing it." Everywhere he turned, Rousseau professed to find only wisdom and serenity. "What is certain is that this

49

Town appears to me one of the most charming in the world, and its inhabitants the most wise and happy men I know. Freedom is well established here, the Government tranquil, the Citizens thoughtful, firm and modest, knowing and courageously sustaining their rights, but respectful toward others. . . ." Filtered through the *idées fixes* defining the imagined city of his desire, Geneva now appeared to him as perfection embodied, a living demonstration of republican virtue and its possibilities. Years later, in his *Confessions*, long after his disenchantment with Geneva, Rousseau described his attitude whenever he crossed back over that fateful drawbridge linking the city of his birth to the world outside. "Never have I seen the walls of that happy city, never have I entered it, without feeling a certain faintness of heart, the product of an excess of emotion. While the noble image of freedom elevated my soul, those of equality, union and the gentleness of mores moved me to tears, and inspired me with a vivid regret to have lost all these goods. How wrong I was, and yet how natural was my mistake! *I believed that I saw all this in my homeland because I carried it in my heart.*"[2]

It is perhaps not surprising, then, to learn from Rousseau's *Confessions* that the climactic event of his return was enacted in a blur of "republican enthusiasm." On July 25, 1754, he renounced Catholicism and was admitted again to Holy Communion in the church of Calvin. The final obstacle to becoming once more a Citizen of Geneva was at last removed.

There seems little reason to doubt his professed motives for this conversion: "Ashamed of being excluded from my rights as a Citizen by the profession of a cult other than that of my fathers, I resolved to return to the latter." The natural religion he had since come to on his own was unaffected by this outward show of duty: in his unique inward faith, his conscience remained clear. "I thought that the Gospel being the same for all Christians, and the root of dogma being different only among those who meddled in explaining what they could not comprehend, it belonged to the Sovereign alone in each country to fix the cult and this unintelligible dogma, and that it was in consequence the duty of the Citizen to concede the dogma and to follow the cult prescribed by law."[3] Without any great inner reformation, then, Rousseau pledged allegiance anew to the civic religion of Geneva—if only to preserve and honor outwardly that personal patriotic zeal which had led him back to the city.

Genevans welcomed him with the curiosity and interest befitting someone internationally renowned. He was warmly hailed in some quarters, cooly received in others. To some magistrates and members of the oligarchic elite, he was automatically suspect for being '*un homme de bas*,' a man of the lower classes, and a religious traitor at that. For his part, Rousseau had become too contemptuous, through his contact with the powerful of Paris, to pay court to the patricians of Geneva. He now regarded his ostensible superiors with a certain disdain:

> Why is it that, having found many good men in my youth, I find so few at
> an advanced age; has their breed been exhausted? No, but the order where
> I have need of seeking them today is not the same one where I found them

then. Among the people, where great passions speak only at intervals, the sentiments of nature most often make themselves heard. In the most elevated estates, they have been absolutely stifled, and under the mask of sentiment it is never anything but interest or vanity which speaks.

However earnestly Rousseau might try to hide it, this was not the sort of disposition liable to win firm friends among the ruling class. Such sentiments were scarcely anathema, however, to those simple Genevans who comprised the bulk of the Citizenry. Professors and pastors flocked to his side and helped him win reentry into the church. Above all, he was a hero to the watchmakers of the faubourg de Saint-Gervais, the artisan district where his father had worked and lived.[4]

He quickly became friends with several of the politically prominent Citizens and Bourgeois. Perhaps the closest of his new acquaintances was Jacques-François De Luc, by trade a watchmaker, by avocation an author of works refuting Mandeville and other unseemly rationalists. An ardent representative of the Genevan popular party, De Luc treated Rousseau as an ally as well as a friend. In the estimate of one historian, De Luc was "the very model of the Genevan bourgeois. He had all the faults and all the merits of his class. He was very pious, very honest, very patriotic and 'republican,' very stiff and very tedious. He found his pleasure in political intrigues and patriotic festivals."[5] De Luc was Rousseau's kind of man—although even Rousseau admitted to ennui when forced to read his friend's rambling essays. We may nevertheless assume that he listened with some interest to the grumblings of the patriot, a man jealous of the Citizens' power—and indignant at any attempted usurpation of it by a patrician elite. By the end of the summer, Rousseau could scarcely have harbored any illusions about the controversial nature of Geneva's government.

Yet Rousseau's dedication of the *Second Discourse* to Geneva remained unchanged. He showed it to De Luc but otherwise seems to have kept it a secret. Since, at the time, he took some satisfaction in his reception by the city, he may well have decided not to test the tolerance of the magistrates by the premature publication of a portrait that, in its evocation of democracy, might seem less than fitting to some of them.[6]

It was not as if he were doing no serious political thinking: during this period, he worked on a translation of Tacitus (never completed) and sketched parts of the "Political Institutions," his projected magnum opus. He also expressed interest in writing a history of the Valais, the mountainous Swiss district bordering the eastern shore of Lake Léman across from Geneva. But, apart from conversations with professed democrats like De Luc and a handful of ministers, as liberal as they were literate, Rousseau seems to have kept to himself, venturing out for walks or to feed the fish of Lake Léman, enjoying the attention his appearance in public elicited. Toward the end of his stay, he spent a week boating round the Lake with De Luc and his family, taking in many of the sights he would later use as the natural backdrop for *La Nouvelle Héloïse*.[7]

It remained a productive and pleasant visit. In October, when he finally left

Geneva, Rousseau, "pressed by the good man De Luc," announced plans to return permanently the following spring.[8] He would never see his native city again.

Exile

His absence was at first puzzling. For some years afterward, Genevan friends like De Luc would urge him to return, even volunteering money to pay for the trip. Rousseau always refused. Why?

In the *Confessions*, he implies that it was a simple matter of government hostility. "As . . . my discourse on inequality . . . was dedicated to the Republic, and as this Dedication might not please the Council, I chose to await the effect it would have in Geneva before returning there. This effect was not favorable."[9]

Rousseau had some reason to be apprehensive about the Small Council's reaction. In November, 1754, the minister Perdriau, after obtaining an advance copy of Rousseau's piece, probably through an indiscretion of the publisher, warned the author not to flout the customary government censorship. The minister was worried as well about the novel content of the encomium. Rousseau's response was adamant. He had composed his dedication only because he had been "struck by the conformity . . . between the Constitution of government that flows from my principles and that which really exists in our Republic." Had his approach led him to apparent innovation? "So much the better," Rousseau writes defiantly. "In commendable things it is always better to set an example than to be given one, and I think my reasons for imitating no one are only too just." Prior censorship? He had considered submitting his dedication to the Small Council but had decided against it. "The decision of my Censors would be without appeal, I would see myself reduced to shutting up or to publishing under my own name sentiments of others, and I want to do neither one nor the other. My experience has made me take the firm resolution to be henceforth my own Censor." If the Council reacted badly, so much the worse for the Council.[10]

But the Small Council did not react so badly. Despite Rousseau's mounting anxiety—he demanded that printed copies of the *Second Discourse* be rushed to Geneva before being distributed elsewhere—the Council accepted his dedication without a murmur of public dissent. In private, to be sure, one of the Syndics dispatched a rather icy note of appreciation to Rousseau. It may have been a disappointment to have his passionate apotheosis treated with such formal reserve by the civic authorities. Yet, given his failure to have the text censored, and given the substance of the dedication—which, in the context of Geneva's political struggles, could be read as a manifesto for the popular party of the Citizens and Bourgeois—Rousseau could scarcely have expected a warmer reception. After all, the members of the Small Council were not fools. As the former First Syndic, Du Pan, delicately wrote him at the time, "In your dedicatory epistle, you have followed the movements of your heart, and I fear that you flatter us too much. You represent us as we ought to be, not as we are." (A contemporary reviewer made a similar point: "Whether or not in the course of this long narrative there are facts which belong effectively to the State that M. Rousseau has in view, the greatest number are scarcely relevant to anything but *Utopia*, and the author has followed a kind of verve that has swept him along, rather than painting objects in their exact reality.")[11]

Rousseau himself seemed pleased enough at the time by Geneva's official response. As he wrote to a friend in the city, "I can scarcely express the joy with which I learned that the Council had accepted the Dedication . . . in the name of the Republic."[12] But if it was not hostility from the Small Council, then what *did* prevent him from returning to his homeland?

In part, he was charmed by the alternative. Back in Paris, M. d'Epinay, then his friend and patron, offered him the use of a small cottage called the Hermitage, located outside Paris near the forest of Montmorency. The serene natural setting appealed to Rousseau's "peaceful nature" and "love of solitude."[13]

He also expressed concern about how he would support himself in a city the size of Geneva. In France, he had decided to live the life of an artisan and earn his keep as a music copyist. But he fretted that this "arduous profession," which barely supported him near Paris, would prove inadequate if he moved to Geneva. Besides, copying music that would be performed at the private affairs of the wealthy scarcely seemed a vocation fit for a republic like Geneva. "How absurd and irresponsible it would be for me to let myself nourish among my compatriots the frivolous tastes I condemn, and which are already only too widespread among them."[14]

And then there was Voltaire. Shortly after Rousseau had left Geneva, the great man had arrived, winning permission from the authorities to settle on republican territory just outside the city. In the *Confessions*, Rousseau makes it sound as if he had already decided against being anywhere near Voltaire by 1754. "I realized that he would make a revolution there, and that I was going to discover in my homeland the tone, the airs and the mores that had driven me from Paris; that it would be necessary to fight constantly, and that I would have no other choice in my conduct than that of being an insufferable pedant, or a cowardly and bad citizen." After the publication of the *Second Discourse* in 1755, it is true that Rousseau had cause to be leery of Voltaire. In a celebrated letter acknowledging a complimentary copy of the *Discourse*, Voltaire, who thought it a work of folly, said so: "I have received, Sir, your new book against the human race; for which I thank you. . . . No one has ever used so much intelligence to try to render us Beasts. It raises the desire to walk on four paws when one reads your works." At the time, though, Rousseau muted any reservations. In a letter to a Genevan friend in December, 1754, he wrote that Voltaire could "hardly trouble the peace which reigns among our men of letters." His presence, Rousseau concluded, "can only be honorable for our town." Even Voltaire's caustic note about the *Second Discourse* left him unruffled. When *le Mercure de France* printed their exchange of letters on the matter in October, 1755, Rousseau welcomed the publication, remarking that it did him honor.[15]

Rousseau had more pressing reasons for keeping his distance from Geneva, though. In 1755, he was not forced into exile, either by the hostility of the Small Council, the absence of work, or the presence of Voltaire. Rather, he *chose* the role of exile for himself. If he stayed in Paris, that was in large part because he preferred the retirement of solitude to the responsibilities of Citizenship.

After all, being an active Citizen of Geneva had its problems. For Rousseau, it might mean joining men like De Luc in a struggle to defend the sovereignty of the Citizens—and that meant not only tangling with gifted rivals like Voltaire, but also dealing directly with whatever uneasiness the Small Council might feel about the substance of Rousseau's own "ardent and patriotic zeal." It meant not only confronting the ruling class, but also risking defeat at its hands. Such an unpredictable situation could not have seemed appealing to the daydreamer, a man who feared his eloquence as a writer would founder in public speaking. He was not interested in constant struggle. He had no wish to be perceived as a troublemaker causing dissension in what ought to be a happy and harmonious community, like the Geneva Rousseau himself had imagined in Chambéry.[16]

By remaining in exile near Paris, by contrast, he remained free to think for himself. Living in isolation at the Hermitage, he could preserve his own unique perspective on the world of politics. Without having to worry about prior censorship or the difficulties and dangers of political action, he could follow his "helvetic muse" wherever his wandering thoughts might lead. "There are some circumstances in which a man can be more useful to his fellow citizens outside of his fatherland than if he were living in its bosom," writes Rousseau in *Emile*. "Then he ought to listen only to his zeal and to endure his exile without grumbling; this very exile is one of his duties."[17]

By the time he wrote these words, Rousseau knew that the Geneva dear to his heart was at odds with the Geneva he had seen in 1754. Even living in his own *patrie*, the dreamer will be an exile. Forced to choose, Rousseau would rather preserve the integrity of the dream. The result, in his stance toward Geneva, is a kind of tough-minded innocence—intolerant of imperfection, impatient with detailed diagnosis, scarcely interested in the subtleties of reform, yet equally unhappy with the violent dislocations a civil war would surely bring.

Doubts

Rhetorically, he begins to compare the austere purity of the Swiss mountain villages with the growing luxury of the commercial plains below. His image of democracy becomes bifocal. At first, this polarization illuminates the dangers besetting Geneva: by depicting the virtuous mountain dwellers of Neuchâtel, Rousseau can remind his compatriots of what will be jeopardized if the city succumbs to those arts that are only the ornament of inequality. As he might have perceived dimly in 1755, his foil would be Voltaire.

When Voltaire moved to Geneva in 1755, he brought with him an ardent desire to be the toast of theatrical audiences everywhere, an ambition he had nursed through the composition of more than fifty plays. Once he arrived, he outfitted his country estate with a private theater, where he mounted productions of his own plays. But he soon ran afoul of a Genevan law banning theatrical presentations. Undaunted, Voltaire moved just beyond republican territory, to a new estate where he continued to entertain Genevan worthies with fine wine, fine food, fine talk, and, of course, more plays. For the seventh volume of Diderot's *Encyclopedia*, he even prevailed upon his friend d'Alembert to pay glowing tribute to the enlightenment of Geneva and then counsel the erection of a civic theater. In the unusually lengthy entry that resulted, d'Alembert included an account of the city's ministers as free-thinking deists, while duly proposing that Geneva confirm its progressive reputation by lifting its ban on public spectacles.

By itself, this proposal would not have been displeasing to the upper class of Genevans, already much taken with French fashion. But to the run of frugal Citizens, long fed up with the flaunting of wealth, the thought was quite appalling. Moreover, the whole city, led by its ministers, was put in an uproar by the implication that these sturdy Calvinist divines were not preaching the Trinity or the truth of revelation. On December 9, 1757, the Council of Geneva agreed that some measures be sought "in order to have this article changed or suppressed."[18]

When Rousseau finally read the article in the *Encyclopedia*, he, too, was displeased, albeit for his own reasons. Apparently urged on by some of his Genevan friends, and sensing his own image of the city implicitly challenged, Rousseau contemplated an independent response. By February of 1758, he had decided to write a reply that, while mentioning d'Alembert's theological slanders, would otherwise focus entirely on his proposal for a theater in Geneva.

In the *Letter to D'Alembert* that he published in the summer of 1758, Rousseau warns his compatriots to "avoid becoming corrupt if there is still time. Beware of the first step which is never the last one, and consider that it is easier to keep good mores than to put an end to bad ones." To make his fears vivid, he introduces his argument by detailing the virtues possessed by the rural inhabitants of Neuchâtel; he then invites his readers to imagine the results if a theater were established in this sylvan setting. Such an innovation, he suggests, would inevitably entail a lot of unhappy consequences: slackening of work, increase of expenses, decrease in trade, institution of taxes, introduction of luxury, ultimately the growth of inequality. In a monarchy like France, such developments would be relatively inconsequential; there, virtue is long gone anyway. But in a democracy like Geneva, these events would be catastrophic: they would sound the death knell for civic freedom.[19]

Similar doubts are more frankly conveyed in *La Nouvelle Héloïse*, the novel Rousseau was then writing. Here also a contrast is drawn between the simple Swiss mountain dwellers Saint-Preux visits and the prosperous Genevan merchants Claire describes to Julie. But in this case, Claire does not hold out much hope for arresting the degeneration she observes. The Genevans, she writes, "have generosity, intelligence, astuteness; but they love money too much—a fault I attribute to their situation, which renders its use necessary, since the territory does not suffice to sustain the residents. It thus happens that Genevans, dispersed in Europe in order to enrich themselves, imitate the airs of foreigners. . . . Thus the luxury of other people makes them scorn their ancient simplicity; proud freedom appears to them ignoble; and they forge for themselves chains of money, not as a shackle, but as a trinket."[20]

But Rousseau's doubts about Geneva remained largely hidden, even if his continued absence from the city gave mute testament to them. And while his regained Citizenship won him a badge he could wear proudly elsewhere, Genevans in turn found his distant authority convenient enough for their own purposes. In 1756, when a debate arose over taxation, both sides cited on their behalf Rousseau's views on "Political Economy" in the *Encyclopedia*.[21] His remoteness from the scene, coupled with his public silence on current affairs, enabled magistrates as well as ordinary Citizens to find aid and comfort in his writings.

Rousseau himself showed no great eagerness to clarify the implications of his thinking for the internal affairs of Geneva. Perhaps he lacked a clear position; perhaps he was still simply ignorant of Geneva's constitution. On the one hand, he was not unwilling to risk provoking the Small Council by his idealized portrait of Geneva as a democratic republic. On the other hand, he was not averse to flattering these same magistrates by hailing their wisdom, perhaps in the hope of winning from them reforms that he deemed desirable. His vacillations can be seen in the first drafts of Claire's letter about Geneva in *La Nouvelle Héloïse*. In a deleted passage, he has her remark that Geneva, by letting foreigners meddle in its affairs, has forfeited its genuine freedom; in a later version, he has her praise the sage magistrates of the city; and, in the final version, he adds some critical remarks on luxury, but only after deleting the blunt assertion that "freedom and poverty are inseparable."[22]

A similar ambivalence can be detected throughout the *Letter to d'Alembert*. Although he appeals directly to the magistrates to save Geneva from corruption by continuing its ban against theatrical presentations, he also says that he is speaking to "the many," and he defends at length the city's political circles, at the time hotbeds of agitation for the popular party. As we have seen, hostility to French manners and opposition to a civic theater were positions more congenial to the common Citizens than to the magistrates, many of whom cordially enjoyed their evenings *chez* Voltaire.

In effect, Rousseau seems to propose an unlikely alliance of concerned ministers, the popular party of the Citizens and Bourgeois, and any magistrates sympathetic to their plight. Yet even this must remain mere speculation. For, as Michel Launay has put it, Rousseau was "a political writer of a particular type: one who writes and also hides himself, one who wishes to act and yet ignore the results of his action, one who wants to guide but who refuses to respond to those who demand of him that he guide."[23]

At the time, he could ill afford to alienate any potential allies, particularly in

Geneva. In publishing his *Letter* attacking d'Alembert's "seductive picture" of an enlightened Geneva, Rousseau also broke publicly with Diderot, once his closest friend among the philosophers of Paris. To add injury to insult, he did so just as Diderot and the *Encyclopedia* were coming under the fiercest attack yet from the French clergy.[24] Of course, Rousseau, writing from his French retreat, was free to portray Geneva as a city of virtue surrounded by savants eager to lure its Citizenry into the pursuit of undignified pastimes. Without running much risk of angering the authorities in Geneva, he could denounce as frivolous the entertainments Voltaire and d'Alembert wished to export. But then it would be rather unseemly to take sides in the political disputes still dividing the city.

Forgoing any direct expression of his views in the *Letter to d'Alembert*, he therefore retreated to veiled allusions, preferring to exhort his compatriots through the filter of his favorite spartan imagery. His true feelings are perhaps most vividly conveyed, however, through his reminiscences of growing up in the city. Thus, near the end of the *Letter*, in the midst of urging on Geneva the example of Sparta, he pauses in a footnote to recall an impromptu celebration by the regiment of Saint-Gervais that he had witnessed as a child. His prose suddenly soaring in rhapsodic cadences, he graphically depicts the patriotic joy he shared with his father as they watched six hundred artisans in uniform relax after a day of military exercises. He remembers how his father, swept up by the sight and trembling with emotion, embraced him while imploring, "Jean-Jacques, . . . Love your country. Do you see these good Genevans? They are all friends, they are all brothers; joy and concord reign in their midst." It is an image of *temps perdu* that leaves a bittersweet aftertaste.[25]

It will not be the last time that Rousseau indirectly criticizes his contemporaries by imagining a time when the world was happier. Such memories, beyond the solace they afford the writer, set an example that others ought to feel worth preserving. No wonder Rousseau singles out for commendation the motto closing d'Alembert's article on "Geneva": *O fortunatos nimium, sua si bona norint* ("O fortunate and more than fortunate, if only they knew their own good"). This, indeed, is the deceptively conservative note on which he ends his own homage to Geneva: "May it transmit to its descendents the virtues, the freedom, and the peace which it has inherited from its fathers"—good Genevan fathers like the watchmakers he grew up with in the faubourg de Saint-Gervais. "This is the last wish with which I end my writings; it is the one with which my life will end."[26]

When he wrote these words, Rousseau was having one of his periodic bouts where he felt himself to be on the verge of death. In the *Confessions*, he explains how his heart "mixed the sentiments" of his physical suffering "with the ideas which meditation on my subject had engendered in me." Thinking about Geneva alleviated the pain. While writing "with a zeal that overcame everything," he "shed delicious tears," and felt as if he "had reentered into my element."[27]

Some of his compatriots, however, were not so moved. Once again, the minister Perdriau expressed his misgivings. Another acquaintance, the patrician doctor Tronchin, who had been involved in the official protest of d'Alembert's essay,

was also uneasy with Rousseau's effort, particularly his emphasis on the circles.
"Those public amusements and circles," he cautioned, "are a source of distrac-
tion, loss of time and dissipation, which passes the upright limits of a necessary
amusement, and which palpably harms domestic education." A civic education,
such as the Greeks practiced—even a remote approximation, such as Rousseau
had implied that the circles could provide—had no place in Geneva. To Tronchin, a purely private education was quite sufficient. "This country, my friend, is
not what you imagine it to be. . . . Geneva does not resemble . . . Sparta."[28]

The point was not lost on Rousseau. Busy at work on the Swiss idyll of *La
Nouvelle Héloïse*, freshly enthralled by his own image of Geneva, he felt increasingly estranged from the civic authorities who received his picture of their perfection so ungratefully. In 1759, he wrote to the Genevan pastor Vernes: "Having
almost become a child again, I am moved in recalling the songs of my childhood
in Geneva; I sing them with a faint voice, and I end by weeping over my country,
thinking that I have outlived it."[29]

3

The Social Contract

THE *Social Contract*, Rousseau's great masterpiece of political theory, was first published in 1762. By then, the "Citizen of Geneva" had become one of the most celebrated authors of his day. If his *First Discourse* had created a scandal, the *Second* had confirmed his notoriety. Both had won him the respect of his peers and the interest of a wider audience. The publication of the *Letter to d'Alembert* had sparked gossip about life among the savants of Paris, while the continuing popularity of his opera *Le Devin du village* ("The Village Sooth-sayer"), first performed in 1752, assured him a living as a music copyist. Above all, though, it was *La Nouvelle Héloïse*, his epistolary romance of love and death in Switzerland, that transformed Rousseau into a figure of passionate importance to a broad mass of readers, as their sobbing, ecstatic letters to him reveal. Published in 1761, his novel became one of the best-selling books of the eighteenth century.

Rousseau, though, was not yet satisfied. Much of his time he devoted to fin-ishing *Emile*, his vision of a perfect pedagogy. And in the *Confessions*, he recalled that "of the diverse works that I had in hand, the one which I had meditated on for the longest time, the one which I had devoted myself to with the greatest relish, the one on which I wanted to work all my life, and the one which, in my opinion, ought to put the seal on my reputation was my *Political Institutions*" — the work that became the *Social Contract*.[1]

Observing the Defects

The initial impetus for this work had come in 1743 and 1744, during a visit to Venice, where he was a diplomatic secretary in the employ of the French ambas-sador. Venice had long occupied a place of pride within the republican tradition of political theory. In his *Discourses on Livy*, Machiavelli had cited it alongside Sparta as an archetype of republicanism in a small city-state. Rousseau himself mentions reading a history of Venice as a youth. By the middle of the eighteenth century, though, the city had fallen into a period of decline, and its government had become a narrow oligarchy. What Rousseau found in his daily chore of writing dispatches on affairs in the city was not the Venice eulogized in the history he had read in his youth or in the great republican treatises, but rather a "dissolute State" aswarm with seedy courtiers seeking favors from a "hereditary Aristocracy."[2]

Disillusioned and cast out of Venice after a spat with the ambassador, Rousseau at first decided, almost instinctively, to repair to Geneva, apparently hoping to revive his spirits there "while awaiting a better lot." But he never forgot the disappointing institutions he had seen from the inside in Venice. "By observing the defects in that Government so vaunted," and by noting the discrepancies between the republican ideal he still felt drawn toward and a real political world that repelled him, Rousseau developed a sustaining interest in political institutions and their role in shaping men.[3]

Over the next fifteen years, Rousseau periodically turned back to the difficult questions first raised by his experience in Venice: "What is the nature of Government proper to form a People who are the most virtuous, the most thoughtful, the most wise, finally the best, taking this work in its most lofty sense. . . . What is the Government which by its nature always holds itself closest to the law? Moreover, what is the law?" In the meantime, his revelation on the road to Vincennes and his subsequent discourses on the sciences and on inequality had convinced him that the root of the ills he observed lay not in human nature, but rather in the institutions of modern society. "I had seen that all depended radically on politics, and that, in whatever way one set about it, no people would be anything but what the nature of its Government made it to be."[4]

His trip to Geneva in 1754 had renewed his interest in these matters—especially since "the notions of law and freedom" prevalent there had seemed to him "neither just enough nor clear enough for my liking." Sensing that he had something to say about the principles at stake in Geneva's ongoing political debates, friends there pressed him to address these issues directly. By 1761, Rousseau was ready. Once again, a discrepancy between his imagined ideal and a contradictory reality motivated him to formulate "some great truths useful for the happiness of humankind, but above all for those in my homeland."[5]

He had been working on his "Political Institutions" for some time. It had occupied his attention in Geneva in 1754, and he had also devoted thought to the project while living near Montmorency. Although several early fragments of this work survive, Rousseau himself reports that he destroyed most of the materials when he decided that the scope of his original plan was beyond his powers. Some idea of this scope may be gleaned not only from the image of Alpine democracy we have examined, but also from his subsequent political essays on Corsica and Poland. If the whole of human existence was rooted in politics, then it should be the task of good political institutions not merely to secure the property and protect the person of each inhabitant, but also to cultivate the capacities and develop the good sense of each citizen. To these ends, the art of politics needed to consider the economy and constitution of the household, the beliefs of the civil religion, even the structure of public play. In a note among the surviving fragments, Rousseau lists some of the things that interested him: "the greatness of nations; government; of laws; of religion; of honor; of f. [finance?]; of commerce; of travel; of sustenance; abuse of society; culture of sciences; examination of Plato's Republic."[6]

What eventually appeared in 1762 as the *Social Contract* thus represents but a fraction of a much larger work. It scarcely conveys the range of Rousseau's interests, the full depth of his thinking about politics. Yet in it, Rousseau displays and defends his original principles and labors to distill into ideas the essence of his thought. For this, finally, is the book he offers to both posterity and his comrades—those citizens concerned about Geneva's political reformation.

The Principles of Political Right

The argument of the *Social Contract* may be briefly outlined. Since debate still surrounds its central categories, we must pay special attention to making plain the sense here given to his contested concepts—particularly his ideas about the contract, the general will, sovereignty, and government. For the moment, I will therefore focus on formal principles, rather than on Rousseau's prudential maxims for realizing them.[7]

Rousseau assumes that all human beings are by nature free: "Man is born free," even if everywhere he appears in chains. By birth a "master of himself," no individual, "under any pretext whatever," can be legitimately subjected to another "without his consent." This "natural law" of freedom is insufficient, however, to found any "natural right." For a "right"—a binding entitlement—to obtain among men and to have any force, a shared moral sense and some ability to reason with ideas are required; in his undeveloped natural state, man lacks both. Man's natural freedom, coupled with his lack of natural rights, poses the problem the *Social Contract* sets out to solve. In order to establish right, man needs to observe conventions that can develop his morality and reason without stifling his free will. The "fundamental problem," then, is this: "Find a form of association that defends and protects the person and goods of each associate with all the common force, and by means of which each one, uniting with all, nevertheless obeys only himself and remains as free as before."[8]

His book takes its title from his solution. In his usage, "the social contract" is that act "by which a people is a people," an act in which all unanimously agree to live together as a community. Through this act of mutual consent, the possibility of cooperation and collective agency first arises. But why should an individual willingly set limits on his natural freedom and immerse himself in a community? Part of the answer is that only in cooperation with his fellows can the individual develop his powers and secure from others recognition for the goods in life he feels entitled to. Another part of the answer is that a genuine community, because it is based on "the most voluntary act in the world," because it is rooted in a unanimous consent that expresses a real common interest, because it "obligates or favors all citizens equally," and because the association has "no other object than the general good," can never appear to the associated individuals as an obstacle to their own free will: "As long as subjects are subordinated only to such conventions, they do not obey anyone, but solely their own will."[9]

The "general will" is Rousseau's designation for that collective ability to do and to forebear doing that arises through this "act by which a people is a people." It is the free will of each, reincarnated through the "contract" as a shared power to define and direct the affairs of a community. At this point, we enter the realm of rational fiction. "Instantly, in the stead of the individual person (*au lieu de la personne particulière*), this act of association produces a moral and collective body, composed of as many members as the assembly has voices, each receiving by this same act its cohesion (*unité*), its common *self* (*moi commun*), its life and its will."[10] There is a certain irony in the clinical precision of this account: for what, in the Alpine republic of Rousseau's dreams, appeared as an organic heritage, handed down from time immemorial—namely, the salutary mores and manners that comprised the "common self" of his rustic citizens—now appears, equally miraculously, as the instantaneous result of a discreet "act."

Yet even in the *Social Contract*, the general will ideally expresses a concrete reality: the *moi* common to each in the community, that aspect of each individual's character constituted by shared experiences and those things held in mutual esteem. Every genuine community, of whatever size or purpose, embodies such a joint sense of self and the possibility of cooperative agency that flows from it. The general will, in other words, merely designates that part of our experience as individuals which moves each of us, in certain contexts, to say "We," and to act in accordance with that identification. There are thus as many general wills as there are genuine communities. For Rousseau, unlike Diderot, who used the phrase before him, the general will is no innate endowment of every individual as a member of the species. In principle, it is neither universal nor inborn, but instead a potential—call it solidarity, fellow feeling, or altruism—that is only developed "by the habit of judging and feeling in the bosom of society and according to its laws."[11]

As a reality, thinking and acting in terms of the general will raises to the level of an explicit joint purpose what, in any vital community, already exists as a disposition tacitly held in common. As an ideal, on the other hand, the general will provides a standard of altruistic motives and shared intentions against which to measure the fallibility of self-interested men, who are often unwilling to look beyond their own private concerns. In this respect, the general will even admits of a mathematical formulation: "Take away from these . . . wills the pluses and minuses that cancel each other out, and the remaining sum of the differences is the general will." What defines the generality of this will is no average of the various concerns different individuals will always have as a matter of course, but rather the sum of those concerns shared by all—a core of common interests, perhaps achieved through compromise, that is amenable to concerted endeavor. The empirical and the ideal are internally related in this idea. Faced with any collection of real individuals, it is possible to arrive at their common will by filtering out everything of interest to only one or a few individuals within the group; and it is only in terms of these shared interests that the actions authorized by the group ought to be oriented. Although, in a genuine community, the general will, like the feeling of "We want," thus belongs in the class of palpable and familiar phenomena, an easily abstracted part of every individual's habitual beliefs and behavior, it can simultaneously appear, particularly in less cohesive societies, as a more remote imperative, something like the dutiful sense that "I ought" to be concerned with my fellows, whatever my spontaneous inclinations.[12]

To define the various aspects of the community created through the social contract and animated by the general will, Rousseau deploys the following technical terms: the "public person," which used to be called a "City," today is termed a "Republic" or "body politic." Insofar as this body is passive, it is called by its members the "State"; insofar as it is active, they call themselves "Sovereign." Taken as a whole, the members of the "public person" are known as "the people"; taken individually, each is termed a citizen when he participates in the sovereign, a subject when he submits to the laws of the state. Within this context, government is a derivative power, an agency authorized by the sovereign citizens to coordinate their relations according to laws they have all agreed to, the better to implement their shared intentions. Government thus designates "an intermediate body established between the subjects and the Sovereign for their mutual correspondence, charged with the execution of the laws and with the maintenance of freedom, civil as well as political." The definition of legitimacy, finally, depends on the line drawn by these terms between government and sovereignty: "In order to be legitimate, it is necessary that the Government not mistake itself for the Sovereign (se confonde avec le Souverain), but rather that it be a minister (ministre) to it."[13]

Since sovereignty is defined as the body politic in action, and since the general will, as we have seen, is but a name for the power of cooperative agency, it is not surprising that Rousseau calls sovereignty "the exercise of the general will." Yet by linking the two concepts, he adds an important dimension to the idea of sovereignty. For sovereignty now encompasses the duality of the empirical and the ideal already encoded in the concept of the general will. That is why Rousseau says clearly in the first draft of the Social Contract that "the sovereign is by its nature only a moral person, that it has only an abstract and collective existence, and that the idea one links to this word cannot be merged with the idea of a simple individual."[14]

Ideally—when it evinces a genuine community of free wills, straightforwardly and cooperatively oriented toward common goods—any sovereign, like any truly general will, can be considered, almost by definition, "always right (toujours droite)," taking droit in its double sense of something straightforward as well as something one is legitimately entitled to. Rousseau assumes that no one would harm himself of his own free will; by extension, no community would harm itself of its own general will. As a rule, people want to be happy: "Why is the general will always right and why do all constantly want (*veulent*) the happiness of each among them, if not because there is no person who does not apply this word *each* to himself, and does not think of himself while voting for all?" [15]

Yet, as a matter of fact, the actual members of an actual sovereign may be too confused, too distracted, or too oppressed to be able to express lucidly and cooperatively their shared wants, too self-absorbed or too fearful to animate steadfastly a joint public endeavor in pursuit of them. Then the "will of all"—a mere average of the separate, particular concerns of each individual—finds expression, rather than the general will—that is, the resolution of each on what shared interests are worth pursuing with others. Moreover, even a steadfastly cooperative people, though entitled to what it wants, sometimes lacks foresight in pursuing what it wills, or even thoughtfulness in choosing what it desires: "The general will is always right, but the judgment that guides it is not always lucid," particularly when a people is not accustomed to exercising freedom in public. [16]

From this circumstance arises the need from the start for a wise set of conventions, designed to help each individual kindle for himself the light of intuitive understanding he possesses. "From the lights of the public results the union of understanding and will in the social body." While good institutions engender this result spontaneously, Rousseau concedes the need at the outset for a "great Legislator," such as Lycurgus or Calvin, to design the best conventions for a given people and to set the rules in motion. Yet the authority invested in the lawgiver is not unlimited. According to Greek tradition, the truly great legislator leaves the scene once his work is done. And so it is with Rousseau's lawgiver: he is not a magistrate, nor is he a part of the sovereign. "He who drafts the laws, therefore, does not or should not have any legislative right." On the contrary, his constitution cannot be considered legitimate "until it has been submitted to the free vote of the people." [17]

A sovereign people, thus suitably illuminated, continue to act together through legislation. Laws, according to Rousseau, "are properly only the conditions of the civil association"; therefore "the People subjected to the laws ought to be their author." He means this literally: on questions of law, only the associated individuals in assembly may arrive at a trustworthy determination of their common interests; only these free individuals may pledge themselves to obey the laws, and, through this act, make these laws their own. To insist, as Rousseau does, that sovereignty ought to be "inalienable" and "indivisible" is not, then, to abridge the freedom of the individuals, it is rather to protect it, by impugning the adequacy of "representative government" as a surrogate for direct self-rule. [18]

Insofar as all laws enacted by a sovereign in assembly are thoughtful expressions of a steadfast general will, they evince a common interest in common goods and apply universally and equally to all. While the specifics of these laws will vary from people to people, Rousseau nevertheless conjectures that certain goods will be generally wanted by all peoples. "If one seeks what precisely comprises the greatest good of all, which ought to be the end of every system of legislation, one will find that it comes down to these two principal objects: *freedom* and *equality*." Among the things each individual generally gains through the social contract, then, and among the things that most sovereigns will be concerned to protect by law are: civil freedom, defined and limited only by the general will; civil equality, which extends the obligations and rights of citizenship to all without distinction of rank; and property, a guaranteed sphere of one's own, tangibly signified by an entitlement to possessions held privately. The apportionment of this property, it should be added, is just as important as the entitlement to it: laws will only serve the rich—and thus appear as a burden to all those others subjected to them—unless private property is distributed equitably among the inhabitants: "The social state is only advantageous to men insofar as they all have something and none of them has too much." Securing the goods men commonly desire thus depends on a joint pursuit of justice that transcends merely formal considerations.[19]

As we have summarized it thus far, there are several noteworthy aspects of this argument. One is its striking attempt to reconcile the freedom of the individual with the ideal of a perfected social order. The concept that Rousseau uses to mediate these two concerns is the general will, simultaneously an existing standard, abstracted from real individuals with a will and interests of their own, and an ideal measure, applied to individuals and societies, to gauge the extent of their solidarity and fellow feeling. Another significant feature of the argument is its abstractness. As a consequence, the *Social Contract* lacks any sustained discussion of mores and manners, allowing the problem of civic education to emerge instead through the suggestive cipher of the "*moi commun*" and the iconic figure of the great Legislator, that semidivine and entirely incredible demiurge charged with shaping at a single glance the customs, tastes, and intuitive understanding needful to make a people capable of self-rule.[20]

There is yet another aspect of Rousseau's argument that cannot be avoided any longer, one that is particularly vexing in the present context: namely, the evaluation offered of different forms of government. On the face of it, his views on these matters are conventional; he gives the three pure forms of government as democracy, aristocracy, and monarchy. He allows for the possibility of a legitimate monarchy, states that an elective aristocracy is "the best," and also says, in no uncertain terms, that democracy is "not suited for men."[21]

Since Rousseau also says that "a true Democracy has never existed, and never will exist," we are faced with a problem.[22] If Rousseau was indeed a partisan of democracy, it should be possible to base this contention, at least in part, on evidence drawn from the *Social Contract*, his most important work on political theory. But the evidence at hand seems to contradict our thesis.

Before attempting to resolve this apparent dilemma, however, it will be helpful to ponder two related issues: first, the rhetorical situation of Rousseau's book; and second, his implicit stance in it toward Geneva—both the real city on the shores of Lake Léman and the democratic city of his dreams.

The Rhetoric of Reasoning

In writing his short treatise on political right, Rousseau had in mind at least four different audiences. First of all, he wished to address a small group of enlightened readers and interested scholars. Occasionally, he writes as if they will be his only audience, since his work contains such "difficult material" that it will be "fit for few readers." Yet he also wished to speak to the literate general public, and at one point in the *Contract*, he directly appeals to "you modern readers." He was particularly concerned to reach readers in Geneva, as we have seen. Yet modern readers were not the only ones on his mind. He also wanted to write "a book for all times," a work that would "put the seal on my reputation." Last, but not least, he wished to compose a work abstruse enough to avoid attracting censorship—a book so purely "philosophical" that its contents would not appear threatening to public peace.[23]

His concern with these audiences shaped his rhetoric. To satisfy all four simultaneously, the most rigorous use of reasoning seemed appropriate. Among Rousseau's works, the *Social Contract* is unusual in its relatively unadorned style, as well as in its circumspectness and difficulty. Drawing on his considerable knowledge of the natural law tradition, he cast the work in the form of a scholarly republican treatise.[24] The casual reader might think it notable only for its careful definitions and lucid economy of argument.

In the first draft of the book, he imagines that he is trying to convince an "independent man" not unlike the person he had been before his revelation on the road to Vincennes: someone unimpressed with the putative authority of others, skeptical about trusting his own sentiments, and thus infected by a certain vanity and a one-sided recourse to reasoning. Yet Rousseau expresses the hope that "reason which led him astray will bring him back to humanity." Without building on the intuitive understanding and feeling for right natural to a man of conscience—a man like himself after his personal reformation—Rousseau will attempt, through reasoning alone, to convince the skeptic of his own position. He will do so, in part, by granting the skeptic his own preoccupation with utilitarian interests and, in part, by attempting to reconcile "what right permits with what interest prescribes, so that justice and utility are never found divided." Despite the wealth of illustrations from ancient writers, the *Social Contract* is thus a treatise specifically tailored to a modern audience of individuals with a modicum of reason and interests of their own. Its argument is designed to convince even a selfish man whose heart is closed to anything but the cold light of logic. Rousseau will use interest to surmount interest. He will fight reason with reason. And if he is successful, any enlightened reader will be won over to the merits of living in a social order that can teach him to prefer his "properly understood interest" to his present vain interests; he might then be led to become "good, virtuous and sensitive," in addition to being a man of reasoned beliefs.[25]

A reasoned treatise promised the further advantage of securing the understanding of posterity, while averting the wrath of local magistrates. By composing a densely argued essay, apparently of interest only to experts in jurisprudence, Rousseau might reassure any censor that his argument was abstract, impractical, and hence harmless. At the same time, by subjecting the desires awakened in his reveries to the discipline of definition and justification, he could minimize the element of subjective caprice, while opening his thoughts to the judgment of anyone able to appraise ideas. For "only reason is common," it alone enables the mind to communicate across barriers of language, time, and space.[26]

Similarly, reasoning might establish an ideal of practical relevance to contemporary readers. As Simone Weil once put it, even if "the ideal is just as unattainable as the dream," it "differs from the dream in that it concerns reality; it enables one, as a mathematical limit, to grade situations, whether real or realizable, in an order of value from least to greatest."[27] And Rousseau, it is clear, intended the *Social Contract* not as a gloss on a daydream, nor even as a testament to his own feelings, but rather as an essay on the real possibilities of a real world, of use for passing judgment on real political institutions.

The proof of such possibilities he finds preeminently in ancient history, in the evidence of institutions that has come down to us from Greece and Rome. "The limits of the possible in moral things are less narrow than we think," he insists: "Let us reckon what can be done by what has been done." A similar concern with reasoning about real political institutions—and his interest in engaging a wider audience of modern readers—shows in his allusions to contemporary affairs in France, England, and particularly Geneva. Geneva is the object of some ten references, most of which depict it as that rarity among modern regimes, "a free State."[28] In the circumstances of Geneva, it seems, a legitimate form of association is feasible even today.

But what precisely was Rousseau's attitude toward Geneva? Should his expressions of praise be taken at face value? Was he trying to convey any specific political position to his Genevan readers? Was he endorsing the aristocratic form of its government as "the best" possible in a modern "free State"? Was he really interested in the practical politics of Geneva at all? By pursuing the difficult question of how Rousseau intended the *Social Contract* to be read in Geneva, we may be brought a little closer to resolving our previous question: What is Rousseau's message about democracy in this, his most important work on politics?

Hidden Intentions

A settled answer to any question about an intended reading is, of course, all but impossible. Yet we have noted how Rousseau was pressed by friends in Geneva to publish a work addressing their political situation. In the *Confessions*, Rousseau himself speaks of writing the *Social Contract*, in part, for the use of this audience. But how did he expect these readers to receive his formidably recondite argument?

One key may be a remark about Machiavelli. In the context—a paragraph about the virtually insatiable desire of Kings for absolute power—it seems so offhand as to verge on being a non sequitur: "While pretending to give lessons to Kings, he gave great ones to the people. The Prince of Machiavelli is the book of republicans." [29]

Sometime after his fate in Geneva was sealed, Rousseau added to this terse digression a kind of explanatory note, first published when his collected works appeared in 1782:

> Machiavelli was an honest man and a good citizen: but being attached to the house of Medici, he was forced, during the oppression of his fatherland, to disguise his love for freedom. The choice of his execrable Hero alone makes manifest enough his secret intention, and the contrast between the maxims of his Book on the Prince and those of his discourses on Titus Livy proves that this profound statesman has had until now only superficial or corrupt Readers. [30]

Could it be that Rousseau followed a similar plan in the *Social Contract* and, during the oppression of *his* fatherland, chose to disguise *his* love of freedom—specifically, the love of freedom expressed in his own preference for democracy?

While hasty censors might be misled, uncorrupted and careful readers, anxious to learn lessons addressed "to the people," would then be extended an invitation not simply to read closely, but also to *decipher* this text, by exploring internal discrepancies, by comparing this book with others by the author, even by reading parts of it as a fable.

Thus alerted to the symptomatic significance of explicit contradictions, a Genevan reader concerned with freedom during the oppression of his homeland—a member of the democratic party, say—might notice that the Roman Republic, in a footnote in the *Contract*, is called "a true democracy," thereby casting doubt upon the self-evident confidence of the assertion made twice in the main body of the text that "a true Democracy has never existed." [31] Interested in the meaning of such contradictions, a partisan reader might then set beside the account of democracy given in the *Social Contract* such other accounts as the one in the dedication to the *Second Discourse* or the one in the *Letter to d'Alembert*. The curious reader would there see our author applaud "democratic government, wisely tempered," and find democracy defined as a social order "in which the subjects and the sovereign are only the same men considered in different relations"—a passage paralleled in many respects by the definition of legitimacy in the *Social Contract*. [32]

Our reader, if he were still concerned about these matters, particularly in view of Rousseau's apparent deference to aristocracy, might also ponder some other puzzling passages, for example the one in book IV of the *Contract* where Rousseau compares the Genevan bourgeoisie with the Venetian aristocracy: "A number of poor Venetian noblemen never come close to any magistracy, and all they get out of their nobility is the empty title Excellence and the right to attend grand

Council. This grand Council being as numerous as our general Council in Geneva, its illustrious members have no more privileges than our simple Citizens." As Michel Launay has pointed out, to suggest "that all the Citizens and Bourgeois of Geneva form an aristocracy" was "to contest the pretension of the Small Council to reserve the exercise of aristocratic government for itself." But there is more. Remembering what Rousseau writes elsewhere in the book about Venice—he calls it a "dissolute State" and the worst kind of aristocracy—does not make his statement that "the bourgeoisie of Geneva represent exactly the Patriciate of the Venetians" sound particularly flattering to the state of Geneva. The message might be deciphered as follows: like Venice, Geneva is not an "aristocracy properly so-called"—that is, one elected by the sovereign. Instead, it is ruled by an inbred clique of families who effectively exclude the majority of qualified citizens from exercising their legitimate right to sanction all laws in person, to review those elected to execute them, and to hold high office themselves.[33]

This kind of coded critique, coupled with the unusual abstractness of the argument, may be the sort of thing Rousseau had in mind, both when he evokes Machiavelli's "secret intention," and when, in the *Confessions*, he describes his own "indirect method" in composing the *Social Contract*. On the one hand, he might provide arguments of use to partisans of the popular party. On the other hand, he might also win over some of those other compatriots whose "ideas were neither just enough nor clear enough" for his liking. An "indirect manner" of speaking to *this* Genevan audience allowed him "to approach gently the vanity of its members," while keeping open the possibility that they might "pardon me for having been able to see a little further in this area than them."[34]

Realizing the Principles of Right

Let us look more closely at the best social order possible, as suggested by the maxims of the *Social Contract*. For if we can show an affinity between this exploration of real possibilities and the image of Alpine democracy, we may get a clearer idea of what Rousseau may have left to the imagination of sympathetic readers.

Before we begin, though, an important caveat must be entered. Throughout the *Social Contract*, and particularly when he presents maxims for implementing his principles, Rousseau is at pains to protest that he is not seeking to establish "absolutely which is the best Government," insisting instead that each form of government is the best in certain situations, the worst in others: "Freedom, not being a fruit of all Climates, is not accessible to all peoples."[35] On the other hand, he also implies that some peoples—for example, those in his own "free State"—are more fortunately situated than others to realize the principles of political right; for them, the contingencies of circumstance do not preclude a measure of perfection. Bearing in mind the ambiguity thus surrounding his notion of "the best Government"—an ambiguity of some significance for the uses subsequently made of the *Social Contract*—consider the picture of possible perfection that emerges through its maxims.

First of all, he would emphatically choose a city over a nation, and a city with genuine citizens rather than mere residents. The effective expression of a steadfast general will—that is, the thoughtful articulation and pursuit of common interests—presupposes a community intimate enough to permit sharing common hardships as well as common pleasures, a community of men close enough to form among themselves a vital "common self," realizing a sort of pacific *esprit de corps*. The best place for developing such a shared way of life and, with it, a sense of fellow feeling generally, would be a city of moderate size, where reciprocal bonds of affection might make the associates into willing compatriots brought together by inclination as much as duty. "We conceive of the general society [of mankind] on the basis of our particular societies; the establishment of small Republics makes us consider the large one; and we only begin properly to become men after having been Citizens." [36]

Such a city-state ought to be "neither too large to be well governed nor too small to be self-sustaining." A limited size would mean that "each member can be known to all," while limited though adequate resources would insure that there are "neither rich nor poor." A state "that does without other peoples, and which all other people can do without," Rousseau's preferred site would thus accommodate an independent and peaceful society of equals, tolerating "neither opulent men nor beggars," its compact size helping to focus the power of public freedom. "The closer together a numerous people is, the less the Government can usurp from the Sovereign." In such a city-state, the popular "leaders deliberate as safely in their rooms as the Prince in his council, and the crowd assembles as quickly in the public squares as the troops in their quarters." [37]

The government of this best possible city must be republican, because "every legitimate Government is republican." Since a republic, by definition, is a society ruled by the general will, great care is taken not to confound the government with the sovereign people who comprise the general will. Although those meritorious individuals honored by elevation to high office offer a means by which probity, thoughtfulness, experience, "and all the other reasons for public preference and esteem become so many new guarantees of being well governed," these magistrates elected by the sovereign are, "in a word, ever ready to sacrifice the Government to the people, and not the people to the Government," for, in their wisdom, they know that a government ought always to be minister of the sovereign, never its master. [38]

The best possible sovereign people, on the other hand, while distinguished by the "perfect independence" of each citizen from all the rest, ought also to be animated by a passionate civic zeal: when matters of freedom and law are to be debated, "everyone rushes to assemblies." When the people meet together—and Rousseau emphatically says that the "legislative power belongs to the people and can belong only to it"—these independent citizens renew their common bonds through the tangible reaffirmation of their common interests. These interests are rooted in shared mores so "upright and simple" that "very few Laws" are necessary, fewer new ones need be introduced, and "the first man to propose them merely says what all have already felt." Because everyone in this public process "necessarily subjects himself to the conditions he imposes on others," an "admirable agreement between interest and justice" arises. Yet the trustworthiness of this accord depends on each citizen giving "only his own opinion (*n'opine que d'après lui*)," so that laws emerge from the independent judgment of each on the common interests, rather than from the collusion of groups united by special interests. "In perfect legislation, the individual or separate will ought to be null; the will of the body proper to Government greatly subordinated; and, in consequence, the general will or sovereign always dominant and the unique rule of all the others."[39]

The quality and character of the laws enacted by the sovereign are so critical that the best possible institutions will be designed, in part, to safeguard the integrity of opinion expressed at these assemblies. Chief among these institutions is the religion of the city, which ought to promote belief in "the happiness of the just, the punishment of the wicked, the sanctity of the social Contract and the Laws." Intolerance is the one thing a civil religion should proscribe: protecting the inevitable diversity of opinion among men is one of the basic conditions for preserving a healthy sovereign. "Wherever theological intolerance exists, it is impossible for it not to have some civic effect; and as soon as it does, the Sovereign is no longer Sovereign, even over temporal matters: then Priests are the real masters; Kings are only their officers."[40]

A variety of political devices protects the integrity of the sovereign in this best possible society. There will be "fixed and periodic" assemblies "that nothing can abolish or postpone." The purpose of these assemblies is explicitly to renew the social bonds through which a people remain a people and to answer two questions: "Does it please the Sovereign to preserve the present form of Government?" and "Does it please the People to leave the administration to those currently entrusted with it?" "The instant the People is legitimately assembled as a Sovereign body"—and it is worth stressing that "the Sovereign can only act when the people is assembled"—"all jurisdiction of the Government ceases, the executive power is suspended, and the person of the lowest Citizen is as sacred and inviolable as that of the highest Magistrate." Such periodic assemblies remind the elected "deputies of the people" that they are not virtual "representatives" with a charter to do as they will, but rather commissioned agents (*"commissaires"*) bound by the wishes expressed directly by the people themselves, according to *their* will. The governors therefore serve only at the sufferance of the people, who may remove them or even abolish the form of government under which they serve. The legislative power of the sovereign, by contrast, is absolute, limited only by the sense of mutual respect that defines the truly general will and by the veneration a people will naturally feel for ancient laws justly administered. But "the instant the Government usurps sovereignty, the social compact is broken, and all the simple Citizens, recovering by right their natural freedom, are forced but not obligated to obey."[41]

Apart from the new detail in its discussion of sovereignty, the best possible society of the *Social Contract* bears an obvious resemblance to the city portrayed in Rousseau's previous images of Alpine perfection. It is not surprising, then, to have the treatise open on a note resonant with the fantasia of his dedication to the *Second Discourse*: "Born a citizen of a free State and a member of the sovereign, the right to vote there, however feeble may be the influence of my voice on public affairs, is enough to impose on me the duty of educating myself about them. How happy I am, whenever I meditate about Governments, to find in my research new reasons for loving that of my country!" He had been similarly forthright seven years earlier in the *Encyclopedia* article "Political Economy." There, in his first published thoughts on public affairs, he had also spoken of Geneva's significance for him: "In order to display here the economic system of good government, I have often turned my eyes toward the system of that republic, happy thus to find in my homeland the example of wisdom and happiness which I would like to see reign in all countries."[42] This, of course, is the same "system" he had called a democracy, both in the dedication and in his *Letter to d'Alembert*.

Yet, if the *Social Contract* opens by evoking the earlier dedication, it is but a muted echo. While the best possible society of the *Contract* bears some resemblance to Geneva, it is primarily to the Geneva of Rousseau's dreams. Here, the new detail in the discussion of sovereignty is crucial. When his ideas about sovereignty are set beside his coded critique of the government actually existing in Geneva, the extent of his disenchantment suddenly becomes palpable. True, he still writes as if Geneva, perhaps alone among modern states, preserves the possibility of realizing his principles of political right. But this also means that if Geneva continues to fall short of the ideal, if it fails to realize these principles, then its rulers and Citizens will have no excuses. They will simply have missed a rare opportunity.

By suggesting all of this, however obliquely, Rousseau was walking a tightrope. It was awkward enough that he had previously insisted on calling his idyllic Geneva a "democracy," thus honoring a relatively insignificant part of the city's avowedly mixed regime with a term that held less than comforting connotations for most of its ruling magistrates. But to insinuate unflattering comparisons between Venice, Rome, and Geneva; to paint again, only now with clear ideas, a picture of perfection at odds with the established government of Geneva; finally, and worst of all, to have the fine points of a legitimate sovereignty spelled out in terms that violated the spirit as well as the letter of the city's current constitution: all of this was new, dangerous, and potentially explosive—particularly in his homeland. Call it a simple republic or call it an elective aristocracy, in this context the semantic formalities of naming forms of government scarcely mattered. Leaving behind ecumenical subtleties and throwing caution to the winds, Rousseau, through his maxims for preventing "the abuse of government," stipulated a set of stringent conditions—conditions strikingly similar to those reforms urged in previous years by the democrats among the simple Citizens of Geneva.[43]

It was this faction that had spurned the decree of "aristo-democracy" and had sought to recast the city purely and simply as a democracy; it was this party that had demanded all power for a truly sovereign General Council. Was it not this tradition that Rousseau now made his own and defended with all the force his reasoning could command?

Completing the Contract

The *Social Contract* is, by design, an enigmatic book. A work "for all time," it can also be deciphered as a democratic treatise for Geneva: a critique disguised as a eulogy, an impassioned plea for freedom cast as a sober argument. An intentionally daunting essay, its labyrinth of logic both conceals—and points to—Rousseau's own *pris de position*, a daring set of convictions that he must have decided to reveal, however circumspectly, only after long and hard thought. Sharing his project with no one, not even Diderot, he had labored in secret over the years, afraid that his book "would appear too bold for the century," wanting therefore to invest in it "uniquely all the force of reasoning, without any trace of bile or bias."[44]

Moreover, as Rousseau confides in the first draft, there is something unfathomable about the book's key concept, the general will—something strange enough and novel enough in its bearing on the idea of sovereignty to have left previous men of politics utterly in the dark: "It is here that all legislators have lost themselves." And if the polished surface of his prose in the final version of the *Social Contract* rationally circumscribes the wonder of a phenomenon like the free will—a phenomenon, after all, that is said to mediate between the body and the soul, between the given and what seems right, and, when generalized in association with others, between the individual and what is common—this show of precision cannot remove or even quite conceal the mystery at its heart. "In the constitution of man, the action of the soul on the body is the abyss of philosophy."[45] Terrified or confused before this abyss, all previous lawgivers have gone astray, whether in ignoring or in trying to repress the power of free will that constitutes not only "the action of the soul on the body," but also the legitimate rule of laws over men.

Indeed, as Rousseau's own language spirals in upon itself, the serpentine prose of the *Social Contract* solicits the very capacity it is designed, in part, to bring into public view, its argument structured with an open tension between the given and what seems right, a tension that the author leaves the reader free to resolve for himself. Different readers will complete the text in different ways. For some, it will be a solace, for others a handbook. On the one hand, to comprehend it at its face value as a treatise on the principles of political right, fit for all times and all places, is to preserve the tension as a spring for moral judgment, the last refuge of hope. On the other hand, to decipher it as a treatise on the principles of democracy, fit for but a few times and a few places, is to focus the force of the tension and to charge the argument with a surprisingly concrete cogency. Then this book for all seasons becomes a practical guide for realizing a community of free individuals—a possibility that appears only infrequently, at fortunate historical moments.

Rousseau seems to have expected his book to be appropriated in both of these ways. In each case, he had the same kind of ideal reader in mind: someone willing to summon his *own* imagination, feelings, and intuitive understanding, exercising his *own* freedom to think through for himself the ideas Rousseau reasons about. In the midst of his trials after publishing the *Social Contract* and *Emile*, he put it this way in a fragment: "In order to understand the language of the inspired, it is necessary to be inspired oneself. Without which all that we say about the obscure and the inconceivable is for us only words without ideas. It is as if they said nothing to us."[46]

One person to whom his words would presumably mean something is Emile, the man Rousseau imagines to be specially trained in the exercise of freedom. In book V of *Emile*, where Rousseau's paradigmatic curriculum comes to a climax with a précis of the *Social Contract*, the tutor advises Emile to master both "the principles of political right" and the "positive right of established governments." "The only modern in a position to create this great and useless science," according to the tutor, "was the illustrious Montesquieu." But he, unlike Rousseau, "was careful not to discuss the principles of political right," contenting himself with representing actually existing systems of right. Nevertheless, "whoever wants to judge soundly of governments such as they exist is obliged to unite the two; it is necessary to know what ought to be in order to judge properly about what is." Unfortunately, in inspiring someone to think through such issues, there is a difficulty, recognized by the tutor in two pointed questions: "What does it matter to me? and What can I do about it?"[47]

Emile, for one, discovers that there is very little indeed that he can do about it. Fortified with Rousseau's principles of political right, he wanders throughout Europe in search of a wise government. Yet in all of his travels, he encounters no legitimate laws, no genuine sovereignty, no real freedom in society. As the tutor laments, "Laws! Where do they have them and where are they respected? Everywhere you have seen reign under this name only individual interest and the passions of men." Yet Emile's quest is not entirely fruitless. His healthy judgment will still be of use to him for preserving his integrity in the midst of a world teeming with injustice and oppression. And he will know, in the depths of his soul, that he is by nature free: though he has found freedom "in no form of government," he has realized for himself that it exists "in the heart of the free man, he takes it with him everywhere."[48]

For other thoughtful men of good faith in other circumstances of greater promise, however, Rousseau hoped that his teaching would be of more practical import. Late in his life, taking stock of a fate he felt to be sorrowful, he alleviated his grief by remembering the plans for civic freedom he had once tried to share with his fellows. Had he not "worked for his homeland and for those small States constituted like it"? Had he not sought to communicate "great truths useful for the happiness of humankind"?[49] Were these gestures so blameworthy that his books should be banned, his ideas reviled?

And so the enigma remains. Yet, from the very depths of Rousseau's thinking—that is, from his inevitably ambiguous and incomplete effort to define the language of politics anew—springs the continuing vitality of the *Social Contract*. In his reveries, he envisioned a shared form of life that, by showing respect for the free will in general, cultivated in all individuals equally the best that each, with the help of others, could become. And while the *Social Contract* does not— and cannot, by itself—indicate clearly the way to realize this vision, it does decisively display an idea of freedom within an ennobling social order. Thus Rousseau defended and preserved the desire at the heart of his invisible city. By writing a reasoned treatise, his dream of democracy became, as he had hoped, "a book for all times."

(1762–1764)

The Citizen Exiled

"HERE BEGINS the work of darkness in which I have been enshrouded for the past eight years, without ever having been able, try as I might, to pierce its frightful obscurity. In the abyss of ills in which I am submerged, I feel the shock of the blows aimed at me, I perceive the immediate instrument, but I can see neither the hand which directs it nor the means by which it is brought into play."[1] Thus opens the final book of the *Confessions*, Rousseau's melancholy narrative of his flight and persecution in the aftermath of publishing the *Social Contract* and *Emile*. That these were dark days for Rousseau can scarcely be denied. But we must nevertheless recapture for ourselves the link between his own words and the fury directed against him. By describing the public outcry over Rousseau's books, we can perhaps shed some light on the "frightful obscurity" in which he felt trapped.

In April, 1762, the *Social Contract* was published in Amsterdam, shipped to Dunkirk, and boated as far up the Seine as Rouen, there to await official clearance for the last leg of the journey to Paris. Rousseau had carefully planned for the *Social Contract* to appear shortly before *Emile*, in part to prevent the treatise from being "smothered" by its more imposing companion, in part to give the smaller book all the benefits of the free publicity he anticipated would attend the publication of *Emile*, by design a more accessible work.[2]

As had been his custom, he insisted on signing both works, refusing the cloak of anonymity sported by most other controversial writers of the day. And, as usual, he warned Malesherbes, the King's *Directeur de la librairie*, that the *Social Contract* would soon be published. Although by law the official charged with superintending the French book trade, Malesherbes was in fact a friend of the *philosophes*, helping their publishers outwit the legal labyrinth of the *ancien régime*. Anticipating what might arouse clerics and the conservative nobility, Malesherbes made it his personal policy to advise authors on the rephrasing or deletion of potentially inflammatory material. If the author cooperated, he would then grant a "tacit permission" to sell the book in France. In this fashion, Malesherbes and the publishers finessed a semilegal protection against piracy for these books, even if it fell short of providing the full legal privileges afforded by the royal imprimatur, which required a more rigorous censorship. Rousseau himself was on cordial terms with Malesherbes. Only recently, he had confided to him a series of four autobiographical letters. Yet, in the case of the *Social Contract*, in distinction from even *Emile* and despite the pleas of his worried publisher, Rousseau inexplicably failed to solicit Malesherbes's advice.[3]

The Trial Begins

His failure proved costly. In May, the *Directeur de la librairie* felt compelled to forbid any copies of the *Social Contract* to enter France. As two disappointed booksellers explained in a letter to Marc-Michel Rey, Rousseau's publisher in Amsterdam, "M. de Malesherbes has received the copy of the *Social Contract* you addressed to him. After the reading he has made of it, he says that entry is impossible." Alarmed at the prospect of bundled books lying idle on the docks at Rouen while pirates smuggled their editions into Paris, Rey cast about for ways to win the work some kind of approved entry. Malesherbes indicated that anonymity for the author might help. Would Rousseau perhaps be able in this one instance to follow the example of such illustrious authors as Montesquieu and remove his name from the book in question?[4]

Confronted with this idea, Rousseau's will stiffened. Resisting Rey's entreaties to remove his name from the *Social Contract*, he explained in a letter that, after all, he was "proud of having written" this book "which contains nothing but what is most fitting to the sentiments of an upright man and good Citizen, nothing that I should refuse to acknowledge, and nothing that I am not prepared to uphold before any qualified tribunal." What tribunal Rousseau might consider qualified remained unclear. Yes, he was "aware that, as far as my own person, my behavior and my writings are concerned, I owe obedience and respect to the laws and government of the country in which I am living." But his ideas did not belong to France, they were not something that its government could properly dispose of. "As far as my principles as a republican are concerned, they have been published in a Republic, and, in France, no magistrate, no tribunal, no legislative body, no Minister and not even the King himself, has any right to question me on such matters, or to ask me to account for them in any way whatever."[5]

While dickering over the *Social Contract* continued, *Emile* was launched with a tacit permission from Malesherbes, who had encouraged its publication. On May 24, the first copies were put on sale in Paris. Almost immediately, the book came under attack; within a week, the public outcry was so intense that Malesherbes was forced to ban it. Police began seizing copies. Educated circles in Paris were electrified. This was Rousseau's biggest bombshell yet. In the words of one contemporary witness, readers found the book filled "with very bold things against Religion and Government." On May 31, the same diarist described the growing agitation: "Rousseau's book is creating a greater scandal than ever.

Sword and Censor are united against the author, and his friends have indicated to him that he has reason to fear for himself."[6]

In the midst of the uproar, the *Social Contract* was all but forgotten, despite Rousseau's plan. Clandestine as well as counterfeit copies remained hard to come by in Paris, while in the provinces officials continued to confiscate the book until well into the fall. Since the commotion over Rousseau centered on *Emile*, selling the *Social Contract* seemed relatively unrewarding as well as risky. A curious situation arose, in which many pirates ignored the *Social Contract* but reprinted *Emile*, eager to cash in on the controversy surrounding it.[7]

The authorities proceeded apace. On June 7, the faculty of the Sorbonne, calling Rousseau "a great master of corruption and error," condemned *Emile*, primarily on religious grounds—the idea of natural goodness contradicted the Church's doctrine of original sin. Two days later, the Parliament of Paris followed suit, making clear that the bravado involved in signing such an impious book ought not to go unpunished. But political issues were at stake as well. According to the attorney for Parliament, Rousseau's work contained not only impieties but also "propositions that tend to give a false and odious character to sovereign authority, to destroy the principle of obedience that is his due, and to weaken the respect and love of peoples for their Kings." Even the author's recourse to imagination was deemed unfit: "The maxims which are propagated form as a whole a chimerical system, as unworkable in its execution as it is absurd and condemnable in its plan."[8]

Though faced with possible arrest, detainment, and trial, Rousseau struggled to remain detached. On the evening of June 9, he was pacing about his lair as usual, trying to summon sleep by reading the Bible. Given the ominous events of the day, it is not surprising to hear that he was abnormally restless. His anxiety, however, merely led him to linger over the Holy Scripture. "That evening, finding myself more aroused than usual, I continued my reading even longer, and I read completely the book which ends with the Levite of Ephraim if I am not mistaken, it is the book of Judges. . . . This history greatly affected me, and I was engrossed in a sort of dream, when suddenly I was seized from it by a noise and a light." The nightmare was beginning.

A messenger entered with a note of warning. "The agitation is extreme," Rousseau was told. "Nothing can avert the blow, the Court demands it, the Parliament wills it; at seven o'clock tomorrow morning a decree for your arrest will be issued, and they will arrange to have you seized."[9] The peril was finally palpable. The next day, Rousseau fled from Paris, his hopes suddenly fixed again on his homeland.

The Charge: "Such Extreme Freedom"

Prudence dictated a certain caution, however, in his approach to Geneva. In 1761, the Consistory there had detected impieties in *La Nouvelle Héloïse* and had asked the Small Council to take some action. Nothing had happened—but Rousseau was now wary enough to decamp for Switzerland, there to await the reaction of Geneva's government.[10]

As his corrspondence with Rey indicates, he was anxious that his latest works be well received in his native city. By the end of May, Rousseau's publisher had talked Malesherbes into releasing the impounded copies of the *Social Contract*, so that Rey could try to vend his wares outside France. Geneva seemed a likely market. But booksellers there, once they had seen the treatise, were reluctant to stock it. "Not a single bookshop has been willing to carry it," Rousseau complained to a Genevan friend at the end of May: "It is true that the book has been prohibited in France, but this is precisely why it ought to be well received in Geneva, for even I prefer Aristocracy to all other government."[11]

In the context, such ingenuousness seems bizarre. Perhaps Rousseau had actually convinced himself that his book was innocuous, despite the public protest closing in on him in Paris. Or perhaps wishful thinking offered an easy way to ward off despair. In any case, Rousseau, while still in Paris, persevered in his efforts to reach a Genevan audience, apparently trusting that its response would be favorable.

At the beginning of June, Rey finally managed to ship two hundred copies to a Genevan bookseller, who depleted his stock within several days. By the middle of the month, one of Rousseau's most eager Genevan partisans, the pastor Moultou, could write to him rejoicing that the *Social Contract* "is read avidly. Even your enemies have to admit that, of all your books, it is the one where your genius is displayed with the greatest vigor. What force! What profoundness! You are even superior to Montesquieu! Your work ought to terrify all tyrants . . . ; it excites the freedom in all hearts."[12]

What so thrilled Moultou and other members of the popular party could scarcely fail to arouse the distrust of the patricians. Was not Rousseau in the *Social Contract* taking "the part of the people against the magistrates," as Voltaire later explained to d'Alembert?[13] Watching the enthusiasm of men like Moultou and De Luc, the members of the Small Council certainly had cause to wonder.

Rousseau's previous record was less than reassuring. Slightly embarrassed by the dedication of the *Second Discourse*, the magistrates had been less than flattered by the *Letter to d'Alembert*; just the previous year, they had heard complaints from the city's religious elders about the *La Nouvelle Héloïse*. From the outset the *Social Contract* was suspect, whatever its pretensions to being an abstract and purely philosophical treatise.

Once officials actually began to *read* the book, their worst suspicions were confirmed. Once again, Rousseau confronted them with an apparent eulogy. Once again, by virtue of the veiled recommendations contained in its familiar inaccuracies, this eulogy seemed to be taking sides in a long-standing civil dispute. Once again, the absent Citizen could be read as endorsing an untoward popular power and urging dangerously democratic innovations. But by now, Rousseau ought to know better. Books were burning in Paris, their author, the most celebrated "Citizen of Geneva," was in flight, his eyes set on his homeland.

The magistrates were not pleased. Things were dangerously close to getting out of hand.

The best measure of their discomfort is the reaction of the public prosecutor Jean-Robert Tronchin, the official responsible for evaluating Rousseau's books. Despite his office and Rousseau's hatred for him—he nicknamed him "*le Jongleur*" (the charlatan)—Tronchin was by no means the author's most implacable enemy. Tronchin even willingly conceded that *Emile* and the *Social Contract* were "two books that sparkle with audacity and genius." But that only made more troubling the "pernicious errors" Rousseau had mixed with his "sublime truths." In an official report to the Small Council, Tronchin carefully outlined the dangerous political ideas he had found in his reading of Rousseau's new books.

In the eyes of Tronchin, Rousseau's "errors" were multiple: political, religious, even rhetorical. Encouraging liberties of interpretation on matters of faith was so radically subjective a form of Protestantism that it posed an implicit threat to the church established by Calvin. Any doubts raised by the account of natural religion in *Emile* were only deepened by the chapter on civil religion in the *Social Contract*. Faced with such ideas, Tronchin nevertheless conceded that "if there were in *Emile* . . . only those extreme maxims which are scattered there, the Piece ought only to be regarded as a philosophical dream," a chimera so obviously unreal as to require no censorship. The problem was that Rousseau had expressed his "philosohical dream" in "licentious pictures all the more Seductive" than the ideas, insofar as they were "more skilled and animated."[14]

Tronchin reserved his most caustic comments, though, for Rousseau's political views. He was especially disturbed by the author's contention that the institution of government is *not* a contract. By insisting on this point, the *Social Contract* ironically discredited the very interpretation of the contract—as a compact mutually binding on "those who govern and those who are governed"—that patrician partisans had stressed for more than a generation. With a similarly wary eye, Tronchin scanned Rousseau's maxims in book III: the suggestion that the fundamental laws can be changed whenever the will of the people in assembly changes; the requirement that magistrates serve not as autonomous representatives, but only as commissioned agents, elected and open to recall by the Citizens in assembly; and, finally, the advice that such assemblies of the Citizens be regularly scheduled in advance. What were these maxims, if not a reiteration of virtually every specific demand raised by the most radical Citizens and Bourgeois in the decades since the death of Pierre Fatio? If put into practice, such maxims would hand victory to the democrats as well as power to the simple people.[15] Was this Rousseau's intention?

It certainly looked that way to Tronchin. In his official report to the Small Council, the prosecutor carefully summarized the dangerous political ideas he had discovered in his reading of Rousseau's new books:

> In the *Social Contract*, after deriving the authority of Governments from the purest of Sources, after developing successfully the immense advantages of

the Civil State over the State of Nature, the author quickly restores all the disorders of this primitive State: The constitutive Laws of all Governments seem to him always revocable; he does not perceive any reciprocal engagement between those who govern and those who are governed; the former only appear to him as instruments that Peoples can change or dissolve at their pleasure.

He supposes in the general Wills of peoples the same instability as in the particular wills of Individuals; and starting from the principle that it is the essence of the Will of Nations, like that of Individuals, not to be able to constrain itself, so that it is as unstable as it is indestructible, he sees all forms of Government only as provisional forms, as Experiments that one can always change; this is not, in his case, a Metaphysical principle that is too rigorous, perhaps, to ascribe to it any consequences; it is, according to him, the basis of all Governments. He knows no means of preventing usurpations other than fixing Periodic Assemblies (chap. xiii), during which the Government is Suspended and where, without requiring a formal convocation, they question Separately and on the plurality of Votes whether they will conserve the customary form of Government and the established Magistrates.

These Periodic Assemblies—which are expressly prohibited by our Laws, and which would render Freedom even more crushing than Servitude—can only be regarded as a kind of delirium; yet such extreme Freedom is the Deity of the Author: it is to this Idol that he sacrifices the most Sacred principles. Finding in the Gospel precepts which limit this deadly independence, a Christian Republic in his eyes is only a contradiction in terms, Religion only a support for tyranny, and Christians only Men fit to grovel in the most vile Slavery.

Tronchin concluded that religion and government had never been "more directly attacked."[16]

The Verdict

On June 11, 1762, the Small Council of Geneva had formally opened its investigation of *Emile* and the *Social Contract*. A committee of scholars was appointed to review the books independently of the public prosecutor. The city was already divided over Rousseau's latest works, even if few people could possibly have found time to read both. On the one side, copies of the French condemnation of *Emile* circulated widely; on the other, partisans like Moultou tried to stir up sympathy for Rousseau by defending his good faith. At the time, public distrust of the absent Citizen apparently ran high, at least in those circles frequented by a highly placed diplomatic envoy: as the official French observer reported on June 14 to the Duke de Choiseul, the French minister of foreign affairs, "The *Social Contract* and the *Treatise on Education* of J.-J. Rousseau have created a sensation here, Sir. They regard these two works as very dangerous. The Council has confiscated the few copies that the bookstores have received, and has named commissioners ... to examine and review these works. If the public voice is heard, they will be condemned in withering terms." [17]

On June 18, the magistrates met to hear the report from its committee of scholars. The committee concluded that the *Social Contract* "contains a system pernicious to sovereign authority, *destructive* of society and *of all government*, and very dangerous for our Constitution." The next day, the Council heard from the public prosecutor. Once Tronchin's more detailed report had made explicit some of the practical implications of Rousseau's ideas, there seemed little reason for debate. Rousseau's strategy of an indirect discourse on politics had failed miserably. After perfunctory discussion, the magistrates of the Small Council voted on June 19 to condemn unequivocally both *Emile* and the *Social Contract*. With a few modifications, Tronchin's comments were published to explain why. But the Council did not stop there: in Rousseau, they now sensed a menacing mind, the kind filled with thoughts as unsafe as they were unpredictable. Against the prosecutor's advice, they thus decided to issue a warrant for the author's arrest should he ever happen to set foot in his homeland again. Once more, the gates of Geneva slammed shut before Rousseau. [18]

Meanwhile, on June 14, Rousseau had arrived at Yverdon, in the canton of Berne, then a Swiss district with a republican regime even more oligarchic than Geneva's. After the proceedings in Geneva had reached their dismal climax, Rousseau's status in Berne also became precarious. The authorities there were no more eager than their friends in Geneva to harbor this man of unseasonable thoughts. On July 1, the government of Berne accordingly ordered the author out of the canton. A week later, it was explained that the *Social Contract* was a "book expressing doctrines extremely contrary to government." Rousseau's plight was now so desperate that he felt himself forced to seek refuge in Neuchâtel, since 1707 a Prussian principality, and thus the only Swiss monarchy. Here at last, he found a temporary resting place, thanks largely to the hospitality of Frederick II, the titular head of Neuchâtel, the reigning King of Prussia, and a monarch renowned for his adroitness at power politics as well as his fondness for the new philosophy. In Frederick the Great, Rousseau at last found a ruler unafraid of his political theories. [19]

But he was too caught up in his own destiny to worry much about the ironies in his current predicament. His mind was elsewhere. From afar and with deepening disappointment, he watched events unfold in Geneva. It is not clear what he now expected to happen. He was not about to beg forgiveness from the Small Council; nor was he eager to recant his religious views to reassure any wavering ministers, as Moultou urged. He was probably gripped by mixed emotions. On the one hand, he wished to ignore completely the politics of a situation that seemed hopelessly beyond his control. Given his awareness of the forces arrayed against him, it was not in his character to muster enthusiasm for a protracted struggle; instead, he lectured the impetuous Moultou on the need for caution and calm—just at the moment Moultou was zealously defending his good name in Geneva. On the other hand, he had scant interest in abandoning his ideas to the misunderstanding and abuse of others. At stake were the possibilities that he prized most, the insights he considered truly original, the intuitions that he had struggled the longest to make lucid.[20]

His ambivalence is vividly conveyed in a letter he wrote on August 10, 1762, to Marcet de Mézières, one of his oldest friends in Geneva. Putting him under an oath of secrecy, Rousseau revealed that he had already resolved to renounce his Citizenship at a propitious moment: "I need repose, I love peace." He then describes his own stoical detachment and drifts into a surprisingly militant exhortation, only to conclude with an ominous image of apocalyptic judgment:

> I am scarcely disturbed any longer about what happens in Geneva, nor about the manner in which I am treated there; the more they henceforth do, the better the hand they will deal me. However, this indifference scarcely goes so far as leaving behind my homeland, the decay of which I lament with bitterness, and in which I am interested as much as ever. If, then, you believe that, in the manner of discussing my case, there is some means which tends to restore freedom and the rights of the bourgeoisie, use it, act in my name, and don't worry about what can only have a bearing on me: for whatever you may believe, my honor does not depend on the procedures of the magistrates in Geneva. Their violence is already known in Europe, and the public has already chosen sides between them and me.[21]

Choosing sides? Them and me? Assailed from a variety of quarters, engulfed in suspicion, Rousseau had already begun to lose his grip on reality, even in this fairly sensible letter. Embroidering a number of legitimate grievances against a number of real opponents, he imagined himself the victim of a vast and inscrutable conspiracy only vaguely connected with the unprecedented political ideas he had set loose in the world. As he insisted in another letter to de Mézières, his ideas boiled down to two simple yet just principles: "the first, that rightfully the Sovereignty belongs always to the people; the second, that Aristocratic government is the best of all."[22] To Rousseau, it seemed self-evident that no honorable man could take exception to these notions. Surely *they* were not alarmed at the innocent doctrine of the *Social Contract*, clearly *they* must be wicked men out to torment his very soul, for reasons that inevitably remained obscure.

On September 4, 1762, he explained his suspicions to another correspondent:

> Pursued by Voltaire, by his worthy friend the charlatan Tronchin, and by their numerous Clique in Paris and Geneva, I have been successively banished from my homeland, from the Canton of Berne, and would have been from this State, if . . . the order of the King of Prussia had not curbed for a while the fury of the Voltaireans, violent defenders and avengers of the cause of God against my irreligion. . . . Innocence and truth no longer have voices by which to make themselves heard. No man in Europe dare take on

my defense, and when I will be base enough to take it on myself, they will not permit me to speak. . . . They dispose of the time that remains for me to live, but they will not prevent me from dying in peace.[23]

That fall, while Rousseau surrendered to gloomy conjectures about the progress of the plot against him, a group of some four hundred Genevan Citizens almost blocked the reconfirmation of Jean-Robert Tronchin as public prosecutor, a gesture of protest sparked by Tronchin's role in condemning Rousseau. In the aftermath, friends like De Luc and Moultou kept plying their exiled compatriot with reassurances, urging him to keep faith while they awaited a more auspicious moment to renew their agitation on his behalf. "My dear fellow citizen," comforted Moultou in a New Year's message, "you have reason, Europe has decreed it, and before this tribunal you are greater than those who judge you. But I hope that they will blush in the end. . . . However that may be, they are afraid of you, and they have a cheap market in men who have fear. For the rest, when you write, put in your letters from time to time things that I can show which paint the true Citizen and the man who does not fear injustices, because he feels that he is not wrong."[24]

Sunny talk did little to relieve the exile's distress. After he had completed a reply to the criticism of *Emile* made by Monseigneur de Beaumont, Archbishop of Paris, Rousseau and his Genevan allies, after some debate, settled on a waiting game. De Luc and Moultou still believed that if Rousseau apologized before the Small Council, even if only for statements *liable* to misinterpretation, then the Council would relent and allow the Citizen to return home without prejudice. Rousseau himself, however, remained adamant: he categorically refused to genuflect before the Small Council, insisting that his sentiments were honorable and his ideas clear enough as published. Since no other conciliatory gestures were forthcoming, all concerned now hoped that the *Letter to Christophe de Beaumont* might turn things around. Perhaps Rousseau's defense against a Catholic critic would also placate some of his Protestant critics, while rekindling interest in the case among ordinary Citizens.[25]

To some extent, such expectations were rewarded. On April 26, Moultou wrote that "Your work has had all the Success we could have desired. . . . There is not a Wise man in Geneva who does not believe you to be a Christian." But by now, Rousseau's friends were grasping at straws. Within a few weeks, their hopes were dashed again. After provisionally permitting the sale of Rousseau's letter in Geneva, the Small Council decided to crack down, confiscating a new edition of the work when one was published in the city. Even more ominously, this prohibition failed to elicit any widespread protest from the Citizens and Bourgeois, perhaps by now as dispirited by the whole affair as Rousseau himself.[26]

Renunciation

Feeling abandoned by his friends and persecuted by his enemies, Rousseau decided that he had taken as much as he could take. Several years later, he described his uncharitable disposition in no uncertain terms. "After having waited in vain for more than a year for some protest against an illegal procedure, I finally made my decision, and seeing myself abandoned by my fellow Citizens, I decided to renounce my ungrateful fatherland, where I had never lived, from which I had received neither goods nor assistance, and in which, as a prize for the honor I had attempted to bestow on it, I found myself disgracefully treated by unanimous consent, since those who ought to have spoken said nothing."[27]

On May 12, 1763, he sent his official letter of renunciation to the First Syndic. "I have tried to honor the name Genevan," he wrote.

> I have Loved my Compatriots tenderly; I have neglected nothing in order to make them love me; no one Could have been less successful. I wish to gratify them even in their hatred: the final sacrifice which remains for me to make for them is that of a name which was once dear to me. But Sir, my Fatherland, though becoming foreign to me, can never become indifferent to me (*ma Patrie en me devenant étrangère ne peut me devenir indifférente*); I remain bound to it by a tender Memory, and I only forget Its insults. May it prosper always, and see Its glory grow: such that it may abound in Citizens who are better and Above all happier than me![28]

Rousseau's Genevan allies were taken unawares. They were both upset by the rashness and stung by the form of the renunciation. On May 18, De Luc expressed his exasperation to Moultou: "It appears to me that we could have certainly Wished that our fellow Citizen had not spoken as generally as he did about the hatred for him he attributed to His Compatriots. You yourself know that he is cherished by the greatest number of them, that the hatred of which he complains with justice only lies in a small number of people who are less than admired generally."[29]

Yet whatever their surprise and chagrin, most of Rousseau's old friends rallied round him once more, jolted from any lethargy by the vehement suddenness of his gesture. As Moultou wrote, "I have shed tears for your fatherland, and felt admiration for you: I would never have advised you to take the decision you have taken, but you were right to do so. It was the only one worthy of you."[30]

In the event, if Rousseau had intended to stir up more trouble under the pretext of making his peace with Geneva, he could scarcely have laid a better plan. On June 18, 1763, De Luc and a group of some forty Citizens and Bourgeois presented a "representation" to the Small Council, protesting the illegality of its proceedings against Rousseau.[31] With the tacit blessing of Rousseau himself, a second representation followed in August, a third in September. All three petitions were declared inconsequential and vetoed by the Small Council.

With these preemptory rejections, *l'affaire Rousseau* began to acquire a broader significance. For such vetoes could not help but raise all over again the long festering question of just how much power the common Citizens in fact possessed. After all, if any popular petition could be summarily dismissed by the Small Council, what meaning had the "right of representation" granted by the Mediation of 1738?

Geneva was polarized politically once more. On the one side stood the *Représentants* of the Citizens and Bourgeois, heirs to the democratic movement who sought not only to establish their right of representation against the veto of the Small Council, but also to invest more power in the General Council as a legitimately sovereign body. On the other side stood the *Négatifs* of the established government, members of the patrician elite who sought not only to resist all claims on behalf of the General Council, but also to protect the sole authority of the Small Council in deciding whether any given representation had merit.

This was the context in which Jean-Robert Tronchin anonymously published his *Letters Written from the Country*, ostensibly an impartial pamphlet defending the official position of the government in terms designed to mollify the Citizens and Bourgeois. Throughout his polemic, the prosecutor exploited the prospect of chaos. While conceding that the General Council was, by right, the source of all legal power in Geneva, Tronchin took it as a sign of wisdom that the Council did not regularly challenge the transfer of these powers to the Small Council, a transfer the sovereign council had prudently contracted to make. If things were otherwise, if the Citizens called a meeting of the General Council every time they had a minor complaint to voice, the laws would constantly change and only disorder would ensue, with results all too well illustrated by the fate of Athens, where such extreme democracy degenerated into mob rule. Yet some rash Citizens, he charged, now appeared ready to sacrifice stability for the sake of a distrust in authority—a distrust that no form of government could ever wholly allay.[32]

The prosecutor thus deftly shifted the burden of proof. Had not the magistrates of Geneva over the years amply demonstrated their good will? Did the treatment of Rousseau by itself warrant making radical and unsettling changes in the current constitution? Did Genevans really prefer the constant turmoil of democracy to the security of the present regime?

4

The Past Recaptured

ROUSSEAU finally felt willing to justify himself before Geneva. Urged on by friends there, he agreed in October, 1763, to compose a response to his patrician critics. His allies, pleased to have resurrected his interest in their cause, took pains to expedite his efforts. In December, De Luc journeyed to Neuchâtel with a bundle of documents. At his leisure, Rousseau now began to explore the written evidence of Geneva's constitution, past and present.

From the distance he had forced upon himself, the exile prepared both to defend his ideas and to use them, by judging the integrity of Geneva's current state and suggesting some ways to reform it. He had no trouble choosing a title for his essay. Answering Tronchin's *Letters Written from the Country*, Rousseau's title would be *Letters Written from the Mountain*, as if to evoke as well his own contrast between the mountains and the plains, between the simple virtues of the Neuchâtel peasants and the opulent vanity of the Genevan elite.

Freed from the necessity of indirection by his abjuration, Rousseau could clarify, if he wished, his original intentions in the *Social Contract*. Since the Small Council had reacted as if he had written a dangerously democratic treatise, now would be the time to correct this misapprehension, if such it be. Yet, as we shall see, Rousseau, while pledging allegiance to stability and good order, also makes plain that his aim in the *Social Contract* was not purely philosophical; that one field of the practical possibilities he had in mind was Geneva; that his preferred polity, given these possibilities, was a democracy; and that freedom, the hallmark of democracy, sometimes even warrants enduring a little instability.[1]

A Book for Geneva

Rousseau's reply to Tronchin opens with a defense of *Emile* and the *Social Contract* against the condemnation of the Small Council. The first five letters explain his views on religion. In uncompromising terms, he describes his own outlook on the Reformation, repeating the need for shared religious dogmas but stress-

87

ing also the freedom of each individual to interpret for himself the meaning of Scripture and the mystery of existence.[2]

The sixth letter is a resumé of the *Social Contract*, emphasizing the genetic aspects of his theory. True laws, he repeats, are "a public and solemn declaration of the general will on an object of common interest." The legislative power therefore ought to be vested in a sovereign people. Yet to execute the laws, a people requires a government, and this smaller body tends, in time, to encroach on the legislative power of the people. As this happens, the state, following a "natural progress," changes its constitution, passing insensibly from the form of government encompassing the greatest number, democracy, to the one encompassing the least, monarchy. Finally, when the laws are subordinated entirely to the particular interests uniting the group of men who happen to rule, the community is torn asunder, "the State is destroyed," and there remain "only masters and slaves." Although proclaiming again his admiration for aristocracy as the best form of government, Rousseau also reiterates his distinction between sovereignty and government, underlining one moral of his cautionary tale with a concise assertion: "The best of governments is aristocratic; the worst of sovereignties is aristocratic."[3]

This, then, is the *Social Contract* as its author now represents it to his Genevan audience. He wonders how certain members of that audience will interpret his account. "I divine it. You will say to yourself, 'Here is the history of the Government of Geneva.'" And Rousseau, far from disavowing this interpretation, seizes on it, writing, in apparent haste, prose that bristles with elliptical accusations:

And in effect, this primitive Contract, this essence of Sovereignty, this empire of Laws, this institution of Government, this manner of restraining it by various steps in order to balance authority by force, this tendency to usurpation, these periodic assemblies, this adroitness in destroying them, finally the coming destruction you threaten and I wish to prevent; is this not, point by point, the image of your Republic, since its birth until this day?

He has written neither a utopia nor a seditious tract. "I have taken your Constitution, which I found noble, as a model for political institutions; and by proposing it as an example for Europe, far from seeking to destroy it, I have shown the means of preserving it."[4]

That his principles were modeled, in part, on the ancient constitution of Geneva proves that they are neither imaginary nor destructive, as his enemies have alleged. It still seems bizarre to him that a book eulogizing Geneva could have been burned by its civic authorities. But then, in a rueful phrase directed at those authorities, Rousseau stakes out the position he will defend in the remaining letters: "I painted an existing object, and you wished that this object had changed its appearance. My book bore witness against the outrage you were going to attempt; this is what I have not been pardoned for."[5]

It is not Rousseau but his accusers who contemplate treasonous changes.

Some magistrates wish to destroy Geneva's "primitive contract," whereas his own goal has been to demonstrate its enduring vitality. The *Social Contract* commends a restoration, not a revolution: and to prove his point, Rousseau will evoke for us Geneva as it once was, before the predations of the patriciate eviscerated the city's "democratic constitution."[6]

A Saga of Decay

"Nothing is more free than your legitimate state; nothing is more servile than your current state." With this antithesis, Rousseau historicizes the tension between the possible and the actual, a tension already encoded in the principles of the *Social Contract*. No longer treated simply as an abstract result of reasoning, these principles now appear inscribed in the past itself. By displaying and defending them, our author thus intends to rescue a tradition in jeopardy. In such a context, "If a novel abuse is introduced, it is no longer an innovation to propose a new remedy; on the contrary, it is an attempt to reestablish things on their old footing."[7]

In the past, according to Rousseau, the backbone of Geneva's freedom was the frequency with which its General Council met. At meetings of the Council, the Citizens ratified all laws in person and reviewed the behavior of the magistrates elected by them. In effect, the power of the Citizens associated in assembly was unlimited: they were sovereign in fact as well as in theory.[8]

Unfortunately, if the legitimate consitution of Geneva offers a model of civic freedom, the "natural progress" of its state provides a paradigm of decay. As with all democratic states, the government has constantly increased its power at the expense of the sovereign. In particular, the Small Council has managed to acquire for itself the sole power of convening the General Council, virtually insuring that any abuses of power by the magistrates will go unchecked. "If you are Sovereign Lords in the assembly, in leaving it you are no longer anything. Dependent Sovereigns four hours per year, you are subjects the rest of your life, surrendered without reserve to the discretion of others."[9]

The only remaining check on the abuse of power in Geneva is the right of representation granted to the Citizens and Bourgeois by the Mediation of 1738. This right enables a group of Citizens to protest injustices to the Small Council. Between assemblies of the General Council, the ability to make representations is the only protection enjoyed by the people, it is the only way that they can superintend the administration of the laws, it is the vital vehicle for preserving their sovereignty.[10]

The current constitution is not completely without virtues. By granting to the Small Council an exclusive right to introduce new laws, it wisely protects against capricious innovations. Yet the full benefits can only be obtained when the power of the Small Council is balanced by the Citizen's right of representation: for this is "the only means possible to unite freedom to subordination, and to maintain the Magistrate in dependence on the Laws without altering his authority over the people."[11]

By its refusal to heed recent representations from the Citizens and Bourgeois, and by its false claim to a "negative right" of vetoing any representations it deems irrelevant, the current government of Geneva only confirms its contempt for the ancient constitution. As a result, the democracy in Geneva threatens to degenerate still further. By discouraging regular assemblies of the General Council and by challenging the right of representation, the government has attempted to assert a monopoly on public opinion and political power. There is no better way to usurp sovereignty. "Persuade all that the public interest is the interest of no one, and by this alone servitude is established; for when each will be under the yoke, where will be the common freedom? If each who dares to speak is crushed in the same instant, where will be those who want (voudront) to imitate him, and what will be the organ of generality when each individual keeps silent?"[12]

How, indeed, is it possible to justify what amounts to an unlimited executive veto on the will of the people, particularly when the Citizens of Geneva so rarely occupy themselves with politics? Most worry about public affairs "belatedly, with repugnance, and only when a pressing danger forces them to." Most of them are too interested in tranquil commerce to risk disrupting it through rash acts. The danger here is not intemperate lawmaking and constant turmoil, as patricians like Tronchin pretend, it is rather the opposite: the Citizens of Geneva, "absorbed in their domestic occupations, and always cool toward anything else, only ponder the public interest when their own is attacked." In this context, it is scarcely relevant to counter the claims of the popular party by brandishing the classical image of democracy. "Is it a more difficult thing to establish rule without servitude among some hundreds of men naturally sober and cold, than it was at Athens among an assembly of several thousands of citizens whom, they tell us, were hot-headed, hot-tempered, and often frenzied?" In the setting of Athens, fear of mob rule may have had some foundation—but not in Geneva, where the bulk of the Citizens and Bourgeois are industrious family men, comprising a truly independent "middle order between the rich and the poor, between the heads of State and the populace."[13]

This order, "comprised of men nearly equal in fortune, in status, and in lights, is neither elevated enough to have pretensions, nor low enough to have nothing to lose." The discipline of labor has given these simple Citizens a firm sense of propriety in their own effective freedom, while the tranquility of their households has let them develop a thoughtful autonomy, as well as an intuitive understanding of what is right for them all. They agree that "their great interest, their common interest, is that the Laws be observed, the Magistrates respected, the constitution sustained, and the State be tranquil."[14] Rousseau thus finds in the watchmakers and other artisans of the Genevan bourgeoisie a decency and modesty, a delicacy of moral perception, a certain steadfastness—above all, a gravity of mien, as befits men who know their rights, grasp their duty, and exercise their will.

By contrast, the wealthy patricians wallow in opulence, while the poor suffer in abject misery: "The rich hold the Law in a purse, the poor prefer bread to freedom." When the wealthy monopolize public affairs, they design laws not to obey them, but to rule through them, to strike fear into others in their name. Why raise objections to recognizing the legitimate sovereignty of the General Council when the real and present danger to the laws comes not from the people, but from an "odious Oligarchy"?[15]

Besides, even supposing that abuses of freedom were as common as abuses of power, there is one essential difference. Since abuses of freedom hurt directly the people who abuse it, problems caused by too much freedom tend to be temporary and easily corrected; by contrast, since abuses of power benefit directly the rulers who abuse it, problems caused by too much power tend to continue without limit, too often ending in the destruction of those who are enslaved. Given a choice, Rousseau does not hesitate: "It is better that a people be unhappy by its own faults than oppressed at the hands of another."[16]

To preserve the freedom of Geneva's state, Rousseau proposes several reforms to insure that the right of representation is scrupulously observed. In cases where the Small Council can see no point to a representation, the disputed petition could be referred to local assemblies where Citizens, through delegates, would vote on the representation and decide whether in their opinion the spirit of the laws had in fact been violated. Another possibility would be to schedule periodic General Council meetings where the agenda would be restricted to a vote on any outstanding representations.[17]

Yet the modesty of these recommendations may be somewhat misleading. As the fine print indicates, Rousseau is intransigent on the key point: "The general Council is not an order in the State; it *is* the State." In principle, its sovereign power is absolute, unlimited: "it can do all, or it is nothing." In every case of dispute between the General Council and the Small Council, whenever the meaning and scope of the law is in doubt, the General Council alone is the final judge. In such instances, it is always up "to the general will to decide"—for in the legitimate constitution of Geneva, "this will is the supreme judge and unique sovereign." The polarized situation in the city only makes a frank discussion of the differences in a General Council meeting all the more imperative: "In a Democracy where the People is Sovereign, when internal divisions suspend all forms and silence all authorities, the people alone remain, and where then proceed the greatest number, there resides Law and authority."[18]

Despite its current disrepair, Geneva's veritable constitution, taken as a whole, is "good and healthy." If the right of representation and the sovereignty of the people are respected, "your Government becomes the best that ever existed: for what better Government can there be than one where all the parts are balanced in a perfect equilibrium, where the individuals cannot transgress the Laws because they are subjected to Judges; and where these Judges cannot transgress the Laws either, because they are watched closely by the People?"[19] Rousseau thus ends on a hopeful note, exhorting his erstwhile compatriots to assemble themselves once more, in order to restore a lost sense of community.

Since in this situation laws newly ratified by all the Citizens are needful, "Deliberate with your fellow Citizens," but "only count the voices after pondering them (*ne compte* *les voix qu'après les avoir pensées*)." If this mutual rededication is to be appropriately thoughtful, some voices ought to carry more weight than others. "Challenge unruly youth, insolent opulence, and venal indigence; no salutary counsel can come from these quarters." Instead, Rousseau hopes that the assembly will be persuaded by the virtuous and honest men in its midst:

> Consult those of an upright mediocrity secured against the seductions of ambition and poverty; those of an honorable old age crowning a life beyond reproach; those whom long experience has versed in public affairs; those who, without ambition in the State, want no status other than that of Citizen; finally, those who, having pursued nothing but the good of the fatherland and the maintenance of the Laws, have merited by their virtues the esteem of the public and the confidence of their equals.[20]

In the considered voices of such honorable men, steadfastly oriented toward shared interests, the city of Geneva still preserves a unique possibility: to renew its "primitive Contract," by reuniting its Citizens and allowing the people, sovereign once more, to rule itself, in accord with the pattern of its ancient constitution.

History as a Fable

There is one slight problem with this hopeful ending: in the words of one modern scholar, Rousseau's *Letters Written from the Mountain* contain "an incontestable distortion of the past." What our author pretends to read from the past, he has in fact read into it. The principles he claims to find in the ancient constitution of Geneva are in effect the principles of the *Social Contract* projected backward. To take only the most glaring example: Rousseau frequently talks as if regularly scheduled meetings of the General Council were a prominent feature of Geneva's traditional constitution. Yet as he must have known from the documents and books before him, such was not the case. Periodic assemblies, established only by a reluctant concession under popular pressure in 1707, had been prohibited again in 1712. In fact, the General Council, according to modern historians, had always been a consultative body, convened at the discretion of the Small Council to discuss whatever issues the Small Council chose.[21]

Such distortions cast doubt on claims that either the *Social Contract* or the *Letters from the Mountain* were modeled on any actual constitution of Geneva. Such doubts are only deepened by a letter to De Luc written late in 1763, in which Rousseau says frankly that "I have never studied the constitution of your Republic, I have no knowledge of the facts cited in the representations and responses; I know the history of your government only from Spon [a contemporary French history of Geneva], and I see that everything important is suppressed [in it]."[22] Affinities and links between Geneva and the *Social Contract* must be sought elsewhere, it would seem. But what about the *Letters from the Mountain?* If Rousseau was not constructing a factually accurate chronicle of Geneva's past and present constitution, what *was* he doing with history?

It is not as if he had made it all up. Once he started work on the *Letters*, it is certain that he read widely: in his notebooks are extracts from a number of books and documents on Geneva's constitution and history. Shortly after complaining to De Luc of his ignorance, Rousseau immersed himself in a variety of narratives. By the time he was done, he probably knew about all that could be known about the political aspects of Geneva's past.

Moreover, in conversations with De Luc and others, he presumably would have become familiar with the traditionally partisan ways this past had been interpreted. He would have heard about the ancient constitution as it was revered by members of the popular party, and he would have learned about their conjecture that sovereignty in Geneva belonged, by customary right, to the Citizens assembled in the General Council. Recently, he had received a historical sketch from Toussaint-Pierre Lenieps, a Genevan acquaintance living in Paris and a man banished from his native city in 1731 for agitation against the government. Lenieps's essay, which has not survived, apparently summarized the documentary evidence that could be used for refuting the official patrician histories. In October of 1763, the old exile explained his conclusions to Rousseau: "I have stressed the necessity of recalling the Government to first principles, contended that there was never a prescription against the sovereign, and that the sovereign was the Will of the greatest number of Citizens, as gathered by their votes."[23]

But these were not the only—or even the most important—sources of Rousseau's understanding. For we have omitted several other sources: for example, his own firsthand impressions of Geneva and his own desire to seek solace in a past that seemed happier. Above all, we have omitted the continuing work of Rousseau's imagination. "My imagination, which in my youth always worked ahead . . . now works backward," Rousseau tells us in the *Confessions*. The dreamer's gaze, when directed toward the past, "compensates me with these sweet memories for the hope I have lost forever. I no longer see in the future anything that holds me; only a return into the past can charm me." Such a reversion to the past becomes all the more attractive in situations of apparent adversity. "It is a very strange thing that my imagination never becomes more agreeably aroused than when my condition is the least agreeable. . . . I have said a hundred times that if ever I were placed in the Bastille, there I would paint the picture of freedom."[24]

It was in a similar mood that Rousseau probably approached his essay about Geneva. Unwelcome in most of Europe, confined to the principality of Neuchâtel, exiled from his fatherland, and thus cut off from the font of his formative experiences, Rousseau undertakes to restore what, after all, is a condition for the feeling of personal identity: through an act of willful recollection, he recreates a narrative unity for himself, one that permits him to enjoy a temporal continuity not with the Geneva that has forsaken his ideals, but rather with the undefiled city that once embodied them—or so he imagines.

Under the circumstances, such a meditation on Geneva's past was by no means of merely personal import. As the efforts of Lenieps show, Rousseau was not the only one interested in portraying an archaic city worthy of the finest first principles. For that matter, there is no reason to believe that the desire for an ennobling sense of temporal continuity is confined to isolated individuals. The creation of idealized mythic histories caters to the need for a narrative identity shared by the members of a community. In this context, appeals to the authority of antiquity reinforce the presumption, however illusory, of an enduring tradition held in common, an abiding foundation that comforts all who honor its memory, if only by its apparent immunity to the corrosive play of time and fate. Of course, such appeals may be made by different groups for different reasons. One way of seeing the past may come to constitute a shared identity exploited to the advantage of a privileged few. But then the past is also open to partisan reinterpretation, in order to win a purchase on the present for those slighted in the authorized tradition.[25]

In his recourse to the semifictional device of an ancient constitution, Rousseau in fact was taking up a quite conventional mode of political theorizing, one that extends back to the Greeks and forward to our own reverence for founding fathers and revolutionary heroes. J. G. A. Pocock has defined this mode as "the attempt to settle fundamental political questions, notably those involving law, right and sovereignty, by appeal not directly to abstract political concepts, but to the existing 'municipal' laws of the country concerned and to the concepts of custom, prescription and authority that underlay them, as well as to the reverence which they enjoy by reason of their antiquity"—an attempt which necessarily involves "the study, critical or otherwise, of their origins and history."[26]

Yet, as Pocock himself notes, critical historiography rarely plays much of a role in this mode of theorizing. Instead, the idea of the "immemorial" serves both to solicit and to conceal a certain amount of creative license in the work of partisan chroniclers. For if the hallowed first principles of the ancient constitution remain shrouded in the mists of time, who can say with certainty just what these principles are?

The convention of appealing to an ancient constitution thus proved peculiarly congenial to Rousseau's temperament. "My sorry head can never subjugate itself to things," he once confessed. "It cannot embellish, it wants to create. Real objects are painted more or less as they are; it only knows how to adorn imaginary objects." In any narrative of the past, he is liable to soar beyond the evidence—but that in no way discredits an account most valuable for the virtuous sentiments it arouses, the moral lessons it teaches. "I may make omissions in the facts, transpositions, errors in dates; but I cannot fool myself about what I have felt, or about what my feelings have made me do."[27] Convinced of the integrity of his own feelings and intuitive understanding, Rousseau will, in part, trust to them. And while he is speaking here about his autobiography, his comments are not irrelevant for appreciating his approach to narrative in general, history included.

He certainly believed that poetic invention had a place in the writing of history, just as he believed that the modern science of critical historiography completely misunderstood the practical utility of remembering the past. We moderns, he charged, no longer "know how to get any true advantage from history; critical erudition absorbs everything, as if it really mattered whether a fact is true, provided that a useful teaching can be drawn from it." The historian, thought Rousseau, ought to be considered a kind of poet—the only poet worthy of being admitted to an ideal republic.[28]

In this view, history is most valuable when it follows the examples of those "poets who can find in the invention of their fables" an edifying "union of merit and fortune" that is "most appropriate to please and even to instruct us." Such a historian "combines from one point of view the facts and the heroes appropriate to elucidate both."[29] By portraying heroes mastering fortune, he can graphically show the meaning of virtue and the significance of fate.

Such an inspiring juxtaposition of facts and heroes, which Rousseau himself first discovered in Plutarch, can be found in all the great ancient historians. In teaching himself, Rousseau had learned much from them. Their stories could still arouse the desire to emulate great deeds. Even if modern scholarship were to prove that every fact in them were false, their value would scarcely be diminished, for "the ancient historians are filled with views that one can use." On the other hand, Rousseau personally prefers a modicum of objectivity and some fidelity to the evidence, if only to permit every reader to judge for himself the men depicted. Thus Thucydides, rather than Plutarch, strikes him as the "true model of historians."[30]

Yet in history, as in autobiography, empirical accuracy is merely a necessary, and not a sufficient, condition. The utility of any narrative ultimately depends on neither the veracity of the facts, nor even the shared identity any well-crafted history may create; it depends rather on the pure nature of the characters portrayed, the virtuosity of the deeds described, the ennobling perfection of the panorama displayed. That is why Rousseau came finally to affirm that "sensible men ought to regard history as a tissue of fables whose moral is especially fitting for the human heart."[31]

When Saint-Preux designs a curriculum for Julie in *La Nouvelle Héloïse*, he therefore prohibits modern history, in part because of the pedantry typical of modern historiography, in part because the decadence of modern men and nations does not present a fertile field for the poetic historian who wishes to record with some degree of detachment a story that remains rooted in real events. But Saint-Preux makes one exception: the history of their homeland, Switzerland. Switzerland is excepted, not because Saint-Preux and Julie happen to have been born there ("Do not be dazzled by those who say that the most interesting history for each is that of his own country"), but because Switzerland is "a free and simple country, where one finds ancient men in modern times." Thanks to this fact, Switzerland can become the subject of a truly "interesting" history—the kind where one finds "the most examples of mores, characters of all types, in a word, the most instruction."[32]

Reconstituting the Lost City

Rousseau himself, as we know, contemplated but never completed a history of the Valais. He did, however, compose a short fragment on the "History of Geneva" while at work on the *Letters Written from the Mountain*. By examining this unfinished sketch, first published in 1861, we may obtain a clearer impression of his method and interests in the writing of history—a history that somehow managed to lead him back to the ancient constitution of democracy in Geneva.

In many respects, Rousseau approaches his task as he approached his *Second Discourse* on the origins of inequality. In both cases, he expresses at the outset a certain disdain for "facts"; in both cases, he nevertheless shows familiarity with a broad range of empirical evidence and scholarly studies; yet in both cases, he embroiders this information so liberally that many readers have felt driven to describe the results as a kind of fiction, with only a dubious claim to any rigorously scientific knowledge of the past.[33]

At the outset of his fragment on Genevan history, Rousseau asserts that the constitution of a modern country can be adequately elucidated only through some sort of genealogy. "I am obliged, in order to explain the present government, to return to its source and to clarify frequently that which exists by that which is long since past." However, he is equally emphatic that his concern for origins cannot be limited by what little evidence survives. The first principles that interest him remain "lost in the night of time." His purpose, therefore, "is not to plunge myself into antiquities; I have forsaken all that is only critical or erudite research in order to confine myself to that which takes me a little closer to my subject."[34]

But what takes him "a little closer"? What can help him find his way "in the night of time"? What, indeed, is the role he accords the evidence "erudite research" has uncovered? In the midst of his sketch, Rousseau gives a clue. He avers that "one can form, in a fairly simple fashion, an exact idea of this government, without entering into an examination of the facts disputed by the parties." He proposes advancing a "pure hypothesis," one where "it does not really matter whether the fact is true. It suffices that one can deduce the entire system of the constitution from this pure hypothesis, long accepted in practice."[35]

The entry on "hypothesis" in Diderot's *Encyclopedia* has this to say about the term as Rousseau's contemporaries used it: "It is the supposition made about certain things to account for what is observed, although the truth of these suppositions cannot be demonstrated." At best, the content of a hypothesis seems plausible: "We are obliged to be satisfied with probable reasons." In circumstances where our evidence is perforce uncertain, however, a hypothetical account is better than no account at all: "A beginning is necessary in all research. . . . There are unknown truths, like undiscovered countries, to which the correct road can be found only after having tried all the others."[36]

We may thus expect that Rousseau's own "pure hypothesis" about Geneva will stand at the intersection of fact and fable, empirical conjecture and poetic invention. And while such a hypothetical narrative will not be able to explain how precisely the ancient constitution of Geneva came into existence, the author believes that it may at least aspire to show us "very exactly what it was, and this is the sole object I propose in this work." In this task, facts are secondary; but that does not make the writing of this hypothetical history either useless or arbitrary. As he avows in the *Second Discourse*, "the hypothetical history of government is an instructive lesson for man in all respects." And though the Genevans "have acquired or conserved rights whose origin in history we cannot see," the nature of these rights nevertheless forms a fit topic for orderly inquiry, an inquiry he tells us that he is pursuing "by induction."[37]

Let us try to picture Rousseau's method. Before him, he has assembled a library of documents and narratives. In reading this literature, some episodes in Geneva's past appear uncontroversial, incontrovertible; others, though obscure, have the status of unimpeachable legend, even if the specific significance accorded them remains open. This is the raw material Rousseau works over by "induction," attempting to move from particular pieces of evidence to generalizations about the shape of the past.

This process of induction may be either directed by the author's reason or left open to the free play of his imagination: the availability of both possibilities is one methodological implication of Rousseau's remarks on poetry and the writing of history as fable. While winding through the labyrinth of uncertain evidence about Geneva, Rousseau might permit the wandering thoughts of his reveries to grope toward the original pattern, hoping, perhaps through an inspired intuition, to depict the general outlines of the archaic city as it once must have been. Or, if he has formed convictions about the necessary shape of the original city from other sources, he might allow his own principles to supply a tentative map for the evidence, determining the order of the facts on the basis of the ideas he has clarified through reasoning, quite independently of this particular evidence. Through a judicious blend of both procedures, he might hope to transform scraps of the past into a cohesive narrative that, besides being plausible in itself, can support a useful deduction of present conditions from a hypothetical origin.[38]

That Rousseau proceeded along something like these lines is suggested by the peculiar structure of the history he sketched. On the one hand, he brings the ancient city to life with a number of vivid details, allowing himself to elaborate an ennobling image of a more perfect past. On the other hand, he incorporates into the past a number of ideas familiar from the *Social Contract*.

"It scarcely seems probable," he writes, that Geneva "would not have lost, under so many masters, the exercise of a right that all peoples have naturally."[39]

This right he clearly feels he has every reason to assume a priori, on the basis of his principled knowledge of politics. Its apparent absence in the documentation of Geneva's past, far from posing doubts about its existence, functions instead as a warrant for letting his imagination fill the gap. Its absence, in turn, is explained by the hypothesis that a succession of unjust rulers have intentionally suppressed or destroyed all evidence of it. The author is thus in quest of an original right that he expects will have been repressed. The memory of right appears locked in combat with the forces of injustice, an unequal contest which only independent reasoning and the tempered use of imagination can settle aright—reason by helping to fix what appears to be the true form of things, imagination by helping to surmount the amnesia wrought by the forces of repression.

And what, according to Rousseau, is the original right that most Genevans have undoubtedly forgotten about, but that "all peoples have naturally"? Freedom. According to his own best reasoning, it is freedom that every person and all peoples possess by nature; it is freedom that defines us all as human; it is the memory of our natural freedom that the forces of domination seek to efface; and it is the redeemed image of freedom that Rousseau has recovered in his reveries. This is the crux of Rousseau's "pure hypothesis." The original right of Geneva to freedom suffices to "deduce the entire system of the constitution," whatever the facts about its current composition may seem to be.[40]

To ask *how* a people is free, indeed, seems to Rousseau not only a question difficult to answer, given the lack of evidence; it also seems a question that is not worth trying to answer. "It always seems to me odd that one asks of a free people why it is free, which is rather like asking a man with two arms why he is not one-armed. The right of freedom arises from freedom itself." The questions for empirical research posed by the pure hypothesis of an original freedom are quite different: How could the public exercise of freedom ever have been eliminated from social life? How could the political significance of freedom ever have been effaced from human memory? For if freedom is "the natural state of man," it is not thus with domination: its "right has need of being proven when it exists. When it no longer exists, it no longer has any right."[41]

The Golden Age in Geneva

The substance of Rousseau's history must thus concern the injustices of domination, particularly when he follows closely the available evidence. This is one reason why, in the *Letters from the Mountain*, Geneva's history appears as a saga of decay.

Things were once better, though. And at the hypothetical origins of Geneva, we may expect to find the untarnished first principles displayed in the *Social Contract* rearranged, through the medium of Rousseau's imagination, in the graphic form of a golden age: the very image of freedom, before decline overtook this legitimate state.

Yet, like any useful story of national origins, this picture of forgotten rights must be painted with enough fidelity to accepted facts and traditional legends to make the portrait seem plausible. By assembling evidence of the archaic city and by letting his reveries cast some light on what otherwise would remain "lost in the night of time," Rousseau's reasoned ideas may thus be made into an ennobling and persuasive panorama of bygone community, an ostensibly shared origin, opening up a new perspective on a new narrative identity—one that calls into question both the official tradition and the present decadence of his native city.

Once the origin of the city in a common freedom is hypothesized, the only things lacking to make the story of archaic Geneva an exemplary topic for an exemplary poetic history are the apparent absence of a hero or a great Legislator. Despite the impression left by the *Social Contract*, Calvin comes on the scene too late to count: "The whole of the current constitution existed before the reformation." Rousseau conjectures that "the prior foundation of freedom produced . . . the reformation; for the Genevans, having started to taste independence, wanted it whole, and turned against the church the arms they had already turned against the dukes."[42]

Rousseau's sketch for a "History of Geneva" thus opens by mourning the absence of a sovereign intelligence at the basis of modern states. Unlike the great cities of antiquity—at least as described in the fables of Plutarch—modern states "have not been formed of a piece and founded, so to speak, at one go. . . . Among us, the name of legislator is no longer anything but an abstract name, more appropriate to represent what gives force to the laws than who writes them. There is no longer any legislator but force, no longer any laws but the most powerful interest." A similar position is implicit in the cipher of the great Legislator in the *Social Contract*: such a figure at best symbolically condenses—and makes manifestly essential—the otherwise diffuse and complex process of shaping the interests of independent individuals into a cohesive community of belief and behavior.[43]

Despite the lack of Genevan history of a real legislator in the ancient sense, it turns out that the city is not without a hero of sorts, or even a great Legislator in the modern sense. After all, Calvin, through his edicts, did play a part in transforming the mores and manners of Geneva; and he certainly symbolizes the import of these features in civic life. As for a hero, Rousseau in his sketch finds one in the bishop Adémarus Fabri, commonly credited with granting civil and political liberties to the city in 1387, in a kind of Genevan "Magna Carta." Like the Magna Carta in England, Fabri's edicts in Geneva came to assume fabulous proportions for subsequent generations. Finding a new use for an old legend, Rousseau made of Fabri an archaic *porte-paroles* for his own views, hailing the bishop for being the first to recognize the rights that "all people have naturally."[44]

On Rousseau's telling, the story of Geneva begins in earnest after the decline of Rome into a brutal imperialism. In those gloomy times of "calamity and oppression," Geneva was a city subjected to the absolute dominion of distant emperors; after their fall, it became the equally abject prey of neighboring feudal lords. In this setting, the appearance of Christianity proved a veritable godsend. The church extended some solace to a people cruelly dominated by foreign masters. With no legitimate civic law to protect them, the city's residents gratefully appealed to "the law of Christ, which is the law of humanity." The bishop of Geneva thus came to be endowed with great authority, an authority the common residents of the community viewed as a shield not only against the predations of foreign powers, but also against the pretensions of the city's counts. In time, the wealthy elite within the town effectively became "vassals" of the bishop.[45]

According to this fable, "the bishop at first was elected by the people, according to the custom of the primitive church." Yet even after this custom was abrogated, as it inevitably was, the bishop found his temporal authority limited by his spiritual mandate. Whatever its injustices, the ecclesiastical rule of the bishop was thus infinitely preferable to the feudal rule of princes—for "the feudal system had degraded human nature" to the point where "there were no longer any men, properly speaking."[46]

The franchise extended by Bishop Adémarus Fabri ushers in the age of gold.

The origin of the franchises and freedoms of the people of Geneva is lost in the night of time. But in the celebrated act of the bishop Adémarus Fabri, this bishop himself recognized that the franchises that he confirmed had been handed down from time immemorial. However, one may only assume that in the disorders which followed the ruin of the Roman Empire, no people, no town, had conserved the least shadow of freedom. The feudal system, founded on the slavery of the vanquished, was not fit to resurrect it. The bishops, sole protectors of the people, rescued them from submission, and the municipal rights of the town of Geneva were only established upon those of the clergy. The [bishop], who owed his power to the people, repaid his debt with interest: he founded freedom. . . .

Protected externally by its sovereign and internally by its franchises, Geneva feared neither its master nor its neighbors, it was far more free than if it had been entirely republican.

Its municipal administration was also as democratic as possible. The people recognized neither classes, nor privileges, nor any other inequality among its members; it acted either by itself in the general council, or by its attorneys, called syndics, who were elected annually by the people, and who were accountable to them for their administration; no intermediary order was interposed between the syndics and the people, and this is the true character of democracy. We will see how this character gradually changed with the establishment of a [small] council. Of course, by the people, I mean only the body of the bourgeoisie, as do the edicts of the republic, where this name is used in the same sense. It is not known when the true right of the bourgeoisie begins, only that it is very ancient, and that the title of bourgeois of Geneva was an honorable one for the bishops.[47]

Another image of Alpine perfection, this is yet another picture of the best society possible, given the principles of the *Social Contract*; it is the "primitive contract" alluded to in the *Letters from the Mountain*; and it is emphatically a democracy.

We can now better understand what Rousseau was doing with history in his *Letters*. When set beside Geneva's modern institutions, the ancient constitution purports to offer graphic evidence of what has been lost, what is in jeopardy, and what may be worth saving. A contested heritage of civic freedom is at stake, and the comparison between the democracy of the past and the government of the present throws into bold relief the dangerous powers currently exercised by the Small Council. By reorganizing the historical evidence through the use of reasoning and imagination, Rousseau has painted a newly detailed picture of the ancient constitution. The burden of proof is thus shifted: it is now the government that must justify its understanding of Geneva's institutions; it is now the patricians who must explain their fear of civic freedom.

Moreover—and this is of the essence, rhetorically—while all usurpers must demonstrate the right of their usurpation, Rousseau, as we have seen, believes that no such burden falls on whoever defends the "right of freedom." The importance of this belief becomes apparent at several junctures in the *Letters from the Mountain*. For example, in one of the passages where he asserts that the general will is the rightful sovereign in Geneva, he forestalls objections by referring to this "immemorial right," which, being founded on "constant usage," has "no need of a lengthy explanation."[48]

Rousseau strikes a similar pose when faced with the apparent absence of any edicts before 1707 spelling out the putative rights of the General Council. In his view, such silence merely indicates that the ancestors considered these rights to be completely self-evident. If the right of representation was never specifically granted before 1707, that merely shows that "it follows, of itself, from the nature of your Constitution." The proper warrant for the rights claimed by the Citizens and Bourgeois is not positive law, but the unwritten tradition recalled by Rousseau. Thanks to his account, Genevans should be able to appreciate with renewed clarity the true nature of their ancient and legitimate laws. And if some obscurity still surrounds these primordial rights—and particularly if the government attempts to play on this obscurity to refute the rightful claims of the people—then this will be but one more sign of the patrician attempt to usurp the sovereignty of the Citizens: "unhappily, they have taken great care to efface thoroughly the ancient traditions, which today would be of great use for clarifying the Edicts." Such selective amnesia is self-serving. "The Magistracy may have its reasons for finding a clear thing obscure; but that does not destroy the clarity of it."[49]

Rousseau's argument, needless to say, forms a closed system of belief. Unfalsifiable, his hypothetical history is immune to counterargument. It is a partisan effort to use the past to redeem the present. But then, Rousseau's purpose in his *Letters from the Mountain* was not to convince with reasons. If he had not accomplished that in the *Social Contract*—and to judge by the reaction of the Small

Council, he obviously had not—then he would resort to "another order of authority, which can win over without violence and persuade without convincing."[50] His is a noble lie. In the *Letters from the Mountain*, the image of Alpine perfection becomes a self-conscious *myth*.

Beyond Utopia: A Myth for Moderns

"We have need of myths," it is said in Plato's *Laws*, "for the enchantment of the soul." Rousseau also talked of enchanting souls, by letting them behold images of "sublime institutions." Such paradigmatic images, he believed, are capable of inspiring a kind of reformation: "they give a new soul to those who draw near them to receive their oracles."[51] And if the mythic cities of classical antiquity enchanted Rousseau himself, he in turn fashioned for modern men an enchanting image of his own, in the shape of yet another mythic city: Geneva, homeland of freedom, the picture of democracy.

Yet, however mythical parts of his image may be, Rousseau's city—and let the point be stressed—is *not* a completely nonexistent utopia, it is not simply "nowhere." His Geneva, he insists, is no purely imaginary city, such as he considers Plato's Republic.[52] For Geneva, after all, was and is a real place with real possibilities: it is a place where we can enlist empirical evidence to conjecture about how "sublime institutions" might have actually arisen and declined; it is a place where men of insight, integrity, and imagination can, without insurmountable obstacles, conjure up a picture of realizable perfection, based on experience and a shared sense of a neglected legacy; it is, finally, a place where lost rights can perhaps still be reclaimed and restored, by men of wisdom, courage, and virtue jointly exercising their common freedom.

Moreover, a Geneva magically reformed through the meditation of a zealous patriot may offer a picture of more practical import than either Sparta or Rome, let alone the utopias of Plato and Thomas More. "Ancient peoples are no longer a model for moderns," says Rousseau; "they are too alien in all respects."[53] Images of the great ancient cities can still show modern men what citizenship and virtue ought to mean; but they cannot provide a pattern of much use for transforming the societies these individuals inhabit.

"One can only make men act in terms of their interest. I know it." So Rousseau reiterated his own convictions late in life. Anyone sharing such convictions can learn more from Rousseau's Geneva than from Plutarch's Sparta, for Genevans are neither Spartans nor Romans, "not even Athenians." They are "merchants, artisans, bourgeois, preoccupied with their private interests, their trade, their gain; men for whom even freedom is only a means of acquisition without obstacle and of possession in security." Coming from Rousseau, this kind of language might be construed as an unmitigated critique, were it not for the author's praise, both here and elsewhere, for the gentle manners engendered by domestic institutions and industrious labor, manners uniquely conducive to the tranquil exercise of a legitimate sovereignty. If civic freedom can be thus secured, even a measure of abundance has its place in Rousseau's best of all possible worlds. "With freedom, wherever affluence reigns, well-being also reigns." Of the Geneva he imagines regenerated through periodic festivals, he remarks in the *Letter to d'Alembert* that "it would be the image of Lacedaemon if a certain lavishness did not prevail here; but this very lavishness is at this time in its place, and the sight of the abundance makes that of the freedom which produces it more moving."[54]

In this context, as Rousseau states at the outset of the *Social Contract*, the task of the modern legislator is to take "men as they are"—namely, individuated and partially civilized creatures, each uniquely defined, not only by a free will, but also by the variety of interests he pursues in private—and to make the changes expressed in these traits compatible with an ennobling, rather than demeaning, sense of society. In other words, our legislator must elevate modern man to a point where, instead of regretting a past he has left behind, he will "ceaselessly bless the happy moment that tore him away from it forever, and that changed him from a stupid, limited animal into an intelligent being and a man." Such a society would foster not just dutiful citizens, but also distinct individuals, each educated, like Emile, to develop his own particular talents, pursuing by himself interests appropriate to preserving his independence among others: even if he is momentarily engulfed "in a social whirlpool," it suffices that such a reformed modern "not let himself get carried away by either the passions or the opinions of men, that he see with his eyes, that he feel with his heart, that no authority govern him beyond that of his own reason."[55]

In Rousseau's mythic image of Geneva, we have already found a place where someone like Emile could be raised and find a home, able to exercise his freedom in public as well as in private. In Rousseau's Geneva, we have also found a model of "laws as they can be." In effect, the ancient constitution of Geneva, like the ideas of the *Social Contract*, shows us how to reconcile "what right permits with what interest prescribes."[56] The emphasis is worth pondering: it is *interest*, not right, that "prescribes"—but only within rightful limits when institutions enable the associated individuals, discerning for themselves the interests they share, to make these interests the substance of their laws, on their own authority and for their own particular reasons.

By trying to make sense of his own odyssey from experience to memory, from reverie to reasoning, from the particular to the universal and then back again, from principle to myth, Rousseau tried to recapture the essence of his own contingent origin, as a "Citizen of Geneva," only now perfected by the self-conscious artifice of imagination, made compelling by reasoned ideas, made persuasive by a selection of historical evidence.

Is being inspired by his mythical picture of a real modern city therefore any more rational or useful than beholding an avowedly utopian image? Do we face a proof of possibility? A tacit concession of impossibility? A solace for the hopeless? A spur to action?

Toward the close of the *Letters Written from the Mountain*, Rousseau had this to say to his Genevan readers: "This state, being the worst into which one can fall, has but one advantage: it can only change for the better." As so often, he was exaggerating. Far from being "the worst," Geneva still possessed, by his own reckoning, an unusual potential for perfection. But the point of his fable remains unaffected. To be able to change only for the better—"This is the sole resource of excessive suffering; but this resource is great when men of sense and heart feel it, and take advantage of it."[57]

For those who consider Rousseau an unrelieved pessimist, absorbed in the past for purely moral or contentious or nostalgic reasons, this passage must seem puzzling. He doubtless believed in a cycle of decay: no cheerful teleologist, he had no faith in happy endings. He left the construction of historical theodicies to Kant and Hegel after him. But he also dreamed that one day, if fortunes were favorable, one man of virtue and boldness, frankly addressing moderns "of sense and heart," could make intuitively clear to each the interest they all shared in overturning domination and letting their legitimate freedom flourish. Working together as a community, such a people might then turn the wheel of time, and manage, if only for one precarious instant, to surmount their common suffering in the pleasures of a shared freedom. It was a desperate dream, really. Decay was inevitable. But as the bishop Adémarus Fabri proved, a real rebirth is feasible too. In principle, it is always possible, taking heed of our origins and probable destiny, to change our pattern of life. Because we are all naturally free, redemption is possible: we can always begin anew.[58]

André Breton once avowed that "I believe in the future resolution of these two states, dream and reality, which are seemingly so contradictory, into a kind of absolute reality. . . . It is in quest of this surreality that I am going, certain not to find it, but too unmindful of my death not to calculate in some slight degree the joys of its possession."[59]

Was Rousseau's desire really so different? "They treat the golden age as a chimera," the tutor tells Emile, "and so it always will be for anyone whose heart and taste have been spoiled. It is not even true that they miss the golden age, since their regrets are always idle. What, then, would be required to give it a new birth? One single but impossible thing: to love it."[60]

5

The Idea of Democracy

THE GOLDEN AGE was, for Rousseau, an era of freedom and democracy.[1] But what precisely does Rousseau mean by "democracy"? How does he evaluate it? In his approach to democracy, what seems novel enough to be noteworthy?

It is time to begin taking the measure of Rousseau's idea. Unfortunately, this is no simple task. At the outset, we face a conundrum of his own creation.

Confusion almost inevitably arises from his use of two divergent definitions. One of them is explicit and traditional, the other implicit and unusual. On the one hand, democracy is defined as a form of government, and this is the way he uses the term throughout most of the *Social Contract*. On the other hand, democracy is defined as a form of sovereignty, and this is the way he seems to use the term most of the time in most of his other political writings. Since the import of democracy varies according to which of these definitions is being used, it is helpful to start by clearly separating the two—something Rousseau himself did not always do.[2]

A Form of Government

The account of the forms of government given in the *Social Contract* is apparently orthodox. Following the conventions of the republican tradition, which we shall examine shortly, Rousseau defines democracy as one of three possible pure forms, alongside aristocracy and monarchy. In this context, he at first distinguishes democracy from the others by a numerical criterion: if the executive administration is entrusted to all of the people, or at least to a majority of them, then that government is a democracy.

Obviously, any such definition covers a broad range of institutions. But in the course of his discussion, Rousseau considerably restricts this range by introducing a second, administrative criterion. According to this criterion, a "true" democracy exists only when "the people remain constantly assembled to attend to public affairs." As soon as the people "establish commissions" and delegate any responsibility whatsoever, the "form of administration" has changed. By this second—and oddly strict—definition, Athens under Pericles could not be accounted a true democracy; and it is in this context that Rousseau asserts that "a true Democracy has never existed." As if to seal that verdict, the succeeding paragraphs make the necessary preconditions of democracy—smallness, simplicity, equality, austerity—sound impossibly daunting.[3]

For the most part, Rousseau seems emphatic in his preference for aristocracy as a form of government, especially in the *Social Contract*. An aristocracy he defines as a government restricted "to the hands of a small number, so that there are more simple Citizens than magistrates." But Rousseau did not prefer just any aristocracy. A hereditary aristocracy he called "the worst of all the Governments." Only "elective aristocracy"—a form where the majority of simple citizens pick magistrates from their own ranks—was truly praiseworthy as the "best" form of government: "It is Aristocracy, properly speaking."[4]

Rousseau felt an elective aristocracy preferable to democracy for a variety of reasons. Perhaps the most important was that an aristocracy avoided the confusion, inevitable in a complete democracy, between the government and the sovereign. If a sovereign people administered its own laws directly, there would be a constant need to apply general laws to particular persons. With this need would come a constant temptation for any member of the sovereign acquainted with the person involved to consult his particular interest in the matter, rather than heeding the interests he believes shared by his peers in general. If these same administrators, their own private concerns thus aroused by executing a law, then had to turn their attention, as members of the sovereign, to *making* the laws, there would be some risk that their lingering interest in personal preferences might inhibit the impersonal meditations appropriate to formulating rules for the community. Such a possibility Rousseau considered more catastrophic than the abuse of laws by government, since, without a sufficiently general will embodying a real consensus within a community, such abuses could never be properly rectified.[5]

There were three other reasons for preferring an elective aristocracy to a democracy. First, it enabled the most upright men in a community to make an example of their virtue and good will—an example all the more important in a modern society, in which people had become all too accustomed to seeing cunning and avarice rewarded with prestige and power. Second, by electing talented individuals to high office, ambitions could be checked by the love of distinction, while the people were taught "that the merit of men offers more important reasons for preference than does riches." Third, the administration and execution of the laws was more likely to be stable and orderly when it was overseen by a small group of "venerable Senators" rather than the entire citizenry. By the same token, a small group was better equipped to handle diplomacy expeditiously; the merit of these men would enhance the prestige of the state in foreign affairs.[6]

These reasons have sometimes been taken as definitive. On this basis, some critics have argued that it is simply wrong-headed to continue calling Rousseau a democrat, particularly in any radical or unfamiliar sense.[7]

But taken out of context, this list of reasons for preferring an aristocracy to a democracy is quite misleading. For one thing, it omits the central role assigned to simple citizens as sovereign lawmakers. In this capacity, after all, the people are charged not only with ratifying all constitutive laws, but also with preventing the abuse of these laws by the government; in their periodic assemblies, they can recast the form of government at will, as well as scrutinize the behavior of their governors. And while Rousseau often insisted that he was no advocate of democracy as a form of government, it must be added that he was equally emphatic in denying the value of aristocracy as a form of *sovereignty*: "The worst of sovereignties is aristocratic."[8]

A Form of Sovereignty

Let us turn, then, to democracy as a form of sovereignty. Here, the *Social Contract* is of only limited help. For while the sovereign is there described as the heart of the body politic and the very "principle of political life," and while it is said that the only legitimate government is republican—that is, a government subjected to laws sanctioned directly by a sovereign people—Rousseau in the *Social Contract* avoids overtly linking democracy with his definition of sovereignty.[9]

He had been less circumspect in the *Letter to d'Alembert*, where we find a reasonably clear indication of democracy as a form of sovereignty: "in a democracy, ... the subjects and the sovereign are only the same men considered in different relations. . . ." Similarly, in the *Letters from the Mountain*: "In every State the Law speaks where the Sovereign speaks. Now in a Democracy where the People is Sovereign, when internal divisions suspend all forms and silence all authorities, the people alone remain, and where then proceed the greatest number, there resides Law and authority." Apart from its ill-considered assumption of majority rule—by the principles of the *Social Contract*, any such rules of voting must be agreed to unanimously beforehand—this is about as compact a definition of a democratic sovereignty as one could want.[10]

These are not isolated instances in Rousseau's writing. He often refers to a city where the people are sovereign as a democracy. Thus his Geneva is described as a "democratic government [*sic*], wisely tempered," "a free and democratic State." By way of comparison, the Swiss cantons of Zurich and Berne are called "aristocratic States," implicitly because the government in these cantons is not subordinated to a sovereign assembly of the people.[11]

What did Rousseau expect from a democratic sovereignty of the people? Since democracy as a form of sovereignty is virtually synonymous with the legitimate republic detailed in the *Social Contract*, a full answer would require repeating the argument of that treatise. His central justification for a democratic sovereign—freedom—will be discussed at length in a final chapter. We may nevertheless mention here three of the reasons why Rousseau valued democracy as a form of sovereignty, giving some preliminary indication of whether these reasons are particularly unusual.

First of all, he held the belief, familiar to us, that a democratic sovereign offered a valuable check on the abuse of power. As he explained in the *Letters from the Mountain*, "Injustice and fraud find protectors often; but never is the public one of them. It is here that the voice of the People is the voice of God." One function he expected an assembly of all citizens to perform, then, was to elect directly the members of a government and to scrutinize their conduct once they were in office. (Although in calling the voice of the people the voice of God, Rousseau was merely invoking something of a republican truism, *vox populi vox dei*, he seems to have taken the motto rather more seriously than some of his predecessors.)[12]

Rousseau also felt that democracy could engender a measure of wisdom in all men. The practice of self-rule would teach the individual self-discipline, while giving him a firsthand feeling for shared norms and whatever reasons were behind them. Through a frank exchange of opinions, a people together could come to an intuitively clear understanding of a common ground. Another function he therefore expected an assembly of citizens to perform was to approve directly all laws, including, at regular intervals, the constitutive laws of the city. Such a democratic sovereign would keep alive the ancient ideal of a civic pedagogy: "Born a Citizen of a Free State, the right to vote there, however feeble may be the influence of my voice on public affairs, is enough to impose on me the duty of educating myself about them." In such a setting, the individual's "faculties are exercised and developed, his ideas are extended, his feelings are ennobled, and his whole soul elevates itself." (These are sentiments worthy of Pericles or Protagoras, perhaps, but an honorable civic education was not the sort of virtue most republicans since Plato had been in the habit of ascribing to democracy. In this context, Rousseau's view of the people was highly controversial. As Socrates is made to remark in one of Plato's dialogues, "I only wish that ordinary people had an unlimited capacity for doing harm; then they might have an unlimited power for doing good, which would be a splendid thing, if it were so. Actually, they have neither. They cannot make a man wise or stupid; they simply act at random.")[13]

Finally—and this is a point closely linked to his view of freedom—Rousseau believed that only a democratic sovereign could enable a society to achieve a transparent unity, reconciling the individual to a world shared willingly with others. A community constituted directly by the citizens comprising it, "being formed only of the individuals who compose it, could have no interest contrary to theirs." More than a juridical desideratum, democracy for Rousseau represented the resolution of a powerful yearning for peace and harmony—for a city of whole men at one with their human nature, their free wills joined in mutual respect, living together in a homeland that felt like a home. "All institutions that put man in contradiction with himself are worthless." A third function Rousseau expected an assembly of all citizens to perform, then, was to realize, as the basis of law and right, a framework of reciprocal recognition and moral equality. By suspending all relations of master and slave, a democratic sovereign promised the end of alienation—that is, the abolition of involuntary subjugation. (So far as I can see, this hope for democracy was unprecedented in political thought, although some antecedents for it may be found in theology. It is a dream of harmony that will haunt subsequent thinkers, particularly Karl Marx, who renewed Rousseau's desire for ontological communion through his own early writings on "true democracy.")[14]

The Two Forms Compared

At first glance, it is difficult to know how to evaluate Rousseau's two definitions of democracy. To which should we assign a greater weight? What is their relative significance in his political thinking? We may begin to answer these questions by noting an essential asymmetry between Rousseau's idea of sovereignty and his discussion of government.

According to his principles, all three pure forms of government may possibly be legitimate: democracy, aristocracy, and even monarchy. These forms, far from being mutually exclusive, may be profitably mixed and matched to the needs of governing a specific people. Thus, there is no question of an absolutely best form of government.

It is different with sovereignty. In the *Social Contract*, Rousseau does not even detail the range of possible forms of sovereignty. In a discussion of right, he apparently considers their conceivable variety irrelevant. A sovereign is either legitimate, or it is not. Peculiarities of situation and culture cannot mitigate the judgment, either: a people is either fit for freedom, or it is not.

If, in his discussion of governments, Rousseau makes a show of his open-minded willingness to mix and match, in his analysis of sovereignty, he bluntly poses a fundamental decision that no appeal to contingencies can evade. Sovereignty poses an either/or: it is an all or nothing-at-all proposition. "The fundamentals of the State are the same in all Governments." On this point, he is perfectly explicit in the *Social Contract*: "Sovereign authority is everywhere the same," everywhere it resides by right in the people. Anything less than a democratic sovereignty means that a society lacks a proper foundation. In that case, reasons for obedience change their character: they become prudential and circumstantial, rather than moral and obligatory. For "if the established order is bad, why should one accept, as fundamental, laws that prevent it from being good?"[15]

Rousseau thus had at his disposal two technical vocabularies of unequal gravity and scope, one defining the different legitimate forms of government, the other defining the one true form of sovereignty. Most often, when he spoke of democracy—and then in the most glowing of terms—he seems to have had in mind a form of sovereignty. About democracy as a form of government, he had less to say; what he did say was neither consistent nor particularly kind.

In his political writings, he would sometimes slip from one vocabulary to the other. Sometimes, he simply reverted to a more colloquial usage, as in his description of Geneva as "a democratic government, wisely tempered." It makes for a confusing scene. But we should not let the disarray in terminology obscure the novelty of what Rousseau is saying or the revolutionary twist he has given to the idea of democracy.

In the Tradition

To grasp the originality of his idea, however, it is necessary to turn our attention in a new direction. We have already indicated that the motivations for Rousseau's thinking were manifold, ranging from memories and daydreams to the polemics of democratic partisans in Geneva. But thus far, we have not lingered over his world of books or the ideas in their pages; we have yet to specify the meaning of democracy in the tradition he inherited.

In this regard, the education he happened to receive while growing up in Geneva is quite misleading: for the currency there of democracy as a slogan of public debate was highly unusual, an anomaly largely confined to the Geneva of his day. In the rest of eighteenth-century Europe, by contrast, democracy was a recondite term of theory, the province of philosophers and professors of jurisprudence, not preachers and artisans claiming political power; when educated men used the word at all, it was as a term of opprobrium.[16]

Moreover, Rousseau's own genius in the *Social Contract* was invested in recasting whatever slogans he might have borrowed in the form of clear and distinct ideas, valid universally. On this level, his predecessors and avowed peers were not his compatriots, but the republicans of the past, the classical authors who had first defined the vocabulary of political thought. We must therefore survey the place of democracy in the realm of their ideas: for it is only against this theoretical background that Rousseau's transvaluation can stand forth and be seen for what it is.

In the tradition of thought that begins with Plato and is transmitted through Aristotle, Polybius, Cicero, Machiavelli, and Montesquieu, democracy is approached as one pure element among three. In a properly constituted republic, it will be appropriately mixed with elements of aristocracy and monarchy to secure the public good.

Within this tradition, writers for many centuries adhered to the classical terminology of Plato and Aristotle. Democracy was customarily defined by picking a particular cluster of criteria from the stock of possibilities they had established. The most universal and least interesting criterion was numerical. According to Aristotle, "the supreme authority must necessarily be either One, or Few, or Many."[17] Democracy represents the supreme authority of the many. In a democracy, it is not sagacity or expertise, but the sheer weight of numbers, the opinion of the majority, that determines the course of the state.

Aristotle, like Plato, also offered an administrative criterion. In a democracy, where all of the citizens are eligible to hold office, they generally appoint officers by lot, rather than by election. In ancient Greece, elections were considered a device typical of aristocracies, since their ostensible purpose was to pick "the best." The drawing of lots, by contrast, was designed to give each citizen an equal (because random) opportunity to serve in office. Although this criterion obviously derives from a description of Athenian practice in the fifth and fourth centuries B.C., it was still employed by Montesquieu: "Suffrage by lot is natural to democracy."[18]

A class criterion was also available in Plato and Aristotle. "Democracy," Socrates reports in the *Republic*, "comes into being when the poor win, killing some of the others and casting out some, and share the regime and the ruling offices with those who are left." According to Aristotle, "the real difference between democracy and oligarchy is poverty and wealth. . . . Where the poor rule, that is a democracy."[19]

Plato emphasized as well a variety of psychological criteria, specifying the type of souls bred in a democracy. The typical democrat "lives along day by day, gratifying whatever desire occurs to him. . . . There is neither order nor necessity in his life." The proliferation of desires and the "unleashing of unnecessary and useless pleasures" marks democracy as a culture of "insolence, anarchy, wastefulness and shamelessness" and lends to the deliberation of its assemblies a frightful disorder.[20]

Democracy, finally, was defined by the two goods its citizens were said to worship in excess, to the point of mass obsession: freedom and equality. Plato evoked the greed within a democracy for "a great and unseasonable freedom." Similarly, Aristotle blamed democracy for engendering the false opinion that "those who were equal in any one respect were equal absolutely, and in all respects; because they are equally free, they claim to be absolutely equal."[21]

This brief survey of classical criteria for defining democracy already suggests why democracy was not the government of preference for Plato or Aristotle, or, for that matter, for any major political thinker before the eighteenth century. For them all, democracy left to its own devices was an inherently unstable form of association, inhabited by men of huge appetite and vainglorious ignorance, its *telos* an unbalanced freedom, an undue equality, its fate a grotesquerie of disorderly debate and disastrous ambition, epitomized by Athens' defeat by Sparta in the Peloponnesian War. From this perspective, it seemed a foregone conclusion that any democracy would collapse eventually into ochlocracy. As Cicero summarized this doleful upshot of self-rule, "the absolute power of the people degenerates into the irresponsible madness of a mob."[22]

It is not surprising, then, to learn that the classical republicans ranked democracy low in the hierarchy of civic forms. In the *Republic*, Plato described the logical cycle of birth and decay in the *polis*. Democracy, which paves the way for tyranny, is shown to be the least desirable form of lawful government. Two centuries later, this cyclical schema was taken over, slightly modified, and made straightforwardly historical by the Greek historian of early Rome, Polybius:

> We should therefore assert that there are six kinds of governments. . . . Now the first of these to come into being is monarchy, its growth being natural and unaided; and next arises kingship derived from monarchy by the aid of art and the correction of defects. Monarchy first changes into its vicious allied form, tyranny; and next, the abolishment of both gives birth to aristocracy. Aristocracy by its very nature degenerates into oligarchy; and when the commons inflamed by anger take vengeance on this government for its unjust rule, democracy comes into being; and in due course the licence and lawlessness of this form of government produces mob rule to complete the series.

Treating as paradigmatic the legislation of Lycurgus at Sparta and the laws of the Republic at Rome, Polybius valued a constitution capable of withstanding the process of decay. The durability of the state, he conjectured, lay in the proper mixture of the three lawful pure forms: monarchy, aristocracy, and democracy. Cicero also proposed tapping the best of the three forms: the paternal love a king feels for his subjects, the wisdom in counsel shown by aristocrats, the vigor and perseverance with which a people desires freedom. By balancing out the strengths and weaknesses of pure forms, a mixed regime might hope to obtain a lasting lawfulness, navigating the winds of time "like a well-trimmed boat."[23]

Now, according to most thinkers in the republican tradition, the people—the democratic element—had a useful role to play in such a ship of state, if only as ballast below deck. Because they were jealous of their freedom, the people made alert watchdogs, vigilant in their guard against official injustice. The very passions of the people, which generated a certain *esprit de corps*, could also be harnessed for the enhancement of civic power. Aristotle admits that the many show "military virtue," while Machiavelli, dreaming of a renascent Italian empire, was eager to exploit popular ardor: "The best armies are those of armed peoples," not paid mercenaries.[24]

Paying attention to the people in a mixed regime also seemed a sensible exercise in prudence, forestalling rebellions before they could take root. To avert a revolution fueled by popular resentment, Aristotle, in his celebrated pragmatic recipe for a stable "polity," advised giving the people some share of power, preferably through carefully supervised participation in public affairs: "A state in which many poor men are excluded from office will necessarily be full of enemies." Though commoners as individuals should be excluded from high office ("their folly will lead them into error"), the people as a whole struck Aristotle as exhibiting a modest and not unhelpful degree of common sense: "When they meet together, the people display a good enough gift of perception, and, combined with the better class, they are of service to the state (just as impure food when mixed with what is pure sometimes makes the entire mass more whole-some . . .)."[25]

The trick, obviously, was to refine the impurities of the popular passion for freedom. Permitting commoners to elect their leaders from a slate of aristocrats was one particularly attractive possibility. Cicero was willing to grant this right to the people but urged that voting be held in public, so that eloquent figures of authority could cue popular opinion: "I am conceding freedom to the people in such a way as to ensure that the authority of the aristocracy will prevail." Machiavelli held similar hopes: "As Cicero says, the people, though they are ignorant, can grasp the truth, and yield easily when, by a man worthy of trust, they are told what is true." And Montesquieu, while adducing England as a modern paradigm of mixed government, advised that the people "ought to have no share in the government but for the choosing of representatives, which is within their reach."[26]

At the same time, the classical republican writers agreed that the chief danger to a mixed constitution came from the democratic element. According to Aristotle, the participation of the people pressed a state inexorably toward a general system of "freedom based on equality," jeopardizing stability and an order of authority based on true merit: "Always it is the desire for equality which rises in rebellion." Polybius foresaw the day when prosperity had made the masses fat, idle, and eager to play a larger role in the state; their mounting demands for more freedom would eventually destroy the equilibrium needed to preserve a lawful mixed regime. Machiavelli cautions that the people, left to themselves, are "promoters of licence," while Montesquieu, like Aristotle, worries about the "spirit of extreme equality." Cicero speaks for a tradition when he warns that "freedom itself punishes with slavery a people whose freedom has no bounds."[27]

Three points about the position of democracy in the republican tradition deserve to be underlined. The first is that democracy in itself, as a pure constitutional form, was all but universally despised and disparaged; for many centuries, professional thinkers had scarcely given it a second thought. The second is that democracy, even in the context of a mixed constitution, was suspect as a prime source of decadence. In establishing a mixed republic, the question, How much democracy? was paramount; in answering it, the burden of proof always fell on anyone who counseled more freedom for the people.

The third point is this. In the wake of the English Civil War, where parliamentary partisans had mobilized republican theories in the struggle against the monarchy, this renovated tradition generated a chronically confusing tendency to conflate republicanism per se with a qualified defense of a more "democratical" republic—that is, a mixed regime with its monarchic element weakened and its representative legislature strengthened. While the question, How much democracy? thus became of some importance, addressing it directly and lucidly became peculiarly difficult—particularly given the low regard in which democracy as a pure form was still held.

In the Enlightenment

Symptomatic of the convoluted approach to democracy taken by Enlightenment republicans is the position of Algernon Sidney. Through the posthumous publication in 1698 of his *Discourses Concerning Government*, and thanks to the halo of martyrdom surrounding his name—a kangaroo court had ordered him beheaded for treason in 1683—Sidney became one of the most respected republican authors of the eighteenth century, his works widely read in France and America as well as in his native England. As he tried repeatedly to make clear, his preference for a popular republic and his opposition to absolute monarchy in no way made him a supporter of democracy: "As to popular government in the strictest sense (that is pure democracy, where the people themselves, and by themselves, perform all that belongs to government), I know of no such thing; and if it be in this world, have nothing to say for it." A proper grasp of civic freedom showed that it could in no wise be assigned to the form of democracy. "In asserting the liberty, generally, as I supposed, granted by God to all mankind, I neither deny, that so many as think fit to enter into society, may give so much of their power as they please to one or more men, for a time or perpetually, to them and their heirs, according to such rules as they prescribe; nor approve the disorders that must arise if they keep it entirely in their own hands."[28]

Reading Sidney's hedged prose and trying to imagine in all this a "textbook of revolution," it seems no wonder that democracy could become the source of so much confusion during the eighteenth century. Even in places like the American colonies, where the question, "How much democracy? became a pressing practical concern, the baroque complexities of the republican tradition, with its abiding distrust of pure democracy, its ancient emphasis on mixed regimes, and its modern tendency to equate the democratic element with a representative legislature, limited sharply the kinds of aspirations to self-rule that could be expressed and justified authoritatively.[29]

This kind of approach to democracy prevailed until well into the eighteenth century. The conventional wisdom of Rousseau's immediate milieu is summarized with welcome clarity by Jean-Jacques Burlamaqui (1694–1748), a Genevan professor of law whose uncluttered style won him a wide audience. Since "in Democracies, the Sovereign is a moral Person, composed and formed by the reunion of all the Heads of families into a single will, there are three things absolutely necessary for its constitution. 1°. That there be a certain place, and regulated times for deliberating in common on the public Affairs." Disorderly assemblies leading to lawlessness would otherwise make stable government impossible. "2°. It must be established for a rule, that the plurality of suffrages shall pass for the will of the whole." Otherwise nothing would ever get done, since unanimity is virtually impossible to obtain on every issue. "3°. Finally, it is essential . . . that Magistrates should be established, charged with convening the assembly of the People in extraordinary cases, expediting ordinary affairs in its name, and executing the Decrees of the Sovereign Assembly; for since the Sovereign Council cannot always sit, it is evident that it cannot attend to everything by itself." By Burlamaqui's definition, we may note, Rousseau's "elective aristocracy" would count as a democracy.[30]

But even such a cautiously defined democracy was not much to the liking of Burlamaqui, who, in this respect, remained a loyal son of the Genevan ruling class. The problem is familiar: "It is not freedom that is lacking in Popular states, rather they have too much of it, it degenerates there into license. . . . It is their ordinary lot to fall prey to the ambition of some Citizens, or to that of foreigners, and thus to pass from the greatest freedom to the greatest slavery." Because democracies harbor this unfortunate propensity, they need to be tempered in a mixed regime. "Let us conclude from this inquiry into the different Forms of Government, that the best are either a limited Monarchy, or an Aristocracy tempered with Democracy, by some privileges in favor of the body of the People."[31]

Certainly, shifts in emphasis within the republican tradition were under way. No less an authority than Montesquieu had linked democracy with the cardinal principle of virtue—an association that caused commotion at the time, but one that Rousseau himself felt appropriate.[32]

An even more favorable impression is left by M. le Chevalier de Jaucourt's essay in Diderot's *Encyclopedia*, perhaps because the separate entry on democracy perforce removes the topic from its normal context. In this essay, first published in 1754, de Jaucourt defines democracy as "one of the simple forms of government, in which the people as a body have sovereignty. Any republic where sovereignty rests in the hands of the people is a *democracy*; and if the sovereign power is found in the hands of a part of the people only, it is an aristocracy." Yet while de Jaucourt praises democracy for shaping citizens capable of "great actions and heroic virtues," imbued with "a continual preference for the public interest" and animated by "the love of equality and frugality," he also feels that the energetic principle of democracy—which, following Montesquieu, he defines as virtue—must sooner or later decay. The vice of instability thus consumes even de Jaucourt's relatively sanguine version of simple democracy:

> It would be a happy thing if popular government could conserve the love of virtue, the execution of the laws, mores and frugality; if it could avoid the excesses, namely the spirit of inequality that leads to aristocracy, and the spirit of extreme equality that leads to despotism alone: but it is indeed rare that *democracy* may preserve itself from these two dangers for long. It is the fate of this government, admirable in principle, to become almost infallibly the prey for the ambition of some citizens, or of a foreigner, and thus to pass from a precious freedom to the greatest slavery.[33]

Once it is conceded that democracy is "admirable in principle," we have come a long way. Indeed. But de Jaucourt, like Montesquieu, also remains bound by the conventions of republican theory; his admiration for democracy stops far short of an endorsement. As he says at the outset of his article, "I do not think that *democracy* is either the most convenient or the most stable form of government; . . . I am persuaded that it is disadvantageous to great states."[34]

Inverting the Cycle of Governments

At first glance, Rousseau's own discussion of democracy may not seem terribly striking or original, even against this backdrop. Particularly when he writes about democracy as a form of government, he pays almost exaggerated obeisance to the conventions of republicanism. Like de Jaucourt, he avers that democracy is admirable in principle: "If there were a people of Gods, it would govern itself Democratically." However, for sublunary souls, such perfection is quite impossible: "A Government this perfect is not suited to men."[35] Yet, even in the *Social Contract*, nuances in his argument imply the true novelty in his perspective.

Consider, first of all, the position of democracy in his theory of governmental cycles. In the *Social Contract*, we learn not only that "Government makes a continual effort against Sovereignty," but also that this "inherent and inevitable vice" eventually leads all governments to degenerate, either through the diminution of the citizens involved in government, or, eventually, through the dissolution of the social compact. "The Government shrinks when it passes from a large to a small number, that is, from Democracy to Aristocracy and from Aristocracy to Royalty. That is its natural tendency."[36] Rousseau here inverts the position republican theorists conventionally assigned democracy in the cycle of governments.

To be sure, Rousseau's inversion was not unprecedented. Montesquieu had begun his discussion in the *Spirit of the Laws* with democracy, although he seemed to attach little significance to this order. More interesting are Pufendorf's remarks in *Of the Laws of Nature and Nations* (1672). "In the first place we will examine the nature of a *Democratical* government," says Pufendorf, hastening to make his own opinion clear, "not that we think it to excel the other forms, either in dignity, or splendor, or in real usefulness and advantage." Why, then, the priority of democracy in his order of presentation?

> Because in the greatest part of the world it appears to have been the most ancient; and because reason shows it to be more probable, that many men, being in a condition of natural freedom and equality, when they resolved to join in one body, should at first be inclined to administer their common affairs by their common judgment, and to constitute a Democracy. Nor is it to be supposed that a father of a family, as yet free and independent, who upon weighing the inconveniences of a separate life, voluntarily joined himself to those of his own condition, in order to form a civil community, should, in a moment, have so far forgot his former state, under which he disposed of all things, relating to his own safety, as he pleased; as to be willing to submit himself immediately to a single director, with regard to

the common interest, with which his own private security has a necessary connection.[37]

Given his own regard for things ancient and natural, Rousseau, when reading Pufendorf, would likely have found such remarks suggestive. If, as Rousseau himself believed, men in society ought to live as closely as possible according to the pattern of an undefiled nature, and if pure democracy as a form of government stands closest to this pattern, then democracy, *even as a form of government*, would seem to possess many estimable merits, despite the conventional criticisms apparently endorsed in the *Social Contract*.

And indeed, whenever Rousseau discusses the cycle of governments, a positive impressive of democracy is consistently conveyed. We have encountered a democratic form of government at the origin of civic freedom in Geneva. We also learn from the *Second Discourse* that "those whose fortune or talents were less disproportionate, and who were the least removed from the State of Nature, kept the supreme Administration in common and formed a Democracy."[38] Because it embodies a community of equals, democracy is the form of government most appropriate to men not far removed from their natural freedom.

When we look a little more closely at Rousseau's position in the *Social Contract*, it turns out that this primitive and complete democracy has other advantages as well. Most significantly, perhaps, it solves the riddle of how the institution of government is to be accomplished. "The difficulty," Rousseau writes, "lies in understanding how there can be an act of Government before the Government exists, and how the People, which is only Sovereign or subject, can become Prince or Magistrate in certain circumstances," for example, in the particular acts through which it elects magistrates to public office and regulates the form of administration under which they serve. "Here again is revealed one of those astonishing properties of the body politic. In this case, the operation is accomplished *by a sudden conversion of Sovereignty into Democracy*," meant here solely as a form of government, "so that without any noticeable change, and solely by a new relation of all to all, the Citizens, having become Magistrates, pass from general acts to particular acts, and from the law to its execution." This shows "the peculiar advantage of a Democratic government," for, in this form, the government itself "can be established in reality by a simple act of the general will." Indeed, confides Rousseau in the *Social Contract*, "it is not possible to institute a Government in any other legitimate way without renouncing the principles established above."[39] In other words, the constitution of political right, wherever it legitimately occurs, necessarily involves an act of complete democracy—that is, a democratic form of government animated by a democratic form of sovereignty.

From this perspective, Rousseau's approach to democratic government begins to assume an unfamiliar shape. Democracy may be a form of government suited only to Gods, as his preemptory conclusion informs us in the *Social Contract*. But democracy is also the form of government instinctively assumed by free men at the origins of society, and it is the only legitimate means for instituting the principles of political right today.

Like the pieces of a puzzle, other comments by Rousseau now falls into place. In a foreword to his unfinished "Constitutional Project for Corsica," Rousseau writes that all decay in government can be laid to one cause. Decline occurs whenever "one too far separates two inseparable things." And what are these two inseparable things? "The body which governs and the body which is governed. By primitive institution, these two bodies form but one; they are only separated by the abuse of the institution." [40]

In the sequel, moreover, it happens that the decline of the state springs, according to Rousseau, not from the licentiousness of a mob, but rather from the very prosperity of democracy, which, irony of ironies, creates an abundance conducive to the spread of inequality. At first, the population grows apace with the surplus goods; there is general prosperity. With trade comes increased power for the government; taxation and skill at diplomacy become important. The development of the community begins to undermine its original *raison d'être*: "The larger the State grows, the less freedom there is." Some men become wealthy. The government becomes smaller, restricted in membership, focused in force; the wealthy begin to monopolize public affairs. It is not the artisans or even the poor who are the prime source of decay. "Everywhere the rich are the first corrupted." As the affluence of a few leads to the impoverishment of the rest, a growing class of poor also become corrupted: the threat of starvation makes them more interested in bread than freedom. That leaves those of an upright mediocrity; but eventually even this middle class of artisans, increasingly shut out of public affairs and abandoned to purely private pursuits, becomes disinterested in the joint exercise of freedom, which has grown difficult in any case. An insensible and divided sovereign makes an easy prey for the corrupt elite, who now dominate a compact and vigorous government, wielding prestige and power for selfish gain. It is only a matter of time until the freedom once shared is disregarded entirely. At this point, the original community dissolves, "and another is formed within it that is composed solely of the members of the Government, and that is nothing any longer for the rest of the People except its master and tyrant." [41]

So turns the cycle of government for Rousseau. Ending in a governing tyranny of those who arrogate authority to themselves, it begins with a pure democracy. Passing insensibly from democracy to aristocracy to monarchy, the government finally ends by usurping altogether the powers of the democratic sovereign, thereby abrogating the social contract at the basis of all legitimate states. For Rousseau, the saga of decay is the story of a disappearing democracy.

Redefining Sovereignty

Merely by inverting the conventional cycle of governments, Rousseau implicitly revalued the idea of democracy. But his greatest innovation was almost certainly his redefinition of sovereignty in terms of democracy—an unconcealed reversal that turned the received wisdom inside out. Once more, to appreciate his novelty, we must first sketch the theoretical context he worked within, and against.

Before Rousseau, sovereignty was a word for power, force, empire, and the ability to command: it defined the dominion of monarchs, not the rights of man. Barbeyrac, in his French translations and commentaries on Grotius and Pufendorf, used the term *souveraineté* to render the Latin phrases *summa potestas* and *summum imperium*; but there was no consensus on this rendering, and other French translators preferred the term *empire*. When Hobbes transported his own Latin concept of *summum imperium* into English under the rubric of the "sovereign," he defined the word to carry all the implications of unrivaled power conveyed by the original Latin.[42]

Most modern writers shared this understanding of the term. Among them, the vicissitudes of sovereignty strictly paralleled the vicissitudes of real power. Sovereignty could be acquired by conquest, consent, election, or inheritance; it could be assigned to one man, to an elite, or to an entire people; under a mixed constitution, it could be divided among different estates, distributed among different elements, a share for a plebeian legislature, a share for an aristocratic parliament, a share for a royal family; or, under an absolute monarchy, it could rest in the will and whim of one man alone, his every wish an imperial command.

The forms of sovereignty were thus as fungible as the forms of government. But if there was any one among them with a special claim to realize the essence of sovereignty, it was absolute monarchy; and if there was any one among them that seemed to suspend that essence, it was pure democracy. As Pufendorf wrote at the outset of his discussion of sovereignty. "The question before us is but little concerned with democracies, under which those who command, and those who obey, are distinguished by a moral respect only, and not a physical." For Pufendorf, sovereignty in essence involved naked force, not mutual respect. This was also the reasoning behind Burlamaqui's definition: "The relation there is between a Sovereign and subjects forms a sort of society between them; but of a particular kind, which we may call a *society of inequality*: the Sovereign commands, and the subjects obey. THE SOVEREIGN *is* therefore *he who has the right to command in the last resort.*"[43]

To be sure, there was a rival tradition. Among some theorists, regal or ecclesiastical claims to dominion had been countered by referring to the dominion of a people. The legitimacy of a government's power was said to spring from popular consent. Gierke has traced such a tradition back to the Middle Ages, and it reappears in Calvinist writers during the Reformation. Thus the Huguenot author Mornay, in his *Vindiciae Contra Tyrannos* (1579), asserted that "kings receive their royal status from the people; that the whole people is greater than the king and above him; that the king in his kingdom, the emperor in his empire, are supreme only as ministers and agents, while the people is the true proprietor." Over a century later, similar views were expressed by Locke. And by the eighteenth century, as we have seen, the Citizens and Bourgeois of Geneva were pressing their own claims to power explicitly in terms of popular sovereignty.[44]

But in France and elsewhere, the perspective prevailing in Rousseau's day was royalist, the dominant theoretical position that formulated by Bodin two centuries before, in his attack on the Huguenot heresies in *Six Books of a Commonweal* (1576). In the first of these books, entitled "Of Sovereignty," Bodin defined his topic as "the most high, absolute and perpetual power over the citizens and subjects in a commonwealth." In French public affairs for long afterward, sovereignty remained synonymous with absolutism, the unlimited power of the King. In 1766, Louis XV, in a proclamation prepared by his lawyers, reasserted the scope of his empire: "Sovereign power resides in my person alone. . . . It is from me alone that my policies take their existence and their authority; . . . it is to me alone that legislative power belongs, without dependence or division; . . . all public order emanates from me."[45]

Within this context, Rousseau's use of sovereignty, even if not unheralded, was decisive and unequivocal. The synonym for sovereignty was no longer *empire*, but *volonté*. Its essence was to be found not in a monarchy, but in a democracy. By thus redefining sovereignty, Rousseau shifted its implications and transformed its content. The slogan of absolute monarchs became a word for self-rule.

At the heart of Rousseau's state stood not force, but freedom; not commands, but reciprocity. The personalized and unbounded power of a king disappeared before the impersonal power of a people—a power limited by the extent of their shared interests and by the strength of their mutual respect. In Rousseau's hands, sovereignty became a moral ideal, a psychological reality, a way of developing the free will inherent in every man.

And yet the political implications of his innovation were no less radical for being couched in terms that he himself considered abstract and moral: if his idea of sovereignty was to have any chance of being realized, certain kinds of political institutions were necessary.

The sovereignty he defined could not, in principle, be divided or alienated. It belonged to a people as a whole, and only to them. They alone could rightfully exercise it; they alone could stipulate its significance; they alone could decide what interests they shared, what goods to pursue in common, what limits to impose; only their joint freedom could warrant the legitimacy of this venture. Such a sovereignty of the people could not be acquired by conquest, election, or succession; it could not be assigned to one man, to an elite, or to an elected group of representatives; it could not be divided between a legislative, an executive, or a judicial council. A legitimate sovereign could not be aristocratic, let alone monarchical. It could not be realized in a mixed republic, even one with a strengthened legislature. It would be directly democratic—or it would not exist at all.

By making democracy the only real embodiment of sovereignty, Rousseau not only ruled out any form of absolute monarchy, he also realigned the world of republican discourse. The primacy of an indivisible and inalienable sovereign meant, in practice, that every legitimate republic must, at base, be simple: a pure democracy. The question, How much democracy? was no longer paramount. The burden of proof was shifted. After reading Rousseau, the question was reversed. All republican government, if it would be legitimate, had to rest on the free will of a people. In this setting, the real question was not How much democracy?, but How much aristocracy?, How much monarchy?—and these questions only a sovereign people could rightfully decide.

The Hidden Masterpiece

We now have a clearer notion of what was unusual in Rousseau's idea of democracy. When his own striking and original image of Alpine democracy is recalled, a very strong conclusion becomes surprisingly credible: Jean-Jacques Rousseau, Citizen of Geneva, effected, virtually single-handed, an epochal transvaluation in the meaning and appeal of democracy.[46]

Moreover, Rousseau himself thought that this was precisely what he had done, even if he did not normally suppose it diplomatic to say so openly. In the *Letters from the Mountain*, though, he let the secret out. "The democratic Constitution," he writes, "has up till now been poorly examined. All those who have spoken of it either have not understood it, or have taken too little interest in it, or have had an interest to show it in a false light. Not one of them has sufficiently distinguished the Sovereign from the Government, the legislative Power from the executive." This is not surprising. For "there is not a State where these two powers have been thus separated." Even where existing arrangements have approximated some such separation, "people have preferred in any case to confound them," hopelessly confusing matters of sovereignty and government. As a result, misleading concepts of democracy abound; they are embedded in the ways of speaking that we have inherited.

Previous theorists are of little help on this score. Some of them, raised on the classical image of Athens, "imagine that a Democracy is a Government where a whole People is Magistrate and Judge," only to be repelled by the disorder they foresee. Others, who have always been "subjected to Princes," see "freedom only in the right to elect leaders"; they give the false impression that "whoever commands is always the Sovereign."

Yet, as anyone can intuit from Rousseau's own imagery, there is no disorder inherent in democracy, when seen from his perspective; and there is much more to freedom in *his* democracy than elections and obedience. At last, he implies, the democratic constitution has found a theorist honestly interested in its intricacies, a thinker willing to show it in a true light. For Rousseau, after all, democracy is not merely a topic of study. It is the city of his dreams.

In the city of Rousseau's reasoning and reverie, we face a constellation of unique individuals and shared institutions, an organic structure of conventional beliefs and common behavior, mostly unwritten and unspoken, yet entirely geared to enabling each on his own to balance perceived needs, habitual tastes, spontaneous wants, and a thoughtful sense of what seems right—a society of whole men and virtuous citizens, where good is done spontaneously, as if by instinct. The essence of freedom in the democratic constitution is therefore unobtrusive;

when it is functioning properly, its operation does not constantly solicit reflection. "The democratic Constitution is certainly the Masterpiece of the political art: but the more admirable its artifice, the less it belongs to all eyes to see through it."[47]

Democracy. "The Masterpiece of the political art"—and yet an artwork bound up with mysteries and hidden by design, its beauties kept a secret by the enigma of free will, the reticence of a wise teacher, and the threat of hostile government censorship. Here is the key to Rousseau's political thinking.

It is also the starting point for any account of the influence that thinking has exercised—for Rousseau's new perspective on democracy was there for all to see in his most seductive fictions, and yet hermetically contained in his most daunting treatises. The contradictions of his legacy spring, in part, from the crosscurrents at play within it. The figural element of his thinking leads the reader on, while the logical course of his argument, often posed through riddle and paradox, draws him up short. In his writing sounds an unfinished resonance.

Yet if his ideas are difficult, his images are anything but. When he eulogized Geneva and Switzerland, he wrote a poetry of politics, a foundation and complement for his own best reasoning. In these siren songs, as in his own ideas, he invested his highest political hopes. And then he cast them off, let them go, setting his thoughts adrift, lost in a world in which he felt like a stranger.

(1764–1778)

The Reluctant Visionary

O NCE HE HAD unveiled the hidden masterpiece of his political art, Rousseau tried to act as if the political career of his ideas was at an end. After publishing his *Letters Written from the Mountain*, he wished to withdraw altogether from the turmoil of public life. Fantasies of Alpine perfection no longer commanded his interest. Disabused of his hopes for Geneva, he had momentarily disburdened himself of his political reveries. As he wrote, shortly after renouncing his Citizenship: "In detaching myself from a chimera, I have ceased to be a man of visions."[1]

Given his disenchantment following the censorship of *Emile* and the *Social Contract* throughout Europe, it is likely that his Alpine dreams had become a painful reminder of reality, rather than a pleasant escape from it. In a note written while he was still at work on the *Letters*, he spoke of how Geneva no longer existed as a genuine *patrie*, either for him or for its Citizens: the *pays* that remained dishonored his memory and its own best possibilities by presenting a mere simulacrum of civic freedom. Shortly afterward, he described the change in his own feelings to Lenieps. "The most profound indifference has replaced my old zeal for the homeland; for me, it is as if Geneva no longer existed. Neither Reason nor indignation has produced this change in me. It happened by itself, my will played no part."[2]

Rage

Yet, until his accounts were finally settled with Geneva, he could not tear himself away. Even when he had completed writing the *Letters from the Mountain* in June of 1764, he was not finished with his project: for the essay had yet to be published and distributed, and Rousseau must also have wondered about its reception. The General Council of Geneva was scheduled to elect Syndics in January of 1765. All concerned felt that Rousseau's book would win its widest audience if it appeared before these elections. To insure that the timing was right, it was decided to hold a secret meeting between the author and some of his allies from the popular party.

Under the pretext of visiting a spa for his health, Rousseau set out on foot, on August 1, telling friends that his destination was Aix-les-Bains, a hot springs resort eight miles north of Chambéry, in the kingdom of Savoy. His route took him out of Neuchâtel and the protection of King Frederick, through the canton of Vaud, probably to the city of Nyon on Lake Léman; from there, he boated to Thonon, also on the shores of the lake, but located in Savoy. In a contemporary letter, Rousseau describes some of the sentiments aroused by the trip. "Crossing the lake and seeing from afar the spires of Geneva, I surprised myself by sighing as cravenly as I used to do for a perfidious mistress."[3]

These are not the words of a man resigned to his fate. Indeed, his suspicions were still running high; he could still feel bitter, the dupe of a whore. A man in his situation might well have relished some kind of revenge. After all, as Rousseau had explained some months earlier to Lenieps, his enemies in Geneva had leagued with the cabal plotting against him in Paris, all in an awful attempt to turn the truth inside out, as if to plunge his mind into darkness: "I understand nothing of the peculiar course of the world; and I am completely astonished to learn that it is I who am evil and impious, while they are upright men and good Christians."[4] Ignoble enemies lurked in the city he had once loved.

Once in Thonon, Rousseau arranged with his Genevan colleagues to coordinate their polemics against the patricians. The appearance of two publications was planned for maximum impact. Rousseau's *Letters* would come first, followed a few weeks later by another pamphlet attacking the government position. "I conceived and executed this enterprise so secretly," Rousseau tells us in the *Confessions*, "that at a rendezvous in Thonon with the heads of the *Représentants* to discuss their cause, where they showed me a sketch of their response, I said not a word about mine, which was already finished, fearing that some obstacle to its publication would set in if the least hint of it reached either the magistrates or my private enemies."[5] If substantive issues were not discussed, however, a secret code for handling future correspondence was. Rousseau, in turn, apparently promised to pressure his publisher into meeting a December deadline.

He never did take a bath in the hot springs at Aix. Instead, he hurried back to Neuchâtel, where he made meticulous arrangements with Rey in Amsterdam for printing and shipping his book "by Christmas," as he tirelessly kept repeating in letter after letter to his publisher. The first copies of the *Letters from the Mountain* were to be smuggled to one of the *Représentants* inside Geneva "in a securely fastened packing-case, wrapped in oil cloth with another layer of stout material on top, labeled *standard cloth*."[6]

Whether it was necessary or not, the surreptitious planning paid off. In December of 1764, the first copies of Rousseau's *Letters from the Mountain* appeared in Geneva, right on schedule.

Nothing is less important for the public, I admit, than the material in these letters. The Constitution of a small Republic, the lot of a small individual, the exposé of several injustices, the refutation of several sophistries; all this in itself holds nothing notable enough to deserve many Readers: But if my subjects are small, my aims are large, worth the attention of all upright men. Leave Geneva in its place and Rousseau in his prostration; but Religion, but freedom, but justice! Whoever you are, these are not beneath you.[7]

It is a deceptively mild foreword.

Rousseau's latest publication was another bombshell. In Geneva, it wreaked havoc. Gone were the mixed signals of the *Social Contract*. Replacing them was a straightforward and detailed criticism covering virtually every facet of public affairs in Geneva. After reading the *Letters Written from the Mountain*, some patricians must have felt nostalgic for the somber abstractions of the *Contract*. But it was too late. The damage was done. The ruling magistrates, obviously stunned, were reduced to an almost incoherent public statement of censorship: "The Council, superior to these atrocious imputations, has disdained to expose them by the ordinary ways of Justice, too disproportionate to their enormity."[8]

Events were out of control in Geneva. On January 1, 1765, several days after Rousseau's tract had appeared, there followed the second *Response to the Letters Written from the Country*. At the meeting of the General Council that month, a slight majority of the Citizens and Bourgeois refused to vote for a single Syndic from the slate of candidates chosen by the Small Council. Attempting to shrug off the embarrassing rash of abstentions, the government stumbled onward, its authority severely eroded, its leaders muttering in their private correspondence about Rousseau, this "charlatan of virtue" who was making their rule so damnably difficult.

Spirits soared, meanwhile, among the partisans of the popular party. What distressed the patricians quite invigorated the militant Citizens; they hailed Rousseau's latest book as the "Gospel of Freedom." The stakes were being raised all over again: this was no longer a parochial affair concerning the fate of one expatriate, it was no longer even a legal dispute over the right to make representations; once the voters' strike had begun in January, 1765, political affairs in Geneva became a frank struggle by the Citizens for more power, specifically the power of the General Council to elect anyone it pleased to high office.[9]

Rousseau's account of these days in the *Confessions* is bizarre. At one point, he speaks of the *Letters from the Mountain* as if someone else had written them, sarcastically describing "the terrible explosion against that infernal work and its abominable author." In the next breath, he tells us of "the stoical moderation" any careful reader will find in these *Letters*, a moderation all the more admirable given "the painful and cruel outrages" perpetrated against the author. Then, in the oddest twist of all, Rousseau accuses the *Représentants* of abusing his work: "Instead of making a trophy out of the *Letters from the Mountain*, they bent it to make a shield, they had the cowardice to render neither honor nor justice to this writing made in their defense and at their solicitation, neither citing it nor naming it, although they tacitly drew upon its arguments."[10]

This accusation is simply untrue. In February of 1765, the *Représentants* had dutifully—and vigorously—protested the decision of the Small Council to censor Rousseau's latest work. Admittedly, they did not quote passages from his book in this effort.[11] But who would have supposed that such citations were necessary? What did Rousseau want?

Retreat

Apparently what he wanted was some peace and quiet. If that was indeed his aim, it is no wonder that the *Letters from the Mountain* could appear to him, in retrospect, as an "infernal work." A trail of smoke seemed to follow it wherever Rey marketed the book. Burned in Berne and at the Hague, it was forbidden in Neuchâtel, censured in Geneva, condemned by the Court of Holland, committed to the flames in Paris.[12]

Even at the time, Rousseau scarcely seemed to care. When the *Letters* first appeared in Geneva, he had taken a polite interest in the reaction there; expressing hopes for the success of the popular cause, he wished his allies well. But once finished with pleasantries, and obviously distressed by the rising temperature of events, he soon changed his mind and attempted to break all his ties to the city. He had seen class conflict come to a head in Geneva once before, in 1737. One image of that event was still etched in his memory: seeing a father run one way to defend the government, while his son rushed off in the opposite direction to mount the barricades alongside the Citizens and Bourgeois. The sight convinced him, he says, "never to take part in any civil war, and never to uphold freedom by arms."[13]

Fearful of fueling any more discord in Geneva, Rousseau tried in effect simply to ignore the chaos he had helped unleash. With astonishing smugness, he preached to his embattled allies, lecturing them on the restraint shown by the virtuous in a political storm: "One could not go any farther without exposing one's country and public repose, which the wise man ought never to do. When there is no longer any common freedom, there remains one recourse, and that is to cultivate personal freedom, that is to say, virtue."[14]

He was not at all certain, however, that such arguments would carry the day and close the case, at least so far as his own responsibilities were concerned. On February 24, 1765, he therefore dispatched a letter to De Luc announcing that he would no longer respond to any letters from him. "For myself, I am taking the only course that remains open to me, and I am taking it irrevocably. Since with intentions so pure, and with so much love for justice and for truth, I have only managed to produce ill on the earth, I will no longer try to produce anything, and will retire within myself. I do not want to hear talk about Geneva or about what happens there. Here ends our correspondence."[15]

But the agitation in Geneva would not go away at his bidding. Old friends still solicited his advice, and he still worried fitfully about the fate of his native city. Two years later, after his former ally, the exile Lenieps, had been imprisoned in France for directing seditious activities in Geneva, word reached Rousseau that Genevan officials claimed to have found among the papers of Lenieps handed over to them "a plan of legislation for our republic, which overthrows our constitution, created and written in the hand of J. J. Rousseau." Rousseau wrote back to his Genevan informant, protesting his innocence. He also made certain that an exculpating note was appended to one of the autobiographical works he was preparing for posthumous publication. In this note, without naming Lenieps directly, Rousseau recalled that one of his friends had attempted to arouse the Citizens against the magistrates in Geneva on his behalf, but against his advice. "I thought differently" about such agitation, he explains, "and in writing either to them or to him, I never ceased pressing them to abandon my cause and to postpone to a better time the defense of their rights." In his sporadic correspondence with friends in Geneva, he now consistently struck the pose of conciliator.[16]

The author who dreamed of courageous deeds, heroic figures, and a democracy of virtuous men obviously had no interest whatsoever in the disorderly and unpredictable consequences of action, no taste at all for the risks of radical change. He would write his books. Others could worry about the implications and consequences. Does this show Rousseau to have been an indecisive coward? An irresponsible firebrand? A wise pacifist? An exemplary stoic? Or simply a very sorry case of self-deceit and bad faith? Whatever the moral verdict, Rousseau's political position had become strategically untenable.

The Armchair Federalist

Long before he died in 1778, Rousseau had taken leave of this world. In truth, he was "alone upon the earth, having no brother, neighbor, friend or society other than myself." His heart was no longer in the quest to answer the great questions of politics. He wondered whether justice was really the lot of terrestrial creatures and found his own thoughts turning toward Providence. He desperately hoped that God, noticing his plight, would confirm his innocence.[17]

But he was not quite finished with politics yet. Aroused by the image of himself as a latter-day legislator, he responded to requests from Corsica and Poland for his constitutional ideas. Although his sketch for Corsica remained incomplete, and he showed no interest in publishing the results of either effort, the surviving manuscripts indicate that he took both commissions seriously. Unwilling to be regarded as a quixotic dreamer, he took pains to meet practical requirements, casting himself as a prudent statesman, a lawgiver of moderate means as well as inspiring aims. If we conclude that he is not quite convincing in the role, that is but one final tribute to the all-consuming force of his original vision.

In the present context, his constitutional proposals for both Corsica and Poland are most notable for the attention paid to crafting a system of federal government—"the only one which combines the advantages of large and small states." If it were at all possible to avoid wandering off into "chimerical projects," it was essential at the outset to correct the "radical vice" of modern nation-states: their sheer size. On this score, his advice was the same to both Corsica and Poland: "Apply yourselves to extending and perfecting the system of federative Governments."[18]

In the *Social Contract*, he had urged large countries to avoid the centralization of power in capital cities, and "to make the Government have its seat alternatively in each town, assembling there in each of them by turn the States of the country."[19] He now tried to apply this federal maxim in practice.

The most difficult case before him was Poland: a large nation with a sharply divided ruling class, a vast mass of dependent serfs, and an unhappy location that aroused the expansionist desires of Russia on the one hand and Prussia on the other. Yet the Poles were not entirely without resources for reform, according to Rousseau. They possessed provincial assemblies of notables, called dietines, which, he believed, might be revitalized to achieve at least a simulacrum of broadly based sovereignty. But while he advised the Poles to "perfect the form of the Dietines," he also gently reminded them that these representative assemblies could never become truly legitimate until the people as a whole were admitted into public life: "The law of nature, this holy, imprescriptible law, which speaks to the heart of man and to his reason, does not permit that one thus restrict the legislative authority, and the laws do not oblige anyone who has not voted for them personally, like the deputies, or at least through representatives like the body of the nobility."[20]

He was thus driven to admit the necessity of representative government in Poland, at least for the foreseeable future. He nevertheless remained dissatisfied with the device of representation. In an attempt to ameliorate its inherent flaws, he recommended frequent elections, the regular rotation of elected officials, and the binding instruction of legislative delegates by those who elected them. About the ultimate basis of even this limited approximation to true sovereignty, he was unequivocal. The government of a large nation could never surmount the legacy of "feudal barbarism" unless it enfranchised the poor and dispossessed, that part of the state which is "the most numerous, and sometimes the most healthy."[21]

In a remote, rural, and relatively poor country like Corsica, by contrast, Rousseau foresaw far fewer problems inhibiting the institution of more legitimate laws. He had declared in the *Social Contract* that Corsica was the one country left in Europe "capable of legislation." Their interest piqued, some Corsicans asked Rousseau for an indication of just what he had in mind. What he had in mind, he responded, was a democracy. "Weakened by a long slavery, devastated by long wars," this island state first of all had "need of reestablishing itself." Such a rebirth was feasible when "the Government is Democratic." Yet, here also, a federation of regional assemblies seemed necessary:

> The rustic system, as I have said, involves a Democratic state. Thus the form that we have to choose is given. It is true that there are some modifications to be made in its application, because of the largeness of the island; for a purely democratic government belongs in a small Town rather than in

a nation. One cannot assemble all of the people in a country like those in a city, and when the supreme authority is confided to deputies, the government changes and becomes Aristocratic. What Corsica requires is a mixed Government where the people only assemble by parts and where the depositories of their power are often changed. . . . The districts and particular jurisdictions they have formed or conserved to facilitate the gathering of taxes and the execution of orders are the only possible means of establishing democracy among the whole of a people who cannot assemble at one time in the same place.[22]

Ambivalence

Such avowedly pragmatic remarks force us to confront again the status of Rousseau's maxims for realizing the principles of political right. What about nations and peoples like the Poles, who seemed unable to meet his minimum conditions for democracy? These conditions—compactness of size, simplicity of mores, equality of fortunes, a taste for freedom—have been met by very few modern countries. Where, besides Geneva and Corsica, were his ideas about sovereignty even remotely practicable?

Given the obvious obstacles, Rousseau was ready to concede almost everywhere the need for aristocratic government. Under the circumstances of modern Europe, where men, long enslaved within feudal relations of domination, had received an education in servility rather than self-reliance, an aristocracy of the wise, elected by the whole of a people, seemed to him salutary. How else could men learn to distinguish virtue from vice, how else could they learn to exercise their free will in concert with others?

But what about a democratic *sovereignty*? What about realizing the only form of society fully in accord with "the law of nature"? Was this a practical possibility for modern men?

Here Rousseau wavered. Unyielding in his prescriptions for Geneva, encouraged by the prospects in Corsica, he hesitated before the obstacles in a large nation-state. In his constitution for Poland, he felt himself obliged, in the name of realism, to make concession after concession, limiting, step by step, however reluctantly, the extent of popular participation in legislation, insisting all the while on the overriding import of his most uncompromising maxims and principles: the true ideals animating his advice to Poland "are established in the *Social Contract*"; his suggestions on how to vote "are discussed with the greatest care in the *Social Contract*." But he vacillated on how frankly to express himself. Thus, in the final fair copy he dispatched to his Polish correspondents, he omitted this passage: "For the rest, I have discussed this matter in the *Social Contract*, and for anyone who wants to reckon well my sentiment on anything, this is where it is necessary to search."[23]

So the question remains. What about those many states and peoples who apparently fail to meet the minimum conditions for instituting a democratic sovereignty? Is there another way to approach this question? Can the emphasis perhaps be reversed?

Instead of adapting law to circumstance, what about transforming the circumstances to support just laws? Others might regard such a feat as an act of folly. But to men of boldness and virtue, it might pose a heroic challenge. Then the minimum conditions for democracy would become a list of necessary reforms. To institute a democratic sovereign would require, from the outset, the decentralization of administrative and legislative power, the reintegration of town and country, the elimination of luxury trades, a leveling of fortunes, and a generalized distribution of property. It would require educating men to be free. The difficulties in the way of democracy would then merely indicate the revolutionary changes required to institute it.

Rousseau himself was no champion of rash ventures. Discord unsettled him. In the *Social Contract*, he stated that "all good institutions should be modified in each country according to the relationships that arise as much from the local situation as from the character of the inhabitants. . . . Each people must be assigned a particular system of institutions that is the best, not perhaps in itself, but for the State for which it is destined." He also told the Corsicans that wise legislators, heeding given conditions, were reluctant to transform "relationships of harmony." They ought to "form the government to fit the nation."[24]

But he also added, in the next sentence, a remark that has an entirely different flavor: "There is, however, something far better to be done, and that is to form the nation to fit the government." The trouble with previous statesmen, he once wrote, is that they have "incessantly mended, whereas it would have been necessary"—if one truly wanted "to raise finally a good Edifice"—"to begin by clearing the site and setting aside all the old materials." Besides, as he put it in the *Second Discourse*, "time will necessarily bring about . . . revolutions" in the forms of government, and the far-sighted legislator might well await that epoch when "new revolutions dissolve the Government altogether or bring it closer to its legitimate institution." Had he not himself described the great Legislator in the *Social Contract* as a man who "ought to feel himself in a position to change, so to speak, human nature"?[25] Even while scaling down his desires and protesting his practicality, Rousseau found it difficult to let go of his dreams.

An Open Question

In January of 1767, he wrote to a friend in Geneva, trying once again to make clear the innocence of his own political convictions: "You have been able to see in our communications that I am not a visionary and, in the *Social Contract*, that I have never approved of Democratic government."[26]

Yet, several months earlier, while in the midst of drafting his proposals for a new—and democratic—constitution for Corsica, Rousseau had spoken in different terms. "Never mind, without thinking of the impossibility of success, I shall occupy myself with these poor fellows, just as if my reveries could really be of some use to them. Since I am devoted to chimeras, I want to forge for myself at least agreeable ones. In musing about what men might be, I shall try to forget what they are." A similar tone appears at the close of his proposals for Poland, when he addresses his reader directly: "Although I think differently from other men, I do not flatter myself that I am more wise than they, nor that [my reader] will find anything in my reveries that can really be useful to his homeland."[27]

And so his unfinished and unpublished practical projects, like all of his previous political writing, fitfully charted the uncertain region between dream and reality, between impossible ideals and remote possibilities. It was the same terrain he had mapped out in the *Social Contract*. But the treacheries of attempting, in practice, to travel the path indicated by his thinking had virtually convinced him to abandon the attempt. The dangers of action were intolerable.

Even at the time he wrote the *Contract*, the intransigence of his desire had been bracketed with a question mark. "The Sovereign can only act when the people is assembled," he flatly declares. "The people assembled, it will be said! What a chimera!" He admits it, he agrees that to us it seems a dream, but how would it have appeared to our most illustrious ancestors? And what about our descendants, how will it appear to them? "It is a chimera today, but this was not the case two thousand years ago: Have men changed their nature?"[28]

6

The Oracle and the Revolution

H AVE MEN changed their nature? In 1789 and after, some people in France
were willing to find out.

Nature tells us that man was born for freedom, and the experience of centuries shows him a slave. His rights are written in his heart, his humiliation
in history. The human race reveres Cato, and bends beneath the yoke of
Caesar. Posterity honors the virtue of Brutus but allows it only in ancient
history. . . . But do not say, O Brutus, that virtue is a phantom! And you,
founders of the French Republic, take care not to despair of mankind, or to
doubt for one instant the success of your great enterprise! The world has
changed, it must change again. What is there in common between what is
and what was? Civilized nations have succeeded the wandering savages of
the deserts; fertile harvests have taken the place of the ancient forests that
once covered the globe. A world has appeared beyond the limits of the
world; the inhabitants of the earth have added the seas to their immense
domain. . . . Everything has changed in the physical order; everything must
change in the moral and political order. Half the revolution of the world is
already accomplished; the other half must be achieved.[1]

In these words of Robespierre, uttered in the midst of the terror, the desire for
civil freedom has become unambiguously revolutionary, a militant call to arms.

The past is a challenge for the future. Compared to the ancients with their
courage and virtue, modern man stands exposed as a creature of mean-spirited
timidity, the product of humiliation and servitude. That much Robespierre could
have read in Rousseau. But the Citizen of Geneva had never taken the next step.
Judged by his accomplishments in taming his physical environment and conquering a new world, modern man seems elevated, ennobled, a creature of bold
ventures and fresh horizons, the product of a renaissance of reason. We are thus
challenged not merely to resurrect the moral and political marvels of antiquity,
but furthermore to outdo and surpass them, spurred on by our own unprece-

dented progress in transforming "the physical order." A revolution in technology has occurred. A revolution in social relations must follow: the time has come for all men to reclaim their natural dignity. That is the unique opportunity created by the French Revolution. By restoring right and virtue through the cooperative exercise of free will, on the basis of popular sovereignty, human nature must be given the chance to show its essence anew. Only then will we be able to say honestly whether men have changed their nature or not.

Few today doubt Rousseau's impact on Robespierre. But serious doubts have been raised about his influence on the political theory and practice of the revolutionary generation as a whole. In the most recent study of the topic, it has been argued that "individual loyalty to Rousseau's memory," however widespread, by no means entailed "actual knowledge and application of Rousseau's political theory, as stated in the *Social Contract*." Properly understood, his political theory can, in any case, scarcely be called revolutionary. From this perspective, the many counterrevolutionaries who appealed to Rousseau's authority showed greater fidelity to his real ideas than their more famous radical counterparts. "The conservative exposition of Rousseau's theory was more exact and more closely related to Rousseau's texts than the interpretation of the revolutionaries."[2] Faced with such doubts, it is clear that Rousseau's relationship to the French Revolution needs to be reconsidered, particularly if we wish to claim that he was "the great democrat of the eighteenth century."

In order to complete our account, we must therefore turn our attention to the influence of Rousseau's way of thinking on the political course of the Revolution—the event in which modern concepts of democracy first gained currency. It is a compelling passage of history, complex enough to prohibit quick summary, rich enough to repay close study. Much research remains to be done, particularly in the areas that interest us. Adequately exploring the many questions about Rousseau and the Revolution would require, as a start, a detailed *histoire de livres*, tracing, so far as that is possible, the circulation of his different books and attempting to clarify their impact on different audiences. An inventory and dating of the numerous Rousseau icons of the period would be helpful; so would a fresh survey of revolutionary oratory and of instances of Rousseauist rhetoric contained therein. Such a comprehensive critical treatment, difficult in any case, cannot be attempted here.

What can be attempted is a new telling of a small and relatively minor part of a much larger story. Using the recent work of historians and our own understanding of Rousseau's thought, it should be possible to dispel many of the doubts raised by skeptics and to explore an alternative hypothesis about the nature of his political influence and the reasons for it. It is also worth describing not only the popular cult of Rousseau, but also the public debate over the meaning of modern democracy. For, as we shall see, Rousseau's dream of civic freedom did not want for converts, critics, and even the most Machiavellian of disciples.

Rousseau and the French Audience for Enlightenment

The first doubts about the influence of Rousseau on the French Revolution were raised by Daniel Mornet. In 1910, Mornet published a study of five hundred private French libraries, using auction catalogues for the years 1750–1780. In his survey, Mornet found but one copy of the *Social Contract*. By way of comparison, he uncovered forty-one copies of Voltaire's *Philosophical Letters* and no less than a hundred and eighty-five copies of Rousseau's *La Nouvelle Héloïse*.[3]

It seems certain that the *Social Contract* was the least read of Rousseau's books among the prerevolutionary generation in France. As the author had feared, his political treatise was for long overshadowed by *Emile* and his own novel. In this respect, Mornet's findings are roughly corroborated by the royalty payments Rousseau himself received. He got 7,000 livres for *Emile*, 4,860 for *La Nouvelle Héloïse*, and only 2,200 for the *Social Contract*.[4]

Yet even for the *Social Contract*, the figure, by the standards of the day, is not insubstantial—particularly since the work was barred from France and was vigorously proscribed throughout much of Europe. The figures are also slightly misleading. For one thing, they do not indicate copies of the *Social Contract* sold after Rousseau's death in the many different editions of his *Collected Works*. For another thing, they pit the *Social Contract* against two of the best-selling books of the eighteenth century: *La Nouvelle Héloïse*, for example, went through at least seventy-two editions between 1761 and 1800—a stunning total. The most recent bibliography lists twenty-six editions of *Emile* between 1762 and 1788, with seven more appearing between 1789 and 1800.[5] All of these figures fail to reflect the traffic in counterfeit and pirated editions—a major market for prohibited works in eighteenth-century France.

In 1762 alone, at least eight pirated editions of the *Social Contract* appeared, in addition to the two editions that Rousseau authorized Rey to publish in Amsterdam. After the first flurry of interest had abated, new editions, mostly unauthorized, continued to pop up: two in 1763, one in 1766, one in 1775, and a cheap pocket edition in 1782. These underground editions are hard to trace; their low quality and illegality would generally have kept them off the shelves of fine libraries like those examined by Mornet. Yet the continued publication of counterfeit editions suggests a steady, if modest, market, even for Rousseau's most abstruse tome.[6]

But who in eighteenth-century France was likely to be reading such works? How far beyond an educated and relatively affluent upper-class audience did book reading extend? What was Rousseau's probable audience, and how did he reach it?

Recent research indicates several different audiences for an author like Rousseau, reached through several different channels. In the first place, Enlightenment authors were read by the wealthy patrons of the new learning, men and women who could easily afford the price of well-made books. By the end of the eighteenth century, this fashionable upper-class audience had broadened to include provincial notables, local lawyers and doctors, some commoners in the royal bureaucracy, even a few clergymen, military officers, and members of the provincial parliaments. Such readers could certainly afford single copies of books by Rousseau and Voltaire. A few of them built libraries large enough and fine enough to auction; Mornet's survey provides a glimpse of their purchasing habits.[7]

But the French audience for Enlightenment literature was not confined to the affluent. Beyond the elite of the ancien régime, a writer like Rousseau found readers among *petites gens* like the watchmakers of Geneva. In France, skilled artisans—compositors, carpenters, jewelers, and the like—occasionally bought books, although apparently not in anything like the quantity of their Genevan counterparts. For such men of modest means, most fine books were out of reach. But this did not mean that they were without reading matter. On the one hand, they had access to paperback editions, both pirated and legitimate, scaled down in size, quality, and price. Cheap editions of proscribed works were often sold alongside pornography in handwritten secret circulars listing "livres philosophiques," a trade name for such banned titles as *Venus in the Cloister*, *The Falsity of Miracles*, and *Contract social par Jean Jacques Rousseau*, to cite a portion of one such clandestine offering. On the other hand, most *petites gens* could read such books without buying them. They had only to pay dues of one or two livres a month to join one of the *cabinets littéraires* which booksellers established at the rear of their stores. These reading clubs usually stocked the latest prohibited works, since these were constantly in demand, if only as objects of curiosity. Here again, Rousseau's books kept company not only with other Enlightenment treatises, but also with pornography and scandalous satires on the royal family.[8]

Of course, there was a still wider audience that books, whether bought or borrowed, rarely reached, at least directly: the vast audience of peasants and common laborers, many of them illiterate. There is some doubt whether news of the Enlightenment penetrated to these lower levels of French society before the Revolution. Yet there is no question that this class had its own ways of transmitting information. In the countryside and on city streets, itinerant *colporteurs* hawked paperback books out of backpacks, catering to an audience interested mainly in almanacs, prayer books, songbooks, sentimental sagas, handbooks of etiquette, and works on astrology and magic. At evening gatherings in remote villages, such tracts would sometimes be read aloud by a literate member of the community, while women sewed and men repaired tools. Topical songs were also used to convey news and gossip within this predominantly oral culture. Even here, though few of the poor could possibly have read him, Rousseau's name was probably not entirely unknown: as one popular ditty from 1754 explained, "Quite gratuitously do you cultivate the arts, O people of France/All success is denied to you/In a few words he has said so, Jean-Jacques, Jean-Jacques, Jean-Jacques."[9]

We may conclude, then, that an author like Rousseau, in one form or another, reached a reasonably broad audience—broader, certainly, than one might conclude from simply reading Mornet. As the literary historian Robert Darnton has recently documented in detail, "Voltaire and Rousseau did speak to an enormous public."[10]

In the present context, moreover, it is worth stressing that a careful reading of the *Social Contract* was by no means the only way that a person could acquire some awareness of Rousseau's political convictions. The *Discourses*, the *Letter to d'Alembert*, and especially *Emile* and *La Nouvelle Héloïse* were all exceptionally controversial and widely circulated texts, as even the skeptics are forced to concede. We have already seen how Rousseau's *image* of democracy is conveyed in these very works. In addition, anyone interested in Rousseau's political ideas could always consult the précis of the *Social Contract* in book V of *Emile*—an approach taken by the prosecutor for the Parliament of Paris in 1762. For those unwilling to tackle the big books, there were also available excerpts and collections of Rousseau's most memorable epigrams. Finally, for those who could not read at all, there were songs to sing and stories to tell, songs and stories about Rousseau the outlaw, chased across Europe, and about Rousseau the martyr, the man who suffered for trying to tell the truth.[11]

The Prerevolutionary Cult

During the decade before the Revolution, an extraordinary cult arose around Rousseau, devoted to the promulgation of his principles and the public worship of the deceased hero. The decisive turn in his reputation came with the posthumous publication of the *Confessions*. Their appearance in 1781 made Rousseau a topic of impassioned debate once more; but now the discussion was focused on the integrity of his character, the authority of his moral witness. This self-professed commoner, the proud son of a Genevan watchmaker, made such a persuasive case for his own innocence and good faith that popular opinion rallied to his side. By 1782, sympathy for Rousseau among the playgoers of Paris had become so fashionable that a revival by the Comédie-Francaise of *Les Philosophes*, a popular lampoon by Charles Palissot, had to be cut short at one point, so that rioting would not erupt over the scene showing Jean-Jacques squatting on all fours eating a lettuce.[12]

Icons and paintings depicted the magnitude of Rousseau's achievement. One engraving from 1782 shows the author arriving in the Elysian fields, where he is being greeted by the other immortals. A caption explains that "Socrates, surrounded by Plato, Montaigne, Plutarch and many other philosophers, advances to the edge of the river Lethe in order to receive J-J Rousseau. Diverse geniuses dispute the benefit of withdrawing the immortal works of this philosopher from the bark of the navigator Caron. Satisfied to have finally found the honest man for whom he has searched, Diogenes blows out his lantern. In the background can be seen Tasso and Sapho, in the middle distance Homer and the great warriors he has celebrated, while behind them Voltaire is talking with a high priest."[13]

There was an outpouring of polemics, essays, and plays, all devoted to Rousseau. While pilgrims made an earnest effort to commune with his shade, *The Ghost of J-J Rousseau*, "a comedy in two acts," regaled its audience with episodes from his afterlife. Visits to Rousseau's tomb on the Isle of Poplars at Ermenonville became so frequent that a guidebook to the place was published in 1788: "It is to you, friend of Rousseau, it is to you that I address myself; you alone are able to sense the affecting charm of such a site. In these solitary places, nothing can distract you from the object of your love; you see it; it is there, let your tears pour out; never will you have wept sweeter or more justifiable tears." Visitors spoke of séances with his soul and demonstrated their solidarity by sacrificial burnings of Diderot's complaints about Rousseau. After one such encounter, a devotee exclaimed that "it is he himself who has talked with me; . . . the divine Rousseau, a man so good, so simple, and sublime. . . ." The simplicity of the Citizen was palpable in such relics as the wooden clogs he wore. A visiting duchess spent an afternoon at Ermenonville hobbling about in them, presumably to participate, however remotely, in the plebeian lot of an artisan's son.[14]

Rousseau's confirmed readers in the period include a number of figures who would become important actors during the Revolution. Above all, of course, there was Robespierre, who in his youth was reputed to have caught a glimpse of the old man at Ermenonville. But there were also Mme de Staël and the Comte de Mirabeau, Mme Roland and Charlotte Corday; Bertrand Barère, later a member of the Committee of Public Safety; and Sylvain Maréchal, later author of the "Manifesto of the Equals." Jean Paul Marat showed familiarity with Rousseau's terminology in his book of 1774 entitled *The Chains of Slavery*, reserving the term *sovereign* for the people rather than the king; and in 1789, Gracchus Babeuf, who at the time had little firsthand knowledge of Rousseau, took careful notes on Marat's argument.[15]

Whether directly or indirectly, through reading books, seeing icons, or hearing stories, details of Rousseau's ideas, images, and life filtered down through French society. For many, the anecdotes and slogans were merely part of the cultural atmosphere and of no great consequence. But for others, they were a primary focus of interest, the object of zealous enthusiasm: more than mere readers, members of the cult fancied themselves acolytes of a new gnosis, beneficiaries of an inner revelation, the disciples of a rediscovered nature.

If details about the development and extent of this cult remain obscure, the outlines of the phenomenon are clear enough. In France in the decade before 1789, Jean-Jacques Rousseau became the object of a popular adulation that, in its breadth, intensity, and religious fervor, far outstripped anything associated with any other eighteenth-century writer. And while the feelings of these prerevolutionary followers were largely aroused by reading his novel and his autobiography, it is not as if his picture of an idyllic Switzerland and his own tortured life had nothing to do with politics.

Once the Revolution was under way, it required no great leap of imagination to hear Rousseau lauded by Saint-Just as the archetypal "revolutionary man." His biography could easily be construed as a political fable. Was not the *Confes-*

sions one man's testimony to the indignities of oppression? Was it not French society that had corrupted the good nature—and crucified the saintly character—that Rousseau claimed as his own? In the bitter words of his last work, the *Reveries of a Solitary Stroller*, "The most sociable and loving of human beings has been proscribed by unanimous consent."[16]

Even Rousseau's avowedly apolitical texts could thus be read from a double perspective, as Jean Starobinski has pointed out. "Some will see in him the prophet of a purely interior revelation, while others will hail the unbroken victim of the ancien régime, the indomitable and finally triumphant adversary of an unjust and unreasonable order."[17] The possibility of this double perspective gave to the cult of Rousseau a volatile content that the onset of the Revolution merely ignited.

The Cult Politicized

In *La Nouvelle Héloïse*, Julie writes to Saint-Preux in terms that may explain how some members of the revolutionary generation felt.

> I should think that a soul once corrupted is so forever, and no longer returns to goodness by itself; unless some sudden revolution, some abrupt change of fortune and situation, in a stroke alters its relations, and, with a violent shock, helps it to recover a good position. All its habits being broken and its passions modified in this general revolution, it sometimes recovers its primitive character and becomes like a new being recently come from nature's hands. Then the memory of its preceding baseness can serve as a shield against a relapse.

With passages like this in mind, the revolutionary generation left it to later historians to wonder whether Rousseau himself would personally have endorsed storming the Bastille. This much was obvious: a violent shock had occurred; old habits had been shattered, old relations transformed; *en masse*, the French people now found themselves in an unusual and remarkably "good position." Rousseau was their prophet. "You trust in the present order of society without thinking that this order is subject to inevitable revolutions," the tutor remarks in *Emile*. "The Great become small, the rich become poor, the monarch becomes subject; are the blows of fate so rare that you can count on being exempted from them? We are approaching the state of crisis and the century of revolutions."[18]

When the Paris Opera reopened after the fall of the Bastille, the first work it presented was Rousseau's *Le Devin du village*—to benefit the families of those patriots who had died while assaulting the fortress. The outbreak of the Revolution brought with it a redoubled number of essays and artifacts devoted to Rousseau. Effortlessly, the cult was politicized, polarized, broadened. Distressed by the unseemly crush of new converts, whom she feared would dishonor his manes, Mme de Staël dutifully trekked out to Ermenonville to inscribe on Rousseau's tomb a cautionary quotation from his work, declaring that freedom was not worth the life of an innocent man. The radical republicans who published *Révolutions de Paris* doubtless had different quotations in mind, but they, too, felt the urge to pay homage to the Citizen of Geneva; Sylvain Maréchal used the pages of the journal to drum up money for erecting a statue.[19]

Meanwhile, the orators at Versailles and the publicists in Paris turned toward the sage of Ermenonville, hoping to borrow some of his rhetorical fire. Politicians picked over the Citizen's corpus, eager for slogans, metaphors, and edifying sentiments. They had no difficulty finding them. Even in his most daunting treatises, Rousseau had written with an uncommon clarity, in prose bristling with passion and boldness. The *Social Contract* quickly became the revolutionaries' vade mecum.[20]

In many quarters, Rousseau was hailed as the father of the new French constitution. In 1790, in a speech to the National Assembly supporting the idea of raising a statue to Rousseau, it was declared that "You should see in Jean-Jacques Rousseau ... the precursor of our great Revolution; you should recall that he taught you how to form men for freedom, when you were on the eve of making the French a free people. . . . The Social Contract has been for you the charter in which you have rediscovered the right usurped from the nation, and above all the imprescriptible right of sovereignty." Other advocates, while admitting that the Revolution had not followed all of his principles, argued that Rousseau nevertheless deserved to be treated as a founder of the new French nation: "Now, gentlemen, Rousseau was the first to establish in a system the equality of rights among men and the sovereignty of the people, right beneath the eyes of despotism." A speaker in the Jacobin Club agreed, describing Rousseau as the patron of all peoples who love freedom.[21]

While the orators paid homage to Rousseau's genius and debated his paternity of the new constitution, a number of new pamphlets about him appeared, beginning in 1789. Republican writers enlisted his authority in defense of the Revolution and invoked his definition of popular sovereignty—for example, Avocat Morisse in an *Essay on the Nature and Exercise of the Authority of the People in a State.* Rousseau was also cited in criticism of the monarchy, by Jean-Baptiste Salaville in his essay *On the Organization of a Monarchical State, or Considerations on the Vices of the French Monarchy and on the Necessity of giving it a Constitution.*[22]

Conservatives, by contrast, attacked Rousseau as a dangerous radical. In *Observations on the Social Contract,* an erudite essay written in 1762 but not published until 1789, the Jesuit P. Guillaume-François Berthier harshly criticized the idea of popular sovereignty. "An essential fault throughout the *Social Contract* is to place sovereignty in the body politic, so that when the government is monarchical, the community does not stop being sovereign; the king is then, and can only be a magistrate and executor of the will of the people: this is to avow neither monarchy nor aristocracy, but simply a democracy; in this the author contradicts all the notions given us by the books of saints and works of philosophers on the power of kings in a monarchy, and on the principles of a nation in an aristocracy." To underscore his argument, Berthier points out that neither Grotius, Pufendorf, nor Locke—not even "Algernon Sidney, otherwise so favorable to democracy"—had refused to recognize the legitimate dominion of a monarch. "In a word, I think that it will be impossible to cite any publicist, before the author of the *Social Contract*, who has refused sovereignty to kings."[23]

Similar misgivings were broached in Achille Nicolas Isnard's *Observations on the Principle which has produced the Eighteenth-Century Revolutions in France, Geneva and America*. This effort to discredit Rousseau enlisted the authority of Cicero, Montesquieu, and the tradition of natural law. According to Isnard, Rousseau wished to replace the eternal laws of nature with the ephemeral laws emanating from an irrational majority of men. "The social contract," he warned, "contains the dangerous principle which has produced the revolutions in his homeland, which has torn America from England, which can tear France from the house of the Bourbon, and which perhaps, for the misfortune of Europe, will still ferment in heads agitated by a superficial acquaintance with politics. . . . This is the fatal principle which has carried away the Genevans, the Americans, and the French: the Law is the act or the expression of the general will."[24]

From Geneva to Paris

However fanciful the ascription of Rousseauist heresies to the American revolutionaries (almost all of whom were far more impressed by Montesquieu and such British republicans as Sidney), Isnard does draw attention to a real connection that should not go unnoticed.[25] By pausing to recapitulate the events linking the political ideas of Rousseau, the Genevan disorders of 1765, the Genevan revolution of 1782, and the French Revolution of 1789, we may obtain a clearer impression of why a writer like Isnard found the principles of Rousseau so deplorable.

In 1765, after Rousseau had mustered the mettle of the Genevan Citizens and Bourgeois with his *Letters Written from the Mountain*, an extended period of turbulence had followed there. In 1766, the refusal of the Citizens in the General Council to elect a single Syndic brought government to a virtual halt. Both sides refused to negotiate. The stalemate drove the Small Council to appeal to Berne, Zurich, and France for help in mediating the dispute. Despite an initial disagreement among the mediating powers, the opinion of France prevailed: the French king could not stand by idly while "the orders in the State" next door were overthrown and replaced by an "absolute Democracy." Under foreign pressure, and with the application of French economic sanctions, a semblance of orderly administration was restored.[26]

But the popular party was unbowed. In January of 1768, the General Council met three times, and three times refused to elect any Syndics. On top of these refusals came news that arsonists had torched the new civic theater that had been constructed by patricians despite popular opposition (and Rousseau's own advice). Some of the Citizens now armed themselves, while many of the circles—the political clubs defended by Rousseau in the *Letter to d'Alembert*—declared themselves "en permanence," self-proclaimed centers of popular agitation and political power. Alarmed at the prospect of civil war, moderate patricians finally prevailed upon the Small Council to make some concessions. Through a last-ditch compromise, the "Edict of 1768," the General Council was granted a slightly greater role in electing the Small Council. A complete breakdown of order was thus narrowly averted.

In the years afterward, however, tensions and unrest continued. The democratic contagion in Geneva went unchecked. Discontent spread from the Citizens to the disenfranchised Natives, a growing class of residents still denied any political rights. Meanwhile, hard times and high prices put the pinch of necessity on the unsatisfied demands for civic freedom. The popular party grew restive again. In 1781, after several years of economic distress, the leaders of the Citizens and Bourgeois decided to strike an alliance with the Natives. At a meeting of the General Council that year, the Citizens introduced and ratified a new law granting civil status and the title of Bourgeois to all Natives who had resided in the city for three generations or longer.[27]

Executing this law would have swelled the General Council overnight from twelve hundred to more than sixteen hundred members. But the magistrates were not about to stand by and watch while the scales of power were thus tipped in favor of the popular party; besides, such unilateral acts of law were unconstitutional according to the edicts and tradition accepted by the Small Council. On April 7, 1782, the First Syndic of Geneva announced that the acts of the General Council could no longer be considered binding.

The Citizens and Bourgeois of Geneva this time responded by staging an insurrection. The longstanding clandestine organization of the civic militia through the circles now paid off: with the help of the Natives, the popular party quickly commanded the streets. By April 9, they were masters of the city. Although most patricians were placed under house arrest, a few escaped to seek outside help. While the Citizens built fortifications and mobilized the population, news of the uprising spread across Europe, raising anxieties in a number of ruling councils.

An alarmed official from Berne denounced the Genevan revolutionaries as "sectaries of J. J. Rousseau and other false philosophers of the day." The French foreign minister took a similarly dim view of events; soliciting the aid of Sardinia, which had jurisdiction over the kingdom of Savoy, the French minister warned that the Genevans were drawing inspiration from Rousseau's dangerous theory that "Sovereignty lies with the people, who alone can give it or take it away." The Sardinian foreign minister, agreeing to cooperate, wrote back that "the government which we must eliminate is that of an unrestrained and tumultuous democracy."[28]

Eventually, a deal was struck between France, Sardinia, Berne, Zurich, and the patrician refugees from Geneva. After a short siege, the city surrendered to the invading armies on July 2, 1782.

Even in defeat, the revolution had repercussions far beyond the walls of Geneva. Among the leaders of the insurrection was Etienne Clavière, who became the French minister of finance in 1792. Observing events on the spot were Brissot, the future leader of the Girondins, and Mallet du Pan, who would later blame the French Revolution on Rousseau. And upon hearing of the uprising in France, Mme Roland, already an enthusiast in the Rousseau cult, exclaimed that "virtue and freedom find refuge only in the hearts of a handful of honorable men; a fig for the rest and for all the thrones in the world!"[29]

The events in Geneva thus formed a muted prelude to the explosion in France. In case anyone had forgotten the details, François d'Ivernois, the son of an old Genevan ally of Rousseau's and an activist in the recent uprisings, in 1789 published an updated edition of his *Historical and Political Description of the Last Revolutions in Geneva.* Furthermore, in a pleasing instance of what the surrealists call *hasard objectif,* the first insurgent atop the Bastille on July 14, 1789, was a man named Humbert: a journeyman watchmaker, a former resident of Geneva, and a witness to its revolution of 1782.[30]

The Revolutionary Cult

As the official French response to Genevan unrest makes plain, it was no accident that Rousseau was immediately singled out in 1789 by conservative writers anxious to attack the principles behind the French Revolution. No other eighteenth-century political theorist was so closely linked to a popular insurrection. Long before 1789, Rousseau was perceived, by both Genevans and interested foreign observers, as an untoward advocate of "absolute Democracy," a man committed to an unbridled principle of popular sovereignty. Other writers before Rousseau may have used some of the same language. But no one before him had been so obviously driven by an overriding vision of direct self-rule by an entire people. And no one before him, it seemed obvious at the time, had ever managed, if only by sheer force of their eloquence, to stir up so much trouble. This, at least, was the opinion of Achille Nicolas Isnard.[31]

As the new situation unfolded in France, events only confirmed Rousseau's centrality to the political self-consciousness of the revolutionaries. With great fanfare, a series of lectures on the *Social Contract* was announced in 1790 by Claude Fauchet, an eager visionary who foresaw a universal confederation of mankind, united through the principles revealed by the French Revolution. The inaugural lecture attracted the abbé Sieyès, Condorcet, Mme Roland, Brissot, Camille Desmoulins, and Tom Paine, an honored onlooker at such affairs despite his inability to speak French.[32]

While Fauchet projected his own enthusiasm for an ecumenical age of harmony through an amorphous and highly idiosyncratic survey of Rousseau, other activists were eager to enlist his authority for more clearly defined purposes. The editors of the journal *Révolutions de Paris,* for example, turned to Rousseau for his wisdom about the defects of representation. "Sovereignty cannot be represented, says Jean-Jacques, it consists essentially in the general will, and the general will can never be represented. . . . Every law which the people in person has not ratified is null: it is not a law." Urging vigilance lest the National Assembly become a new aristocracy, this journal's anonymous writer warned that the Commune of Paris was not yet sufficiently "democratic or popular." Direct participation in lawmaking was the best protection against any resurgence of despotism. Such participation was all the more important in France, where the people were unaccustomed to involvement in public affairs; only through lawmaking could their horizons be broadened, their capacity for virtue developed. "Without mores, each prefers himself to the fatherland, particular passions conspire against the general will, and there cannot exist a public spirit."[33]

Such ideas were readily transmitted through the avalanche of newspapers, journals, pamphlets, and books unleashed by the Revolution. Some three hundred and fifty new journals appeared in Paris during its first two years, while roughly two hundred new printing shops were opened. Some of these establishments found it profitable to cater to the unprecedented demand for the *Social Contract*. Between 1789 and 1799, at least thirty-two French editions were published. In 1792, to take a sample year, there were three authorized editions and five counterfeits; in 1794, a pocket, Bible-size edition was issued for the use of soldiers at the front.[34]

This eruption of print spilled across class lines. Journals aimed at an artisan audience, such as Marat's *L'Ami du peuple* and Hébert's *La Père Duchesne*, found popular favor and were widely discussed, if not carefully read. Alongside the booksellers to the affluent flourished the *colporteurs*, who continued to peddle cheap printed matter to the peasants and urban "sans-culottes"—those artisans and laboring poor so dubbed because they disdained the *culottes* or knee breeches worn by the wealthy.

With the old restrictions on hawking books lifted overnight, the *colporteurs* were free to respond to the growing popular interest in political topics. Modifying their inventory, they dropped many devotional titles and added political pamphlets and extracts from Enlightenment authors. (Some perennial favorites remained in vogue: *Poor Richard's Almanac* was still widely circulated, as was a popular work on the occult entitled *Explanations of Dreams*.)[35]

Familiar genres of popular literature were transformed by the Revolution. Traditional handbooks of etiquette were gradually replaced by new, revolutionary handbooks—for example, *Republican Civility, Containing Principles of Propriety Derived from Morality, and Other Useful Instructions to Youth*. Advice on rectitude betrayed a newfound emphasis: "Today, there is but one rule to follow in the commerce of life: be free, modest, steadfast and loyal with everyone." Old almanacs were also replaced by new, topical ones, including an *Almanac of the Most Beautiful Thoughts of Rousseau*. Finally, the *colporteurs* carried revolutionary songbooks, with many new hymns making explicit or implicit reference to Rousseau. One declared that "The free French cherish you / You created a *patrie* for us," while another, entitled "Hymn to Freedom and Equality," had its audience singing that "Freedom is only in the law / The law, the supreme will of all / This is my work, it is made by me / Submitting to the laws, I obey myself." Through such songs—and through evening neighborhood gatherings, where the latest speeches, newspapers, and pamphlets were read aloud—the slogans and name of Rousseau made their way into the oral culture of the lower classes.[36]

A succession of official honors and ceremonies kept Rousseau before the public eye. In 1790, a bust of the Citizen was installed in the National Assembly, and copies of the *Social Contract* and *Emile* deposited at its base. Political clubs and popular societies followed this lead, and a bust of Rousseau was also installed in the Jacobin Club.[37]

Rousseau played a prominent role in revolutionary iconography. In one early engraving, the hall of the National Assembly is shown on the horizon, set back from an embankment overlooking a choppy sea. In the foreground, next to an overturned hull, are splashing helplessly a nobleman, a magistrate, and a bishop, his miter bobbing beside him. Hovering above this scene of shipwrecked privilege, floating in a puff of cloud, is a winged cherub with a small flame flickering from the top of his head, in one hand clutching the *Social Contract*, in the other aiming a mirror reflecting the rays of the sun, which is overhead and out of view, into the cavernous hall of the National Assembly.[38]

There were also new plays about Rousseau, one celebrating his youth in Geneva, another showing his last hours at Ermenonville. Relics became cherished collectors' items, and one source tells of the pleasure Anarcharsis Cloots took in his treasure: "My fingers have touched this snuff box, my heart has quivered, and my soul has become more pure." Rousseau even appeared on a deck of patriotic playing cards, as one of the four sages chosen to replace the outlawed images of kings.[39]

The cult of Rousseau did not lose in fervor what it gained in scope. An extraordinary account published in 1791 provides a glimpse of one postrevolutionary pilgrimage to Rousseau's tomb. According to the author, a group of dedicated republican friends of the "citizen philosopher" witnessed a miracle at Ermenonville. Upon arriving, the group had first summoned "Rousseau, dear and sacred ghost." They had then formed a ring around his tomb and offered oblations to his "fiery spirit." After the ceremony, while absorbing inspiration from the spot—one of the group tried his hand at composing music in the style of the deceased, another experimented with automatic writing—the shade of Rousseau, mirabile dictu, responded in kind, offering his salutations: "Generous and sensible nation! Brave Frenchmen! Compatriot citizens! Friends!" After this rousing fraternal welcome, Rousseau thanked the congregation for their confidence, congratulated them on the new French constitution, and asked them to extend forgiveness to his enemies, as well as congratulations to various members of the National Assembly. On their return to Paris, the awestruck members of the group dutifully complied—or so we are told.[40]

Montage and Misreadings

It was no accident that Rousseau's voice could appear as if from *un autre monde.* For if the Revolution created previously unimaginable prospects, Rousseau's

imagination, once endowed with such unanticipated practical cogency, illuminated the political landscape with an uncanny light. The most unhistorical and
undialectical aspects of his thinking—particularly his emphasis on universal
principles of political right—helped make his ideas appear immediately appli-
cable. The saintliness popularly ascribed to him only made his ideas seem all the
more trustworthy: the integrity of the man bespoke the truth of his revelations.
Even Rousseau's preoccupation with antiquity acquired an incendiary aura. Juxtaposing pictures of a golden age with their own memories of oppression under
the monarchy, readers could create for themselves a powerful sense of previously
denied possibilities, possibilities made palpable once before in the glories of the
classical world—republican institutions and virtuous heroes that might flourish
in a regenerated France, too.[41]

   The urgency of this message was not confined to a small band of political
cognoscenti. With Rousseau, the idea of the true republic held out hope—for
freedom, happiness, and dignity—to all men equally. In the context of a universal upheaval, his reasoned precepts and fictional panoramas could, without difficulty, be seen to promise a kind of millenial renewal, the redemption and liberation of everyman. Locke may have more overtly condoned revolution, but it was
only Rousseau who raised the prospect of salvation: of a just social order where
citizens would become virtuous, souls would be purified, and all men would feel
free at last. Inspired by this democratic moral promise, and freshly aware of the
political principles he had bequeathed them in order, they now assumed, to realize this promise, it is no wonder that so many in the revolutionary generation
should look upon Rousseau as a founding father, a great legislator, an epony-
mous hero. The myth of Rousseau had its reasons—as did the political struggle
to claim his authority.[42]

   He thus appears as *le révolutionnaire malgré lui*. Yet if Rousseau's status as the
patron saint of the Revolution was, by 1791, reasonably secure and all but universally acknowledged, his canonization was by no means to the liking of conservatives or, for that matter, to the taste of the more cautious republicans, wary
of the implications of his subtle language, a language so like the old natural law
terminology and yet so charged with incalculable new resonances. In this respect, political writers during the Revolution rarely display a strict regard for
Rousseau's own apparent convictions. Rather, one discovers a panoply of misreadings, mapped according to divergent interests, motivated by a variety of
social situations, shaped by the onrush of unforeseen events, facilitated by the
ambiguities and tensions contained in Rousseau's own style of writing, particularly in his greatest political masterpiece, the *Social Contract*.

   The ongoing conflicts over authority in the new state prompted forced readings, as proxy power struggles were waged on the field of his texts. Rousseau's
practical maxims were pitted against his ideal principles, his ideas were held
against his images, his epigrams were torn out of context. Of course, these readings usually violated the canons of scholarly exegesis. But they were not without
their own significance, if only because they show the importance attributed to
Rousseau's new way of thinking.

At stake was the power to define the new world of politics. Rousseau had been hailed for revealing the principles of the Revolution in terms like "general will," "sovereignty," "freedom," "equality," and "democracy." While Rousseau had not invented these terms, he had made them his own. But what precisely did he mean by them? What could they mean to Frenchmen in the circumstances of the Revolution? What kinds of institutions were entailed by his principles? How could they be realized in the present situation? And who was to decide?

The struggle was thus joined. Anyone interested could read or hear about a monarchical Rousseau, a Girondist Rousseau, a Montagnard Rousseau, a sans-culottes Rousseau, even eventually a Thermidorian Rousseau.

Having failed in the attempt to persuade Frenchmen that Rousseau was a dangerous radical, an increasing number of conservative writers took the opposite tack. By 1790, they had begun to offer sober appraisals of his virtues as a prudent statesman. In a number of efforts at co-optation, the critical apparatus of traditional pedantry was enlisted to discredit the common understanding of Rousseau as a revolutionary hero. In J. J. O. Meude-Monpas's *Elegy to J.J. Rousseau*, praise is heaped on the *First Discourse*, which is appreciated as a prescient warning of the disorders entrained by universal enlightenment. "Under all its aspects, the progress of science will be the principle of insurrection and of the reversal of order. . . . For if the peasant, the artisan, persuade themselves that men are equal (which is morally and physically repugnant), they will abandon their social station. . . . Thus Rousseau had good reason to declaim against the progress of human knowledge." [43]

Charles François Lenormant's *J.-J. Rousseau, Aristocrat* advanced a more complex thesis. After arguing that the abstract ideals of the *Social Contract* were, of course, impractical, and therefore at odds with the new constitution, Lenormant proceeded to turn his own argument upside down, claiming that Rousseau's own sensible maxims for implementing his principles were equally at odds with the impractical ideals of the new constitution. Other conservative writers celebrated the wisdom of Rousseau's stoicism and pointed out his apparent preference for aristocracy in the *Social Contract*. They reminded readers that Rousseau had said not only that a true democracy had never existed, but also that such a form of government was unsuitable for men. Besides, if democracy required a small city, simplicity of mores, and a rough equality of fortunes, then any reasonable observer would admit that the French nation could not meet these conditions. The *Social Contract*, the conservatives stressed, was only a utopia, not a blueprint for action. [44]

Moderate Jacobins were no more eager to have Rousseau's name cited in support of some wild scheme for popular sovereignty. Thus Fauchet, in his lecture series on the *Social Contract*, cautioned his audience that Rousseau, despite the basic soundness of his principles, had endorsed many absurdities, doubtless because he had written in an era when darkness still shrouded the minds of men. His unfortunate circumstances also accounted for his gloom about progress, an opinion Fauchet otherwise found all but unintelligible. Nor was he impressed by the Genevan's sweeping condemnation of representation; here also, Rousseau had failed to appreciate the constructive role that wise rulers could play in fostering the progress of universal enlightenment.[45]

Brissot was equally adamant on this point. Though admiring Rousseau's outlook on many matters, the Girondist leader also criticized his extreme views on sovereignty. In 1791, he remarked that "Rousseau would not have slandered the representative system if he had been able to see, as in America, a brake on the undertakings of representatives in periodic conventions. The representative system only becomes tyrannical when this brake does not exist. But conventions were not well known at the time Rousseau wrote." However, such criticisms did not stop the Girondins from invoking Rousseau's authority whenever it seemed convenient. In a Girondist almanac, epigrams of Rousseau were even cited in *support* of representative government—and in criticism of simple democracy.[46]

Robespierre, Rousseau, and the Sans-Culottes

And so we come at last to the heart of our story, the role played by Rousseau's way of thinking in the political aspirations of Robespierre and the sans-culottes— the two parties that brought the debate over popular sovereignty to a practical climax of the greatest theoretical significance. It is through their appropriation of Rousseau's key terms that the idea of a modern democracy first crystallizes as a practical objective. To be sure, some journalists were calling for a more "democratic or popular" government as early as November, 1789. In 1791, Brissot had also advocated "a popular monarchy, tending to the popular side. Such is my democracy." (It may be recalled that Brissot himself had heard the term used favorably before—in Geneva, in 1782.) But similarly honorific uses of democracy seem to have been infrequent before May 31, 1793, the date when an armed insurrection of the Parisian sans-culottes helped bring Robespierre and his colleagues to power.[47]

Before describing their stormy struggle over the meaning of modern democracy, however, it will prove helpful to consider more closely the cast of actors. To make plain how their political differences acquired importance, we must also paint, if only in the broadest strokes, a bit of a very complicated panorama, for the surrounding events often gave meaning to their words and cause for their deeds.

On the one side stands Maximilien Robespierre, the chief theoretician and most eloquent orator of the Montagnard faction of the Jacobin party. On the other side stand the plebeian sans-culottes, the common people of Paris, many of them, by 1792, armed members of the Parisian National Guard: the men and women who had stormed the Bastille on July 14, 1789, who had invaded the Tuileries on August 10, 1792, who had raped and pillaged in the September Massacres of that year, who accounted the history of their political freedom as a succession of similar *journées*—moments of violent upheaval when the people rose in a mass, sometimes for loot, more often for bread, but also on principle, as if to avenge in a day the wrongdoing of years.[48]

By the spring of 1793, the king was dead, the country at war, the government beset by treachery on the front and economic chaos at home. The constitution enacted in 1791 was in abeyance, rendered obsolete by its allowance for the veto of a monarch and its provisions assuring the legislative power of propertied representatives, elected indirectly, through less than universal suffrage. The king had been dethroned by the insurrection of August 10, 1792. The next day, the unicameral National Legislative Assembly, meeting under the old constitution, had dissolved itself and called for elections—for the first time, by direct universal manhood suffrage—of representatives to a National Convention. An interim body outside the old laws, authorized by the people to create an entirely new instrument of sovereignty, the Convention was also to become, in an atmosphere of perpetual crisis, a body effectively vested with unlimited power.[49]

The Convention had met for the first time on September 20, 1792. There could be no turning back: a restored Bourbon monarchy posed an unconscionable threat to the Revolution and its leaders. Two days later, the first French Republic was declared. Uppermost in the delegates' minds was national defense, the prosecution of a war that was not going well for the French. In addition, the fate of the king had to be decided. Under pressure from the people of Paris, the Convention that winter tried the king for treason, found him guilty, and recommended the death penalty. On January 21, 1793, Louis Capet, once known as King Louis XVI, was beheaded on the guillotine.

As the French armies meanwhile recorded some victories abroad, sporadic debate continued at home over what shape the new state should take. On October 11, 1792, a committee led by Condorcet was authorized to draft a new constitution appropriate to the postfeudal epoch of freedom. Once the king had been executed, only the people, in principle, remained—the people and their elected agents in the Convention. But how directly should the sovereignty of the people be expressed? How popular should the new republic be? What was to be done about the persistent threat of counterrevolution? And what was to be done about those reluctant to build a new society, the many tradition-bound peasants and pious Catholics who probably constituted an inchoate and cowed majority in the country at large? Though the Republic was, by declaration, a troubled reality, its destiny and final design remained unclear.

From the outset, the Convention was riven by factional intrigue. Two ill-defined groups within the ruling Jacobin party, the "Girondins" and "Montagnards," vied to dominate events. Many of the Girondins had counseled leniency for the king and expansion of the war abroad; many of the Montagnards had urged the execution of the king and rejection of any scheme for an international revolutionary struggle. The Girondins, led by Brissot, looked to support from the provinces and success on the front. The Montagnards, led by Robespierre, looked to support from the people of Paris and victory at home—over the Girondins.[50]

This, in rough outline, was the political climate in which Maximilien Robespierre articulated his political principles. His thinking grew from a sturdy confidence to his own virtue, a belief some thought ostentatious moralism but a posture credible enough to earn him popular esteem as "the Incorruptible." His sentiments were shaped by compassion for the poor, a feeling first aroused during the prerevolutionary days when he was a struggling lawyer and a "poor man's advocate" from the provincial capital city of Arras. His basic ideas, by contrast, were secondhand, if deeply felt, most of them, if the internal evidence of his rhetoric can be trusted, borrowed from the book he is reported to have kept at his bedside: the *Social Contract* of Jean-Jacques Rousseau.[51]

A man of rural accent and humble demeanor, Robespierre was driven, as one biographer has put it, "not by cruel ambition but by common hopes and fears." Unlike many politicians, he tried to live by a thoughtful personal creed, a few simple principles animated by a palpable passion for justice. Periodically throughout the Revolution, he communicated these ideas in speeches that combined the moral witness of a sermon, the conceptual precision of a lecture, and the measured cadences of classical oratory. His persuasiveness earned him authority, his evident sincerity won him respect. As Mirabeau sized him up in his earlier years, "That man will go far; he believes all he says."[52]

Robespierre held that an eternal natural law, inscribed in the hearts of all men, provided the basis for sound legislation, and led all men naturally to desire the good. The problem was that this natural goodness had been compromised by oppression: "We are raising the temple of freedom with hands still shackled by the chains of servitude."[53] If the aim of legislation was to reconcile public and private interests, it could only accomplish this task by building virtue upon a renewed popular awareness of natural law. This was the true basis of republicanism.

Virtue could be maintained in a state where "all the low and cruel passions will be curbed, all the beneficent and generous passions awakened by the laws, where ambition will be a desire to deserve glory and serve the fatherland.... And what is the *patrie* if not the country where one is a citizen and a member of the sovereign?" Robespierre trusted that the natural tendency of men to desire the good would become manifest in the aggregate, when a people acted in concert as a sovereign body: "Morality, which has disappeared in the majority of individuals, only rediscovers itself in the mass of people and in the general interest." The goodness of the poor was especially to be trusted, since the simplicity imposed on their existence kept them from luxury and the prejudices that typically accompanied it. "The people, that large, industrious class . . . is untouched by the causes of depravity. . . . It is closer to nature." When a mass of essentially decent people was left free to pursue its natural inclinations and was not led astray by false leaders still attached to the prejudices of the old order, "the general will governs society as the particular will governs each isolated individual."[54]

Given this set of principles, it is scarcely surprising that Robespierre drafted a dedication to Rousseau, discovered after his death among his papers: "It is to you that I dedicate this work, manes of the Citizen of Geneva! . . . Divine man, you have taught me to know myself, . . . you made me appreciate the dignity of my nature and reflect on the great principles of the social order. . . . Called to play a role in the midst of the greatest events which have ever shaken the world; assisting in the agony of despotism and the revival of true sovereignty; . . . I want to follow your venerated path . . . happy if . . . I remain constantly faithful to the inspiration which I have drawn from your writings."[55]

In the present context, the details of Robespierre's political program are less important than the principles he invoked to justify it. As the most effective spokesman for the Jacobin party, he was instrumental in setting the terms of political debate at the height of the Revolution. Moreover, by the force of his imagery and integrity of his sentiments, Robespierre exhibited the eloquence to make these terms matter—a virtue Rousseau himself had admired in the figure of the ancient orators.[56]

Robespierre's eloquence was not lost on the Parisian sans-culottes.[57] During the course of the Revolution and under the influence of its leaders, the city's poor—independent craftsmen, apprentices, shopkeepers, some salaried laborers—evolved an ad hoc but sophisticated system of political institutions, comprising a crisscrossed network of legally sanctioned sectional assemblies, which they came to dominate, and voluntary popular societies, which became extralegal centers of political power. Formerly cut off from public affairs, these artisans, at least the most militant among them, now enjoyed the pleasures of debate, agitation, and direct action; they felt, in many cases doubtless for the first time, that their fate was really in their own hands.

They were rude and bullying. They could be intolerant of differences that threatened the sacred unity of the reborn nation. They tended to treat with suspicion any divergence of opinion, particularly when it was pressed by men of the upper orders. They distrusted the dandy down the block, who had once intimidated them all. Many of them were fiercely chauvinistic. Patriotism meant, if necessary, coerced participation, an allegiance under duress. Enthralled by violence, some of them behaved as viciously as the old oppressors they were so intent on sweeping aside. They were not scholars. At best, they were autodidacts.[58] At worst, they were superstitious and gullible, easily manipulated by rumors of treason. Inflamed by an unfamiliar sense of dignity, they found little cause to ponder the meaning of their newfound slogans. Because they needed to, they worried more about the supply of bread than the limits to freedom. Many of them could barely sign their own name. And yet they helped bring the principles of the Revolution to life.

By the summer of 1793, the sans-culottes of Paris had developed a distinct political perspective. At the base of their demands was the ideal of popular sovereignty. Like Rousseau, they meant it literally. When a people met face-to-face in their neighborhood assemblies to discuss politics and to ratify laws, that was when a people was sovereign. The agents they elected to administer the laws ought never to be left unattended; their behavior needed to be scrutinized constantly. It was every patriot's duty to instruct as well as to censure these officials, whenever necessary. To insure that the will of the people prevailed, the sans-culottes demanded the right to recall unsatisfactory agents (they refused to call them "representatives"). They also felt that all legislation, before becoming law, ought to be ratified by the people at their own local assemblies. Militants finally argued that these sectional assemblies ought to meet "en permanence," as legal centers of everyday popular power and civic education, as well as extraordinary tribunals protecting the virtue of the people against the corruptions of government.

When they did not get results, many sans-culottes felt that even more direct action was justified. As one neighborhood activist, Guiraut, impatiently explained to the revolutionary tribunal of the *Contrat Social* section in Paris, "The time has come when the sections must rise and present themselves *en masse* before the Convention, telling it to make laws for the people, and above all laws which suit them; they should give it three months, and warn it that if by the end of this time, laws have not been passed, we will force them through at the point of a sword." The ultimate resort of the people—and the ultimate foundation of sovereignty—was, according to the sans-culottes, insurrection: the armed uprising of the citizenry.[59]

To articulate their objectives, the sans-culottes, like Robespierre, had at hand a readymade vocabulary, even if not in the form of bedtime readings from the *Social Contract*. Instead, they absorbed Rousseauist ideas more obliquely, through the speeches of Robespierre himself and through the papers and pamphlets read aloud at sectional assemblies and societies. When Leclerc, writing in the journal *L'Ami du peuple*, advised the sans-culottes to remain vigilant, he naturally resorted to the idiom of Rousseau: "Above all, remember that when people are 'represented,' they are not free, so do not use this term loosely. . . . There is no way of 'representing' the General Will. . . . Your magistrates, whatever their function, are only your agents (*mandataires*)."[60]

Other aspects of the sans-culottes ideal also have a familiar ring. The sans-culottes extolled the discipline of labor and denounced the corruptions of luxury. While wishing to protect the small property owner, they urged an equalization of fortunes and some restriction on the amount of property that could legally be possessed. A life of honorable mediocrity would protect man's natural goodness from the vices of privilege. In a pamphlet entitled *Conversations between a Citizen of Philadelphia and a French Republican*, happiness is ascribed to the upright manners of the healthy artisan: "Let us enter the dwelling of a patriot. There we will find simple mores, a frugal table, a mother who suckles her son." On June 5, 1793, in an address to the Convention, an anonymous member of a Parisian section promised that "in place of this fatal splendor that puts equality to flight, of this thirst for gold and wealth that corrupts and debases a part of the Republic, we will substitute simplicity, honorable austerity, rustic hearths where temperance, moderation, and virtue dwell." Rousseau's Fabricius would have been right at home.[61]

Robespierre's Plans for Popular Sovereignty

Robespierre also found such rhetoric congenial. With his own severe temperament and beliefs, he was a political figure well suited to forge an alliance between the more militant gentlemen and professionals who frequented the roughly
six thousand Jacobin clubs throughout France and the craftsmen and laborers
who crowded the assemblies and societies of its capital city. Indeed, his personal
convictions already formed a bridge.[62]

On May 10, 1793, in one of his most important speeches to the Convention,
Robespierre himself reinforced this bridge by giving the political aspirations of
the sans-culottes his carefully qualified stamp of approval. A contribution to the
ongoing debate over a new constitution, his speech took as its topic representative government. In it, in language very close to Rousseau's own, we can see one
practical attempt to think through the implications of popular sovereignty.

The problem to be faced by every great legislator, Robespierre declared, is "to
give to government the force necessary to have citizens always respect the rights
of citizens and to do it in such a manner that the government is never able to
violate these rights itself." History shows that this problem has rarely been solved.
A saga of domination, it tells of rulers oppressing subjects, of "government
devouring sovereignty," of the rich debasing those whom they have helped render poor. Yet, however impoverished the majority of the people may be, "the
interest of the people is the public good." By contrast, "the interest of the office-
holder" is always a "private interest." Fortunately, the very modesty of circumstances forced on the people protects them against corruption: "It is labor, austerity, and poverty that are the guardians of virtue." Guiding the great legislator's
work therefore ought to be this "incontestable maxim: *that the people is good and
that its delegates are corruptible; that it is necessary to seek protection against the vices of
despotism of government in the virtue and sovereignty of the people.*"[63]

Robespierre proceeds to detail some ways to protect this popular sovereignty
and bring its virtue to bear on government. In the first place, he commends a
number of legal restraints on magistrates, including short terms in office, a prohibition on holding more than one office at a time, the careful separation of
legislative and executive officeholders, and, finally, the strict accountability of all
elected officials, an accountability guaranteed by the right of recall, by periodic
investigation of official behavior, and by the strict punishment of any corruption.
The correlative of such safeguards against government tyranny is the continued
vitality of local assemblies: "Leave to communes the power to regulate their own
affairs themselves in all that does not essentially affect the general administration
of the Republic. In a word, render to individual freedom all that does not belong
naturally to public authority, and you will have left that much less of a prize for
ambition and imperiousness. Above all, respect the freedom of the sovereign in
primary assemblies."[64]

But such elaborate safeguards still do not strike Robespierre as sufficient.
Elected officials must be made constantly aware of their moral responsibilities.

For this purpose, France needs some form of permanent "publicity"—some way of facilitating the direct scrutiny of the people over their government. "The entire nation has the right to know the conduct of its agents." And while it would obviously be impossible to have the whole nation watch while the National Assembly meets, Robespierre proposes, as a practical compromise, building "a vast and majestic edifice, open to 12,000 spectators.... Under the eyes of so great a number of witnesses, neither corruption, intrigue nor perfidy dare show itself; the general will alone shall be consulted, the voice of reason and the public interest alone shall be heard."[65]

Without a number of such devices to protect their sovereignty, there is no way to preserve a free people from the ambition of bad governors. "A people whose agents are only accountable to other agents do not have a Constitution, since it remains possible for the latter to betray the Constitution with impunity, and to let others betray it. If this is the sense attributed to representative government, then I admit that I approve of all the imprecations pronounced against it by Jean-Jacques Rousseau." On the other hand, with such devices empowering the people themselves as a tribune, Robespierre avows that it is possible to organize a state "equally far removed from the tempests of absolute democracy and the perfidious tranquility of representative despotism."[66]

The Constitution of 1793

On May 31, 1793, the sans-culottes, acting in their capacity as armed members of the Parisian National Guard, seized control of the city in a bloodless uprising. In the days that followed, they demanded the arrest of the Girondist leaders, whom they accused of counterrevolutionary plotting. Recent evidence of Girondist ill will included an unsuccessful attempt to jail Jean Paul Marat and the simultaneous incarceration of Hébert, a partisan of Marat and the publisher of *Père Duchesne*, by then perhaps the journal most popular with the sans-culottes. On June 3, the Convention, besieged by armed militants, capitulated, authorizing the arrest of twenty-nine delegates, and thus handing undisputed supremacy in the assembly to the Montagnards.[67]

Once in power, the victorious faction hurried to reward its supporters and reassure the rest of the country with a new constitution. After months of protracted debate and accusations directed by the Montagnards against the Girondins, a new design of government was rushed out of a new committee in a week, rammed through the Convention over token opposition, and sent on to the primary assemblies of the French people for their approbation. The hurried byproduct of a tumultuous ten days of insurrection and intrigue, the Constitution of 1793 was a patchwork of federalist provisions drafted by Condorcet, amendments offered by Robespierre, and the demands for direct democracy pressed by the sans-culottes.

Hérault-Séchelles, who supervised the final draft, explained to the Convention that the new design was "no less *democratic* than representative," providing ample opportunity for the voice of the people to be heard. The Committee would be "happy," he reported, if its labors had managed to "resolve the problem of J.-J. Rousseau in the *Social Contract*"—the problem of how a legitimate sovereign could survive in a large state. "We each had the same desire, that of attaining the most democratic result. The sovereignty of the people and the dignity of man were constantly before our eyes. A secret sentiment tells us that our work is perhaps the most popular that has ever existed."[68]

The circumstances surrounding the composition and fate of this document suggest that it was, at least in part, a piece of cynical propaganda, intended as mere window-dressing. It nevertheless warrants our attention, if only because it represents an authorized monument to the high tide of democratic hopes.

Like its predecessor, the Constitution of 1793 opens with a "Declaration of the Rights of Man and Citizen," modeled on the original Declaration approved in August of 1789:

1. The end of society is the common happiness. Government is instituted in order to guarantee man the enjoyment of his natural and imprescriptible rights.

2. These rights are: equality, freedom, safety, property.

3. All men are equal by nature and in the eye of the law.

4. The law is the free and solemn expression of the general will.

The emphasis here has only been shifted on a few small points: for example, equality not only joins the list of rights but comes before freedom.

Far more unusual are the articles which conclude the new Declaration of Rights:

25. Sovereignty resides in the people. It is one and indivisible, imprescriptible, and inalienable.

26. No portion of the people can exercise the power of the entire people; but every section of the sovereign assembled ought to enjoy, with an entire freedom, the right of expressing its will.

27. All individuals usurping the sovereign should be immediately put to death by free men.

28. A people always has the right of revising, of reforming, and of changing its constitution. One generation cannot subject future generations to its laws.

29. Every citizen has an equal right to consent to the formation of the law, and to the nomination of his agents, or of his delegates (*ses mandataires ou de ses agents*).

30. The public functions are essentially temporary: they cannot be considered either distinctions or rewards but only duties. . . .

35. When government violates the rights of the people, insurrection is for the people, and for each portion of the people, the most sacred of rights, and the most indispensable of duties.

The body of the document, while more sober in tone, was no less sweeping in its implications. Casting aside previous restrictions, the constitution stipulated universal manhood suffrage (a feature of Condorcet's original draft as well). At the foundation of the new republic were to be Primary Assemblies, composed of no less than two hundred and no more than six hundred citizens; in theory, popular sovereignty was thus embodied in local councils where face-to-face interactions would still be feasible. Effective public power was assigned to a National Assembly charged with legislation. Each delegate to this Assembly was to be chosen annually on May 1 by an electorate of forty thousand citizens, created by uniting a number of Primary Assemblies into a regional Department; election would be by a majority of individual votes cast within the Department.

In principle, the people in their Primary Assemblies were assigned the power to accept or reject laws made by their agents. Recommendations of the National Assembly could not become law until they had been published and made available for public scrutiny and debate over a period of forty days. In practice, however, rejecting any given legislative act would have involved a monumental effort: it required a negative vote from nine-tenths of the Primary Assemblies in over one-half of the Departments to put the matter directly in the hands of the sovereign.

The administration of the laws was assigned to an Executive Council. The members of this body were selected through a complex procedure initiated in the Primary Assemblies. Each Primary Assembly elected one delegate to a Departmental Electoral Assembly; this body in turn nominated one person to serve as a candidate for the Executive Council; the members of the National Assembly then selected from the list of candidates provided by the Departments the twenty-four members of the Executive Council. In addition to all this, there was a provision enabling a sufficient number of Primary Assemblies in a sufficient number of Departments to convoke a new National Convention, to draft new laws that another generation of the sovereign might feel appropriate.[69]

In July, this new constitution was submitted to the citizens of France. Although it took till January of the following year for official results of the plebiscite to be tabulated and announced (out of some seven million eligible voters, 1,801,918 had voted for, 11,610 against), a favorable outcome was assumed. The new constitution was thus symbolically baptized on August 10, 1793, in an elaborate *Festival of Nature* decorated, costumed, and choreographed by the artist Jacques Louis David. Perhaps the government hoped that celebrating these new institutions, however prematurely, would fend off fears in the provinces about a sans-culottes tyranny, while placating the sans-culottes themselves by the appearance of a civic freedom that had already been accomplished.

For their part, the militant artisans of Paris showed every intention of taking the new constitution seriously. On July 14, patriots from a number of the sections swarmed into a meeting of the Convention, voicing their acclaim for the document. The startled delegates approved a motion welcoming the visitors, "because they do not appear before us as petitioners, but as members of the sovereign." Throughout Paris, the Constitution of 1793 was communicated through solemn readings at sectional assemblies. Children were encouraged to recite the new Declaration of Rights at neighborhood patriotic societies.[70]

For the radical democrats, however, it was purely a paper victory. By the autumn of 1793, the sans-culottes, increasingly undamped in their assertions of sovereignty, posed a direct and mounting threat to the authority of the government. Still at war abroad and facing economic chaos as well as rebellion at home, the Montagnards found no reason to rush implementation of the new constitution. On the contrary, the continuing agitation in the capital inhibited the consolidation of order.

Matters came to a head on September 5, 1793, when demonstrators surrounded the Convention. A delegation of sans-culottes demanded of the assembly that the remaining enemies of the revolution be promptly purged and punished, that repression and terror become the order of the day, that price controls be imposed on all basic foodstuffs, and that a trustworthy and truly popular army be raised through conscription. The Convention agreed in principle to meet these demands.

But in the following weeks, the government capitalized on the enthusiasm for terror to institute new organs for controlling the popular movement. On September 9, the Convention passed a law prohibiting the de facto permanence of many Parisian sectional assemblies and limiting their meetings to no more than two a week. Though the focus of neighborhood politics in Paris at first merely shifted to the unofficial sectional societies, the sans-culottes found their demands for a legal permanence of the primary assemblies ignored. Instead, on October 10, a centralized revolutionary government was officially declared and granted extraordinary powers. Implementation of the Constitution of 1793 was thus postponed indefinitely; the aims of the new dictatorship were set on a collision course with the political aspirations of the sans-culottes. Though the Convention meanwhile voted to give the nation a new republican calendar, symbolic of the new age dawning, the time of domination was still unbroken.[71]

Virtue and Terror: Robespierre Redefines Democracy

It fell to Robespierre to justify the new policy. In a major address "on the Principles of Revolutionary Government," delivered on 5 nivôse, year II, the Incorruptible announced that the theory behind the present regime was unprecedented. To understand it, the work of previous political philosophers was irrelevant.

"The end of constitutional government is to conserve the Republic; that of revolutionary government is to found it. . . . Under the constitutional regime, it suffices to protect individuals against the abuse of public power; under the revolutionary regime, the public power itself is obliged to defend itself against all the factions that attack it." Such factions were symptomatic of a deeper problem: a diseased and disunited body politic. The virtue of the people was in peril, the citizenry itself torn asunder. Many revolutionaries who used Rousseau's formulas confused the general will with the will of all. But not Robespierre. For him, legitimate public power only belonged to a true sovereign: to the general will of those with virtue. Unfortunately, "there are two peoples in France," he reported several months later. "One is the mass of citizens, pure, simple, thirsty for justice and friendly to freedom. . . . The other is a pack of malcontents and schemers."[72]

When corruption thus threatened to set a people against itself, the preservation of true sovereignty and the preparation of the people for their final freedom required decisive corrective measures. For such purposes, the government needed to undertake something more than a defensive stewardship—something more like a cultural revolution. It needed to reform men to fit the new institutions. The awe inspired by republican rituals, the shared joy of civic festivals, censorship of the press, a civil religion to instill patriotic sentiments—these were all devices that Robespierre turned to in the spring of 1794, apparently in hopes that such indirect efforts at public education might restore the body politic to the soundness of its natural instincts, while innoculating it against any recrudescence of "aristocratic prejudices." But these devices were not enough by themselves, particularly in view of the continuing crisis; more drastic purgatives were needed as well. "If the driving force of popular government in peacetime is virtue, that of popular government during a revolution is both *virtue and terror*: virtue, without which terror is destructive; terror, without which virtue is impotent."[73]

As he delivered this speech on 18 pluviôse, year II, Robespierre and his colleagues were preparing to move against the recalcitrant leaders of the sansculottes. Yet on the eve of this move, Robespierre was careful to justify the government's position in terms his audience might appreciate. He implies that some of the people have fallen prey to "the tempests of absolute democracy." They have staked a premature claim to popular sovereignty. But such rights cannot be exercised until peace has been restored, the constitution firmly established, the mores of the people rid of any lingering "egotism." And even then, Robespierre asserts, direct democracy—apparently, even a democracy so direct as the one he himself had defended less than a year ago—is unthinkable, a self-defeating delusion. Such an untrammeled sovereignty of the people would only succeed in undermining all stability. It would bring disorder and despotism, the ruin of the Republic.

But Robespierre has not altogether given up the goal of a democratic republic. "We wish . . . to fulfill the vows of nature, to achieve the destiny of humanity, to keep the promises of philosophy, to absolve providence of the long reign of crime and tyranny." And what form of government might thus redeem the suffering of the past? Only "a democratic or republican government."

Challenging the distinction between the two, Robespierre avows that they are in fact synonymous. On the one hand, an aristocracy is no more imaginable in a modern republic than a monarchy; on the other hand, a simple democracy such as the ancients practiced is quite unworkable today. "A democracy is not a state where the people, continually assembled, regulate by themselves all public affairs, and still less one where one hundred thousand portions of the people, by measures that are isolated, hasty and contradictory, would decide the fate of the whole society: such a government has never existed and could only exist in order to reduce the people to despotism."

In contrast to such an ill-advised "absolute democracy," a modern republic should have governors able to point out the path of virtue to the people. Properly understood, "a democracy is a state where the sovereign people, guided by laws that are their work, do by themselves everything that they can do well, and by means of delegates everything that they cannot do themselves." Representatives will always have a valuable role to play. "Democracy perishes from two kinds of excesses, the aristocracy of those who govern, or contempt on the part of the people for the authorities that they themselves have established." These authorities ought to teach people how to achieve the good they naturally desire. While the people may sometimes be tossed between the "shoals" of anarchy and tyranny, "the representatives of the people can avoid them both, for the government is always the master of being just and wise, and when it has these characteristics, it is certain of the confidence of the people."

The aim of the revolution thus remains democracy. But to reach this goal, the leaders of the revolution have been forced to take extraordinary steps, they must ruthlessly wage a "war of freedom against tyranny." Only with victory in this struggle can virtue stand unaided by terror. Only then can an orderly "democratic or republican government" finally become feasible. And even then, the new republic must be *representative*.[74]

With this speech, Robespierre joined battle over the meaning of modern democracy—and did so in terms that amounted to a declaration of war, not just on tyranny but also on the form of democracy practiced by the sans-culottes. The indigenous sovereignty of the people was to be replaced, first by a transitional dictatorship ostensibly exercised in order to establish a democratic republic, and then by a representative democracy in which the people, through elections, would hand over power to a government of the "just and wise." Yet, once Robespierre and his colleagues had succeeded in taming the tempests of "absolute democracy," they would also find the popular will broken. When Robespierre was arrested on 9 thermidor, year II, the tocsin was sounded, but few sans-culottes rallied to his side. By alienating the lower classes of Paris, he had destroyed the basis of his own power.[75]

Rousseau and the Rise of Modern Democracy

It is time to step back and take stock of the events we have been trying to survey. In the last half of the eighteenth century, the world of politics underwent a series of revolutions. In the course of these revolutions, democracy was transformed, fitfully at first, from a term of opprobrium into a word of praise, a designation for the most desirable form of government. For this transformation to occur, it was as necessary for someone to transvalue the idea of democracy as it was for this transvaluation to be appreciated in practice. If Rousseau accomplished the one, the men of the French Revolution accomplished the other.[76]

To be sure, the notion of a modern democracy was not unheralded. In America after 1776, it was sometimes said that "representation from the people" made the governments of the new American states "purely democratical." But it was no accident that the word *democrat* did not enter the English language until 1790, under the influence of events in France: even within the theoretical framework of the most radical English-speaking republicans, it simply did not make much sense to talk of a personal or party allegiance to a democracy.[77]

The American debate over sovereignty was also inconclusive. According to the Whig theory that the Americans had inherited from the British, actual sovereignty resided in Parliament; the power of the people was merely virtual, and any attempt by them to claim it more directly could be rebuffed by citing the legitimate authority of the legislature. As Benjamin Rush reminded his readers in 1787, "it is often said that 'the sovereign and all other power is seated *in* the people.' This idea is unhappily expressed. It should be—'all power is derived *from* the people.' They possess it only on the days of their elections. After this, it is the property of their rulers."[78]

Here was a universe of discourse where representative government was essentially a foregone conclusion, even if the nature of the representative relationship remained uncertain. Here also was a universe where the notion of "democratic despotism" made immediate sense, and where the very phrase "popular sovereignty" could be turned against the advocates of popular power. The resulting semantic fog has crippled American political thought to this day.[79]

Thanks to the confusion, the American Federalists could simultaneously hold that the new constitution established "a government wholly popular," since "the people" were represented in all branches; and that this popular representation permitted "the total exclusion of the people in their collective capacity" from the government. As Hamilton put it, "The whole power of the proposed government is to be in the hands of the representatives of the people." To insure the stable dominion of this regime over the people, "divide et impera" was not an inappropriate maxim: by becoming the sole neutral arbiter in the disputes between different factions of the people, the American government assumed a sovereign role that proved, Madison thought, a decisive advance over the unrealistic devices of "simple Democracy."[80]

How different it was in France. The "strange and awkward" arguments of the American Whigs[81] here gave way to the relentless logic of Robespierre and his rivals. The question of popular sovereignty was at last posed in blunt terms, while being a "democrat" became a position that could at least be cogently articulated, if not always made compelling. And I suspect that the roots of this difference may be traced not only to the divergent circumstances of the two revolutions, but also to the divergent vocabularies they assumed: for on the crucial question of sovereignty, Rousseau's thinking marked a striking departure from the kind of republican theory within which the Whigs remained locked.

For any state to be fully legitimate, the sovereignty of the people had to be direct and active. Through this doctrine, Rousseau opened the way for a new discourse about politics—a discourse the French revolutionaries carried on in practice as well as in theory.

Moreover, if Rousseau thus carefully defined a new vision of politics, he also galvanized that vision with an unusual millennial attraction. In this respect, too, his way of thinking was uniquely fitted to dignify and define the events in France: for the French Revolution, in another departure from the American experience, was not simply about the rectification of injustice, it was also about the redemption of nature. As Alexis de Tocqueville remarked, "It was because the Revolution always harked back to universal, not particular, values and to what was the most 'natural' form of government and the most 'natural' social system that it had so wide an appeal and could be imitated in so many places simultaneously. No previous political upheaval, however violent, had aroused such passionate enthusiasm, for the ideal the French Revolution set before it was not merely a change in the French social system, but nothing short of a regeneration of the whole human race."[82]

By juxtaposing the inequities he denounced in society with the virtue he foresaw in both his images of Alpine harmony and his ideas about popular sovereignty, Rousseau himself preserved the desire for a renewed form of life. By extending the boundaries of imaginable perfection and by treating perfect justice as a secular and social (rather than religious and supernatural) phenomenon, the thinking of Rousseau offered popular sentiment a novel sense not only of what seemed possible, but also of what, in auspicious circumstances, might seem worth taking extraordinary risks to obtain: a regenerated society of freedom among equals, a worldly city of peace and happiness. One name for this city was democracy.

That Rousseau fired the enthusiasm and "captured the imagination of the revolutionary generation," even the most skeptical historians do not doubt. But so it was, we may conjecture, that the revolutionary cult of Rousseau helped dissolve traditional beliefs inhibiting the expression of moral outrage, in part by challenging popular convictions about the inevitability of injustice, in part by encouraging the indignant with hopes for a democratic alternative—the prospect encoded in his own principles of political right.[83]

This hypothesis about Rousseau's role in the rise of modern democracy should not be taken, however, as a vindication of the old and justifiably discredited thesis claiming Rousseau as one cause of the French Revolution. As we have seen, his work, though well known before the event, only became the object of widespread adulation after 1789; and this is particularly true of his political work. More important, that event, by transforming the context in which his message was communicated, transformed the ways in which it was received: it was through the Revolution itself that a stimulus for personal insight also became a source of political wisdom.

As unsettled impulse, the desire aroused by an imagined object such as Rousseau's world of civic freedom merely brings into being a sense of emptiness, an awareness that something wanted is lacking. If fulfillment seems impossible, the emptiness may simply be endured as an inevitable frustration. The feeling of a lack may be forgotten or played out in private fantasies of satisfaction. In different circumstances, however, if actually fulfilling the desire seems feasible, it may be self-consciously taken up as a project, an indication of what ought to be done and what aspects of a situation promise gratification. Then the lack becomes a motive for action, and, if cooperation is required, the imaginary object assumes a shared significance. For most Frenchmen involved in the prerevolutionary cult of Rousseau, the desires he aroused, whatever their political aura, remained perforce at the level of daydream and personal longing. For the vast majority, what created an objective space where their desires could become communicable in explicitly political terms was not a book, a myth, or even a revolutionary cult, but rather a tax revolt, a bread riot, a social revolution.[84]

On the other hand, these pressing events were endowed with significance by men who identified themselves through their hopes as well as their fears, through their dreams as well as their hunger. If taxes and food and prices and war mattered to them, so did their common sense of dignity and what seemed right. Once the Revolution was under way, the *Social Contract* played a privileged role in defining such moral terms. Treated as a kind of civic scripture, it was the one text generally held to display the principles of right avowed by all of republican France. Without determining the event, the thinking of Rousseau thus became available for orienting those swept up in it.

In this situation, slogans borrowed from Rousseau became clichés, a pervasive part of the climate in which all of the revolutionaries acted. It is not as if Frenchmen flocked *en masse* to read the *Social Contract*—although after 1789, an abnormally large number did just that. Rather, the images and epigrams Rousseau had used to convey his ideas were vivid enough and memorable enough to enter the oral culture of the lower classes as well as the oratorical repertoire of their leaders. To borrow a metaphor, Rousseau's way of thinking "was taken up like a popular song, whose tune one heard repeated everywhere, even if the words were often got wrong."[85] One discovers, then, not clean lines of influence, but instead, as we have seen, a contradictory jumble of misreadings, a perplexing network of affinities, many of them tacit and therefore difficult to document, all of them consequently open to a variety of interpretations.

Yet the importance of Rousseau for the revolutionary conceptions of self-rule seems no more disputable for all that. The case of Robespierre is reasonably clear: even without being invoked by name, the spirit of Rousseau haunts the central arguments in some of his most important speeches.

Consider also the sans-culottes. Most of the militants were usually preoccupied with such issues as the cost of bread and rumors of hoarding. Most had no direct knowledge of Rousseau's theories. Yet these men were not without means for grasping his message; it might even be argued that many of them had a clearer idea of his main principles than the erudite conservatives who ridiculed their ignorance. In everything from patriotic hymns and speeches to engravings on posters, the interested sans-culotte could encounter Rousseau's ideas second-hand. In the poorer quarters of Paris, these new ideas met with little resistance. On the contrary, many of the aspirations dear to the theorist were treated as intuitively obvious by the lower classes of the capital.

Perhaps that is because it is a relatively small step from the Genevan watch-makers Rousseau grew up with to the French artisans who later joined in idol-izing him. For whatever reasons, the stringent conditions he attached to legiti-mate sovereignty—the devolution of power, simplicity of mores, equality of fortunes, unity of interests, the vigilance of free men—all were welcomed by the independent producers, small shopkeepers, and wage earners of Paris. In the world of Rousseau, they could see themselves. Living in an atmosphere of con-flict lit up by the battle cry of popular sovereignty, they found themselves in a unique position to appreciate this principle practically, to find in an epigram or an image one key to making sense of the unprecedented happenings around them, one tool for spelling out their claims to political power. In this context, to ask whether the sans-culottes had "actual knowledge . . . of Rousseau's political theory, as stated in the *Social Contract*" is to miss the point.[86] Passionately pursu-ing a dream of freedom they had made their own, the militants of Paris instinc-tively gave flesh to Rousseau's ideas and forced them to undergo the vicissitudes of action. That, we may surmise, is another one of the ways in which the Citizen of Geneva informed the rebirth of democracy in the modern world.

The Oracle of Paris

The effect of his ideas Rousseau might well have found surprising. Presumably he would have disavowed the uncontrolled actions he inspired at a distance, just as he had done in Geneva after 1765. But the impact of his *images* Rousseau had every reason to anticipate, if only on the basis of his own theory of rhetoric. Because he had experienced it firsthand, he respected the force of figural lan-guage: beyond commending the pedagogical virtues of symbolism and myth, he resorted to these resources of language in his own thinking and writing.

Contemporaries, moreover, recognized these aspects of his appeal. Even in the unflattering judgment of Condorcet, Rousseau had to be credited with "awakening among our young men an enthusiasm for virtue." He had done so not by dint of original ideas, for, in the opinion of Condorcet, he had not had very many of these. He chided Rousseau for having discovered little in the way of "new truths"; other philosophers had contributed far more to the forward march of science. Condorcet nonetheless conceded that Rousseau's impact on the Revolution far surpassed that of any other modern thinker. The reason, he believed, was the unique force of Rousseau's figural language: "He had the talent of possessing the soul of his readers like the ancient orators possessed the soul of their listeners."[87]

A pamphlet published anonymously in 1790 makes a similar point. According to the author, few revolutionaries properly understood Rousseau. His political ideas were too subtle. Yet such incomprehension scarcely mattered. Far from being treated soberly as the Newton of the moral sciences, Rousseau was in fact being acclaimed as the prophet of a new cult. And that gave him a singular stature: he had become the "oracle" of the republicans.[88]

Rousseau himself once said that if his own most implausible thoughts about political perfection had "any utility" for "numerous peoples and great States" like the French, it was in "changing the objects" of their "esteem," thus arresting, if only for a moment, a degeneration accelerated by "their false appreciations." He also had once appraised classical images of perfection in similar terms, admiring their capacity to reform the spirit of those who contemplated them. Beholding pictures of civic virtue, a kind of rebirth became possible, for such images "gave a new soul to those who draw near them to receive their oracles."[89] As Condorcet bears witness, and as Robespierre and the sans-culottes prove, Rousseau's oracle of democracy did not fall on deaf ears.

Disinterment and Last Rites

Shortly after the *Letters from the Mountain* had appeared in Geneva, one of his followers there told Rousseau of his admiration for his work. "A century longer, sir, and your manly writings will break all the chains of Europe. . . . Even Geneva which rejects you, Geneva one day will honor you." Rousseau's correspondent proved correct on both counts. In December, 1792, the General Council of Geneva annulled the decree against Rousseau; in January, 1793, it placed his bust in its meeting hall; in July, the city held a public banquet in his honor.[90]

In France, the official installation of Rousseau in the pantheon of national heroes occurred after 9 thermidor and Robespierre's fall from power. On 29 fructidor, year II, a report to the National Convention recommended that Rousseau's remains be removed from Ermenonville:

> The *Social Contract* seems to have been made to be read in the presence of the human species assembled in order to learn what it has been and what it has lost. . . . But the great maxims developed in the *Social Contract*, as evident and simple as they seem to us today, then produced little effect; people did not understand them enough to profit from them, or to fear them, they were too much beyond the common reach of minds, even of those who were or were believed to be superior to the vulgar mind; in a way, it is the Revolution that has explained to us the *Social Contract*.[91]

And so it was that on 18 vendémiaire, year III, Rousseau's body was exhumed, and the self-styled simple citizen, the subject of official persecution during his life, was made in death the object of an opulent national ceremony stretching over the next three days.

New decorations, sculptures, icons, and hymns were specially commissioned. A procession of government dignitaries, delegates, and musicians was organized.

At stops along the way from Ermenonville to Paris, local ceremonies consecrated the occasion. Once in Paris, the coffin was placed on public view in the Tuileries gardens, where a replica of the Isle of Poplars at Ermenonville had been built. After a special service at the Convention, the cortege wound through the streets of Paris toward the Pantheon. In the procession were groups of standard-bearers representing various beneficiaries of the author's wisdom: artisans, mothers and children, Genevans, even, for patriotic purposes, war orphans. Bands played Rousseau's most beloved compositions. A cart pulled by twelve horses exhibited a statue of the Citizen. And a copy of the Social Contract, upheld as the "beacon of legislators," was carried in regal splendor on a cushion made of velvet. After the ceremony at the Pantheon, where the president of the Convention laid a wreath and delivered a eulogy, the evening was given over to diverse amusements. At the Place de Panthéon, there was dancing in the streets, while in theatres across Paris, playgoers attended revivals of their favorite spectacles by or about Rousseau.[92]

Similar ceremonies were held in provincial capitals throughout France. At Lyon, the procession, in part a replication of the one in Paris, was designed to display the "dignified character of this friend of humanity and nature." Young men representing Emile and young women representing Sophie carried banners inscribed with edifying extracts from the author's "sacred words": "Man is born free, and everywhere he is in chains." "To renounce one's freedom is to renounce one's status as a man, the rights of humanity and even its duties."[93]

Through such symbolic generosity, the new rulers of France sought to expropriate "the enthusiasm for virtue" still aroused by the revolutionary hero, while dissociating his name from the doctrines of Robespierre. Rumors even spread that the Incorruptible had delayed installing Rousseau in the Pantheon—out of jealousy.[94]

The oracle of the republicans was thus entombed. Having seen the Citizen officially raised to the ranks of the immortals, Rousseau's disciples may have felt that their work was done. In case the more militant among them had any doubts, government repression of indigenous political activity continued apace. The cult of Rousseau diminished in intensity and dwindled in importance. By the defeat of Napoleon in 1815, it was little but a memory. Yet, as the heirs to the Parisian sans-culottes showed, in 1830, in 1848, and in 1871, his ghost could not be laid to rest so simply. Once aroused—and, if only for a fleeting moment, once satisfied—the desire for democracy was not soon forgotten.

7

The Forms of Freedom

THROUGH the story of Rousseau's role in the French Revolution, we have drawn near to the end of our inquiry. We have explored Rousseau's vision of democracy and described the influence exercised by it. We have examined his new language of politics and traced out some of its implications.

There remains the task of appraising the grounds for his transvaluation of democracy. We still need to consider more closely the logic and limits of his original thinking, the cogency of his fundamental beliefs. Are his images of Geneva and his ideas about sovereignty worthy of the loyalty they once inspired? Does Rousseau offer a useful perspective on the world of politics? Or did this stubborn thinker merely rationalize wishes that we may now judge to be barren illusions rather than productive insights? If Rousseau may rightfully be called "the great democrat of the eighteenth century," what conviction can his thinking carry today?

We may begin to approach such questions by recalling Rousseau's position at the juncture of two currents of political theory. In a standard work on the topic, it has been argued that Rousseau's greatest novelty, when compared to the theorists of his own day, lies in his treatment of politics as a vehicle of education: "Whereas according to Locke and Pufendorf, the State has fulfilled its mission when it assures the protection of its citizens and sees to their security, for Rousseau it becomes the essential condition for the intellectual and moral development of man." From the standpoint of our own study, however, Rousseau's greatest novelty, particularly when compared with the theorists of antiquity, appears in a somewhat different area: in his radical stress on the role of *freedom* in any state worthy of being called just.[1]

Both currents in Rousseau's thinking are relevant if we want to evaluate his convictions about democracy. From the ancients he inherited an interest in institutions that perfected the capacities of the human being, while from the moderns he inherited an interest in institutions that solicited the assent of free individuals. Moreover, Rousseau tended to regard these two currents as confluent: he believed that some measure of perfection was, in principle, open to all individuals, thanks to the universal capacity of free will. For Rousseau, the exercise of the will becomes the precondition for educating the human being; and a democratic sovereign becomes the political form facilitating the general exercise of this will. Yet, while his uncompromising emphasis on the freedom of the individual leads Rousseau to his transvaluation of democracy, it is only because he preserves Plato's classical account in one crucial respect: "In a city under democracy you would hear that freedom is the finest thing it has, and that for this reason it is the only regime worth living in for anyone who is by nature free." [2]

That freedom is the greatest good and that a democracy is the only kind of state capable of protecting if not perfecting it are two of the most shopworn propositions in contemporary political writing. As we shall see, for Rousseau as well it is the exercise of free will that justifies democracy; and it is democracy alone that promises to all men equally the civilized enjoyment of a self-confident freedom. By returning to the origin of these propositions in Rousseau's thinking, where they are first clearly joined, we may hope to learn why the connection made sense to him, and whether it makes sense to us.

The idea of freedom holds still greater significance for our study, however. If we, like Heidegger, were to affirm that every thinker thinks but one thought, we would have to say that with Rousseau that one thought is freedom. In the life of his mind, it is the point of departure, the desired destination: his most ineluctable sentiment, what his reveries display, what his reasoning confirms. Freedom is Rousseau's master idea. By closely examining it, we may expect to be led to the heart of his thinking.

We are not the first to find in freedom the key to Rousseau's genius. Hegel thought that Rousseau's idea of freedom was his signal contribution to the spiritual development of humanity. In his *History of Philosophy*, Hegel cavils with the notion of the general will, but only because he finds it flawed by an atomistic individualism that is unworthy of Rousseau's other important principle: that freedom is what distinguishes man from the animals. "The false apprehension of these principles does not matter to us," concludes Hegel: "What matters to us is that by their means it comes as a content into consciousness that man has in his spirit freedom as the downright absolute, that the free will is the concept of man. . . . The principle of freedom dawned on the world in Rousseau, and gave infinite strength to man, who thus apprehended himself as infinite." [3]

Other observers have been less charitable. To proponents of the distinction between a "positive freedom" (to realize mastery of oneself) and a "negative freedom" (to do without the interference of others), Rousseau at best has appeared confused about his own most important concept. Isaiah Berlin, for example, leaves the impression that our author, despite a passing regard for "negative freedom," more often succumbed to an incautious enchantment with "positive freedom," in the process producing, however unwittingly, a monstrous justification for tyranny. [4] Rousseau's idea of freedom is therefore vitiated by contradictions.

Of course, there *are* contradictions in Rousseau's thinking: in many instances,

I would number the tensions they provoke among its most fruitful features. However, his concept of freedom is more coherent than is sometimes thought. In what follows, I will attempt to show this coherence. I will nevertheless conclude by exploring some of the contradictory—and potentially dangerous—impulses at play within Rousseau's idea. Such contradictions illuminate both the vitality of his appeal and the limits to his understanding. If his convictions about democracy are to be of any use to us today, his illusions about freedom are worth dispelling.

Free Will

"To renounce one's freedom is to renounce one's status as a man, the rights of humanity and even its duties." Neither the revolutionaries in Lyon nor Hegel in his appreciation of Rousseau were mistaken in singling out this passage from the *Social Contract*. In it, we find the importance of freedom unequivocally affirmed. Freedom comprises the essence of our nature. It stands at the heart of our morality. It forms the basis of political right. To neglect it is to diminish the capacity to be human. But what is the character of this capacity? And why should freedom play such a prominent role in defining our humanity?[5]

Our perplexity may only be aggravated when we are told that freedom can take a variety of forms. In the *Social Contract*, Rousseau himself distinguishes three general ones: "natural freedom, which is limited only by the force of the individual, and civil freedom, which is limited only by the general will. . . . To the foregoing . . . could be added moral freedom, which alone makes man truly the master of himself."[6] Rousseau discusses each of these three forms in some detail.

At the outset, though, it will help to examine what Rousseau believed to be the common ground of freedom in all its forms. For he held that freedom, whether natural or civilized, whether dormant or developed, exists inalienably in every human being in and through the *will*.

The significance of the will in Rousseau's thinking is attested by its place in the Creed of the Savoyard Vicar. The Vicar preaches freedom of the will as one of his few simple dogmas. It is an article of faith, an unprovable hypothesis. Yet that does not mean that the existence of free will is to be assumed on the Vicar's word or anyone else's. Standing before such mysteries, preachers of faith and learned professors lack trustworthy authority. Often, they merely contradict one another—one reason why Rousseau considered the idea of free will to be "the abyss of philosophy."[7]

Our sense of volition, he believed, is an intrinsically enigmatic phenomenon. In order to become a conviction worth holding, the idea of the free will calls for skepticism and meditation. It defines an experience so fundamentally individualized that its meaning can only be explored by each person on his own. It first appears before the mind as an inescapable feeling, not a clear idea: "I know will only by the sentiment of my own will." This sentiment sometimes seems self-

evident. Up to a point, it can be subjected to reason. But reasoning with empirical evidence cannot establish the existence of the will's freedom with certainty.
To will is a "purely spiritual act about which the Laws of Mechanics explain
nothing."[8] If another person insists that his will is predetermined, there is little
to be said. One can only grope to define the capacity, describe the feeling of
purposeful mastery that accompanies its exercise, and hope that the other person
recognizes something like a similar capacity and feeling within himself.

For someone like the Savoyard Vicar, however, who has plumbed the depths
of his soul and become convinced of the freedom of his own will, there are few
beliefs more passionately held, few intuitions of such cardinal importance. "You
will ask me again how I know there are spontaneous motions, I shall tell you
that I know it because I sense it. I want (*veux*) to move my arm, and I move it
without this movement having another immediate cause than my will. It would
be in vain for someone to try to use reason to destroy this sentiment in me; it is
stronger than all evidence; one might just as well try to prove to me that I do
not exist."[9]

Will is that faculty of the soul which causes there to be spontaneous motion.
A spontaneous motion is one that is self-generated rather than externally caused.
Though such assertions imply a metaphysical dualism that distinguishes the
mechanical motion of "scattered and dead matter" from the spontaneous motion
of creatures endowed with a soul and a will, the difficulties of this dualism need
not detain us. What matters here is that "will" is Rousseau's word for the vital
source of freedom: "All free action has two causes which combine to produce it:
one is moral, namely the will which determines the act, the other is physical,
namely the power which executes it. When I walk toward an object, it is first
necessary that I want to get there, secondly that my feet carry me there."[10]

As this definition suggests, the paradigmatic case of free will involves physically doing something. "The will is known to me by its acts, not by its nature,"
and the sentiment of will is most apparent in such acts as lifting an arm or
walking across a room. To be free is to be able to do as one wants. "Willing and
doing (*faire*) are the same for every free Being."[11]

Because the will can govern physical motion, it appears not only as the locus
of freedom in man, but also as the chief faculty linking soul and body. Yet, while
the physical ability to do as one wants assumes a certain primacy in Rousseau's
account of freedom, willing also can be turned to the movement of images and
ideas in thought. We have already noted the appearance of spontaneous motion
in reverie; in certain instances, to will can mean merely to wish. Willing also
plays a role in "active judgment," which requires the mental movement of objects for comparison. These multiple uses of the will (*la volonté*) can be connoted,
according to the context, by the single French verb *vouloir*: "to will," "to want,"
"to aim at," "to require," "to need," "to wish," "to prefer," "to consent to," "to
mean to," "to try."[12]

As that which commands spontaneous motion, the will, in all of its applications, lies at the root of the potential for change. To borrow a formula of Kant's,

freedom of the will entails the possibility of "spontaneously beginning a series of successive things or states." By acting and by doing, we may transform our physical environment; by dreaming and by judging, we may transform our beliefs. In his unfinished sequel to *Emile*, Rousseau has his naturally educated man, after he has fallen upon hard times and succumbed to the temptations of Paris, write to his tutor in the following terms: "In seeing that the past was no more, I tried to put myself completely in the state of a man who is beginning to live"— as if such an act of will could allow for a kind of reformation and return Emile to the happy habits he had left behind. "I told myself that, in effect, we never do without beginning, and that there is no connection in our existence other than a succession of present moments, of which the first is always the one being enacted (*celui qui est en acte*)." [13]

The free will, however, offers more than the prospect of change and regeneration. The capacity to transform our environment also may be employed for the sake of preserving it. The instrument for pursuing wants may be used to restrain appetites. As Rousseau himself once admitted, his own interest was less in "action than in abstinence"—and here, too, the will plays a crucial role. Through an effort of will, the virtuous man may withstand temptation. The willful person may insist on his principles with stubborn preseverance. In meaning to honor his commitments, the man of good will may extend promises and keep them. The will, in other words, confers an ability not only to command, but also to pledge; not only to initiate, but also to resist; not only to start over, but also to stand one's ground—to forebear doing, as well as to do; to keep to a course, as well as to change it. [14]

This potential perdurability of the will is nevertheless treated by Rousseau as derivative. If the will is to flourish and provide the strength of constancy, it must be exercised, and that, he believes, necessarily involves being able to do as one wants, whether such action involves change or conservation. We may thus imagine the will on the analogy of a muscle: the muscle of the soul, as it were. Like any other important muscle, the will is always there in every healthy human being; but it needs to be exercised to become firm, to remain strong. Without the ability to do, a man may lose the ability to forbear doing. [15]

That the ability of the will to stand firm is derivative does not lessen its importance. In the *Second Discourse*, Rousseau tells us that "it is not so much understanding which constitutes the distinction of man among the animals as it is his being a free agent." But it is not free will *tout court* that distinguishes man; as the Vicar points out in *Emile*, animals exhibit a capacity for spontaneous motion, too. What makes the free will distinctively human, according to Rousseau, is man's ability to employ his will to *resist* instinct. "Nature commands every animal, and the Beast obeys. Man meets with the same impetus, but he recognizes himself to be free to acquiesce, or to resist; and it is above all in the consciousness (*conscience*) of this freedom that the spirituality of his soul shows itself." The irony of Rousseau's position is noteworthy. "Man is only free thanks to the natural law that commands all," he avows. Yet free will, by giving man the flexible power to resist the commands of nature with constancy, makes nature to him forever uncertain.[16]

But how does it happen that the free will comes to resist with constancy a natural instinct or an unnatural passion? What, if anything, may steadfastly guide the will in such efforts? "When I am asked what the cause is which determines my will," answers the Vicar, "I ask in turn what the cause is which determines my judgment; for it is clear that these two causes are only one, and if one well understands that man is active in his judgments, and that his understanding is only the power of comparing and judging, one will see that his freedom is only a similar power or one derived from it."[17]

As the Vicar tacitly admits ("beyond this I understand nothing"), there is some obscurity here. We have seen that man is unique in his use of free will to resist instinct. According to the Vicar, this ability can only be "derived from"—or be "similar to"—the "power of comparing and judging." It now seems that the will, which previously appeared as the ground of judging, may in turn be directed by judgment. Despite the impression left by the *Second Discourse*, it therefore seems that a kind of "understanding"—or something "similar" to it—guides the application of will that is distinctively human. At the very least, the free human being exhibits a special affinity for comparing and judging, and this may be a part of what Rousseau has in mind when he links the uniqueness of man to his *consciousness* of being free. Yet from remarks made elsewhere, it is equally clear that the will may be reliably guided by more than a reasoned understanding. The natural man, for example, has his will directed primarily by the benign instincts of self-love and compassion. And even for modern man, there is a steadier guide than reason per se: "Too often reason deceives us. . . . But conscience (*conscience*) never deceives, it is the true guide of man."[18]

Let us try to summarize the picture of will that has emerged thus far. A capacity of the soul that enables us to initiate or to resist both bodily and mental motion, the will ensures the perpetual possibility of change and starting over. The power of the will springs from the will itself. This "strength of the soul" is the only virtue exhibited by every hero, according to Rousseau. The will, however, may atrophy. Like a muscle, it requires exercise to remain strong. When a person's will has been sufficiently weakened, whether through domination by another person or dissipation from within, it is even possible "to renounce one's freedom"—with results resembling a bedridden invalid unable to walk for having given up trying.[19]

The Goodness of the Will

Rousseau's concept of free will has religious and moral significance. According to the Vicar, man, through the "good use" of his will, can become "the instrument of that great Being who wants (*veut*) the good."[20] But if our free will may thus offer testimony to the goodness of God, its role in explaining the wrongs of this world is considerably less clear.

At first glance, it seems plausible to assume that will gives to man the ability to do bad as well as good: it is the mark of his freedom that he must choose. A means of redemption, freedom would also be a source of depravity. "Man, seek the author of evil no longer," lectures the Vicar: "It is yourself. No evil exists other than what you do or suffer." The "first depravity" of men, he also says, "comes from their own will." And speaking of God, he asks rhetorically, "Did he not give me conscience for loving the good, reason for knowing it, and freedom for choosing it? If I do the bad, I have no excuse. I do it because I want (*veut*) to."[21]

Such comments, however, do not accurately convey the weight of Rousseau's own convictions about the orientation of the will toward good. As the Vicar puts it, "I am not free not to want (*vouloir*) my own good (*mon propre bien*), I am not free to want what is bad for me (*mon mal*); but my freedom consists in precisely this, that I can will (*vouloir*) only what is suitable to me, or what I deem to be such, without anything alien (*étranger*) determining me." A similar conviction appears in both drafts of the *Social Contract*: "No will consents to anything contrary to the good (*bien*) of the being who wills (*veut*)"; "The will always tends toward the good of the being who wills." When the will takes its bearings from the prerational instinct of self-love, it can do no wrong. Every human being naturally desires pleasure. Each naturally avoids pain. "The love of oneself," the tutor informs Emile, "is always good and always in conformity with order." With or without the guidance of conscience and reason, a free man seeks only the good—which, in general, may be defined as what brings a person pleasure and happiness.[22]

Regardless of how the good may be defined in any given context, however, this much seems clear to the tutor as well as the Vicar: "No one does the bad (*le mal*) for the sake of the bad." If we are to take such comments seriously, it follows that the desire for the good inheres in the free will. The "right" of freedom—taking *droit* in its twofold sense of justice and straightforwardness— "arises from freedom itself." So long as it does not err or stray (*errer*), free will can do no harm. All wrongdoing must therefore be considered involuntary, a product of external causes: "I have always the power of will," says the Vicar, "but not always the strength to execute it. When I abandon myself to temptations, I act according to the impulse of external objects." If the will in itself is the cause of no wrong, the source of our ills must be sought elsewhere: in the frailties of the body; in the weakness of the mortal will; in the overriding attraction of tempting "external objects"; or in prejudices, needless passions, and the kind of corrupt society that engenders both.[23]

This curious doctrine—that the free will wants only the good—has a long and distinguished pedigree. A similar idea may be found in Locke. Something like it also appears in the opinion of Socrates upheld by Plato: "No wise man, as I believe, will allow that any human being errs voluntarily, or voluntarily does shameful and base actions; but they are very well aware that all who do shameful and base things do so other than voluntarily." In the Platonic version of the doctrine, the stress falls on *knowledge*, an emphasis expressed in the teaching that virtue *is* knowledge. To know the good is to want it. Wrongdoing occurs because men lack knowledge. But Rousseau alters the formula and transforms the emphasis, for reasons rooted in his own skepticism about the reliability and force of reason.[24]

According to Rousseau, goodness and the desire for the good are rooted in the free will. Will, not knowledge, is what enables man to do good and to forebear doing wrong. In order to be good, the will does not have to be guided by any exceptional intellect. All the good man needs are a few simple ideas and thoughtful convictions, an awareness of conscience, a straightforward love of self and compassion for others. Even though he believed that some form of intuitive understanding could contribute to what he called virtue in society, Rousseau never accepted the Platonic teaching that virtue *is* knowledge.[25] As a result, his own doctrine of free will effected a subtle revolution.

On the one hand, Rousseau answered the question of why evil exists along neo-Platonic rather than Christian lines: wrongdoing occurs only because man sometimes lack sufficient strength of will, not because he wants the bad per se. At the same time, though, Rousseau rejected the ontology of Platonism in favor of his own version of a sort of Lockean Protestantism: only the conscientious individual, using his free will in thought and action, can decipher the meaning of right and execute its precepts in practice.[26] By thus transforming the traditions he inherited, Rousseau managed to translate the Platonic idea that knowledge of the good can be possessed only by a few—which justifies a republic ruled by philosopher-kings—into his own idea of the good as the unhampered exercise of the free will inherent in every individual—which justifies a democracy.

To be sure, Rousseau follows Plato in stressing the cultivation of understanding and virtue once men enter society. For while the free individual wants only the good, both in isolation and at the outset of his association with others, his benign instincts of self-love and pity may be supplanted by the unnatural passions of pride and envy; his nascent conscience may be subdued by other voices from without. A man may be misled. In the complex circumstances of modern society, he may unintentionally do great harm, particularly if he has not acquired a capacity for independent judgment as well as an awareness of conscience.

Rousseau's belief that the free will seeks only the good nevertheless explains his conviction that "there is no original perversity in the human heart," that "the first movements of nature are always right," and that therefore man is naturally good—and reinforces the impression that man's essential nature appears only in the same free will that removes him from the rest of nature. On this reading of Rousseau, it follows that if our original freedom in the state of nature has been lost forever, then the civilized unfolding of free will—through the conventional cultivation of a reasoned understanding attuned to conscience and the healthy instincts of self-love and pity—represents the only renewal of nature—and goodness—that remains faithful to the inner nature of man. To this extent, Kant and Hegel were not mistaken to read Rousseau as their forerunner.[27]

Natural Freedom: The Lost Paradigm

Man in his natural state, conjectures Rousseau, was a creature of self-sufficient solitude. Wandering the earth alone, he was sovereign in his isolation and ignorance. "To perceive and feel will be his first state. . . . To will and not to will, to desire and fear will be the first and only operations of his soul." With blissful simplicity, the undeveloped individual leads an existence ruled only by spontaneous motions, "with no other law than his will." Though he lacks a hut or a family, he is able to unite "fortuitously" with women wandering by. Within him, force and wants coexist in an uncanny harmony. "His desires do not exceed his Physical needs; the only goods he knows in the Universe are nourishment, a female and repose; the only evils he fears are pain and hunger." [28]

Instinctively, he is comfortable with the extent of his grasp. Since all that he wants lies within easy reach, he brooks no frustration, suffers scant grief, and feels at peace with his world. "The spectacle of nature has become indifferent to him by dint of becoming familiar." His serenity is uncrossed by curiosity, unbroken by wonder. Not yet inflamed by imagination, undistracted by regrets, his existence is focused entirely on the present. His heart "asks nothing of him," his conscience lies dormant. [29]

In this "simple, uniform and solitary way of life," the individual absentmindedly delights in a purely self-defined autonomy, a product of de facto autarchy. "I see him satisfying his hunger under an oak, quenching his thirst at the first stream, finding his bed at the foot of the same tree that furnished his meal; and therewith his needs are satisfied." Drifting idly from meadow to hilltop, his native strength prepared "for any event," Rousseau's natural man rarely feels at odds, either with his surroundings or himself. He enjoys the advantage of "always carrying oneself, so to speak, entirely with one." He is happy, he is his own master, and "he prefers the most stormy freedom to tranquil subjection" [30]

Yet even here, man's freedom is not unbounded. It will be recalled that in the *Social Contract*, Rousseau defined the three forms of freedom through their different *limits*. Natural freedom, he says, "is limited only by the forces of the individual." But given the felicity we have just described, it is equally plain that the natural man does not perceive this limit as an imposition or an obstacle, for his wants never outstrip his strength. In this "primitive state," man's "power and desire are in equilibrium"; he feels free and is "not unhappy." Thus Rousseau's most concise definition of natural freedom, as it appears in *Emile*: "The only one who can act according to his will is the one who, in order to act, has no need of hands other than his own: whence it follows that the first of all goods is not authority, but freedom. The truly free man only wants what he can do, and only does what pleases him." [31]

In this definition and in the idyll of the *Second Discourse*, Rousseau recognized the form and appearance of primordial freedom, the essence of man in his undefiled condition. Thinking about man in the state of nature while drafting the *Social Contract*, he also saw before him "perfect independence," "freedom without rule," an "ancient innocence."[32] These images and ideas are worth keeping in mind, as we will encounter them again.

But let there be no mistake. Natural freedom is gone forever. "A man who wanted to regard himself as an isolated being, not depending at all on anything and sufficient unto himself, could only be miserable." The development of society has foreclosed the possibility of spontaneously exercising the kind of freedom man enjoyed in his original state. "By leaving the state of Nature, we force our fellows to leave it, too; no one can remain there in spite of the others, and it would really be leaving it to want to remain when it is impossible to live there. For the first law of Nature is the care of preserving oneself."[33]

That natural freedom is now impossible does not diminish its significance. For Rousseau, it becomes a paradigm, a kind of regulative ideal. In devising a sound curriculum, Saint-Preux in *La Nouvelle Héloïse* declares that "all consists in not spoiling the man of nature in adapting him to society."[34] Similarly, for the tutor in *Emile*, the definition of man's natural freedom becomes his maxim for properly educating his charge for society.

"The truly free man only wants what he can do, and only does what pleases him." There are two equally important elements in this maxim. The first part suggests that a man feels free only when his desires are capable of satisfaction. If he pursues a limited number of manageable wants, a person will generally find that his abilities allow him to do as he pleases. If he pursues a boundless number of unmanageable wants, by contrast, he will often experience the pain of dissatisfaction: his world will seem full of obstacles.

The pursuit of manageable wants is crucial to the second part of the maxim, which states that a man feels free only when he "does what pleases him." The context is important. Rousseau is not saying that freedom involves pursuing any desire whatsoever; that has just been ruled out. Instead, he has in mind a negative condition, perhaps most clearly formulated in a later remark: "I have never believed that a man's freedom consisted in doing what he wanted (*veut*), but rather in not doing what he did not want."[35]

If someone orders me against my will, I feel oppressed. "If someone can constrain my will, I am no longer free."[36] When enabled only to submit to the commands of another, a person develops habits of servility. For want of use, the will withers. Being free therefore depends, negatively, on not being forced by someone else to act in a certain way, and, positively, on the perceived ability to satisfy wants.

Given the character Rousseau attributes to the free will—it is what enables men to do good—the importance he ascribes to stimulating the feeling of freedom is not surprising, for it is through this feeling that intuitive access to the sentiment of will is secured. If the experience of freedom is to be pleasurable rather than frustrating, it should be easier to exercise the will, and thus to keep it healthy, strong, a vital part of a person's existence. "It is the same for freedom as for innocence and virtue—their value is felt only as long as one enjoys them oneself, and the taste for them is lost as soon as one has lost them." This enjoyment, moreover, must be active; the sentiment of the will depends on feeling able *to do*. No wonder, then, that Rousseau in *Emile* finds in the definition of natural freedom "my fundamental maxim." The freedom of natural man provides the only fit paradigm for a modern domestic education aimed at developing and preserving the desire for goodness inherent in the free will. "It is only a question of applying" this idea "to childhood, and all the rules of education flow from it."[37]

To educate a modern child according to this paradigm is essentially to let him elaborate, apparently on his own, a manageable number of wants that do not disturb his pleasurable feeling of being free. Left to his own devices amid the things of nature, he must become inured to the pain he will inevitably suffer, even as he becomes accustomed to the pleasure his mastery of these things may bring. In addition, however, the wise tutor must keep in mind the final destination of his pupil: if his freedom is to survive in the kind of civilization typical of most modern societies, a child must simultaneously learn to take pleasure in ordering a limited existence of his own, so that the appearance of others pursuing different wants need not prove painfully disorienting.

Rousseau himself professed to take delight in such a limited existence. Explaining his joy at inhabiting a tiny island, he remarks that "it is very agreeable, and singularly situated for the happiness of a man who loves to limit himself; for although I may be the only man in the world to whom his destiny has made this a law, I cannot believe myself to be the only one who has a taste so natural."[38]

Emile's tutor seeks to engender a similar love for limits in his pupil. The first book Emile reads will be *Robinson Crusoe*:

> Crusoe on his island, alone, deprived of the assistance of his kind and the instruments of all the arts, providing nonetheless for his subsistence, for his preservation, and even procuring for himself a kind of well-being. . . . This state is not, I agree, that of social man; realistically, it is not going to be that of Emile; but it is on the basis of this very state that he ought to appraise all the others. The surest means to raise oneself above prejudices and to order judgments about the true relations of things is to put oneself in the place of an isolated man and to judge everything as this man himself ought to judge of it with respect to his own utility.[39]

By imagining himself in a situation like Crusoe's, Emile may learn to see in limits the sinecure of his own freedom. He may come to understand natural limits as a necessary and inevitable constraint, even as he discovers the extent of his own powers. But if the desire for an "absolute independence" becomes incoherent in a situation like Crusoe's, one kind of *dependence* becomes impossible (at least for Crusoe): forced subjugation to the will of another.[40]

In this regard, Rousseau felt it important to distinguish between two different kinds of dependence: dependence on things, "which is from nature," and dependence on men, "which is from society." He avers that "dependence on things, having no morality, is in no way detrimental to freedom and engenders no vices. Dependence on men, being disordered, engenders all the vices, and it is by it that master and slave mutually deprave themselves."[41]

Emile is thus led to discover his own distinctively *human* capacities through learning for himself his "dependence on things." On his own, the child can begin to measure the extent of his strength, the adequacy of his understanding, his resourcefulness in getting along by himself. "The true education consists less in precept than practice." At an appropriate age, Emile should acquire a useful trade, undergo the discipline of labor, and become familiar with the range of things he can transform to suit his needs. While thus becoming conscious of his own will in action, he simultaneously becomes able to direct it by himself intuitively, by comparing, judging, and reasoning. Throughout all of these endeavors, he ought never to feel his actions under the command of another, he ought never to feel his own understanding dictated by some ulterior authority. "If ever you substitute in his mind authority for reason, he will no longer reason. He will be nothing more than the plaything of others' opinions."[42]

The trick at all stages of education is to foster in the pupil a feeling of spontaneously satisfying wants of his own, so that he experiences himself as doing only what pleases him, with his own strength and for his own reasons. It is a trick, because appropriate objects for his desires are in fact being plotted throughout his life by the tutor, who covertly stages the situations that Emile confronts. "There is no subjection so perfect as that which keeps the appearance of freedom; one thus enthralls the will itself."[43] The goal of this subterfuge, however, is not naked domination, but rather an extension of Emile's feeling of freedom. By letting him resolve an ascending series of manageable dilemmas, the tutor seeks to engender a pattern of self-reliance through a pleasurable exercise of will.

So it is that Emile insensibly acquires sound habits. Since the "freedom without rule" of the natural man is no longer feasible for social man, the child needs to learn not only to respect limits, but also to observe conventional rules, even if these rules are at first experienced as purely personal predilections which he might change at will. The result should be an adolescent fit for society who nonetheless feels himself a slave neither to his own whims, nor to the will of other men.

By constantly exercising his will in a variety of situations, Emile should, furthermore, become an adolescent adept at solving unforeseen problems on his own. His supple strength of will ought to insure his ability not only to resist needless passions and unreasonable commands, but also to initiate new motions spontaneously, in order to cope with changing circumstances. Thus the tutor's charge, though tacitly informed by sound habits, "does not know what routine, custom or habit is; what he did yesterday does not influence what he does today; he never follows a formula, does not give way before authority or example, and acts and speaks only as it suits him." He is trained to give "faithful expression of his ideas," wherever these may lead. In this context, the capacity of the will to change course and modify wants seems unambiguously providential. "The author of things provides not only for the needs he gives us but also for those we give ourselves," says the tutor; "and it is in order to place desire always at the side of need that he made our tastes change and alter themselves with our manners of life."[44]

There is a paradox here. The same capacity that allows us the leeway to survive in a variety of settings insures that no fixed group of wants can define an immutable human nature. Once he enters into association with others, the freedom of his will makes man forever a creature of conventions. At worst, this adaptability also makes him a slave to fashion: the gift that insures his survival may, in certain circumstances, fuel his unhappiness. At best, though, the flexibiity of will enables a healthy man, even in a relatively complex society, to strike a happy balance between desires and powers, between what he wants and what he can obtain, between what he thinks proper and what others urge him to do.

The inclinations and ideas engendered by an education premised on the exercise of free will ought thus to provide the child with a motile "second nature" that can serve functions similar to the instinctive motions of natural man in his first state, even while laying the grounds for the conscious autonomy of the adult. In the shelter of the household, the rules conducive to survival in society may be taught without diminishing the feeling of freedom or the capacity for change. It might even be said that for Rousseau there are two types of natural freedom, both defined by the happy parity a person manages to maintain between desires and power. The first type of natural freedom is the unpremeditated result of existence in a state of natural isolation; the second type is the planned result of education in a state of domestic isolation.

But if a kind of natural freedom can exist in the modern world, it cannot extend very far. It is a province of childhood. In all of the conditions of natural freedom we have described, the will is guided by instinct, habit, spontaneous reasoning, or the veiled authority of another. Emile's self-reliance is essentially unselfconscious. Moreover, the inculcation of sound habits requires keeping the child at one remove from the larger society, whether within the confines of a healthy Alpine family, or through the more elaborate quarantine contrived by the tutor for Emile (a child of the rich who must, therefore, be protected from a completely corrupt society).[45]

At this point, two possibilities offer the prospect of preserving and extending the individual's feeling of freedom: he may become his own self-conscious master as a man; and he may become the citizen of a legitimate community. Neither of these possibilities requires diminishing freedom; both augment and reinforce the strength of a man's will. One possibility involves developing spiritual stamina, the other involves participating in civic affairs. Since Rousseau thinks the opportunities for civic freedom are extraordinarily rare—and since he thinks spiritual stamina is necessary in any social setting—these two possibilities are of unequal importance. So let us turn next to his idea of moral freedom.

Moral Freedom: The Need for Virtue

The child who has been naturally educated spontaneously enjoys an equilibrium between desires and power. From an early age, he has exercised his body and his senses, in the process learning how to exercise his judgment and understanding. An "active and thinking being," he has gradually "become aware of himself as an individual (*rentré dans son individu*)." Though he wants little, whatever he wishes he obtains for himself. Though he knows little, what he believes, he holds true for reasons of his own. By the time he is twelve, Emile, we are told, has become "laborious, temperate, patient, firm and full of courage."[46]

But the strength of will that makes such traits habitual must undergo two more crucial tests: Emile's "second birth" as a creature of passions, related self-consciously to other men; and his entry into a larger society, with its own distinctive customs and laws.

According to Rousseau, instincts are transformed into passions when the young adolescent becomes aware of his fellows as free agents, ruled by wants and wishes of their own: "We never impassion ourselves over insensible beings. . . . But those from whom we expect good or ill by their inner disposition, by their will, those we see acting freely for us or against us, inspire in us sentiments similar to those they show us." Through experiencing the will of others, the adolescent passes beyond an inchoate attraction and repulsion and comes to define his feelings in terms of friendship and enmity, compassion and envy. In relating himself consciously to others, he becomes aware of himself as a separate individual. He simultaneously begins to perceive wants and weaknesses shared with others, the one engaging his interest, the other his affection. He feels new impulses stirring within. Aroused by his sexuality, he becomes aware of love— and with these developments, earlier limits are swept aside, his feeling of self-sufficiency is shattered. Emile becomes "deaf to the voice that made him docile. . . . He disregards his guide; he no longer wishes to be governed."[47]

Entering society will only extend the challenge of these unruly new passions. Once driven by his newfound appetites into association with others, a man must confront a host of new wants, a range of new powers. Depending on the company he keeps, he may find his simple tastes ridiculed, his painstaking autonomy belittled. When the highborn Emile returns to society, the tutor assumes that he will receive "a second education completely opposed to his first, an education from which he learns to despise what he esteemed, and to esteem what he despised." His strength of will may be assailed and diminished rather than praised and amplified. If his associates are followers of fashion, their needless passions and misleading prejudices may only serve to cloud his judgment and weaken his will. In such a society, "man finds himself outside of nature and sets himself in contradiction with himself." Becoming wholly dependent on others, he may lose the pleasurable sense of being able to do as he wants, he may lose as well the inclination to exercise his will.[48]

The man who wishes to remain free among people who are not must therefore be prepared to undergo a rite of passage that Rousseau paints as full of temptations. To resist the sirens surrounding him, our voyager must develop new reserves of willpower: for "it is only the tepidness of our will which causes all of our weakness, and we are always strong enough to do what we strongly want (*veut*): *Volenti nihil difficile*"—"Nothing is difficult for him who wills." [49]

To reinforce Emile's will, the tutor seeks to enlist sentiment in the service of reasoning, imagination in the service of understanding. He orients the will of his pupil through enchanting images as well as reasoned ideas. Emile will read inspiring histories. He will explore his own religious beliefs. He will be aroused by talk of perfect love. Finally, he will travel throughout Europe in search of a country "where one is always permitted to be a decent man." [50]

Above all, though, Emile must learn to look to himself, to exercise his judgment according to his own lights, to clarify his personal opinions about the meaning of life. He should develop an "active taste for reverie and contemplation," he should acquire the "habit of returning to himself and of searching there in the calm of the passions" for his own sense of proper order. In this way, he may engage his free will in thought and discover for himself "how the first movements of the heart lift the first voices of conscience." [51]

Conscience is the intuitive understanding sparked by love and animated by the free will. Though "formed only by the habit of judging and feeling within society and according to its laws," the Vicar exalts it in transcendent terms. Conscience is a "divine instinct, immortal and celestial voice, certain guide of a being that is ignorant and limited but intelligent and free; infallible judge of good and bad which makes man like unto God." Through conscience alone can a man become convinced that "*justice* and *goodness* are not merely abstract words . . . but are true affections of the soul elucidated by reason." By acknowledging his feelings of love toward others and by using imagination and judgment to clear his own perspective on the right way to act in regard to them, Emile not only is enabled to acquire an impassioned faith in a reasonable creed, he is also encouraged to behave thoughtfully, to be compassionate toward others yet confident of himself, unmoved by debasing prejudices and desires. Because we are free, we want the good; because we are conscientious in our freedom, we love the good. [52]

For Emile to remain happy, "it suffices for him to be free and master of himself." In the *Social Contract*, moral freedom is described as that "which alone makes man truly the master of himself. For the impulse of appetite alone is slavery, and obedience to the law one has prescribed for oneself is freedom." In order to master himself, a man must be willing to act in accordance with his conscience: moral freedom for Rousseau may be defined, in part, simply as this practical commitment to conscientious self-rule. Thus the tutor's advice as he sends his pupil off on his tour of European countries: "Do not expect lengthy precepts of morality from me, I have only one to give you, and it comprehends all the others. Be a man; restrain your heart within the limits of your condition. Study and know these limits; however narrow they may be, a man is not unhappy as long as he closes himself up within them." [53]

But moral freedom involves more than conscious self-rule; it also requires that unnatural strength of will Rousseau calls *virtue*. As the tutor warns his young traveler, "There is no happiness without courage nor virtue without struggle. The word *virtue* comes from *strength*; strength is the foundation of all virtue. Virtue belongs only to a being that is weak by nature and strong by will; it is in this that the merit of the just man consists."[54]

Insofar as Emile's penchants have inclined him spontaneously to limit his wants, he has long enjoyed being free and (by definition) doing good; from the outset, he has done "everything voluntarily and with pleasure," thus adding "the empire of habit to the sweetness of freedom." Once he has learned as well to elucidate his conscience and to limit his wants for reasons of his own, he has already acquired a degree of virtue. But "so long as virtue costs nothing to practice, there is little need to know it. This need comes when the passions are aroused"— and aroused they certainly will be, if only by his upcoming tour of modern societies. "I have taught you not so much to give unto each what belongs to him as to care only for what is yours. I have made you good rather than virtuous: but who is only good remains so only as long as he takes pleasure in being so." This pleasure will likely be severely tested on Emile's travels, when he finally encounters opulence, domination, and injustice firsthand. In such a setting, "the man who is only good is good only for himself."[55]

In his *First Discourse*, Rousseau hailed virtue as the "sublime science of simple souls." Who, then, is the virtuous man? According to Rousseau, anyone has it within himself to develop virtue. Although he must be strong, he requires no superhuman strength: "Diminish desires and it is as if you increase strength; he who is capable of more than he desires has strength left over. He is certainly a very strong being." The man who would be virtuous needs no special knowledge, although he must be willing to consult his conscience and think for himself; he needs no extraordinary talents, although he must be steadfast and straightforward; unless he inhabits an unusually degenerate society or is born to either obscene wealth or crushing poverty, he needs no unusual nurture. As a child, he should have constantly exercised his will; as an adolescent, he should have acquired the ability to do as he wants while limiting his wants to what he feels himself able to do and what he feels it is right to do. The virtuous man, in sum, "is he who knows how to conquer his affections. For then he follows his reason and conscience; he does his duty; he keeps himself in order, and nothing can make him deviate from it."[56] He is a man like the one Emile is about to become.

The tutor at last must confess: the freedom his pupil had felt as a child was merely a simulacrum of natural freedom, the result of manipulation as much as spontaneous impulse. "Up to now you were free only in appearance," the tutor admits. "You had only the precarious freedom of a slave to whom nothing has been commanded. Now be free in fact; learn to become your own master; command your heart Emile, and you will be virtuous."[57]

Thus enlightened about his past and fortified for the future, armed with a homily on virtue and a précis of the *Social Contract,* Emile wanders off into the world, to take responsibility on his own for evaluating different states and for making one of the most difficult decisions of his life: the choice of a country to call his own.

Civil Freedom: The Need for Laws

For want of a legitimate government—a state a free man could willingly call his own—a decision like Emile's proves doubly difficult. Most laws, he discovers, are codes of oppression, used by the privileged to justify their privileges. Most great nations, he discovers, are populated by masters and slaves. None permit true citizenship. None embody civil freedom. As the tutor laments, "Who knows where one can live independent and free, without needing to do wrong (*mal*) to anyone, and without fear of being wronged?"[58]

Yet, according to the *Social Contract*—and Emile's own experience—"common freedom" ought to be a "consequence of man's nature."[59] We have already seen at play the free will of the naturally educated child. We have watched that gift blossom in the virtuous strength of the man accustomed to think and act on his own. Is not some shared form of freedom a logical result of this development?

If moral freedom is defined as "obedience to the law one has prescribed for oneself," then the idea of a common freedom raises the possibility of an association of individuals prescribing an analogous law through and for each of its members. To qualify as truly free in the terms we have so far been using, any such society must be "suitable to men and contain nothing contrary to the natural Laws," including the natural law of free will. It must therefore preserve in each associate the feeling that he is able to do what he wants; and it must permit each to maintain a circumscribed sphere where his powers and desires remain in balance.[60]

A society that meets these conditions promises new benefits, however. In principle, such an association could be structured to reinforce—rather than work against—the free will of each.

But how can any association regulate its affairs without compelling some of its members to do what they do not want to do? "By what inconceivable art could the means be found to subjugate men in order to make them free? . . . To enchain their will with their own assent?" This miracle, according to Rousseau, is wrought by the law—specifically, those legitimate laws established by a sovereign people. In association with others, "it is to law alone that men owe justice and freedom." By the time he wrote the *Social Contract,* he had devised this definition of legitimate laws: "When all the people decree concerning all the people, it only considers itself, and if it then forms of itself a relationship, it is of the entire object from one point of view to the entire object from another point of view, without any division of the whole. Then the matter on which they decree is general, like the will that decrees. It is this act that I call a law."[61]

We are on familiar terrain, so little more will be said here about the general will. While natural freedom is limited only by the power of the individual, and moral freedom is limited, in addition, by the laws an individual, consulting his own lights, prescribes for himself, civil freedom "is limited only by the general will." Rousseau assumes a community united by feelings of solidarity and sharing common interests. A civil framework for exercising their freedom has been created among these men, thanks to the fact—and only thanks to the fact—that each individual has willingly agreed, on his own and in person, to abide by laws that facilitate cooperation while preserving independence: general in their origin, these laws are to be general in their application. Where this fundamental framework is periodically sanctioned unanimously, each individual preserves the feeling of only doing what he wants. He never experiences the law as an obstacle imposed by the will of another. "In giving himself to all, each gives himself to no one, and since there is no associate over whom he does not acquire the same right that he grants the other over himself, he gains the equivalent of everything he loses, and more force to preserve what he has."[62]

Now, among the things "he has"—inalienably and always—are the rudiments of free will and, in consequence, the desire to do good. In this respect, all men are equal, according to Rousseau. And, among other things, what each gains in a legitimate association is "more force" to preserve and develop this capacity, which may now be exercised in public as a shared inclination worth cultivating with others. The strength of will Rousseau called virtue thus acquires a civic dimension: if moral virtue is the conformity of the free will to rules that one has set for oneself, civic virtue "is only the conformity of the particular will with the general will." The individual's freedom, which previously had been rooted in habit and reinforced by reason and conscience, may now in turn be rooted in mores and reinforced by the law.[63]

Thanks to such reinforcements, the will of each wins new protection against wrongdoing and the domination of others. In a community dedicated to developing freedom, the "inner voice" of conscience is amplified: legitimate laws become a "celestial voice that tells each citizen the precepts of public reason, and teaches him to behave according to the maxims of his own judgment and not to be constantly in contradiction with himself."[64] Since legitimate laws are forged anew at periodic assemblies of all citizens, their very mode of existence invites each citizen to enter into himself, to exercise his own best thinking, to come to his own conclusions about what seems generally right, and then to share such insights, to subject them to public debate and scrutiny, in order to secure reciprocal assent to a common framework of moral understanding and legally binding order. Through the possibility of joint endeavor thus created, each acquires new power not only to fulfill a wider range of wants, but also to use his own judgment, in cooperation with his fellows, to reach agreement about what wants can and ought to be commonly satisfied. The opportunities for temptation may thus be reduced: needless desires can be mutually limited. A shared harmony between wants and strength may be achieved. The pleasurable feeling of being free—of being able to do as one wants—is rendered correspondingly more secure.

This may help to explain the tutor's otherwise puzzling remark to Emile: "Inasmuch as the individuals have subjected themselves only to the sovereign, and the sovereign authority is nothing other than the general will, we shall see how each man who obeys the sovereign obeys only himself, and how one is *more free* under the social pact than in the state of nature." Rousseau himself clearly wished as much: "Our sweetest existence is relative and collective, and our true *self* is not whole entirely inside of us."[65]

Having used the term "reinforcement" in relation to freedom, and having quoted, in this context, the controversial idea of a "true self," it may be just as well to consider at this point what sense can be made of Rousseau's most notorious dictum: "Whoever refuses to obey the general will shall be constrained to do so by the whole body: which only means that he will be forced to be free."[66]

There are two aspects of this passage, one having to do with punishment, the other with pedagogy. Each will be discussed in turn. But let us examine, first, how Rousseau thought that a man could become obligated to obey a law; and second, why he expected that punishment might be necessary.

In theory, each citizen in a community regulated by legitimate laws enjoys the right to vote on particular laws according to general procedures that he has personally endorsed. Furthermore, each citizen continues to enjoy the right to urge his compatriots to repeal particular laws, and even to transform the general procedures they have all previously agreed upon unanimously: since the desires and opinions of a free man can always change, it would be "absurd for the will to give itself chains for the future." But so long as each member of an association preserves the power of rejecting the fundamental laws and does not do so; so long as each has willingly agreed to the utility of these laws and the justice of the procedures for enacting and repealing them, even if he disagrees with some particular edicts—so long, that is, as civil freedom is secured through a direct democracy—it is legitimate to take silence on the part of a citizen as a sign of "current and tacit consent."[67] This continuing implicit consent to laws a man has previously endorsed explicitly is what creates a moral obligation to obey them, according to Rousseau.

But in reality, an individual may waver in his concern with civic affairs. In a community like the one Rousseau imagines, each person enjoys "an absolute and naturally independent existence." Different men pursue different interests in private; different wants may be satisfied in different households. In such a setting, a person may sometimes be tempted to pursue his own interests at the expense of others. Ignoring his conscience, he may be momentarily wanting in virtue: he may sometimes lack the independent strength of will to forebear wrongdoing. Even if each has agreed to heed the law in principle, it seems prudent to wonder whether each will always do so in practice.[68]

Lest laws become "an ineffectual formula," any legitimate community may therefore be expected to establish a public power to penalize wrongdoing. If someone violates a particular rule, the justice of the law depends on applying its force "from without." It depends, that is, on punishment. Such punishment must be applied equally to all wrongdoers. Otherwise, if an exception were to be made for an individual, the impersonality of the laws would be violated. But this impersonal enforcement of the law "is the condition that, by giving each Citizen to the Fatherland, guarantees each one against personal dependence."[69]

But this is not all. Punishment has an important pedagogical dimension, as can be brought out by a comparison of Rousseau's position with that of Protagoras in Plato's dialogue of the same name. For Rousseau, as for Protagoras—and unlike Socrates and Plato—virtue can be taught, through involvement in an orderly community, to all men equally. As Protagoras puts it, any man may become virtuous, "by instruction, and by taking pains." The impersonal enforcement of the law guarantees the citizen against all personal dependence not merely by punishing the offender, but by teaching him, and all who watch, just what civic virtue ought to mean. "If a man is wanting in those good qualities which are attained by study and exercise and teaching, and has only the contrary evil qualities, other men are angry with him, and punish and reprove him." They do this, contends Protagoras, not for reasons of vengeance, but in order to instill virtue: "He punishes for the sake of prevention, thereby clearly implying that virtue is capable of being taught." When Rousseau speaks of laws forcing men to be free, he has something similar in mind: "to force them to punish themselves" when virtue fails them, "when they do what they did not want (voulu)." For him, as for Protagoras, one purpose of such punishment is pedagogical: "There is no wicked man who could not be made good for something."[70]

In any case, if the institutions of a community are in proper order, every individual, by exercising his will regularly, both in public and in private, ought to be able to develop virtue on his own. Punishments should occur rarely. Moreover, if they are designed to impart a sense of virtue, the severity of punishments has nothing to do with their effectiveness. "The first of the laws is to respect the laws. Severity of punishments is merely a vain expedient thought up by small minds in order to substitute terror for the respect they can't obtain." Finally, it should be pointed out that civic virtue can at best supplement—not supplant—moral virtue: for civil freedom is real only in and through the free will of each of the associated individuals.[71]

When Rousseau wrote the *Social Contract*, he had in mind his own image of Alpine perfection. In such a democracy, a veritable chain of virtue is unobtrusively forged, reconciling the rights established through the laws with the interests spontaneously pursued by individuals naturally educated in private.

In the family, the Alpine child learns to take pleasure in a simulacrum of natural freedom; he becomes accustomed to the feeling of being free, of being able to do as he wants, while acting within limits he perceives as natural. By the time he has learned a trade, reached the age of reason, married and become a father, he has acquired a measure of material self-sufficiency as well as a taste for moral self-reliance. He is his own master, able to rule himself; by voluntarily limiting the extent of his wants, he preserves the feeling of doing as he wishes. Since, as a child, he has tasted the joys of natural freedom, he now finds pleasure in exercising his will. Since, as a man, he has thought about what it means to prescribe a law for oneself—and since he has come to understand why such laws are essential to preserve a happy balance between desires and powers—he has acquired, besides the strength of virtue and a sensitivity to conscience, reasons of his own for wanting to remain free.

These are just the kinds of sound habits that will make him an ideal associate of Rousseau's ideal Alpine city. There, in the circles he frequents and the civic festivals he enjoys, he can meet men like himself and develop sentiments of solidarity. Through the civic faith professed in public, he feels his own sense of justice and conscience dignified and confirmed. The mores cultivated in such institutions make of him finally a perfectly thoughtful citizen, firm in his own freedom, yet attuned to what he holds in common with others. Before attending an assembly of the sovereign, alone in the circumscribed domain of his family, the father will consult his own lights; when he comes to the assembly, he will give "only his own opinion" but will listen with respect to his compatriots, knowing that they are his peers, animated equally by free will and good faith. And after he leaves the assembly, even if he has disagreed with a particular decision taken there, he will embrace civic as well as moral virtue, by gladly observing the precepts of the general will—gladly, because, as an active member of his community and as a direct participant in the sovereign, the civil law as a whole appears to him as an extension of his own powers as well as a limit he has helped set for himself.[72] In the laws, he feels his free will respected. He therefore respects the laws, of his own free will. That, at least, is the ideal.

The Coherence of Rousseau's Idea

By realizing the principles of political right, Rousseau's idea of the free will completes its worldly odyssey. It is time, then, to examine the coherence of the idea of freedom as it is described by Rousseau. As a start, we may point out some general features.

What do Rousseau's three forms of freedom have in common? First, all three—natural, moral, and civil freedom—are grounded in the exercise of the individual's *will*. Second, freedom in all three forms appears as an inward subjective *feeling*—a quite pleasurable one, whenever a person is able to do as he wants. Third, in all three forms, freedom is nonetheless defined by objective or communicable *limits*, whether natural, moral, or legal.

The coherence of this general idea may be further clarified by considering the definition of freedom offered by Frithjof Bergmann. "An act is free if the agent identifies with the elements from which it flows; it is coerced if the agent dissociates himself from the element which generates or prompts the action." We may compare Rousseau's definition of free will in terms of spontaneous motion. A spontaneous motion, it will be recalled, is one that is generated "within," rather than one that is caused by "external objects." But this distinction presupposes a notion of inner and outer and an identification of freedom through motions that are generated "within."[73]

As Bergmann puts it, "Freedom is a function of identification and stands in a relation of dependence to that with which a man identifies." Insofar as different agents may identify with different elements, we may expect that the feeling of being free can arise in a variety of settings. That the specific sense of freedom may vary with the context is borne out by Rousseau's own discussion of the three forms. These forms are also, in Bergmann's terms, frameworks for three different processes of identification. Looking at these forms again, we may briefly indicate how freedom in each one depends on differing relations between self and world. The naturally free man, being unselfconscious, identifies with the whole world at his command; the morally free man, by contrast, identifies with the "true self" of his conscience elucidated by reason; the politically free man, finally, identifies with the laws and the *moi commun* he shares with his associates. As Bergmann summarizes his point, "The primary condition of freedom is the possession of an identity, of a self—freedom is the acting out of that identity."[74]

Two implications of this general idea of freedom are worth noting. In the first place, although the continued sentiment of freedom may depend on the perceived ability to act differently if so moved, feeling free as a function of identification is not necessarily the result of any self-conscious deliberation—or even of having a particularly striking "choice" to make. Rousseau's natural man acts purely instinctively, with delectable abandon, while his civil man can be "forced to be free." So long as a person identifies with the elements from which his action flows (even if that act is submitting to punishment), he will feel his action to be free, whether or not deliberation or explicit choice figure in it.[75]

In the second place, once the concept of freedom is implicated in a process of identification, the idea of an absolute independence becomes absurd. Without a definable personal identity—without circumscribed wants and interests—willing threatens to become an unfocused exercise in perpetual frustration. As Rousseau's own fondness for islands suggests, to feel free is, in part, to feel secure in a sphere of our own; it is, in part, to be able to do as we want with some confidence that unfamiliar obstacles or constraints imposed by others are not likely to thwart our efforts. Given this dependence of feeling free on a prior sense of a world that we feel comfortable calling our own, the demolition of limits to that world does not necessarily increase our feeling of freedom. On the contrary, the skeptical questioning of patterns of belief and behavior that we have come to take for granted may seem disorienting and unsettling, a disruption of our customary identity, "an extension of our 'empty space,' an increase of our 'desert,'" as Nietzsche once put it. This is one reason why Rousseau thought that moral freedom should be built upon sound habits, while civic freedom needed to sink roots in the familiar customs—the mores and manners—of any given people.[76]

There is, I think, much to recommend Rousseau's general idea of freedom, thus described. Without denying what remains puzzling in the idea of free will, we may perhaps be able to agree that being free is bound up with something like an exercise of will, that is, with a perceived ability to do as one wants. Similarly, without accepting Rousseau's own metaphysical dualism, we may also be able to agree that something like the feeling of being free is a central feature of our own existence. In the words of Merleau-Ponty, we find within ourselves "a power of placing in abeyance, and that suffices to ensure our freedom from determinism." If such phenomenological evidence seems unconvincing, we may also turn to the sociological evidence. Here we discover that determinism, if it were true, would make a wide range of conventional moral expressions, of praise and blame, of honor and punishment, inapplicable or unintelligible. Such observations, as Rousseau would have admitted, cannot "prove" free will, nor can they "refute" determinism. But the apparent role played by the sense of being free in our thinking about our own existence, in our conventional moral concepts, and in the prevailing legal codes, must nevertheless count for *something*, if the thesis against free will is not to become, in turn, an unfalsifiable tautology.[77]

Finally, on the importance of limits for feeling free, Rousseau also seems perceptive. By linking the growth of satisfying inclinations to the provision of an appealing context for identification and by stressing the importance of learning by doing if the experience of mastery is to be vivid, Rousseau displays the principles of a pedagogy designed to delimit a sense of personal wholeness and self-confidence alongside a feeling of freedom, through an ongoing process of pleasurable self-rule. If the focal point of our distinctively human powers can be called the free will, then Rousseau has indeed suggested some of the preconditions, both personal and political, for stimulating rather than stifling it.

Contradictions

There is nevertheless something disturbing about Rousseau's idea of freedom. Two problems seem to me especially troubling: the doctrine that the free will wants only the good; and the impression sometimes left that freedom, as a purely subjective feeling, may be passively enjoyed and covertly manipulated. Let us consider the doctrine of the good will first.

The assumption that no one would harm himself voluntarily is not without a certain plausibility: most of us do not commonly seek out pain and suffering. If right and wrong may be defined in terms of pleasure and pain, we might agree that most people would not willingly do wrong to themselves. And if we follow Rousseau in the belief that man naturally feels pity whenever he sees another suffer, we might also agree that most people would not willingly do wrong to others. But such examples are scarcely exhaustive: for what are we to make of the apparent evidence of ill will? The satisfaction taken by some in masochistic activities seems to challenge the assumption that no one wishes to cause pain to himself, while the joy found by others in sadistic brutality raises questions about just how far an aversion to beholding pain may extend. And what are we to make of alternative accounts of the will? A century after Rousseau, Nietzsche argued that the will in general seeks not pleasure or goodness but rather sheer *power*, a power that may well occasion suffering and (in the language of its victims) "evil."

Of course, there are semantic strategies available to rebut counterexamples and rival theories. Given the right redescription, the problem disappears. The onus can always be shifted. A theory of the will to power may then be treated as evidence of wickedness. Wickedness and wrongdoing in turn may be explained as symptoms of social institutions that have weakened the free will and misguided its natural inclination to do good. Wickedness and wrongdoing are then, by definition, considered involuntary: the only problem is to discover what causes them. But this sort of response succeeds at an extraordinary price: the idea of freedom threatens to dissolve in contradiction.

If free will is the power of spontaneous motion, and if it gives us the strength to do what is good and to forebear doing what is bad, it would seem that it must also give us the strength to do what is bad and to forebear doing what is good. As Rousseau himself tacitly admits when he describes the deliberation essential for maintaining moral and civic virtue, enjoying the power of free will implies, in certain circumstances, having the ability to choose between divergent courses of action, one good, the other bad. A free act is one that might have been done differently: that, it would seem, is a part of what the struggle to be virtuous is all about. If it truly depends on our own decision whether we are able to do good, the reality of that decision must mean that we are also able to do wrong. Both courses are within our power. But if both courses are within our power, it would be an odd linguistic protocol that forced us to say, after the event, that one kind of decision (the bad one) was actually involuntary, while the other kind of decision (the good one) was voluntary.

In rejecting the Socratic and Platonic doctrine that all wrongdoing is involuntary, Aristotle put it this way: "Wickedness is voluntary. If we do not accept that, we must contradict the conclusions at which we have just arrived, and must deny that man is source and begetter of his actions as a father is of his children. But if our conclusions are accepted, and if we cannot trace back our actions to starting points other than those within ourselves, then all actions in which the initiative lies within ourselves are in our power and are voluntary actions."[78]

Strangely enough, abandoning the doctrine that man wills only the good does not entail abandoning many of the other central tenets of *Emile* and the *Social Contract*, even if it does entail forfeiting one of the most seductive aspects of Rousseau's appeal.[79] Theoretically, all that must be given up is the notion that the naturally free man is inherently innocent; and, as we shall see, there are other good reasons to abandon this notion in any case. When it comes to moral and civil freedom, by contrast, the doctrine that man spontaneously desires the good is expendable, for the simple reason that Rousseau himself agrees that the free will, to do good in society, must be specially cultivated and reinforced against temptation. Because the will is weak, and because the implications of interaction in society are complex, understanding and virtue must supplement goodness, and both are taught, not inborn. In his ethics and political theory, the phenomena of ignorance and the weak will in effect fulfill the same function in explaining wrongdoing as the idea of a free will able to choose the bad as well as the good. Thus many of the pedagogical and political devices he designed to fortify the will, awaken conscience, train the intuitive understanding, and punish wrong-doing could also serve to temper and protect against the phenomenon of ill will.

Rousseau himself nevertheless remained devoted to his own doctrine that the free will wants only the good, with some extraordinary results that are worth exploring a little further. If all wrongdoing is involuntary and hence necessary, there would seem to be little point in attempting to redress abuses that must be considered inevitable. Why worry about reforming souls unless the wrongs they do or suffer are within their power? Of course, Rousseau on one level scarcely intended his doctrine as an invitation to inaction. The belief that all men equally contain the capacity to do good served as a summons, a call to exercise our freedom with renewed vigor. Similarly, the assertion that society unjustly shackles and enervates the free will served as an exhortation, a call to transform corrupt institutions.

But consider Emile's own resignation at the climax of an education that has supposedly prepared him for the most sinewy feats of will: "It seems to me that in order to make oneself free, one has to do nothing; it suffices that one not want (*vouloir*) to stop being free. It is you, my master, who have made me free in teaching me to yield to necessity."[80]

Moreover, even if Rousseau did not intend his doctrine as an invitation to inaction, that is how he himself ended up taking it. "I know this; I know that the only good which is henceforth in my power to do is to abstain from acting, for fear of doing harm without wanting to and without knowing it (*sans le vouloir and sans le savoir*)." In the *Reveries of a Solitary Stroller*, we read a familiar refrain: "So long as I act freely, I am good and do nothing but good." But acting inevitably results in unforseen consequences, it always hazards betraying a weakness, an involuntary flaw that might produce harm. In part, Rousseau's aversion to action derives from the irreversibility of its implications once an act has begun: he suffers from a fear of finality. "After so many sad experiences, I have learned to foresee from a distance the consequences of my first movements followed through, and I have often abstained from a good deed, which I had the desire and the power to do, frightened at the liability to which, in what followed, I would sub-mit myself, if I surrendered myself inconsiderately."[81]

Even worse, when the will is weak and thus laid open to external influences, an action runs the risk, in going astray and betraying the actor's intentions, of coming to feel unpleasantly *unfree*, the vital focus of its motion dispersed amid "scattered and dead matter." Because he believed his own will to be weak, Rous-seau came to see in himself "the simple impulse of a temperament determined by necessity." No wonder he withdrew from action: "I no longer even carry out my will, because I am weak." Nothing ventured—but everything gained. For the free will retains its innocence intact: "As for the bad, it has not entered into my will during my life, and I doubt if there is any man in the world who has really done less of it than me."[82] Once he had assumed the innate goodness of the free will, Rousseau was disposed to forego risking that goodness by testing his own will in practice.

There is another aspect of the matter, one that Kierkegaard saw with severe clarity. In his journals, he had high praise for Rousseau's *Reveries*, a work he considered "admirable." But he also felt that Rousseau was "an example of what it means not to be well-read in Christianity." Rousseau had failed to grasp the essence of Christian conflict: a conflict rooted in the deliberate—and agonizing—choice that Christ has given man. "There are analogies in Rousseau's life with the truly Christian conflicts (to do good and suffer for it, to do good and thereby make oneself and others unhappy). That is what he cannot endure; he complains that it paralyzes him so terribly. . . . He is an example of how difficult man finds mortification."[83]

It would be fruitless here to debate the metaphysics of mortification. Rousseau himself certainly felt that he had suffered enough. Whether justifiably or not, many eighteenth-century readers agreed with Rousseau's own estimate. Kierkegaard nevertheless seems to me perceptive on this point. As Rousseau himself once admitted, "I saw that to do good with pleasure, it was necessary that I should act freely, without constraint, and that to take from me all the sweetness of a good deed, it sufficed that it should become a duty for me. . . . In every imaginable thing, that which I did not do with pleasure was soon impossible for me to do."[84]

For Kierkegaard, by contrast, there was no question of effortless goodness, no certainty of inward innocence to fall back on, no comforting belief that being free could finally be reconciled with feeling pleasure. Rather, the authentic Christian life showed man to himself in his finitude and fallibility and made him aware of the abyss separating his own existence from the perfection and absolute transcendence of God. Salvation required not the liberation of a benign inner nature, but rather a painful leap of faith. The free will, far from securing for man a guarantee that he was by nature good, signified his radical contingency, the perpetual possibility that he might fall into wrongdoing. To believe that the free will wants only the good was therefore to mistake radically the meaning of freedom, the pathos of being human.

Kierkegaard's comments also shed some light on the peculiar aura of passivity surrounding some of the most ecstatic feelings of freedom reported by Rousseau. Consider, for example, the spontaneous motions of the daydreamer strolling, lost in his thoughts:

> I can scarcely think when I remain in one spot; it is necessary that my body be set in motion in order to move my mind. The sight of the countryside, the succession of agreeable views, the open air, a large appetite, the good health I earn by walking, the freedom of a country tavern, the distance from all that makes me feel my dependence, from all that recalls me to my situation, all this releases my soul, gives me a great boldness to think, throws

me in some way into the immensity of beings in order to combine, to choose, to appropriate them to me at my pleasure, without discomfort and without fear. I dispose of all nature as its master; my heart strays from object to object, uniting itself, identifying itself with those objects that flatter it, wrapping itself in charming images, intoxicating itself with delicious sentiments.

That the wandering thoughts of reverie may sketch a world of real mastery, we have already suggested in our discussion of Rousseau's Alpine imagery. Yet if imagination sometimes paints a picture of perfect freedom, Rousseau also seems willing to settle for a perfect freedom that is purely imaginary: "In desiring much, he was obliged to achieve very little. . . . His fictions became sweeter than reality itself, they avoided defects as well as difficulties." Having fled the discomforts of exercising the will in practice, he seeks a more pleasurable outlet in thinking, in the self-satisfied contemplation of the purely subjective *feeling* of freedom—a sentiment most "delicious" when the daydreamer spontaneously enjoys, like Rousseau's natural man, an unselfconscious identification with the whole world at his command.[85]

But we need not resort to Rousseau's confessional writings to feel a certain disquiet with the idea of freedom taken simply as a pleasurable process of identification. For how can this process be limited? And who is to establish the boundaries? Emile is tricked into feeling free. As a child, while exercising his will, he believes that he is doing things on his own and drawing conclusions about the world on the basis of his own judgment. Yet, in fact, the hidden authority of the tutor is manipulating the situations Emile must face. It is the tutor, not Emile, who controls the process of identification through which the child develops a self. And it is Rousseau himself who avers that "there is no subjection so perfect as that which keeps the appearance of freedom."[86]

Nor is this sort of manipulation confined to the education of children. Rousseau counsels the wise legislator to use similar guile, by propounding myths to persuade without convincing. Seeking to extend "his respectable dominion over wills even more than over actions," the "true statesman" seeks to mold mores indirectly, laying his plans "in secret," in order to insure that "one . . . enthralls the will itself." "The greatest talent of leaders is to disguise their power in order to make it less odious, and to manage the State so peacefully that it seems to have no need for managers."[87]

In such passages may be found evidence of bad faith, the sentiments of an aspiring autocrat. Yet they simultaneously suggest a certain submissiveness on Rousseau's part. It is as if he longed for someone to grant him a simulacrum of natural freedom by *imposing* limits on his wants, while maintaining the illusion that he is really free. It is as if he would submit passively and without a struggle to an order someone else had forged for him, so long as he felt as if he himself had made the choice. Even punishment he sometimes craves: forced to be free, he might enjoy the delights of freedom without worrying about the difficulties.[88]

Hesitation

Yet Emile, after all, is told of the tutor's deception. He is prepared to take responsibility for his own decisions. Being told to choose for himself marks his coming of age: for, "by a right nothing can abrogate, when each man attains his majority"—that is, "the age of reason"—he "becomes his own master," entitled to rule himself. Emile must thus decide for himself whether he will remain a resident in the community of his birth or become a citizen of another city, with laws more to his taste. The whole point of his education has been to permit him to make just this sort of decision with wisdom and forbearance, by himself and for his own reasons. Similarly, in the *Social Contract*, the avowed purpose of the great Legislator is to fashion sound mores for a people, so that each may pursue the task of self-rule with conscientiousness and understanding, as well as with good will.[89] In both cases, Rousseau, in principle, permits manipulation only so long as such guile allows its subjects eventually to enjoy effective mastery and, with it, the reality of freedom.

Submissiveness in a child and docility in a people may ease the task of the educator and lawgiver; but such traits, by themselves, scarcely enable a man to rule himself. Yet, according to the precepts of Rousseau's pedagogy, both domestic and political, only the man capable of self-rule is worth cultivating. To settle for anything less is to court slavishness, to hobble the will, to humiliate what is truly noble in man. It is to fail in the tasks of an education for freedom. Thus, after advising the Polish aristocracy "to render again worthy of freedom and capable of enduring it those serfs whom they want to emancipate," Rousseau reminds his clients of just what that goal means: "Remember that your serfs are men like you, and that they have in themselves the makings to become all that you are."[90]

But to justify manipulating the appearance of freedom for the sake of acquiring real freedom is to presuppose a distinction between the two. In effect, it is not only to restrict our previous definition of freedom, it is also to concede the preeminence of civilized over natural freedom. If some such distinction can be drawn, however, we will not only have circumscribed the domain and goal of permissible manipulation, we will also have put ourselves in a position to discard the doctrine of the innately good will: for to assert the preeminence of civilized over natural freedom is also to assert the need for virtue beyond the mere inclination to do good.

Assuming a process of self-development through a framework for identification, we previously singled out three features common to all the forms of freedom discussed by Rousseau: the exercise of the will, the pleasurable feeling of being able to do as one wants, and the concomitant identification with natural, moral, or legal limits on what one wants. But these three features are insufficient for distinguishing apparent from real freedom. For a child or a docile people may exercise its will, feel able to do as it wants, respect certain limits, and yet still, in reality, be in the power of another, at the mercy of their will.

If we wish to define freedom more narrowly, then, this list of features must be supplemented. Two further criteria, drawn from Rousseau's own discussions of moral and civil freedom, come to mind. First, the individual who would be really free must be capable of thoughtful deliberation and self-conscious choice: and this requires developing a lucid conscience and an ability to reason on one's own. Second, the individual who would be really free must be able to persevere and take responsibility for the consequences of his action; and this requires developing an unnatural strength of will and the steadfast ability to see an action through, no matter how painful the ramifications.

In a word, real freedom in association with other people requires what Rousseau called *virtue*. Writing late in his life, he put it with, for him, extreme severity: "There is no virtue in following one's penchants, and in giving oneself, when they carry us there, the pleasure of doing good." Rather, "virtue consists in conquering" our habitual impulses whenever "duty commands us to do that which it prescribes us."[91] The unselfconscious spontaneity of natural freedom cannot suffice. One sometimes needs throughtful stamina, the courage of one's convictions. That is what virtue means; and that is what is required to preserve freedom.

Yet Rousseau himself was plagued by faintheartedness on just this point. Despite his dreams of domestic and political situations where duty would not seem like a heteronomous command, he could not get himself to feel the call of conscience as anything but a dreadful imposition. To his own exasperation, duty for him remained dissociated from inclination; he could never happily identify with what his convictions prescribed. And so he confessed that being virtuous "is what I have known less how to do than any man in the world."[92] As a matter of personal taste, he had always indulged himself by enjoying a sort of natural freedom, even if only in his daydreams and wanderings alone.

But if this is Rousseau's most abject admission, his message for his audience remains fundamentally different. While musing on his apparent inconsistency in hoping that Emile will not become an author, he wrote in the margin of his own copy of the book that "I write not to excuse my faults, but in order to prevent my readers from imitating them."[93]

Freedom cannot survive without virtue. That is the conviction Rousseau repeats incessantly, with all the certainty of a man atoning for his errant ways. While the will may be innate, its vitality and strength—its capacity to do good—cannot be assumed, particularly in societies ruled by prejudice, needless passions, and despotic government. And when Rousseau is writing in this key, his thoughts on freedom limn a somber melody indeed:

I laugh at those debased peoples who, allowing themselves to be stirred up by rebels, dare to speak of freedom without having the slightest idea of its meaning, and who, with their hearts full of all the servile vices, imagine that, in order to be free, it is enough to be insubordinate. Proud and holy freedom! If those unfortunate people could only know you, if they realized

at what price you are won and preserved; if they felt how much more austere are your laws than the yoke of tyrants is heavy; their feeble souls,
enslaved by passions that would have to be suppressed, would fear you a
hundred times more than slavery; they would flee from you in terror, as
from a burden threatening to crush them.[94]

Still, this is but half the picture. To take Rousseau whole, we must keep in
mind the lost paradigm of natural freedom: for behind his plea for virtue remains
his hope for happiness. To compare his sobering sermon to the Poles with his
soothing idyll in the *Second Discourse* is to appreciate afresh the crosscurrents
within Rousseau's best thinking, the tensions held within his one overriding
concern, to be free and to remain free.

Rousseau, we might say, coined his own idea of freedom: to appraise its value,
we need to grasp both sides at a single glance. On the one side appears the
freedom of the natural man. It is associated with isolation and inclination, innocence and carefree abandon, indolence and tranquility, an unselfconscious and
spontaneous feeling of solitary wholeness, harboring a sentiment of unbounded
pleasure. On the other side appears the freedom of the civilized man and citizen.
It is associated with duty, virtue and thoughtful reflection, labor and struggle, a
communicable sense of right and wrong, a self-conscious and hardwon feeling
of shared harmony, reconciled to the inevitable griefs of this world.[95]

Rousseau's great pedagogical insight was to stimulate the happiness he ascribed to natural freedom in the service of civilizing freedom. By rooting virtue
in inclination, he wished to make doing good a penchant as well as a duty, an
occasion for satisfaction as well as the result of taking pains. The point of freedom was to be the pleasure it could bring. The Vicar in *Emile* put it this way:
"The supreme enjoyment is in satisfaction with oneself; it is in order to deserve
this satisfaction that we are placed on earth and endowed with freedom." But
elaborating this intuition carried with it a double temptation: to seek an immediate self-satisfaction by reverting, if only in reverie, to the carefree abandon of
natural freedom; and then to imagine that a harmonious world of civilized freedom could miraculously restore, in all of its pure delight, an undefiled innocence,
an uninhibited communion of self with world, a freedom in repose, a lasting
happiness—in other words, "all of the advantages of the natural state."[96] In
thinking through his own idea of freedom, Rousseau could not completely resist
either of these temptations.

The Self-Defeating Dream

On the island of St. Peter in the Lake of Bienne, in the Swiss canton of Berne
just over the border from Neuchâtel, at a time when he was besieged by detrac-
tors, his books burned, his ideas condemned, his name reviled, Jean-Jacques
Rousseau enjoyed several moments of insight that, in their intensity and importance, rivaled the moment of illumination he had experienced sixteen years ear-

lier on the road to Vincennes, when the image of Fabricius had prefigured the long train of ideas that followed. Now he experienced a different sort of revelation. He envisioned not an ancient hero, but personal fulfillment.

While confined to St. Peter, Rousseau devoted himself to botanizing, walks, and meditation. Watching from the banks of the lake while the waves lapped ashore, thinking idly on a bobbing boat as it drifted at the will of the water, he felt the storms within calmed, his thoughts transported, his soul ennobled. By his own strict standards, he had won the right to feel a certain satisfaction. He had published his boldest thoughts in *Emile* and the *Social Contract*. He had stood by his ideas in the *Letters Written from the Mountain*. He had dared to exercise publicly his freedom to think. And he had suffered for it. Only recently he had been forced to spend a night cowering under cover while a mob stoned his house. He had been driven from Neuchâtel in a hail of ill will.

But on this island, disaffected with his fatherland, removed from his friends, and thrown back upon himself, he also experienced as uncanny serenity, a strange sense of power, as if no limits could contain the abandonment he now savored. His reveries set his mind to wandering, their tranquil motion tracing an unlikely feeling, the images passing before him, first comforting and then elevating him, exalted before the picture he finally beheld within, a panorama of perfect happiness. For once, he felt able to say: "*I wish that this moment should last forever.*" Home at last in this unexpected glimpse of grace, he was sure that even "at the Bastille, and even in a cell where no object could strike my sight," he could still have "dreamed agreeably" this dream of perfection:

> If there is a state where the soul finds a position sufficiently solid to settle itself entirely and to gather together the whole of its being, without having need to recall the past or to project the future; where time is nothing for it, where the present lasts forever without marking its duration in any way and without any trace of succession, without any other sentiment of privation or delight, of pleasure or pain, of desire or fear, than this alone of our existence, and which this feeling alone can fill entirely; so long as this state lasts, whoever finds it can be called happy, not with an imperfect happiness, poor and relative, such as one finds in the pleasure of life, but with a sufficing happiness, perfect and full, which does not leave in the soul any void that it feels the need of filling.

In such a state, there would be "nothing external to oneself, nothing except oneself and one's own existence." One would live like the naturally free man "always carrying oneself, so to speak, entirely with one." And "so long as this state lasts, one suffices to oneself, like God."[97]

This, then, is what the perfect happiness of a perfect freedom means: it means the suspension of time in the eternal present; it means plenitude and fulfillment, sustained satisfaction; it means the omnipotent manifestation of goodness in the transparent exercise of will; ultimately, it means being able to lose oneself in a world of one's own, without difference or obstacles. "If I had remained free, obscure, isolated, as I was made to be, I should have done nothing but good, because I have not the germ of any harmful passion in my heart; if I were invisible and powerful as God, I should have been beneficent and good like Him." With a fervor Jean-Paul Sartre would understand, Rousseau seeks Being-in-and-for-itself: he wishes to escape the contingency of freedom by becoming his own foundation.[98]

But this is no politically innocent yearning. The desire for an everlasting presence, for plenitude and happiness, for the advent of a transparent merger of self with world, all are encoded at various levels in his political imagery. At the origins of society, in the golden age, when the first ties were established among families, when "the original festivals developed," when democracy was first instituted, "nothing marked the hours, nothing would oblige one to count them." The image of lasting social grace recurs in Rousseau's picture of Sparta: "Could I forget that in the very heart of Greece rose that City as renowned for its happy ignorance as for the wisdom of its Laws, that Republic of demi-Gods rather than men, so superior did their virtues seem to humanity? O Sparta!"[99] Faced with Rousseau's enthusiasm for that most durable of ancient republics, is it not possible to imagine a society of abiding freedom unselfconsciously exercised, by dint of a disciplined unanimity, an unflawed solidarity, an ironclad virtue?

Consider also the Alpine city of his dreams. In his Geneva, he would not only have been "isolated" and free, he would also have been at rest, able to enjoy a "peaceful and gentle life," invisible in his obscurity, unrent by conflicting impulses, having relations with "those like himself," self-absorbed in a self-confident freedom. His would be a city united only by the good will of free individuals, where the antiquity of the laws was a tribute to their wisdom, where the happiness of the citizens showed the depth of their satisfaction, where the differences between men melted in periodic floods of common feeling, in great festivals of shared ecstasy.[100]

He desired the satisfaction of a lasting freedom. To obtain it, he imagined creating an artificial world of pseudonatural freedom, where men would do good as if by instinct. Yet in pursuing this wish, his political thinking was caught in a cul-de-sac of his own design: 'If the laws of nations could, like those of nature, have an inflexibility that no human strength could ever conquer, dependence on men would then become dependence on things again, reuniting in the Republic all of the advantages of the natural state with all those of the civil state, joining freedom which keeps man exempt from vices to morality which raises him to virtue."[101]

But where conventions exhibit "an inflexibility which no human force can conquer," how can men exercise real freedom? Is the perfection of human freedom merely a willful mimicry of inanimate nature? Do the wisest human conventions constitute an unyielding barrier, as predictable in its effects on men as the motion of "dead and scattered matter"? Rousseau's wishful answers emerge only obliquely, in a train of troubling paradoxes.

He wants a simple, unambiguous situation, where the rules are clear, their force fixed, yet the feeling of free will unimpaired. Fascinated by self-sufficiency, fearful of outstripping his own powers, he was leery of the abundance that freedom makes feasible. He was suspicious of the surplus meaning produced by imagination, the surplus goods produced by labor. He envied a world of restricted goods and simple ideas. He would limit production and impose dogmas. Just as he sometimes tried to deny the unsettling novelty of his own thinking, so also he would try to stanch the flow of time in his invisible city, as if spontaneous motion were a wound to be treated with a tourniquet. The will must be contained within boundaries, its course made true by the force of laws, its steadfast goodness maintained through mutual supervision. If the civilized individual cannot have the world to himself, he can at least imagine a world where everyone would be as much like himself as possible; if he cannot find strength to express the good within, he can at least imagine a world where the laws would give him the strength from without; and if he cannot quite trust the powers at play in this world, he can at least imagine a transformed society where weakness and wrongdoing would not go undetected, because the will of each lies open to the gaze of all. The public eye becomes his surrogate for a hidden God.[102]

Thus far, Rousseau's political thinking has been cast in a sympathetic light. But it is well to mark that point where his desires intersect with our fears: for his image of democracy, in its daydream of perfect freedom, harbors the germ of a nightmare, a nightmare Rousseau briefly perceived for himself when he wrote of the Geneva that had burned his books: "In so small a State where no one can hide in a crowd, who will not live in eternal terror, and not feel at each moment the unhappiness of having his equals for masters?"[103]

Even in his imaginary Geneva, no one can hide in a crowd. To be in public is to be under surveillance. Festivals for men and women ready for marriage will occur in the presence of parents, so that "the eyes of the public are constantly open and upon them, forcing them to be reserved, modest, and to watch themselves closely." When Rousseau proposes a new constitution for Poland, he urges that they "arrange things so that all the Citizens, feeling themselves incessantly under the eyes of the public, can advance and succeed only by public favor. . . . Out of the effervescence excited by this common emulation will be born that patriotic intoxication which alone can raise men above themselves, and without which freedom is but an empty word, and legislation but a chimera." To insure the transparent exercise of a self-confident freedom, Rousseau can imagine stripping men naked and letting the gaze of others freeze their identity. "The good man is an Athlete who is pleased to compete in the nude."[104]

The desperation of this desire may be seen in a letter Rousseau wrote late in his life. On January 15, 1772, the former Citizen of Geneva addressed a request to M. de Sartine, the lieutenant of police in Paris, where Rousseau was then residing. After recounting the plots he felt unfolding around him, he told of the solace given him by the lieutenant's watchfulness. "Although I am by myself the least important of men, I have also, in my singular position, come to be assured that nothing of what I do or do not do escapes your attention: that is one of my surest consolations; and I must confess to you, Sir . . . the advantage of living under the eyes of an honest and vigilant magistrate." Along this path lies a madness that would surrender the self to certify its identity, to prove its innocence, to verify its virtue, to make its freedom unerring.[105]

Of course, the sanctions of the law and the attention of others may well reinforce the will and help a person to do what the law prescribes, what others want, and what he himself may wish to do. The cultivation of freedom, through an education like Emile's and a democracy like Geneva's, may engender satisfying habits, a sturdy group spirit, an inclination to do right by one's fellows. But no institution, no spartan regimen, no "honest and vigilant magistrate," no human authority, however wise and just, can promise an absolution of wrongdoing, the fulfillment of well-being, a final reconciliation of self and world, a salvation of the soul. The will, so long as it preserves the capacity for spontaneous motion, must frustrate any plans for a perfect happiness. To be free is to be open to change, through imagining things otherwise, through judging things differently, through acting to make of things something new. To act is to be capable of error. It is to face contradiction and contingency. It is to be human, with all of the liabilities that implies.

Insofar as Rousseau considered ways to abolish such liabilities, his thinking about freedom, in its impulse and orientation, creates a mirage, the illusion of lasting fulfillment just over the horizon. This wish, rarely stated explicitly, nevertheless haunts his reasoning and gives it an unspoken appeal. It is made to seem credible by the claim that men are naturally free, happy, and innocent. It is made to seem plausible by the prospect of recapturing, in just institutions, "all of the advantages of the natural state." And though Rousseau did not go chasing after this mirage directly, the illusion of a millennial fulfillment was sometimes strong enough to lead him momentarily astray, focusing his thoughts about freedom through his wish that this power of spontaneous motion, standing firm, cease its endless toiling and deliver us back to a state of timeless grace.[106]

It is an understandable wish: Rousseau is not the first person to draw back before the hazards of being free, anxious as well as exhilarated. It is perhaps even a noble wish: his vision of an eschatological Parousia has its lofty antecedents, its well-intentioned successors. But his longing for a lasting fulfillment is a mirage nonetheless: an illusion nourished on contradiction, it is fruitless in its unreality, impossible under even the best of circumstances, at least for mere mortals.[107] By pursuing this particular chimera, we would play false Rousseau's greatest hopes—hopes for a *human* freedom that are still worth pondering today.

Freedom and Democracy

It seems, then, that Rousseau was wrong. But he was also right. The perfectly happy freedom he envisioned he also knew to be impossible. The reversion in reverie to a kind of natural freedom could bring only passing relief from the cares of this world. Even the wisest of institutions could at best facilitate a man's freedom, not lift its burdens entirely.

Besides, a state of truly changeless grace would be boring, a colorless grey on grey, a form of living death. In *La Nouvelle Héloïse*, at just the moment when Julie appears to have won fulfillment, she shoves it aside: "Unhappy is he who has nothing more to desire! It is as if he had lost everything he possessed." In his own daydreams of perfect happiness, Rousseau himself relished the continuing pleasures of spontaneous motion, the unpredictable sense of floating free: "Without movement, life itself is only a lethargy. . . . An absolute silence leads to sadness. It offers us an image of death. Then the help of lighthearted imagination is necessary and presents itself naturally to those whom Heaven has gratified with it. The movement which does not come from without, then, is made within us." But to say this is to gainsay the permanence of our pleasure, for our greatest delight comes from the same gliding freedom that restlessly removes lasting fulfillment from our grasp. In the lives of men, declares the tutor to Emile, "Everything is finite and fleeting. . . . Happiness leaves us, or we leave it." [108]

Well-being cannot last forever. Even the freedom of the natural man Rousseau called "stormy." The enjoyment of satisfaction and repose may be among the momentary fruits of our freedom, but they are not a part of its motile essence. As our author once avowed, "A little agitation gives vitality to souls, and it is not so much peace as freedom that makes the species truly prosper." [109]

Rousseau says all this. He must simply be held to it. His motto for democracy is worth recalling: *Malo periculosam libertatem quam quietum servitium.*—"I prefer a perilous freedom to a tranquil servitude." He had similar words for those alarmed by his ideas in the *Social Contract*: "It is necessary to worry less about authority and more about freedom." Sometimes a choice must even be made between the serene rule of entrenched order and the uncertain dominion of a newfound freedom. "Some men," Rousseau cautioned, "would like to combine the peace of despotism with the sweets of freedom. I fear that they seek contradictory things. Repose and freedom seem to me incompatible; it is necessary to make a choice." [110]

So let us be resolute in choosing a "perilous freedom," let us forgo pursuing the fatal splendors of a perfectly happy pseudonatural freedom, and let us conclude by remembering how Rousseau himself thought that "the sweets" of this flawed but civilized freedom might be obtained through society, rather than in spite of it.

The foundation was to be men of virtue, the framework legitimate laws. The heart would be an association of citizens united by shared interests and animated by a general will. But there was a condition attached to preserving such a civilized freedom. "It is not enough for everyone to be subject to the general will," it is not enough for a beneficent government to execute laws that allow the members of the community to enjoy well-being unselfconsciously. To cultivate a vital will in common, all must participate actively in elucidating its scope and character. Both civic virtue and the legitimacy of the laws depend on vesting ultimate power in periodic assemblies of the people. [111]

"The instant the People is legitimately assembled as a Sovereign body, all jurisdiction of Government ceases, the executive power is suspended, and the person of the least Citizen is as sacred and inviolable as that of the first Magistrate." As a citizen of such a sovereign, each person is empowered to help make the laws and to oversee their execution. "As long as subjects are subordinated only to such conventions," they may be reasonably certain that their wants are determined without distortion, that the laws they endorse are impersonally administered. Then "they do not obey anyone, but solely their own will." [112]

In the context of such institutions, "the aversion to novelty is generally well founded." A willing identification with conscientious decisions made cooperatively is to be expected: few men want to disrupt a world they feel happy to call their own. Yet a truly free people nonetheless retains the capacity not only to elect and dismiss officials at will, not only to exchange pledges of continuing good faith in a common framework, but also to change entirely the form of government, to transform the institutions of society, to reject old laws and pass new ones. Safeguarding this capacity preserves the integrity of civic freedom and reminds any government that its power derives from and is always revocable by one superior power alone: the people. Protecting their collective ability to begin anew is the only reason why it should seem "absurd"—not impossible—for a general will "to give itself chains for the future." For thoughtful citizens enjoying a real freedom, however, any such alienation of ongoing sovereignty would be unthinkable—as unthinkable as a renunciation of their own free will. [113]

The possibility of change is why Rousseau's motto for democracy is apt. It is why freedom may be perilous. It is also why the instant a "people promises simply to obey," "the instant the Government usurps sovereignty," or "the instant a People choose Representatives," the free state is dissolved, "it is no longer free, it no longer exists. . . . As soon as someone says, *What do I care?* about the affairs of State, the State should be considered lost. . . . The instant there is a master, there is no longer a Sovereign, and from then on the body politic is destroyed. . . . The social compact is broken, and all the simple Citizens, by right recovering their natural freedom, are forced but not obligated to obey." [114]

As Rousseau well knew, civil freedom is no imperative realized inevitably in the course of events. It is no rule inscribed unambiguously in the nature of things. On the contrary. To judge from existing states, it is clear that the cooperative exercise of freedom, in Rousseau's terms, is quite needless. However helpful some measure of consent may be, inertia and the diversions of affluence, fraud and the appearance of fairness, cynicism and the dissipation of moral feeling, fear and the surveillance of the police, all are quite sufficient to insure obedience, tranquility, and even the semblance of lawful order.

Faced with such facts, Rousseau himself turned inward. Certain of the freedom of his own will and convinced of the fundamental importance of freedom for all men, he endeavored to shape a new language for politics, molded around the idea of a shared freedom, a general will. In pursuing this idea, he enlisted all of his considerable resources as a writer to persuade, convince, convert. In a sense, it is one mark of his triumph that the images he fashioned, the ideas he labored to make clear, may lead us to conclusions that strike the modern reader as truisms, an unsurprising confirmation of what we today think we have known all along: for example, that freedom justifies democracy.

Yet there is really nothing at all self-evident about the articulation of Rousseau's master idea. The phenomenon of the will remains enigmatic, his effort to define its possibilities incomplete.[115] That the free will is innately good seems dubious. That a perfect freedom might secure a perfect happiness seems illusory, even to Rousseau himself, though the wish may remain.

Rousseau's cathedral of concepts nevertheless remains an imposing edifice, whether we are looking at its unfamiliar floor plan or its commonly admired spires. Designed with the utmost seriousness and erected with genuine artistry, its beauty is not only a solace to Rousseau's moral man exiled in a hostile world, but also a monument to one sort of invisible city, with its reasons as well as its charms. For *if* we could agree that the free will, however enigmatic, is an idea that usefully circumscribes the evanescent power that distinguishes our species from all others, then we might also agree that a democratic sovereign, on something like Rousseau's terms, can lay a special claim to protecting that power and allowing it to prosper, creating from our common freedom a common capacity to do good and to forebear doing wrong, an enduring ability to bring pleasure more often than pain.

Realizing the fruits of our freedom, Rousseau conjectured, depends on mobilizing the will of each to clear, through acting and thinking, a common ground; to affirm, through a self-conscious assent to laws, a common framework; to preserve, through joint effort and individual labor, an association of independent households; and thus to secure, through a cooperation that preserves privacy, a setting appropriate to the uncoerced self-development of every single person. By showing respect for the free will in general, such a community might cultivate in all individuals the best that each, with the help of others, could become.

Freedom thus justifies democracy. But the freedom at issue is unsettling, contingent, "perilous," a capacity susceptible to error as well as alteration, a source of turbulence as well as contentment. And the democracy thus justified is simple and straightforward, built around a sovereign assembly of all citizens.

So what Rousseau found true is not a truism, after all. Instead, his idea of civic freedom seems simply an impractical ideal. But it was a possibility that he thought might be realized in Geneva; it is the great hope still conveyed in his images; and it is the logical result of his own best reasoning. Wanting to give full scope to a civilized freedom, Rousseau foresaw not a monarchy, not an aristocracy, not even a mixed republic. He imagined a new form of direct democracy.

EPILOGUE

Democracy After Rousseau

W HILE HE was First Consul, Napoleon visited the site of Rousseau's original grave, on Stanislas Girardin's property at Ermenonville. According to Girardin, the following conversation took place:

When he reached the Isle of Poplars, Bonaparte stepped in front of Jean-Jacques' tomb and said, "It would have been better for the peace of France if this man had never lived." — "And why, Citizen Consul?" — "It was he who prepared the French Revolution." — "I should have thought, Citizen Consul, that it was not for you to complain of the Revolution." — "Well," he replied, "the future will tell us whether it would have been better if neither I nor Rousseau had ever lived." And he resumed his walk with a thoughtful air.[1]

Given the shape of our history, such pensiveness does not seem misplaced. Nor was Napoleon mistaken in his estimate of Rousseau's importance. Through the revolution that used him to define itself, the Citizen of Geneva helped transform the discourse and avowed destiny of politics, with mixed results that have yet to run their course.

He straddles at least one great divide in these developments. Before Rousseau, democracy was, at best, an admirable but obsolete pure form of government, generally of interest only to students of jurisprudence. After him, it became a name for popular sovereignty, extending to all the promise of a personally fulfilling freedom, exercised in cooperation with others. Once a broad audience had identified its political hopes in Rousseau's terms, the meaning and appeal of self-rule would never be quite the same.[2]

Formerly the picture of disunity and decadence, of licence and mob rule, democracy now connoted harmony and regeneration, the true order of legitimate laws. Formerly the home of immoderate and unhappy souls, their passions outrunning their strength and understanding, democracy at its limit now became the home of whole men, unalienated in their enjoyment of a thoughtful independence, in effective control of their powers, each able to satisfy his wants with self-confidence. In Rousseau, the idea of democracy finally found an able and eloquent advocate, a philospher dedicated to the ideal of self-development. Switzerland joined Athens as a model of civic freedom, while Geneva joined Sparta as a model of civic virtue. No merely picturesque panorama, Rousseau's Alpine imagery helped communicate an epochal transvaluation, rooted in a personal conviction of universal import: all human beings possess, in their own free will, the capacity and the desire for goodness essential to govern themselves. The "democratic Constitution" could now be called the "Masterpiece of the political art."[3]

Of course, many details in Rousseau's vision—the rustic patriarch working the fields, say—do not seem particularly "democratic" to a contemporary reader. His idea of democracy stands at some distance from ideas common today. Rousseau could also be as blind to prejudice as any man. He did not, for example, question whether relations within the family might be based on something more than sentiment, whether the will of women might merit a wider field of sovereignty, too. He did not imagine any ways beyond the family to establish frontiers of privacy within a community.[4] What matters today, though, are not so much the specifics of Rousseau's vision, though many of these doubtless account for his popularity two hundred years ago. What still matter are the abstract ideas conveyed *through* his images, the inchoate longing aroused by them. The figure of the patriarchal farmer suggests not only hierarchical command, but also self-reliance, evoking the notion of mastery in a sphere of one's own—no trivial idea and certainly no obsolete aspiration, either for men or for women.

Because so many of the desires he expressed remain unmet, the principles at play in Rousseau's work offer a focus for regrets that might otherwise remain diffused, amorphous, unfelt. This is not really surprising. Despite all the cautions cloistering his own wishes, the idea of democracy contained in his writing still harbors the force of a revelation. Even if we were to decide that his vision of politics was the illusion of an epoch, Rousseau could at least show us the dimensions of our disenchantment—for we all live in the shadow of his dream, in democracies ostensibly dedicated to the freedom and well-being of each individual.

In this respect, the French Revolution has played a major role in determining how we can read Rousseau. The event illuminates the text—for it was the Revolution, after all, which forced the idea of democracy onto the agenda of modern history. It did so, as we have seen, not in the sense that the revolutionary generation enacted a plot outlined in the *Social Contract*, but rather in the sense that its actions made political ideas like Rousseau's, with analogous possibilities and contradictions, come vividly to life, exposing their promise and risks for all to see. Yet the text also illuminates the event—for it was Rousseau, after all, who became the oracle of the Revolution. While the programs of Robespierre and the sans-culottes prefigure the structure and aims of subsequent democratic movements, the language they both used belongs, indirectly, to the thinker; and it is Rousseau who most clearly reveals the assumptions and limits of these first practical efforts to define the meaning of a modern democracy.

Rousseau's links with the French Revolution have not generally been accounted to his credit. Even sympathetic Marxists are inclined to dismiss him as a regressive theorist of the petit-bourgeoisie, his agrarian ideals fated for failure. Conservatives have long suspected him of demagogic ambitions; more recently, he has been denounced as the architect of a "totalitarian democracy" made all too real in the repressive policies of Robespierre and his colleagues. Whether treated as the representative of a class in decline or the prophet of Stalin's Russia, Rousseau appears as a mere ideologist, his thinking an index of a doomed past or the augury of a grim future.[5]

Faced with such criticism, it would not be hard to show that Rousseau himself was no myopic moralist, unwittingly struggling against the tides of history. If progress simply meant a growing supply of material goods, he was quite reasonably against it, believing that happiness had nothing to do with a proliferation of wants. Similarly, it would not be hard to show that he was no aspiring tyrant, eager to stamp a new order on unyielding human subjects: writing against absolutism in France and oligarchy in Geneva, he rejected the legislative authority of any leader or elite, whether exercised in the name of God or in the name of a people.

Such rejoinders miss the point, however. They make it seem as if the meaning of a political text could be fixed once and for all and then insured against the acts of all those inspired to follow in its traces. Leszek Kolakowski has put it this way:

> We may . . . be certain in advance that no political or religious movement is a perfect expression of that movement's 'essence' as laid down in its sacred writings; on the other hand, these writings are not merely passive, but exercise an influence of their own on the course of the movement. What normally happens is that the social forces which make themselves the representatives of a given ideology are stronger than that ideology, but are to some extent dependent on its tradition. The problem facing the historian of ideas, therefore, does not consist in comparing the 'essence' of a particular idea with its practical 'existence' in terms of social movements. The question is rather how, and as a result of what circumstances, the original idea came to serve as a rallying point for so many different and mutually hostile forces; or what were the ambiguities and conflicting tendencies in the idea itself which led to its developing as it did?[6]

We have examined the ambiguities of the *Social Contract*; and we have explored the conflicting tendencies at work in Rousseau's idea of freedom. Such ambiguities and conflicting tendencies go a long way toward making sense of the multifaceted uses to which his thinking was put during the French Revolution. Prophetic, regressive, unrealistic, a dictator wishing to recast society at will, a stoic clinging to the past, a loser hopelessly tilting at windmills, Rousseau in his own way, at various moments, was all these things, and much more besides.

But let us look a little more closely at the main currents of democratic practice as they have emerged in the wake of a transvaluation thus charged with internal tensions. We have already seen how democracy arose as an articulate ideal during the course of the French Revolution. In 1792, after rejecting a "simple democracy" like that of the ancient Athenians, Tom Paine, in *The Rights of Man*, his influential pamphlet defending the Revolution, endorsed something new: *representative* democracy as the best form of republican government. In 1794, Robespierre made a similar point: a legitimate democracy must be representative, just as a legitimate republic must be democratic.[7]

During the Revolution, there thus appears a new sense of democracy: it becomes a synonym for a popularly elected representative government. However, alongside this familiar understanding (first broached, in different terms, during the American Revolution), there also appear two other conceptions. The sansculottes, who practiced their own form of direct democracy, demanded that popular sovereignty be considered inalienable and ongoing. And Robespierre, in opposing these demands, defended the need, in a democratic revolution, for dictatorship and terror.

What we find inscribed in the course of these events are three divergent definitions of democracy, each of them in some measure indebted to Rousseau's transvaluation: representative democracy, dictatorial democracy, and direct democracy.

Representative democracy requires the abolition of feudal privilege and the institution of equality before the law. It is constituted through the election by universal suffrage of representatives to a national legislative assembly, empowered to make laws in the name of a people. Such a form of democracy is practicable on the scale of a nation-state, provided a people is unified through patriotic enthusiasm and a sense of cultural identity. (Something like this prospect can be found in Rousseau's "Considerations on the Government of Poland.")[8]

A dictatorial democracy concentrates the power of government in the hands of one man or a cadre of enlightened leaders. This power is to be temporary, used only to defeat the enemies of a popular revolution, while transforming the people themselves into dutiful citizens. For this task, however, few means are considered unfit: purges as well as plebiscites, public punishments as well as patriotic festivals—all may help to force a mass reformation, cleansing human nature of its impurities and making men fit for a more pacific form of democracy. (Something like this prospect can be found in Rousseau's image of the great Legislator.)[9]

Finally, a direct democracy, through local assemblies and by the election of revocable delegates to regional and national assemblies, aims to realize lawmaking as an activity undertaken by the people themselves. Here solidarity is rooted in a feeling of affection for those who are nearest, regarded as free men and equals, while the idea of the nation is tied to a federation of cities and rural regions, allowing the devolution of power to neighborhood groups. (Something like this prospect can be found in Rousseau's idea of inalienable sovereignty.)[10]

For the West, the decisive current of democratic practice—leading to the triumph of representative democracy—can be traced back through Robespierre's defense of a national assembly elected by universal suffrage as the only feasible form of modern democracy. At first, the connection between this idea and the Jacobin terror compromised its attractiveness, particularly to respectable reformers in post-Napoleonic Europe. Among moderate men of conscience, repelled by the violence of year II, it became a commonplace to reject Rousseau, Robespierre, and democracy in a single breath. As Benjamin Constant put it, the leaders of the Revolution, "seized" by the words of Rousseau, "embraced philosophy as a prejudice, and democracy as a fanaticism."[11]

Only gradually did the idea of representative democracy become disentangled from this web of frightening associations. It helped that Englishmen like Jeremy Bentham and James Mill came to regard universal suffrage and a radical understanding of parliamentary representation as the keys to political reform. It also helped to have the relatively serene example of self-government in the United States, although its experiment in republican liberty still was not generally called a democracy.[12]

The work of theory that made a difference in this context was Alexis de Tocqueville's *Democracy in America*. It was Tocqueville who most boldly separated the fate of representative democracy from the French Revolution, linking its essential possibilities instead to the experience of the United States. In the process, he cleared the way for a new view of democracy. The choice irrevocably posed by the French Revolution was, according to him, simple: "democratic liberty or democratic tyranny." Thus far, "Democracy has been left to its wild instincts; it has grown up like those children deprived of parental care who educate themselves in the city streets." The Swiss model was no help in this regard. In Tocqueville's opinion, "The pure democracies of Switzerland belong to another age; they can teach us nothing useful for the present or future." It is a tacit tribute to Rousseau's influence that, only by disarming the two most prominent aspects of his legacy, could Tocqueville present the American constitution as an object lesson in how "the most powerful, intelligent, and moral classes of the nation" might tame democracy, "to gain control of it in order to direct it." Tocqueville, in other words, made democracy safe for liberalism. The effect of his work, published in 1835 and 1840, was immediate. In his footsteps followed John Stuart Mill and a flock of others, anxious to temper the rising pressure for self-government, lest a new "tyranny of the majority" result.[13]

In the period between 1848 and World War I, the liberal idea of democracy gradually took shape, in the face of popular struggles to extend the suffrage and limit the influence of wealth and in view of official efforts to exploit nationalism and whip up enthusiasm for imperial adventures. With the approach of World War II, representative democracy was made to seem still more attractive, by contrast with a bleak set of new alternatives: in the aftermath of monarchy and aristocracy appeared the new forms of fascism and Stalinism, or, more generally, "the totalitarian state."[14]

The second main current of democratic practice—leading to the victory of a dictatorial democracy—can be traced back through the reign of terror defended by Robespierre. Near this source stands Gracchus Babeuf, a man inspired by the heroism of the Incorruptible, the aspirations of the sans-culottes, and the Rousseauist theories of his associate Sylvain Maréchal. In 1795, Babeuf and his comrades organized a covert "Conspiracy for Equality" to carry forward the work of the Revolution. They blamed the death of Robespierre and the defeat of his program not only on the treachery of the government, but also on the disunity of the people. The lesson to be learned was that democracy, if it were ever to be realized, required concerted action by a brave, bold, and virtuous elite, able to overturn government tyranny and then to exercise, as a temporary purgative, a vigorous dictatorial authority. The dictatorship was designed to help a corrupt people restore themselves to goodness, while conquering their enemies through the unblinking use of violence. Though Babeuf's immediate goal was to implement the Constitution of 1793, he gave an unprecedented prominence in his program to the redistribution of wealth: justice would prevail only if all men were allotted equal portions of property. Babeuf himself favored some form of communal ownership. But the ultimate aim was moral regeneration, a regeneration to be effected and preserved through direct popular sovereignty, a uniform public education, the dismantling of large cities, the rise of communal festivals, and the institution of new civic religion.[15]

Babeuf never came close to putting his plans into practice. He was arrested and, after a show trial, executed in 1797. But the publication in 1828 of a *History of Babeuf's Conspiracy for Equality*, written by Philippe-Michel Buonarroti, a minor member of the conspiracy, rekindled the memory of Robespierre. Buonarroti treated Babeuf as Robespierre's authentic heir and presented both as martyrs for a coming era of democratic communism. In 1832, Buonarroti's path crossed that of a younger man named Auguste Blanqui, when both were members of a secret society called *Les Amis du Peuple*. Symbolically at least, the legacy was handed down: Blanqui became the most feared master of conspiracy and insurrection in nineteenth-century Europe. Through him, the idea of a democratic dictatorship entered the mainstream of the European socialist tradition. It was thus available for Lenin's use a half-century later, when he evaluated the tactics open to the Russian socialist movement. After the Russian Revolution of 1917, however, his Bolsheviks introduced a new element: the preservation of a *permanent* "revolutionary-democratic dictatorship."[16]

The third idea of democracy has not been so successful. The most obscure current of modern democratic practice—which points toward a federal alliance of direct democracies—can be traced back through the sans-culottes institutions of year II. In a broken arch, there extends a discontinuous tradition of direct democratic action, running from 1794 through the great Parisian uprisings of 1830 and 1848 to the Paris Commune of 1871. In defeat, the Commune became an example for socialists of all stripes, anarchists as well as Marxists. Thirty-four years later, efforts at direct self-government unexpectedly reappeared in Russia, in the form of the soviets of 1905, a form revived in the revolution of 1917. Linked by radical publicists with the Paris Commune and upheld as the true model of socialist democracy, the soviets after World War I inspired a number of workers' councils in Hungary, Germany, and Italy. There have been subsequent attempts at direct self-rule in Spain in 1936, in the anarchist communes; and in Hungary in 1956, in the workers' councils of Budapest.[17]

Marxists, starting with Marx himself, have apotheosized the Paris Commune of 1871. A number of socialist writers have tried to develop the principles implicit in such efforts into a modern theory of direct democracy. In *On Revolution*, Hannah Arendt commemorated these institutions of public freedom. Yet this current of democratic practice remains curiously neglected, as if such instances of active popular sovereignty were, in Arendt's words, "a romantic dream, some sort of fantastic utopia come true for a fleeting moment to show, as it were, the hopelessly romantic yearnings of the people, who apparently did not yet know the true facts of life."[18] Beset by enemies on the right and jealous leaders on the left, these revolutionary efforts at self-rule have all failed to survive the storms of violence they helped unleash.

Among orthodox Marxists as well as sensible liberals, the assumption remains that the common people, left to their own devices and inflamed by fantasies of a pure democracy, are out of step with the implacable imperatives of history, at odds with the need for expert leadership, a shapeless and potentially dangerous mass requiring discipline, enlightenment, and forceful organization. Distrustful of ordinary actors, the managers of the existing democracies command the political stage, ruling on behalf of a "sovereign people" who, in fact, are still ruled over.[19]

Walter Benjamin once wrote that the historian must "seize hold of a memory as it flashes up at a moment of danger. . . . In every era the attempt must be made anew to wrest tradition away from a conformism that is about to overpower it."[20] And so it is with democracy in the wake of Rousseau's transvaluation. What at the outset seemed puzzling, provocative, and even revolutionary, has since become banal, the stuff of everyday prejudice, an ornament for patriotic rhetoric, and, in some countries, just another name for despotism.

And yet merely to survey the divergent fates of three divergent definitions of democracy is to pose anew the question of what democracy can possibly mean. To ask that question is not to argue for a consensus on the definition of a justifiably contested term. Rather, it is to ask all who still speak of democracy to say just what they mean and why; and it is to require of ourselves greater clarity and skepticism about what principles of right may actually take shape in modern society. In this situation, reading Rousseau engenders a certain sobriety about the conditions necessary to delimit and develop an unsettling as well as satisfying freedom; a certain forthrightness about the radically unprecedented institutions at issue in saying, and meaning, that *this* contingent freedom justifies democracy; a certain honesty about the host of difficulties involved in making a practical commitment out of this conviction.

If we try to think through the possible significance of democracy today, Rousseau nevertheless matters a great deal, not least because he stands at the beginning. First in Geneva and then in Paris in 1789 and after, democracy for the first time in two thousand years left the study for the streets, no longer a technical term but once more a living word for the right and power of a people to rule itself. What was won and what was utlimately lost in that migration may be grasped by consulting the thinker who was instrumental in allowing actors in this drama to understand themselves as democrats, struggling to obtain a legitimate freedom. Above all, reading Rousseau can remind us that the advocates of inalienable popular sovereignty lost, by force of arms. In the era of democratic revolutions, the proponents of simple democracy did not win, they were defeated—a defeat made all the more bitter when the victors expropriated the language of the vanquished.

Because Rousseau wrote before that conquest, his thinking can still show us what was at stake. If we discover the importance of a direct involvement in lawmaking to the reality of being free in society, we may also appreciate the risks in treating popular sovereignty as a myth estranged from the very citizens the original idea was designed to empower. If we discover the need to train a people in self-rule, we may also appreciate the perils in letting one group arrogate to itself the powers of a pedagogical demiurge, in the name of some higher harmony. If we discover the significance of feeling able to do as one wants for fostering a self-confident freedom, we may also appreciate the temptations of a covert manipulation promoted by the impossible promise of bestowing a habitual virtue, a tranquil liberty, a socialized salvation. Finally, if we discover the significance of solidarity for the feeling of shared freedom, we may also appreciate the threat in seeking absolute unity, a final end to alienation, a fixed reconciliation of self and society, at the cost, however unintentional, of stunting self-development, by shackling the spontaneous motion of each free will. For, in the most paradoxical reversal of all, Rousseau's self-defeating dream of a perfectly happy freedom takes us to the heart of a deadly ecstasy that would abolish the boundaries defining the free person as a unique individual, with a self worth expressing on its own terms, in activities that may be distinctive as well as typical, creative as well as customary, fallible as well as perfectible.

Rousseau, it is true, understood most of these dilemmas, but that scarcely removes the conflicting impulses contained within the words he struggled to reinvent. Though he cleared a powerful new perspective on politics, his outlook remains rooted in an open question: the question of free will and the possibilities uncovered through it. Insofar as the meaning of that premise can never finally be settled (each must explore it on his own), Rousseau's conclusions must be considered questionable, too. His understanding, like the sense of volition it is built upon, thus remains suspended in irresoluble ambiguities, oriented toward an uncertain eschatology motivated by despair as much as faith. Yet from the discrepancy between doubt and desire arise his own most characteristic images and ideas. Their tensions are what give his approach to politics its appeal and vitality, its depths and its dangers.

Such was the gift of his mind, unafraid to be moved by imagination, yet willing to let reasoning be one measure of his wishes. In the midst of a situation he perceived as infernal, he sifted through the scraps of his life, searching for signs of hope. Seeking a glimpse of a worldly redemption, he allowed himself to imagine a civilized freedom, a state of lasting happiness, a true democracy. By recording what he saw, he gave his images space, he made his ideas endure. Through the city he thus so vividly summoned, he engendered a new way of thinking, a new way of acting, and, above all, a new way of feeling. By conveying all this through his books, he performed the political duty he could never discharge in practice. His virtue was in writing, his courage in communicating a fantasy. By dreaming of himself as an ideal citizen of a Geneva that never was, he interpreted the world anew. And that is how Rousseau has changed it.

Abbreviations

French Texts of Rousseau

C Correspondance complète de Jean Jacques Rousseau. Ed. R. A. Leigh, 32 vols. to date (Geneva, 1965–   ).

D Oeuvres complètes de J.J. Rousseau, 17 vols. (Paris, 1834).

H Oeuvres complètes de J.J. Rousseau, 13 vols. (Paris, 1905).

P Jean-Jacques Rousseau: Oeuvres complètes, ed. Bernard Gagnebin and Marcel Raymond, 4 vols. to date (Paris, 1959–   ).

S Rousseau: Oeuvres complètes, ed. Michel Launay, 3 vols. to date (Paris, 1967–   ).

V The Political Writings of Jean Jacques Rousseau, ed. C. E. Vaughn, 2 vols. (Cambridge, 1915).

In all cases, roman numeral after abbreviation indicates volume number.

English Translations of Rousseau

CO The Confessions of Jean-Jacques Rousseau, trans. J. M. Cohen (Harmondsworth, 1953).

DS Jean-Jacques Rousseau: The First and Second Discourses, trans. Roger D. and Judith R. Masters (New York, 1964).

EM Jean-Jacques Rousseau: Emile, or On Education, trans. Allan Bloom (New York, 1979).

LA Politics and the Arts: Letter to M. d'Alembert on the Theatre, by Jean-Jacques Rousseau, trans. Allan Bloom (Ithaca, 1960).

NH La Nouvelle Héloïse: Julie, or the New Eloise. Letters of Two Lovers, Inhabitants of a Small Town at the Foot of the Alps, by Jean-Jacques Rousseau, trans. and abridged Judith H. McDowell (University Park, Penn., 1968).

OL On the Origin of Language: Two Essays by Jean-Jacques Rousseau and Johann Gottfried Herder, trans. John H. Moran and Alexander Gode (New York, 1966).

PW Rousseau: Political Writings, trans. Frederick Watkins (Edinburgh, 1953).

RS The Reveries of a Solitary, by Jean Jacques Rousseau, trans. John Gould Fletcher (New York, 1971).

SC Jean-Jacques Rousseau: On the Social Contract, with Geneva Manuscript and Political Economy, trans. Judith R. Masters (New York, 1978).

Other Works

ECS *Études sur le* Contrat social *de Jean-Jacques Rousseau,* Journées d'étude sur le *Contrat social,* Dijon, 1962 (Paris, 1964).
ROC *Oeuvres de Maximilien Robespierre,* ed. Société des études Robespierristes, 10 vols. (Paris, 1910–67).

Notes

Introduction

1. According to Alfred Cobban, the fable about Marat and the *Social Contract* originated with Mallet du Pan: see du Pan's *Mémoires* (Paris, 1851), p. 126n. The story of the festival in year II appears in Louis Trenard, "La diffusion du *Contrat social* (1762–1832)," in *ECS*, p. 446. The medallion is reproduced in *S* II, p. 576. For the disoriented dandy, see Gordon H. McNeil, "The Cult of Rousseau and the French Revolution," *Journal of the History of Ideas* (1945):204. For the quote about Castro, see Bernard Gagnebin's introduction to *P* III, p. xxvi. Rousseau even pops up in Mao's China: see Fredric Wakeman, Jr., *History and Will* (Berkeley, 1973), esp. ch. 4 on "The Great Legislator," pp. 43–59.
2. Jules Michelet, *Histoire de la Révolution française* (Paris, 1847–53), vol. I, pp. 59–60, quoted by Cobban, *Aspects of the French Revolution* (London, 1971), p. 19. Lord Acton, *Lectures on the French Revolution*, ed. John Neville Figgis and Reginald Vere Laurence (New York, 1959), pp. 15–16. George H. Sabine, *History of Political Thought* (New York, 1961), p. 570.
3. Bertrand de Jouvenel, "Rousseau's Theory of the Forms of Government," in *Hobbes and Rousseau*, ed. Maurice Cranston and R. S. Peters (Garden City, 1972), p. 487. See Jean Starobinski, *J-J Rousseau: la transparence et l'obstacle* (Paris, 1971), pp. 123, 125–26; Judith Shklar, *Men and Citizens* (Cambridge, 1969), esp. ch. 1, "Two Journeys to Utopia," pp. 1–32, and ch. 4, "Images of Authority," pp. 127–64; Cobban, *Rousseau and the Modern State* (London, 1964), pp. 20–22; idem, *Aspects*, p. 22; Joan McDonald, *Rousseau and the French Revolution 1762–91* (London, 1965).
4. *On the Social Contract; or, Principles of Political Right*, bk. III, ch. 4; *P* III, p. 406; *SC*, p. 85.
5. See François Furet, *Interpreting the French Revolution*, trans. Forster (Cambridge, 1981), p. 204.
6. Evidence for these assertions appears below: see chs. 2, 5, 6, and epilogue. Alcibiades calls Athenian democracy a "patent absurdity" in Thucydides, *The Peloponnesian War*, 6.89. See also A. H. M. Jones, "The Athenian Democracy and its Critics," in *Athenian Democracy* (Oxford, 1969), pp. 41–72. For the con-

ventional view of democratic development, see, e.g., Charles M. Sherover, ed., *The Development of the Democratic Idea* (New York, 1974). Sherover's anthology includes excerpts from Pericles, Aristotle, Cicero, Machiavelli, Locke, Montesquieu, Rousseau, Jefferson, Kant, Madison, J. S. Mill, T. H. Green, and John Dewey. A more sophisticated reconstruction of this kind of a tradition appears in the writings of the British Whig historians of political thought, such as Ernest Barker, A. D. Lindsay, and Harold Laski.

Chapter 1. *The Rhetoric of Reverie*

1. *Rousseau, Judge of Jean-Jacques*, II; *P* I, p. 815. "Letters to Malesherbes," 2; *P* I, pp. 1135–36.
2. *The Confessions*, bk. VIII; *P* I, p. 351; *CO*, p. 328. "Letters to Malesherbes," 2; *P* I, p. 1136. *Discourse on the Sciences and Arts*, pt. I; *P* III, p. 14; *DS*, p. 45. For the character of Fabricius, see Plutarch, *The Lives of the Noble Greeks and Romans*, trans. John Dryden (New York, n.d.), pp. 481–82.
3. *Confessions*, bk. IV; *P* I, pp. 159–60; *CO*, p. 155. *Emile, or On Education*, bk. IV; *P* IV, p. 548; *EM*, p. 253.
4. *Emile*, bk. II; *P* I, p. 344; *EM*, p. 107.
5. On Rousseau's recourse to Plato, see M. J. Silverthorne, "Rousseau's Plato," *Studies on Voltaire and the Eighteenth Century* 116 (1973):235–49. The word *idea* is itself of Platonic origin: see the entry for it in the *Oxford English Dictionary* and Erwin Panofsky, *Idea: a Concept in Art Theory*, trans. Joseph J. S. Peake (New York, 1974).
6. See Plato, *Republic*, 509d–511c. (For the text of the *Republic*, I am relying on Allan Bloom's English translation [New York, 1968].) Cf. Frances A. Yates, *The Art of Memory* (Chicago, 1966), esp. pp. 27–49.
7. *Contract*, bk. II, ch. 7; *P* III, p. 383; *SC*, p. 69.
8. The quote is from Jean Le Rond d'Alembert, *Preliminary Discourse to the Encyclopedia of Diderot*, trans. Richard N. Schwab (Indianapolis, 1963), p. 51. Other accounts of imagination that I found useful in considering Rousseau include Kant's in the *Critique of Pure Reason*; F. C. Bartlett, *Remembering* (Cambridge, 1932); Paul Valéry, "Poetry and Abstract Thought," in *The Art of Poetry*, trans. Denise Folliot (New York, 1958); Jean-Paul Sartre, *The Psychology of Imagination*, trans. Bernard Frechtman (New York, 1966); Jean Starobinski, "L'empire de l'imaginaire," in *La relation critique* (Paris, 1970); Edward S. Casey, *Imagining* (Bloomington, 1976); Mary Warnock, *Imagination* (Berkeley, 1976); and Charles Rycroft, *The Innocence of Dreams* (New York, 1979).

For more on the imagination in Rousseau, see Marc Eigeldinger, *Jean-Jacques Rousseau et la réalité de l'imagination* (Neuchâtel, 1962); and Pierre Burgelin, *La philosophie de l'existence de J.-J. Rousseau* (Paris, 1952), esp. pp. 168–90. For a catalog of passages where Rousseau actually uses the words "*image*" and "*imagination*," see Léo and Michel Launay, *Le vocabulaire littéraire de Jean-Jacques Rousseau* (Geneva, 1979), pp. 347–67.

9. "Essay on the Origin of Languages, which treats of Melody and Musical Imitation," ch. 9; *D* II, p. 350; *OL*, p. 32. *Emile*, bk. II; *P* IV, p. 304; *EM*, p. 81. Ibid., bk. II; *P* IV, pp. 289–90; *EM*, p. 68 (*"fantasie"*—here translated always as "whim"—generally has a negative connotation in Rousseau, unlike *rêverie*).

10. *Rousseau, Judge*, II; *P* I, pp. 815–16.

11. *The Reveries of a Solitary Stroller*, VII; *P* I, pp. 1061–62; *RS*, pp. 136–37.

12. *Confessions*, bk. IV; *P* I, p. 163; *CO*, p. 158. On the etymology of *rêverie* and *rêver*, see Marcel Raymond's remarks in *P* I, pp. lxxv–lxxvi.

13. *Confessions*, bk. VIII; *P* I, p. 294; *CO*, p. 276. *On the Social Contract*, first version (hereafter cited as Geneva Ms.), bk. I, ch. 2; *P* III, pp. 284–85; *SC*, p. 160.

14. René Descartes, "Reply to the Second Set of Objections," in *The Philosophical Works*, trans. Haldane and Rose (Cambridge, 1911), vol. II, p. 52. Thomas Hobbes, *Leviathan*, pt. I, ch. 2. John Locke, *An Essay Concerning Human Understanding*, bk. III, ch. 10, sec. 34.

15. "Moral Letters," 3; *P* IV, pp. 1098–99. Ibid., 2; *P* IV, p. 1091. *Emile*, bk. IV; *P*, IV, p. 568; *EM*, p. 268.

16. *Narcisse*, preface; *P* II, pp. 963, 965.

17. Pascal, *Pensées*, edn. Lafuma, No. 512. Cf. ibid., no. 530: "All our reasoning comes down to surrendering to feeling (*sentiment*). But whim (*fantaisie*) is like and also unlike feeling, so that we cannot distinguish between these two contraries. One person says that my feeling is mere whim, another that his whim is feeling. It is necessary to have a rule. Reason is available but it is pliable to any sense. And thus there is no rule."

18. *Narcisse*, preface, *P* II, p. 959. Cf. *Emile*, bk. IV, p. 670; *EM*, p. 339. For *finesse* as a valued trait in Rousseau, see *Letter to M. d'Alembert on the Theater*; *D* I, p. 331; *DA*, p. 62.

19. *Emile*, bk. IV; *P* IV, pp. 645–46, 648, 651; *EM*, pp. 321, 323, 325. "Origin of Languages," ch. 1; *D* II, p. 330; *OL*, p. 8. Crucial to "guiding" imagination is leading an active and useful life, such as Emile's. See *Emile*, first version (Favre Ms.); *P* IV, p. 231: "It is above all by a flabby and sedentary life that the ardor of the senses is irritated. . . . It is from this disproportion between desire and strength that are forged the monsters of the imagination."

20. *Julie, or the New Héloïse*, second preface; *P* II, p. 21. "Theatrical Imitation"; *H* I, p. 358.

21. *Confessions*, bk, IV; *P* I, p. 174; *CO*, p. 169.

22. *Héloïse*, second preface; *P* II, p. 17. "Letters to Malesherbes," 3; *P* I, p. 1140. *Confessions*, bk. IX; *P* I, p. 427; *CO*, p. 398.

23. *Héloïse*, second preface; *P* II, p. 14. *Reveries*, V; *P* I, pp. 1048–49; *RS*, pp. 116–17. *Rousseau, Judge*, II; *P* I, pp. 815–16. "Letters to Malesherbes," 3; *P* I, p. 1140.

24. On the figurative origins of language, see "Origin of Languages," esp. chs. 1–3; *D* II, pp. 327–34; *OL*, pp. 5–13; and *Discourse on the Origin and Foundations of Inequality Among Men*, pt. I; *P* III, pp. 148–49; *DS*, pp. 122–23. Some ambiguity surrounds Rousseau's location of figural language at the origin: on this, see Paul De Man, *Allegories of Reading* (New Haven and London, 1979), pp. 146–

49. Rousseau's theory has been suggestively dissected in Jacques Derrida *Of Grammatology*, trans. Spivak (Baltimore, 1976).

25. "On Theatrical Imitation"; *H* I, p. 358 (cf. *Emile*, bk. IV; *P* IV, p. 126; *EM*, p. 307: "When Plato paints his imaginary man . . ."). "Moral Letters," 4; *P* IV, p. 1101. Plato seems to temper his antipathy to the irrational in *Phaedrus*, 244a–257b, where Socrates' remarks on madness and eros suggest a rather different perspective on Rousseau's enthusiasm for reverie; cf. *Timaeus*, 71d–72a.

26. See, e.g., *Emile*, bk. IV; *P* IV, p. 656; *EM*, p. 329: "What is true love if it is not a chimera? . . . If he [Emile] takes pleasure in the image" of true love, however, "he will soon hope that it has an original"—and thus search for a proper wife.

As these remarks about reverie and perfection may suggest, the imagination forms one precondition for the phenomenon of "perfectibility" discussed by Rousseau in the *Second Discourse*. Imagination allows the mind to project perfect possibilities into the future: "It concentrates in a single moment the times which are going to follow one another, and sees objects less as they will be than as it desires them because it is free to choose them." (*Emile*, bk. II; *P* IV, p. 418; *EM*, p. 158.) As we might expect, Rousseau attributes parallel paradoxes to perfectibility and the imagination. Thus, in *Inequality*, pt. I; *P* III, p. 142; *DS*, p. 115, we find that perfectibility contributes to man's "enlightenment and his errors, his vices and his virtues." Cf. the passage on imagination in *Rousseau, Judge*, II; *P* I, pp. 815–16. As we shall see, the paradoxes of imagination and perfectibility have a common ground: the free will.

27. Montaigne, *Essays*, trans. Frame (Stanford, 1958), p. 617 (bk. III, ch. 2).

28. "Political Fragments": "A Comparison Between the Two Republics of Sparta and Rome"; *P* III, pp. 538–39. Canceled variants appear in *V* I, pp. 314–15.

(1712–1754) *The City and the Citizen of Geneva*

1. Jean Le Rond d'Alembert, "Genève," in *Encyclopédie, ou Dictionnaire raisonné des sciences, des arts et des métiers, par une Société de gens de lettres* (Paris, 1751–65), hereafter cited as "Diderot's *Encyclopedia*." See Bloom's translation in *LA*, pp. 4–5, 139–48. For eighteenth-century Genevan politics, see R. R. Palmer, *The Age of the Democratic Revolution* (Princeton, 1959–64), vol. I, pp. 111–39; Gaston Vallette, *Jean-Jacques Rousseau Genevois* (Paris, 1911); John Stephenson Spink, *Jean-Jacques Rousseau et Genève* (Paris, 1934), a critical history that provided much of the factual material cited below; and Michel Launay, *Jean-Jacques Rousseau écrivain politique* (Grenoble, 1971), a scrupulous literary and class analysis of Rousseau's relation to Geneva. See also Guglielmo Ferrero, "Genève et le Contrat social," *Annales Jean-Jacques Rousseau*, vol. XXIII (Geneva, 1934), pp. 137–52; and the contemporary—and partisan—account by François d'Ivernois, *Tableau historique et politique de Révolution de Genève dans le dix-huitième siècle* (Geneva, 1782), pp. 173–204. For Genevan affairs generally, the standard modern reference is *Histoire de Genève des origines à 1798*, ed. Société d'histoire et d'archéologie de Genève (Geneva, 1951).

2. All preceding quotes are from d'Alembert, "Genève."

3. For the census of watchmakers, see Palmer, *Democratic Revolution*, vol. I, p. 128. The historian alluded to is Herbert Lüthy: see *P* III, p. clxi. For watchmaking in Geneva, see Antony Babel, *Histoire corporative d'horlogerie, de l'orfèvrerie et des industries annexes*, published as vol. XXXIII in the series *Mémoires et documents publiés par La Société d'histoire et d'archéologie de Genève* (Geneva, 1916).

4. From "Proposals of citizens" made in 1707, quoted in Spink, *Rousseau et Genève*, p. 14. On Fatio, see ibid., pp. 14–15; Launay, *Ecrivain politique*, pp. 19–20; and André Corbaz, *Pierre Fatio* (Geneva, 1913). Rousseau alludes to Fatio several times: see *Letters Written from the Mountain* VII; *P* III, p. 833; and ibid., IX; *P* III, p. 883.

5. Cited in Spink, *Rousseau et Genève*, p. 17.

6. Cited in Launay, *Ecrivain politique*, p. 61.

7. See Spink, *Rousseau et Genève*, pp. 19–23.

8. Cited in ibid., p. 23.

9. Cited in Launay, *Ecrivain politique*, p. 63.

10. On unrest in the militia, see ibid., p. 20n. On the Mediation of 1738, see Spink, *Rousseau et Genève*, pp. 25–28; and Palmer, *Democratic Revolution*, vol. I, pp. 127–29, 130 (on the "right of representation").

11. For Rousseau's childhood—and his life generally—see Maurice Cranston, *Jean-Jacques* (New York, 1983), pp. 9–29; and Jean Guehenno, *Jean-Jacques Rousseau*, trans. John and Doreen Weightman (New York, 1966), vol. I, pp. 3–17. Cf. *Confessions*, bk. I; *P* I, pp. 6–44; *CO*, pp. 17–51. On the literacy of the watchmakers, see Launay, *Ecrivain politique*, esp. pp. 24–25.

12. *Confessions*, bk. I; *P* I, pp. 8, 9; *CO*, pp. 19, 20.

13. See Guehenno, *Rousseau*, pp. 9–10; Launay, *Ecrivain politique*, pp. 17–18; and the remarks in *P* I, pp. 1240–41. Cf. *Confessions*, bk. I; *P* I, p. 12; *CO*, p. 23.

14. *Confessions*, bk. I; *P* I, p. 42; *CO*, p. 49. Cf. the remarks in *P* I, p. 1253.

15. *Confessions*, bk. I; *P* I, pp. 43–44; *CO*, pp. 50–51.

16. See ibid., bk. V; *P* I, p. 215; *CO*, p. 206; and ibid., bk. VI; *P* I, p. 246; *CO*, p. 234. On Barrillot, see *P* I, p. 1334.

17. Rousseau to baronne de Warens, July 24 or 26?, 1737; *C* I, p. 45. By law, Rousseau, as a lapsed Calvinist turned Catholic, was prohibited from appearing in Geneva: see *C* I, pp. 46–47, note e.

18. *Confessions*, bk. V; *P* I, p. 216; *CO*, p. 207.

19. "Epistle to M. Bordes"; *P* II, pp. 1130–33. With a population of roughly 100,000, Lyon was the second largest city in France (after Paris, with 500,000).

20. "Epistle to Monsieur Parisot"; *P* II, pp. 1136–44.

21. *Confessions*, bk. IV; *P* I, p. 152; *CO*, p. 148. Rousseau claims that the setting of *La Nouvelle Héloïse* was modeled on Vevey, a town in Vaud on the shores of Lake Léman. See ibid., bk. IX; *P* I, pp. 430–31; *CO*, p. 401.

22. For a sense of the contrast, compare the account of Geneva in Palmer, *Democratic Revolution*, pp. 111–12, 127–29, with the account of the Swiss canton of Raetia in Benjamin Barber, *The Death of Communal Liberty* (Princeton, 1974), esp. pp. 170–203. For more on Rousseau's early identification with Switzer-

land, see Launay, *Ecrivain politique*, pp. 74–77; and François Jost, *Jean-Jacques Rousseau Suisse* (Fribourg, 1961).

23. *Confessions*, bk. VIII; *P* I, p. 363; *CO*, p. 339.

24. Rousseau to Voltaire, January 30, 1750; *C* II, pp. 123–24. See also Cranston, *Jean-Jacques*, p. 235.

25. Voltaire to Rousseau, c. February 2, 1750; *C* II, p. 126.

26. *Narcisse*, preface; *P* II, p. 967. On the importance he attached to his early education, see *Confessions*, bk. VIII; *P* I, p. 356; *CO*, p. 332; upon hearing that his *First Discourse* had won the prize at Dijon, Rousseau found that "this newly reawakened all the ideas it had suggested to me, animated them with new force, and managed to set fermenting in my heart those first leavens of heroism and virtue that my father, my *patrie* and Plutarch had implanted there in infancy." Cf. *Sciences and Arts*, pt. II; *P* III, pp. 24–25n.; *DS*, p. 57n.

27. *Sciences and Arts*; *P* III, p. 1; *DS*, p. 31. The nature of the alternative is sketched by Rousseau in the last paragraph of the discourse: "O virtue! sublime science of simple souls. . . ." See ibid., pt. II; *P* III, p. 30; *DS*, p. 64.

28. Rousseau to Marcet de Mézières, May 28, 1751; *C* II, p. 154. On the attribution of the first Genevan edition of the *First Discourse*, see *S* II, p. 52n. On the legal question of whether Rousseau had any right to claim Citizenship, see *C* II, p. 126, note g. The moral weight Rousseau attached to the phrase "Citizen of Geneva" may be confirmed by his omission of it in 1761, when he was, in fact, a Genevan Citizen, from the title page of his novel, *La Nouvelle Héloïse*, a work he felt was unfit for his republican epigraph. See the comments in *Héloïse*, second preface; *P* II, esp. pp. 21, 27.

29. *Confessions*, bk. VIII; *P* I, p. 390; *CO*, p. 363. For Geneva as an ideal spot for political inquiry, see "From Jean-Jacques Rousseau, of Geneva. On the Response that has been made to his Discourse" (Response to Stanislas); *P* III, p. 43. Cf. the remarks in *P* III, p. 1261.

30. The published version of the dedication is signed "Chambéry, June 12, 1754"; *Inequality*, dedication; *P* III, p. 121; *DS*, p. 90. The biographer is Guéhenno, *Rousseau*, vol. I, p. 304. On the circumstances of the dedication, see *Confessions*, bk. VIII; *P* I, p. 392; *CO*, p. 365. Cf. the note in *P* III, pp. 1286–88. See also the circumstantial evidence that his dedication was complete before his arrival in Geneva, discussed in *C* III, pp. 17–18, note b. Rousseau was granted Citizenship in Geneva on August 1, 1754. The dedication and the *Second Discourse* were published in June, 1755. In the *Confessions*, bk. VIII; *P* I, p. 392; *CO*, p. 365, he remarks rather cryptically that he had signed the dedication in Chambéry "judging that it would be better so as to avoid all quibbling (*chicane*) to date it neither in France nor in Geneva."

31. On Rousseau's knowledge of Genevan politics in 1754, see Spink, *Rousseau et Genève*, p. 39. At Chambéry, Rousseau was not alone. His common law wife, Thérèse Levasseur, was with him and he was visiting Mme Warens, who had nurtured him through early manhood. See *Confessions*, bk. VIII; *P* I, p. 391; *CO*, pp. 364–65.

32. *Inequality*, dedication; *P* III, pp. 111, 115, 120–21; *DS*, pp. 78, 83, 90.

Chapter 2. *The Image of Democracy*

1. *Inequality*, dedication; *P* III, pp. 115, 111; *DS*, pp. 83, 79.
2. Ibid., *P* III, p. 113; *DS*, p. 81. *D'Alembert*; *D* I, p. 342; *LA*, p. 73. See also "Draft of a Constitution for Corsica"; *P* III, p. 906; *PW*, pp. 284–85: "Where cultivation is more awkward and requires more effort, the Government is Democratic."
3. "Moral Letters," 6; *P* IV, p. 1114.
4. *Héloïse*, pt. I, xxiii; *P* II, p. 79.
5. *Emile* bk. IV; *P* IV, p. 565; *EM*, p. 266. *Héloïse*, pt. I, xxiii; *P* II, p. 78; *NH*, p. 65. On the moral implications of the sublime, using the Swiss Alps as one illustration, cf. Immanuel Kant, *Critique of Judgment*, §29.
6. *Inequality*, dedication; *P* III, p. 115; *DS*, p. 83.
7. *Emile*, bk. V; *P* IV, p. 859; *EM*, p. 474. See also the fragment "On the *Patrie*"; *P* III, pp. 534–36. Cf. *Héloïse*, second preface; *P* II, p. 24.
8. *Inequality*, dedication; *P* III, pp. 119–20, 118; *DS*, pp. 89, 86–87. Cf. *Emile*, bk. I; *P* IV, pp. 245–46n.; *EM*, p. 37n.
9. *D'Alembert*; *D* I, p. 330; *LA*, pp. 61–62.
10. *Inequality*, pt. II; *P* III, p. 168; *DS*, pp. 146–47. *D'Alembert*; *D* I, p. 397; *LA*, p. 128.
11. "Corsica"; *P* III, p. 914; *PW*, p. 295. "Political Fragments"; *P* III, pp. 487–88.
12. *D'Alembert*; *D* I, pp. 397–98; LA, pp. 127–28. "Corsica"; *P* III, p. 914; *PW*, p. 295.
13. Plutarch, *The Lives*, p. 61 (on Lycurgus). For Plato's unconventional doctrines on women and the family, see *Republic*, 451c–461e.
14. *Emile*, bk. V; *P* IV, pp. 699–700; *EM*, pp. 362–63. *Inequality*, dedication; *P* III, p. 118; *DS*, p. 87.
15. *Héloïse*, pt. I, xxiii; *P* II, p. 81.
16. *Héloïse*, pt. V, ii; *P* II, pp. 527, 557; *NH*, p. 345.
17. *D'Alembert*; *D* I, p. 329; *LA*, p. 60.
18. Ibid., *D* I, pp. 329–30; *LA*, pp. 60–61. Rousseau's account is not wholly fanciful: independent observers also described the Swiss artisan as a jack-of-all-trades. See [Samuel Frédéric Osterwald], *Description des montagnes et des vallées qui font partie de la Principauté de Neuchâtel et Valangin*, 2nd ed. (Neuchâtel, 1766), pp. 95–97, quoted in David S. Landes, *Revolution in Time: Clocks and the Making of the Modern World* (Cambridge, Mass., 1983), p. 306.
19. *Inequality*, dedication; *P* III, p. 112; *DS*, p. 79.
20. "Corsica"; *P* III, pp. 938 (on pride vs. vanity), 941 (on labor vs. idleness); *PW*, pp. 326, 329: "Men are naturally lazy: but ardor in labor is the first fruit of a well-ruled society." *Emile*, bk. III; *P* IV, p. 470; *EM*, p. 195.
21. "Corsica"; *P* III, p. 905; *PW*, p. 283. *Emile*, bk. III; *P* IV, p. 470; *EM*, p. 195. On patriotism and "the ground that nourishes" a man, see the fragment "On the *Patrie*"; *P* III, p. 535.
22. "Corsica"; *P* III, pp. 914–15; *PW*, pp. 295–96.
23. *D'Alembert*; *D* I, p. 329; *LA*, p. 60.

24. *Emile*, bk. V; *P* IV, p. 859; *EM*, p. 474. *D'Alembert*; *D* I, p. 365; *LA*, pp. 95–96: ("There are many Citizens and bourgeois who reside [in the countryside] all year, and have no dwelling in Geneva"). Ibid., *D* I, p. 329; *LA*, p. 60.

25. *Inequality*, dedication; *P* III, p. 119; *DS*, p. 88. *Contract* bk. IV, ch. 8; *P* III, p. 468; *SC*, p. 131.

26. On the import of religion as a public force helping the individual to consult conscience, see *Emile*, bk. IV; *P* IV, pp. 634–35n.; *EM*, pp. 313–14n.

27. *Mountain*, II; *P* III, p. 712. On lay preaching in Geneva, see the remarks in *P* III, p. 1293. Rousseau's uncle was a lay preacher, and Rousseau himself briefly considered becoming a minister; see *Confessions*, bk. I; *P* I, pp. 25–26; *CO*, pp. 34–35.

28. See *Contract*, bk. IV, ch. 8; *P* III, p. 468; *SC*, p. 131 (the dogmas will be "without explanation or commentary"); and *Confessions*, bk. II; *P* I, p. 65; *CO*, p. 69 ("a Protestant must learn to decide for himself").

29. *Emile*, bk. IV; *P* IV, p. 607; *EM*, p. 295. *D'Alembert*; *D* I, p. 279n.; *LA*, p. 11n. Cf. *Contract*, bk. IV, ch. 8; *P* III, p. 469; *SC*, p. 131 (contra intolerance—the only "negative" dogma of the civil religion). For more on the relation between civil and natural religion, see Roger D. Masters, *The Political Philosophy of Rousseau* (Princeton, 1968), pp. 87–88; Ronald Grimsley, *Rousseau and the Religious Quest* (Oxford, 1968), pp. 76–86; and Launay, *Ecrivain politique*, pp. 393–412.

30. *Inequality*, dedication; *P* III, p. 112; *DS*, p. 79.

31. *D'Alembert*; *D* I, pp. 368–69; *LA*, p. 99.

32. Ibid., *D* I, p. 374; *LA*, pp. 104–05. Rousseau to doctor Théodore Tronchin, November 26, 1758; *C* V, p. 242.

33. *D'Alembert*; *D* I, pp. 374–75; *LA*, p. 105.

34. *Héloïse*, pt. I, xxiii; *P* II, p. 81. Cf. *D'Alembert*; *D* I, pp. 378–79; *LA*, p. 109: "In the countries of bad mores . . . men are apprehensive about an indiscreet state. . . ."

35. *D'Alembert*, *D* I, pp. 377–78; *LA*, p. 108.

36. Ibid., *D* I, pp. 375, 377; *LA*, pp. 105, 108.

37. For Rousseau on the virtues of the Greek theater, see *D'Alembert*; *D* I, pp. 347–48; *LA*, p. 78.

38. For a harvest festival, see *Héloïse*, pt. V, vii; *P* II, pp. 607–11; for a military festival, see *D'Alembert*; *D* I, pp. 404–05n.; *LA*, pp. 135–36n.; on marriage festivals, see ibid.; *D* I, pp. 397–403; *LA*, pp. 127–33. The classic account of the festival in Rousseau is Starobinski, *La transparence*, pp. 116–21.

39. *Héloïse*, pt. VI, v; *P* II, p. 662 (from a letter about the Genevans Claire has written to Julie); in the first draft, Rousseau speaks of an "epicurism of virtue"; see *P* II, p. 1759. *D'Alembert*; *D* I, p. 405n.; *LA*, p. 136n.

40. *D'Alembert*, *D* I, pp. 400–01; *LA*, p. 131.

41. Ibid., *D* I, pp. 395, 400; *LA*, pp. 125, 126, 131. *Héloïse*, pt. V, vii; *P* II, pp. 607, 608. On the "*moi commun*," see below, n. 44, and ch. 3.

42. *D'Alembert*; *D* I, p. 405n.; *LA*, p. 136n.

43. *D'Alembert*; *D* I, p. 331; *LA*, p. 62. For the characteristics listed below, see *Inequality*, dedication, passim, and *D'Alembert*, passim; my list has been drawn

almost entirely from passages already discussed. See also *Héloïse*, pt. I, xxiii; and pt. VI, vii. And "Corsica"; *P* III, pp. 914–17; *PW*, pp. 295–98.

44. To use Rousseau's technical terms, the *moi relatif* is transfigured by the *moi commun*. On the *moi relatif*, see *Emile*, bk. IV; *P* IV, p. 534; *EM*, p. 243. On the *moi commun*, see "Discourse on Political Economy"; *P* III, p. 245; *SC*, p. 212; *Contract*, bk. I, ch. 6; *P* III, p. 361; *SC*, p. 53; and *Emile*, bk. I; *P* IV, p. 249; *EM*, p. 40.

45. *Emile*, bk. V; *P* IV, p. 818; *EM*, pp. 444–45. For more on virtue, see below, ch. 7.

46. *Inequality*, dedication; *P* III, p. 117; *DS*, p. 85.

47. For "love of humanity" vs. "love of the *patrie*," see the fragment "On the *Patrie*"; *P* III, p. 536.

48. *D'Alembert*; *D* I, p. 335; *LA*, p. 66.

49. See ibid., *D* I, pp. 334–36; *LA*, pp. 66–67.

50. *Inequality*, dedication; *P* III, p. 114; *DS*, p. 81.

51. *D'Alembert*; *D* I, p. 393; *LA*, p. 123. See *Inequality*, dedication; *P* III, p. 114; *DS*, p. 82.

52. *D'Alembert*; *D* I, pp. 380, 343; *LA*, pp. 110, 74.

53. On the legitimate authority of the father, see Geneva Ms., bk. I, ch. 5; *P* III, pp. 298–99; *SC*, pp. 169–70. On the civil religion, see *Contract*, bk. IV, ch. 8; *P* III, pp. 460–69; *SC*, pp. 124–32. On regulating public entertainment, see ibid., bk. IV, ch. 7 ("On Censorship"); *P* III, pp. 458–59; *SC*, pp. 123–24; and *D'Alembert*, passim. On confining private property "within the narrowest possible limits," see "Corsica"; *P* III, p. 931; *PW*, p. 317. On minimizing the exchange of material goods to maximize the force of public honor, see "Corsica"; *P* III, pp. 924–25; *PW*, pp. 308–10. On minimizing monetary taxes by the use of *corvées*, or "common work," see "Corsica"; *P* III, pp. 932–33; *PW*, p. 319. For more on the Swiss practice of "common work," see Barber, *Communal Liberty*, pp. 176–77.

54. *Inequality*, dedication; *P* III, p. 116; *DS*, p. 84.

55. Ibid., *P* III, pp. 118, 114; *DS*, pp. 87, 82. "Corsica"; *P* III, p. 907; *PW*, p. 286. To avoid a sense of familiarity that is, I think, slightly misleading, I will be translating *éclairé* throughout as "thoughtful" (when applied to persons) or "lucid" (when applied to judgment), rather than as "enlightened."

56. On "true talent" in Geneva, see *Héloïse*, pt. VI, v; *P* II, p. 658. On the false power of wealth, see "Corsica"; *P* III, p. 939; *PW*, p. 327. On using the desire for distinction to check self-interest, see the fragment "On Honor and Virtue"; *P* III, pp. 501–02. For more on the value of public honors supplanting monetary rewards, see "Considerations on the Government of Poland and on its Projected Reformation" [xi]; *P* III, p. 1007; *PW*, p. 229.

57. *Inequality*, dedication; *P* III, p. 114; *DS*, p. 82.

58. "Corsica"; *P* III, p. 909; *PW*, p. 288. *Narcisse*, preface; *P* II, p. 965. See also *Contract*, bk. I, ch. 2; *P* III, p. 352; *SC*, p. 47. Cf. ibid., bk. III, ch. 13; *P* III, p. 426; *SC*, p. 100: "The more force the Government has, the more frequently the Sovereign ought to present itself."

59. "Corsica"; *P* III, pp. 940–41; *PW*, p. 329.

60. The question of Rousseau's patronizing attitude toward women is not particularly controversial: he was no advocate of an equality between men and women, as witness the domestication of Sophie in *Emile*, an education so at odds with Emile's own training in freedom. More controversial is Rousseau's attitude toward property qualifications. But see "Corsica"; *P* III, p. 919; *PW*, p. 301; the easiest way to make a country independent is "to attach men to the earth, so to speak, by making it the basis of their distinctions and their rights," and "to affirm this link through the link of the family, by making land a necessary condition of paternity."

61. *Inequality*, dedication; *P* III, p. 117; *DS*, p. 86. To emphasize the religious and individualized connotations of the "inner light" and "receiving the light," I will be translating *lumières* literally as "lights," never as "enlightenment." For more on the Christian antecedents of this idea, see Frank and Fritzie Manuel, *Utopian Thought in the Western World* (Cambridge, Mass., 1979), esp. p. 442.

62. *Inequality*, dedication; *P* III, p. 112; *DS*, p. 79. Cf. D'Alembert, *D* I, p. 385; *LA*, p. 115.

63. See François Jost, *La Suisse dans les lettres françaises au cours des âges* (Fribourg, 1956), esp. pp. 7, 80–101, 312; and James Sime in *Encyclopedia Britannica*, 9th ed., s.v. "Switzerland," pt. III on "Literature."

64. Both Thucydides and Aristotle admired aristocratic leadership, finding in Pericles the last and best of the breed, a rare spirit able to calm the fickle crowd and rule it prudently: see, e.g., Thucydides, *The Peloponnesian War*, 2.59–65; cf. Aristotle, *The Constitution of Athens*, XXVIII. Aristotle has special praise for the brief oligarchic regime of the "four hundred" instituted by a *coup d'état* after Athens' defeat in Sicily: see *Constitution of Athens*, XXIX, XXXIII, and cf. the remarks on oligarchy and wealth in his praise of "polity" in the *Politics*, 1293b–1294a. For Plutarch, following Thucydides, the hero is Pericles: see *The Lives*, p. 212, where Pericles is portrayed as having been "the chief bulwark of public safety" against the "invidious arbitrary power" and "licentious impunity" of the people. Cicero, in *De Re Publica*, I, xliii–xliv, paraphrases the *Republic* of Plato (for which see below), but with a number of subtle shifts even more disparaging of democracy: on this, see Robert Denoon Cumming, *Human Nature and History* (Chicago, 1969), vol. I, pp. 217–22.

Modern historical scholarship has now clarified many of the distortions involved in these classical accounts of Athenian democracy, in part by restoring a context for appreciating the social perspective of the writers. See A. H. M. Jones, *Athenian Democracy* (Oxford, 1969), M. I. Finley, *Democracy Ancient and Modern* (New Brunswick, N.J., 1973), and the informative annotation in J. M. Moore, ed. and trans., *Aristotle and Xenophon on Democracy and Oligarchy* (Berkeley, 1975). For more on the traditional treatment of democracy, see below, ch. 5.

65. Plato, *Republic*, 555d; 561d; 563b–c.

66. Ibid., 492b–c. For the *eikon* of the democratic ship, see ibid., 488a–489a.

67. Joseph A. Schumpeter, *Capitalism, Socialism and Democracy* (New York, 1950), p. 257. For more on this theme in the republican tradition, see below, ch. 5.

68. "Political Economy"; *P* III, p. 246; *SC*, p. 213. *Sciences and Arts*, pt. I; P III, p. 12; *DS*, p. 43. *Inequality*, dedication; *P* III, p. 114; *DS*, p. 82.

69. *Inequality*, dedication; *P* III, p. 113; *DS*, p. 81.

70. Ibid., dedication; *P* III, pp. 111, 115; *DS*, pp. 78–79, 84.

71. For Calvin as a great Legislator, see *Contract*, bk. II, ch. 7; *P* III, p. 382n.; *SC*, pp. 68–69n. When considering Rousseau's city as a "flock of Emiles," it is well to remember that Rousseau himself equates a "natural" education with a healthy domestic one. See *Emile*, bk. I; *P* IV, p. 251; *EM*, p. 4: "There remains *l'éducation domestique* or that of nature."

72. *Inequality*, pt. II; *P* III, pp. 168, 171; *DS*, pp. 147, 150–51. *Sciences and Arts*, pt. I; *P* III, pp. 7–8; *DS*, p. 37. Rousseau criticizes Hobbes for attributing to the state of nature a bellicose existence that in fact results from society: see *Inequality*, pt. I; *P* III, pp. 153–55; *DS*, pp. 128–30; and "That the State of War is born of the Social State"; *P* III, pp. 601–12.

73. *Sciences and Arts*, pt. I; *P* III, p. 8; *DS*, p. 37. *Inequality*, dedication; *P* III, p. 112; *DS*, p. 79.

74. *Emile*, bk. I; *P* IV, p. 250; *EM*, p. 40: "From these two necessarily opposed objects come two contrary forms of institution: the one public and common, the other individual (*particulière*) and domestic."

75. *D'Alembert*; *D* I, p. 330; *LA*, p. 61. As we shall see in even more detail in what follows, the image of Geneva contravenes C. E. Vaughn's contention that Rousseau entertains a "defiant individualism" incompatible with the "defiant collectivism" of the *Contract*; see his comments in *V* II, p. 14.

76. See Montesquieu, *Spirit of the Laws*, bk. XI, ch. 6.

77. *Emile*, bk. I; *P* IV, pp. 250, 248, 249; *EM*, pp. 40, 39, 39–40.

78. The centrality of Alpine imagery in Rousseau makes implausible the standpoint of Shklar in *Men and Citizens*, pp. 3, 5: "One difficulty presented by Rousseau as a utopist is that he offered two models rather than one. One model was a Spartan city, the other a tranquil household. . . . The alternatives are . . . domestic or civic education. Is a man to find his maturity in a recreated Golden Age or as a citizen of a Spartan republic? He cannot have both. . . ." As we should expect, given his picture of Geneva, Rousseau himself is never this emphatic. Cf. *Emile*, bk. I; *P* IV, p. 250; *EM*, p. 40: "To be something, to be oneself and always one, a man must act as he speaks. . . . I am waiting to be shown this marvel so as to know whether he is a man or a citizen, or *how he goes about being both at the same time*" (emphasis added).

79. *Inequality*, dedication; *P* III, p. 120; *DS*, p. 90. *Héloïse*, pt. I, xii; *P* II, p. 60.

80. *Emile*, bk. I; *P* IV, p. 251; *EM*, p. 41. *Contract*, bk. II, ch. 12; *P* III, p. 394; *SC*, p. 77. Cf. George Armstrong Kelly, *Idealism, Politics and History* (Cambridge, 1969), p. 48.

81. See *Emile*, bk. IV; *P* IV, p. 671; *EM*, p. 339: "Loving men because they are similar to him (*qu'ils sont ses semblables*), he will love above all those who most resemble him, because he will feel good in himself, and, judging of this resemblance by the conformity of tastes in moral things, he will be quite comforted (*il sera fort aise*) to be approved in everything connected with good character." Cf. ibid., bk. I; *P* IV, p. 249; *EM*, pp. 39–40.

82. Italo Calvino, *Invisible Cities*, trans. William Weaver (New York, 1974), pp. 164–65.

(1754–1762) *The Exile as Citizen*

1. *Héloïse*, pt. IV, vi; *P* II, p. 419; *NH*, p. 286.
2. Rousseau to Mme Dupin, July 20, 1754; *C* III, p. 16. *Confessions*, bk. IV; *P* I, p. 144; *CO*, p. 141 (emphasis added).
3. *Confessions*, bk. VIII; *P* I, p. 392; *CO*, p. 365.
4. Ibid., bk. IV; *P* I, p. 147; *CO*, p. 144. On Rousseau's reception, see the remarks of R. A. Leigh in *C* III, p. xxi. Cf. Spink, *Rousseau et Genève*, p. 40; and *Confessions*, bk. VIII; *P* I, p. 392; *CO*, p. 365.
5. Spink, *Rousseau et Genève*, pp. 40–41. Cf. Cranston, *Jean-Jacques*, pp. 338–40.
6. See Launay, *Ecrivain politique*, pp. 233–34; and Rousseau to François Mussard, July 6, 1754; *C* III, p. 7.
7. See *Confessions*, bk. VIII; *P* I, pp. 392–94; *CO*, pp. 366–68. Thumbnail sketches of the company he kept appear in *P* I, pp. 1457–59; cf. Cranston, *Jean-Jacques*, pp. 324–50.
8. *Confessions*, bk. VIII; *P* I, p. 393; *CO*, p. 366.
9. Ibid., bk. VIII; *P* I, p. 395; *CO*, p. 368.
10. See Rousseau to Perdriau, November 28, 1754; *C* III, pp. 55–60.
11. Jean-Louis Du Pan to Rousseau, June 20, 1755; *C* III, pp. 136–37. The contemporary review is cited in *P* III, p. 1288. On the reaction in Geneva, see the comments and documentation in *P* III, pp. 1286–88; cf. Spink, *Rousseau et Genève*, p. 43.
12. Rousseau to Jacob Vernes, July 6, 1755; *C* III, pp. 141–42.
13. See *Confessions*, bk. VIII; *P* I, pp. 395–96; *CO*, pp. 369, 370.
14. Rousseau to Jean Jallabert, November 20, 1755; *C* III, pp. 206–07.
15. *Confessions*, bk. VIII; *P* I, p. 396; *CO*, pp. 369–70. Voltaire to Rousseau, August 30, 1755; *C* III, pp. 156–57; cf. Rousseau to Voltaire, September 7, 1755; *C* III, p. 164. Rousseau to Jallabert, December 16, 1754; *C* III, p. 72. See also Guehenno, *Rousseau*, vol. I, pp. 320–24.
16. *Confessions*, bk. VIII; *P* I, pp. 396–97; *CO*, p. 370.
17. *Emile*, bk. V; *P* IV, pp. 858–59; *EM*, p. 474. Cf. *Confessions*, bk. IX; *P* I, pp. 406; *CO*, p. 378; and "Letters to Malesherbes," 4; *P* I, p. 1143.
18. Quoted in Arthur M. Wilson, *Diderot* (Oxford, 1972), p. 281. For the circumstances of d'Alembert's article, see ibid., pp. 280–84; and Palmer, *Democratic Revolution*, vol. I, pp. 116–18.
19. *D'Alembert*; *D* I, p. 380; *LA*, p. 110. For Neuchâtel, see ibid., *D* I, pp. 329–33; *LA*, pp. 60–64. On the special dangers of inequality in a democracy like Geneva, see ibid., *D* I, p. 385; *LA*, p. 115. See also *Confessions*, bk. X; *P* I, pp. 494–95; *CO*, pp. 458–59. Cf. *P* I, pp. 1515–16.
20. *Héloïse*, pt. VI, v; *P* II, p. 658.
21. See Launay, *Ecrivain politique*, pp. 234–36.
22. *P* II, p. 1755. For an analysis of Rousseau's hesitations, see Launay, *Ecrivain*

politique, pp. 341–42. For evidence of Rousseau's political ignorance, see Spink, *Rousseau et Genève*, p. 87.

23. Launay, *Ecrivain politique*, p. 349. On speaking to the *"plus grand nombre,"* see D'Alembert; *D* I, p. 279n.; *LA*, p. 11n. But cf. ibid., *D* I, p. 336; *LA*, p. 67: "As to the choice of instruments of public opinion, that is another question which it would be superfluous to resolve for you and which it is not here the place to resolve for the multitude." On the circles, see the passages discussed above, ch. 2.

24. D'Alembert; *D* I, p. 273; *LA*, p. 5.

25. D'Alembert; *D* I, p. 405n.; *LA*, p. 135n.

26. Ibid., *D* I, p. 406; *LA*, p. 137. What Rousseau in effect has done, of course, is to confront and contrast d'Alembert's "seductive picture" with his own image of Geneva. On the implicit class bias of his hopes for Geneva at this time, see the quite explicit letter, Rousseau to Théodore Tronchin, November 13, 1758; *C* V, pp. 241–42: "It is always an injustice to blame public corruption on Artisans. . . . Everywhere the rich are the first corrupted, the poor follow, the mediocre class goes last. Now, with us, the mediocre class is the watchmakers."

27. *Confessions*, bk. X; *P* I, pp. 495–96, 502; *CO*, pp. 459–60, 465.

28. Tronchin to Rousseau, November 13, 1758; *C* V, pp. 220–21. Cf. Rousseau to Tronchin, November 26, 1758; *C* V, p. 242. For other responses to the *Letter to D'Alembert*, see *P* I, pp. 1517–18.

29. Rousseau to Vernes, November 18, 1759; *C* VI, p. 200.

Chapter 3. *The Social Contract*

1. *Confessions*, bk. IX; *P* I, p. 404; *CO*, p. 377. For fan letters inspired by *La Nouvelle Héloïse*, see, e.g., *C*, viii, pp. 56–58.

2. For Rousseau's characterization of Venice, see *Contract*, bk. III, ch. 5; *P* III, p. 407n.; *SC*, p. 86n. On reading a history of Venice, see *Confessions*, bk. I; *P* I, p. 9; *CO*, p. 20. His dispatches from Venice are reprinted in *P* III, pp. 1045–1234. On Venice as a model republic, see the survey of William Bouwsma, "Venice and the Political Education of Europe," in J. R. Hale, ed., *Renaissance Venice* (London, 1973), pp. 445–66. For Machiavelli's views, see the *Discourses on the First Decade of Titus Livius*, bk. I, ch. 6. For the eighteenth century, see William H. McNeill, *Venice: the Hinge of Europe 1081–1797* (Chicago, 1974), pp. 224–26.

3. *Confessions*, bk. VII; *P* I, p. 323; *CO*, p. 303. Ibid., bk. IX; *P* I, p. 404; *CO*, p. 377.

4. Ibid., bk. IX; *P* I, pp. 404–05; *CO*, p. 377.

5. Ibid., bk. IX; *P* I, p. 405; *CO*, p. 377. On the urging of his Genevan friends, see Launay, *Ecrivain politique*, pp. 356–57.

6. "Political Fragments"; *P* III, p. 473. The date Rousseau abandoned the "Political Institutions" in favor of a work along the lines of the *Social Contract* is uncertain: Robert Derathé believes the first draft of the *Social Contract* dates from around 1759 (see *P* III, pp. lxxxiii–lxxxv). For another example of the range of matters Rousseau associated with political questions, consider his queries for materials relating to his proposed history of Valais: on this topic, see Launay, *Ecrivain politique*, pp. 279–80.

7. My own understanding has also been shaped by the analysis of the *Contract* in Emile Durkheim, *Montesquieu and Rousseau*, trans. Ralph Mannheim (Ann Arbor, 1960) and in Masters, *Philosophy of Rousseau*, esp. pp. 301–06.

8. *Contract*, bk. I, ch. 1; *P* III, p. 351; *SC*, p. 46. Ibid., bk. IV, ch. 2; *P* III, p. 440; *SC*, p. 110. Ibid., bk. I, ch. 6; *P* III, p. 360; *SC*, p. 53. For freedom and the "loi naturelle qui commande à tous," see *Mountain*, VIII; *P* III, p. 842; cf. "Poland" [vi]; *P* III, p. 973; *PW*, p. 185; and see Jean Fabre's comment in *P* III, p. 1760. A distinction can be drawn between the *droit naturel* Rousseau finds insufficient to found a political association and the *loi naturelle* of free will, which obtains universally, whatever the social setting. For an extended discussion of Rousseau's concept of freedom, see below, ch. 7.

    Rousseau vacillates in his approach to natural right. Sometimes he speaks as if eternal norms of right were inscribed in the heart or conscience of everyman, if only he would consult his inner lights. The Savoyard Vicar avows that conscience contains "an innate principle of justice and virtue." (See *Emile*, bk. IV; *P* IV, p. 598; *EM*, pp. 288–89.) Yet, in the first draft of the *Social Contract*, Rousseau himself sarcastically remarks that "if concepts of the great Being and of natural law were innate in every heart, it was surely superfluous to teach them both explicitly." (See Geneva Ms., bk. I, ch. 2; *P* III, pp. 285–86; *SC*, p. 160.) In a sense, all that matters for Rousseau's political position is that such equivocation is thinkable; this suffices to suggest the intolerable fragility of building a theory of politics on questionably natural principles—particularly since Rousseau thinks that the *loi naturelle* of free will makes man, once he enters into association with others, into a creature of conventions in any case. Cf. ibid., bk. III, ch. 4; *P* III, p. 326; *SC*, p. 189.

9. *Contract*, bk. I, ch. 5; *P* III, p. 359; *SC*, p. 52. Ibid., bk. IV, ch. 2; *P* III, p. 440; *SC*, p. 110. Ibid., bk. II, ch. 4; *P* III, p. 375; *SC*, p. 63. On what man wins through association, see ibid., bk. I, ch. 8; *P* III, p. 364; *SC*, p. 56; and below, ch. 7.

10. *Contract*, bk. I, ch. 6; *P* III, p. 361; *SC*, p. 53.

11. Geneva Ms., bk. I, ch. 2, *P* III, p. 287; *SC*, p. 161. On the critical importance of the "concrete reality" expressed (N.B., *not* created *ex nihilo*) by the general will, see *Contract*, bk. II, ch. 10; *P* III, p. 390; *SC*, p. 74: "What people, then, is suited for legislation? One that, though already bound by some union of origin, interest or convention, has not yet borne the true yoke of the laws." In other words, a preexisting, if tacit, *moi commun* is the first condition of legitimate laws.

    On the plurality of possible general wills, see the important passage in "Political Economy"; *P* III, pp. 245–46; *SC*, p. 212: "All the individuals whom a common interest reunites, compose so many ... particular societies." For Rousseau's critique of Diderot, see Geneva Ms., bk. I, ch. 2; *P* III, pp. 281–89; *SC*, pp. 157–63. See also Patrick Riley, "The general will before Rousseau," *Political Theory* VI:(1978):485–515.

12. *Contract*, bk. II, ch. 3; *P* III, p. 371; *SC*, p. 61. That individuals will always have different interests is indicated in ibid., bk. II, ch. 3; *P* III, p. 371n.; *SC*, p. 61n.. "If there were no different interests, the common interest, which would never encounter any obstacle, would scarcely be felt."

13. Ibid., bk. I, ch. 6; *P* III, pp. 361–62; *SC*, pp. 53–54. Ibid., bk. III, ch. 1; *P* III, p. 396; *SC*, p. 78. Ibid., bk. II, ch. 6; *P* III, p. 380n.; *SC*, p. 67n.

14. Ibid., bk. II, ch. 1; *P* III, p. 368; *SC*, p. 59. Geneva Ms., bk. I, ch. 4; *P* III, pp. 294–95; *SC*, p. 167.

15. *Contract*, bk. II, ch. 3; *P* III, p. 371; *SC*, p. 61. Ibid., bk. II, ch. 4; *P* III, p. 373; *SC*, p. 63. For more on why Rousseau assumes that the will is "always right," see below, ch. 7. J. W. Gough, *The Social Contract* (Oxford, 1957), p. 172, points out the two senses of *droit*. Cf. the title of *Contract*, bk. II, ch. 3: "Si le volonté générale peut errer." The French *errer* combines the sense of to wander or to roam with that of to err or make a mistake. Again, the contrast with *droit* as "direct" or "straightforward" is suggested.

16. *Contract*, bk. II, ch. 6; *P* III, p. 380; *SC*, p. 67.

17. Ibid., bk. II, ch. 6; *P* III, p. 380; *SC*, p. 67. Ibid., bk. II, ch. 7; *P* III, p. 383; *SC*, p. 69.

18. Ibid., bk. II, ch. 6; *P* III, p. 380; *SC*, p. 67. On the inalienability and indivisibility of sovereignty, see ibid., bk. II, chs. 1 and 2; *P* III, pp. 368–71; *SC*, pp. 59–61. For more on Rousseau's attitude toward representation, see Richard Fralin, "The evolution of Rousseau's view of representative government," *Political Theory*, VI(1978):517–36.

19. *Contract*, bk. II, ch. 11; *P* III, p. 391; *SC*, p. 75. Ibid., bk. I, ch. 9; *P* III, p. 367n.; *SC*, p. 58n. See also ibid., bk. I, ch. 8; *P* III, pp. 364–65; *SC*, p. 56; and ibid., bk. II, ch. 11; *P* III, p. 392n.; *SC*, p. 75n. As Rousseau's image of Geneva shows, his ideal for property is the self-sufficient farmer, see above, ch. 2.

20. For the enormous tasks assigned the Legislator, see esp. *Contract*, bk. II, ch. 12; *P* III, p. 394; *SC*, p. 77.

21. Ibid., bk. III, ch. 5; *P* III, p. 407; *SC*, p. 86. Ibid., bk. III, ch. 4; *P* III, p. 405; *SC*, p. 85.

22. Ibid., bk. III, ch. 4; *P* III, p. 404; *SC*, p. 85.

23. Rousseau to Marc-Michel Rey, April 4, 1762; *C* X, p. 180 ("fit for few readers"). *Contract*, bk. III, ch. 15; *P* III, p. 431; *SC*, p. 103 (it should be noted that Rousseau's direct address to "you modern peoples" occurs in the midst of one of his bolder exhortations to civil freedom—the chapter attacking representative government). Rousseau to Rey, November 7, 1761; *C* IX, p. 221 ("a book for all times"). *Confessions*, bk. IX; *P* I, p. 404; *CO*, p. 377. On Rousseau's concern with censorship, see, e.g., Rousseau to Rey, May 29, 1762; *C* X, pp. 307–08. See also Michel Launay, "L'Art de l'écrivain dans le *Contrat social*," in Michel Launay, ed., *Jean-Jacques Rousseau et son temps* (Paris, 1969), pp. 125–50, esp. ibid., p. 138, n.69.

24. For a detailed account of Rousseau's relation to the natural law tradition, see Robert Derathé, *Jean-Jacques Rousseau et la science politique de son temps* (Paris, 1950).

25. Geneva Ms., bk. I, ch. 2; *P* III, pp. 284–85, 288–89; *SC*, pp. 160, 163. *Contract*, bk. I; *P* III, p. 351; *SC*, p. 46.

26. *Emile*, bk. II; *P* IV, p. 346; *EM*, p. 109: "Reason alone is common, the mind in

each language has its particular form." Cf. the defense of the *Contract* in *Mountain*, VI; *P* III, p. 812: "Locke, Montesquieu, l'abbé de Saint-Pierre, have treated the same matters, and often with more or less the same freedom. . . . All three were born under kings, lived tranquilly, and died honored by their countries." Why all the fuss about a scholarly tract?

27. Simone Weil, *Oppression and Liberty*, trans. Wills and Petrie (Amherst, 1973), p. 84.

28. *Contract*, bk. III, ch. 12; *P* III, p. 425; *SC*, p. 99. Ibid., bk. I; *P* III, p. 351; *SC*, p. 46.

29. Ibid., bk. III, ch. 6; *P* III, p. 409; *SC*, p. 88. For antecedents of this interpretation of Machiavelli's veiled intentions, see *P* III, p. 1481. For Rousseau on his own interest in Genevan readers, see *Confessions*, bk. IX; *P* I, p. 405; *CO*, p. 377.

30. *Contract*, bk. III, ch. 6; *P* III, p. 1480; *SC*, p. 88n. Masters' discussion in *Philosophy of Rousseau*, p. 310, seems needlessly convoluted, perhaps because he ignores the Genevan context.

31. *Contract*, bk. III, ch. 10; *P* III, p. 422n.; *SC*, p. 97n. Ibid., bk. III, ch. 4; *P* III, p. 404; *SC*, p. 85. For the second reminder that a true democracy has never existed, see ibid., bk. IV, ch. 3; *P* III, p. 443; *SC*, p. 112. For an interpretation of Rousseau's Roman references also focused on their allusions to Genevan problems, see Launay, *Ecrivain politique*, pp. 443–51. Cf. Masters, *Philosophy of Rousseau*, pp. 406–08.

32. *Inequality*, dedication; *P* III, p. 112; *DS*, p. 79. *D'Alembert*; *D* I, p. 385; *LA*, p. 115. Cf. *Contract*, bk. II, ch. 6; *P* III, p. 380n.; *SC*, p. 67n. And ibid., bk. I, ch. 6; *P* III, p. 362; *SC*, p. 54.

33. *Contract*, bk. IV, ch. 3; *P* III, pp. 442–43; *SC*, p. 112. Launay, *Ecrivain politique*, p. 446. *Contract*, bk. III, ch. 5; *P* III, p. 407n.; *SC*, p. 86n. (On Venice, also see ibid., bk. IV, ch. 4; *P* III, p. 453; *SC*, p. 119: a once proud republic, "its laws are only suited to wicked men" today.) Ibid., bk. III, ch. 5; *P* III, p. 406; *SC*, p. 86 (on "aristocracy properly so-called").

34. *Confessions*, bk. IX; *P* I, p. 405; *CO*, p. 377.

35. *Contract*, bk. III, ch. 9; *P* III, p. 419; *SC*, p. 95. Ibid., bk. III, ch. 8; *P* III, p. 414; *SC*, p. 92. Cf. ibid., bk. III, ch. 1; *P* III, p. 398; *SC*, p. 80: "There is no unique and absolute constitution of Government, . . . there can be as many Governments of different natures as there are States of different sizes (*différens en grandeur*)." Note that the emphasis throughout is on *government*, not sovereignty. Cf. below, ch. 5.

36. Geneva Ms., bk. I, ch. 2; *P* III, p. 287; *SC*, pp. 161–62. Cf. *Contract*, bk. I, ch. 6; *P* III, p. 361n.; *SC*, p. 54n.

37. Ibid., bk. II, ch. 9; *P* III, p. 386; *SC*, p. 71. Ibid., bk. II, ch. 10; *P* III, pp. 390–91; *SC*, p. 74. Ibid., bk. II, ch. 11; *P* III, p. 392n.; *SC*, p. 75n. Ibid., bk. III, ch. 8; *P* III, p. 418; *SC*, p. 95.

38. Ibid., bk. II, ch. 6; *P* III, p. 380 and n.; *SC*, p. 67 and n. Ibid., bk. III, ch. 5; *P* III, p. 407; *SC*, p. 86. Ibid., bk. III, ch. 1; *P* III, p. 399; *SC*, p. 81.

39. Ibid., bk. II, ch. 12; *P* III, p. 394; *SC*, p. 77. Ibid., bk. III, ch. 15; *P* III, p. 429; *SC*, p. 102. Ibid., bk. III, ch. 1; *P* III, p. 395; *SC*, p. 78. Ibid., bk. IV, ch. 1; *P* III,

p. 437; *SC*, p. 108. Ibid., bk. II, ch. 4; *P* III, p. 374; *SC*, p. 63. Ibid., bk. II, ch. 3; *P* III, p. 372; *SC*, p. 61. Ibid., bk. III, ch. 2; *P* III, p. 401; *SC*, p. 82.

40. Ibid., bk. IV, ch. 8; *P* III, pp. 468–69; *SC*, p. 131.

41. Ibid., bk. III, ch. 13; *P* III, p. 426; *SC*, p. 100. Ibid., bk. III, ch. 18; *P* III, p. 436; *SC*, p. 107. Ibid., bk. III, ch. 14; *P* III, pp. 427–28; *SC*, p. 101. Ibid., bk. III, ch. 12; *P* III, p. 425; *SC*, p. 99. Ibid., bk. III, ch. 15; *P* III, pp. 429–30; *SC*, p. 102. Ibid., bk. III, ch. 10; *P* III, pp. 422–23; *SC*, p. 98. For "Government is not a contract but a Law," see ibid., bk. III, ch. 18; *P* III, p. 434; *SC*, p. 106; and ibid., bk. III, ch. 16; *P* III, pp. 432–33; *SC*, pp. 104–05. On "the prejudice favoring antiquity," see ibid., bk. III, ch. 11; *P* III, p. 425; *SC*, p. 99.

42. Ibid., bk. I; *P* III, p. 351; *SC*, p. 46. "Political Economy"; *P* III, p. 267; *SC*, p. 228.

43. For Rousseau's coolness toward mixed regimes, see *Contract*, bk. III, ch. 7; *P* III, p. 413; *SC*, p. 91. "On the Abuse of Government and Its Tendency to Degenerate" is the title Rousseau gives to ch. 10 of bk. III of the *Contract*, his chapter introducing the uncompromising maxims which fill out the remainder of bk. III. My conclusions here agree with Vallette, *Rousseau Genevois*, pp. 184–99, 209–11, and contradict Spink, *Rousseau et Genève*, p. 90; also see below, ch. 4, n. 22.

44. *Confessions*, bk. IX; *P* I, p. 405 and n.; *CO*, pp. 377 and 377–378n.

45. Geneva Ms., bk. I, ch. 4; *P* III, p. 296; *SC*, p. 168.

46. "Fragments of the Letter to Christophe de Beaumont"; *P* IV, p. 1028. Also see below, ch. 4, n. 38.

47. *Emile*, bk. V; *P* IV, pp. 836–37; *EM*, p. 458.

48. Ibid., bk. V; *P* IV, p. 857; *EM*, p. 473.

49. *Rousseau, Judge*, III; *P* I, p. 935. *Confessions*, bk. IX; *P* I, p. 405; *CO*, p. 377.

(1762–1764) *The Citizen Exiled*

1. *Confessions*, bk. XII; *P* I, p. 589; *CO*, p. 544.

2. Rousseau to Rey, April 4, 1762; *C* X, p. 180. On Rousseau's plans for the *Contract*, see also Derathé, in *P* III, pp. cix–cx.

3. Almost from the outset, Malesherbes had all but personally supervised the printing of *Emile*. See Guehenno, *Rousseau*, vol. II, pp. 64–67.

4. Jean Dessaint and Charles Saillant to Rey, May 12, 1762; *C* X, p. 240. For Rey's entreaties, see the letters from Rey to Rousseau on May 15 and May 24, 1762; *C* X, pp. 242–44, 289; and Rousseau's response to Rey, May 29, 1762; *C* X, pp. 306–08. Cf. *Confessions*, bk. XI; *P* I, pp. 571–79; *CO*, pp. 527–35.

5. Rousseau to Rey, May 29, 1762; *C* X, pp. 306–07.

6. Louis Petit de Bachaumont, *Mémoires secrets*; cited in *P* I, p. 1557, and Guehenno, *Rousseau*, vol. II, p. 81.

7. On the checkered early career of the *Social Contract* in France, see Derathé's remarks in *P* III, pp. cx–cxi; also see below, ch. 6.

8. The judgment of the Sorbonne is cited in *P* IV, p. clxix; see also Launay, *Ecrivain politique*, pp. 364–65. For the report of Olmer Joly de Fleury, advocate general of the Parliament of Paris, see *C* XI, pp. 262–66 (the passages quoted appear

on p. 265). The Sorbonne's censure was, of course, not purely theological; as one faculty member reminded his colleagues, we ought to "Fear God, respect the King"—two sentiments *Emile* obviously undermined.

9. *Confessions*, bk. XI; *P* I, p. 580; *CO*, p. 535.

10. Ibid., bk. XI; *P* I, p. 581; *CO*, p. 537. Rousseau here leaves the false impression that Geneva had banned *La Nouvelle Héloïse*. Respectable Genevan opinion, however, was hostile to the book, and Rousseau knew of this hostility; see *P* I, p. 1540. The complaint of the Consistory to the Small Council and the Council's decision to do nothing are documented; see *P* III, p. 1634.

11. Rousseau to the minister Paul-Claude Moultou, May 30, 1762; *C* X, p. 312.

12. Moultou to Rousseau, June 18, 1762; *C* XI, p. 108.

13. Voltaire to d'Alembert, September 28, 1763; quoted in Peter Gay, *The Party of Humanity* (New York, 1971), p. 245. Even Moultou had doubts about how Rousseau's apparent pledge of allegiance to aristocracy would wash. After reading the *Contract*, he wrote to Rousseau, on June 5, 1762; *C* XI, p. 29: "If your prefer Aristocracy to all other Governments, I grasp all the limitations that you have made. But do you think that those to whom our democracy is displeasing will accommodate themselves to your Aristocracy?"

14. "Conclusion of the public Prosecutor on two Books entitled of the Social Contract and of Education," June 19, 1762; *C* XI, p. 299.

15. The patrician theory of the contract is discussed in Spink, *Rousseau et Genève*, p. 23. On the impact of partisan politics in the proceedings against Rousseau in Geneva, see ibid., p. 238.

16. "Conclusion of the public Prosecutor," *C* XI, pp. 298–99.

17. Cited in Spink, *Rousseau et Genève*, p. 215; see also ibid., pp. 212–15.

18. The report of the committee is cited in ibid., p. 52.

19. See Charly Guyot, "L'Accueil fait en Suisse au *Contrat social*," in *ECS*, pp. 381–91.

20. See Moultou to Rousseau, June 16 and June 18, 1762; *C* XI, pp. 88–91, 108–10. Also see Rousseau's reply to Moultou, June 22, 1762; *C* XI, pp. 126–28. On Moultou's impetuousness, see Spink, *Rousseau et Genève*, pp. 180–81.

21. Rousseau to Marcet de Mézières, August 10, 1762; *C* XII, p. 169.

22. Rousseau to de Mézières, July 24, 1762; *C* XII, p. 98.

23. Rousseau to Mme de Verdelin, September 4, 1762; *C* XIII, p. 9.

24. Moultou to Rousseau, January 4 [1763]; *C* XV, p. 9. On the protest over Tronchin, see Spink, *Rousseau et Genève*, p. 54.

25. On the debate over Rousseau's disposition toward Geneva, see Charles W. Hendel, *Jean-Jacques Rousseau: Moralist* (Oxford, 1934), vol. II, esp. p. 280. Cf. *P* III, p. clxiv.

26. Moultou to Rousseau, April 26, 1763; *C* XVI, p. 110.

27. *Confessions*, bk. XII; *P* I, p. 609; *CO*, p. 563.

28. Rousseau to Jacob Favre, May 12, 1763; *C* XVI, p. 164.

29. De Luc to Moultou, May 18, 1763; *C* XVI, p. 202.

30. Moultou to Rousseau, May 17, 1763; *C* XVI, p. 193. At this time, some bickering over strategy erupted between De Luc and Moultou: see Spink, *Rousseau et Genève*, p. 183.

31. In the *Confessions*, bk. XII; *P* I, p. 609; *CO*, p. 562, Rousseau claims that "fear of the disorder and trouble that my presence could cause prevented" him from returning to Geneva. Certainly Rousseau feared disorder, particularly for himself; whether he cared so much about trouble for the Small Council is another matter.

32. For the allusion to the classical image of democracy at Athens, see Jean-Robert Tronchin, *Lettres écrites de la campagne* (Geneva, 1763), pp. 112–14.

Chapter 4. *The Past Recaptured*

1. For more on the circumstances surrounding the composition of the *Letters Written from the Mountain*, see Spink, *Rousseau et Genève*, pp. 65–70; Hendel, *Rousseau: Moralist*, vol. II, pp. 286–90; and the remarks of Jean-Daniel Candaux in *P* III, pp. clxv–clxxi.

2. For a summary of Rousseau's position, see Grimsley, *Religious Quest*, pp. 80–84.

3. *Mountain*, VI; *P* III, pp. 807–09. This account is supplemented in an indicative passage deleted from the published version, probably because it touched too directly on one of the topics of contention: "Among these means [for preserving the laws], I take as one of the best periodic general assemblies, in which the Government ought to be rectified or ratified by law, in order to maintain or to restore it to the order that befits it. A Government may be good without such assemblies, but it is difficult to keep it such. The prophetic spirit which sometimes illuminates me has served me too well at this moment, but my prophecies are like those of Cassandra. They always announce ills, people never hear them, and they always come to pass." (See *P* III, p. 1663.)

4. *Mountain*, VI; *P* III, p. 809.

5. Ibid., VI; *P* III, pp. 811, 810.

6. Geneva's constitution is called democratic at several junctures: see ibid., VII; *P* III, p. 832; ibid., bk. IX; *P* III, p. 872.

7. Ibid., VII; *P* III, pp. 813, 820.

8. See ibid., VII; *P* III, pp. 816–17, 825–26; and ibid., VIII; *P* III, p. 850.

9. Ibid., VII; *P* III, pp. 814–15. Cf. *Contract*, bk. III, ch. 15; *P* III, p. 430; *SC*, p. 102: "The English people thinks it is free; it greatly deceives itself; it is free only during the election of the members of Parliament; as soon as they are elected, it is a slave, it is nothing."

10. See *Mountain*, VIII; *P* III, pp. 845, 847.

11. Ibid., VIII; *P* III, p. 850. On the prudence of allowing the Small Council alone to introduce new laws, see ibid., VIII; *P* III, pp. 846–47, 860–61.

12. Ibid., IX; *P* III, p. 893. On the false claim of the Small Council to a "negative right," see ibid., IX; *P* III, p. 870.

13. Ibid., IX; *P* III, pp. 888, 881. Ibid., VII; *P* III, p. 831. Ibid., IX; *P* III, p. 889. See also ibid., VIII; *P* III, p. 861, on "the interest of all" in a "town of commerce" like Geneva.

14. Ibid., IX; *P* III, p. 889. For the identification of artisans with the middle class in

Geneva, see also the letter of 1758 to Tronchin, cited above in (1754–1762), n. 30.

15. Ibid., IX; *P* III, pp. 890, 891–92 (on the rich using the laws). Ibid., VIII; *P* III, p. 863.

16. Ibid., IX; *P* III, p. 891.

17. See ibid., VIII; *P* III, pp. 853–54. One aspect of the constitution Rousseau does *not* mention reforming is the division of the city's population into Citizens and the disenfranchised residents called "Natives." But cf. "History of Geneva"; *S* III, p. 389: Under the older and more legitimate laws, "the sons of inhabitants became bourgeois by their birth, and the word *native* was not known."

18. *Mountain*, VII; *P* III, p. 824: "Le Conseil général n'est pas un ordre dans l'Etat, il est l'Etat même" (cf. the approach of Sièyes in 1789 to the question *Qu'est-ce que le Tiers Etat?*). Ibid., VII; *P* III, p. 826: "Elle peut tout ou elle n'est rien." Ibid., VIII; *P* III, p. 850. Ibid., VII; *P* III, p. 816.

19. Ibid., IX; *P* III, p. 894 (note the slightly incautious and hence canceled sentence that follows in the rough draft, cited in *P* III, p. 1719; Geneva's constitution may be "good and healthy," but its equilibrium is currently questionable: "The balance leans strongly to the side of the magistracy, it is true"). Ibid., VIII; *P* III, p. 844.

20. Ibid., IX; *P* III, pp. 896–97.

21. Candaux, "Introduction" to *Mountain* in *P* III, p. cxcvii (see also his remarks in *P* III, p. 1698). For Rousseau on the former frequency of General Council meetings, see *Mountain*, VII; *P* III, pp. 830–31n.; and ibid., VIII; *P* III, p. 860. For more on Rousseau's distortion of the past, see Spink, *Rousseau et Genève*, pp. 48–49, 74, 79–80.

22. Rousseau to De Luc, October 25, 1763; *C* XVIII, p. 70. This letter supports the judgment of Spink that Rousseau was essentially ignorant of the *facts* concerning Geneva's constitution. However, because he tends to underestimate the importance of Rousseau's ties to the popular party in Geneva, and because he virtually ignores the fertile role played by Rousseau's imagination, Spink is led to a conclusion that is far too strong, I think: namely, that "the *Social Contract* is a work of pure speculation," and therefore that it is "not possible" that the work contains any critique of Genevan institutions, such as the prosecutor Tronchin thought he had discovered. See Spink, *Rousseau et Genève*, p. 90.

23. Toussaint-Pierre Lenieps to Rousseau, October 18, 1763; *C* XVIII, p. 50. On what documents about Geneva Rousseau had read, see the evidence evaluated by Candaux in *P* III, pp. clxxxii–cxc; and Spink, *Rousseau et Genève*, pp. 279–84.

24. *Confessions*, bk. VI; *P* I, p. 226; *CO*, p. 216. Ibid., bk. IV; *P* I, pp. 171–72; *CO*, pp. 166–67.

25. Cf. M. I. Finley, "The Ancestral Constitution," in *The Use and Abuse of History* (New York, 1975), esp. pp. 47–48.

26. J. G. A. Pocock, *The Ancient Constitution and the Feudal Law* (New York, 1967), p. 17.

27. *Confessions*, bk. IV; *P* I, pp. 171–72; *CO*, p. 166. Ibid., bk. VII; *P* I, p. 278; *CO*, p. 262.

28. *Emile*, bk. II; *P* IV, p. 415n.; *EM*, p. 156n. Cf. "Theatrical Imitation"; *H* I, p. 369.
29. "Political Fragments"; *P* III, p. 539.
30. *Emile*, bk. II; *P* IV, p. 415n.; *EM*, p. 156n. Ibid., bk. IV; *P* IV, p. 529; *EM*, p. 239.
31. Ibid., bk. II; *P* IV, p. 415n.; *EM*, p. 156n.
32. *Héloïse*, pt. I, xii; *P* II, p. 60.
33. For the problematic status of the *Second Discourse*, cf. the scholarly notes Rousseau appended to his text, which open with the warning: "Let us therefore begin by setting all the facts aside, for they do not affect the question." (See *Inequality*, pt. I; *P* III, p. 132; *DS*, p. 103.) For an interpretation emphasizing Rousseau's use of empirical evidence, see Robert Wokler, "Perfectible apes in decadent cultures: Rousseau's anthropology revisited," *Daedalus* CVII (1978): 107–34. Cf. Starobinski, *La transparence*, pp. 330–55, esp. p. 341: "Sustained and oriented by ethnographic facts, the imagination can extrapolate boldly. . . ."
34. "History of Geneva"; *S* III, pp. 381, 389.
35. Ibid., *S* III, p. 384.
36. Diderot's *Encyclopedia*, s.v. "Hypothèse." I am relying on the translation in Stephen J. Gendzier, ed., *Denis Diderot's The Encyclopedia* (New York, 1967), pp.137–39.
37. "History of Geneva"; *S* III, p. 384. *Inequality*, preface; *P* III, p. 127; *DS*, p. 97.
38. Cf. Rousseau's own implicit account of his procedure in *Inequality*, pt. II; *P* III, pp. 191–92; *DS*, p. 178.
39. "History of Geneva"; *S* III, p. 384.
40. Ibid., *S* III, p. 384.
41. Ibid., *S* III, p. 393.
42. Ibid., *S* III, p. 396. Cf. the assessment of Calvin in the *Contract*, bk. II, ch. 7; *P* III, p. 382n.; *SC*, pp. 68–69n. Rousseau took a dim view of Calvin as a theologian: see *Mountain*, II; *P* III, p. 715.
43. "History of Geneva"; *S* III, p. 381.
44. In contrast to Rousseau's account, Spon's history makes little of Fabri's contribution, remarking that his edicts "simply confirmed ancient usages." See Mr. [Jacob] Spon, *Histoire de Genève* (Geneva, 1730), vol. I, p. 157n.
45. "History of Geneva"; *S* III, p. 386.
46. Ibid., *S* III, pp. 386, 387.
47. Ibid., *S* III, p. 389.
48. *Mountain* VIII; *P* III, p. 850.
49. Ibid., VIII; *P* III, p. 867. Ibid., VII; *P* III, p. 829n. Ibid., VIII; *P* III, p. 861.
50. *Contract*, bk. II, ch. 7; *P* III, p. 383; *SC*, p. 69. However, there is some question about just how persuasive Rousseau's polemic actually was in the long run—precisely because of its omissions and falsifications. By 1782, we find François d'Ivernois, in his *Tableau historique de Genève*, p. 193, gently disparaging the *Letters from the Mountain*, a "work so admirable in its general principles": "Rousseau knew the trunk of the Constitution, but he did not pursue enough of its branches; he lacked particular facts. . . ."
51. Plato, *Laws*, 903b. "Political Fragments"; *P* III, pp. 538–39.
52. On Plato's *Republic* as a product of imagination, see above, ch. 1. For Rous-

seau's view of his own work in relation to utopias, see *Mountain*, VI; *P* III, p. 810: "Since there has been a Government existing on my model [in the *Social Contract*], I have not tended to destroy all those that have existed. Ah! Sir; if I had written only a System, you may be sure that they would have said nothing. They would have contented themselves with relegating the *Social Contract* to the land of chimeras, alongside the *Republic* of Plato, *Utopia*, and the *Sévarambes*." Deferring to Rousseau's explicit wishes on this matter—and wanting as well to respect a fruitful tension in his thought—I have resisted using the word *utopia* in the present essay. Too often, it functions in studies of Rousseau as a subtly prejudicial term, supporting the smug assumption that only an "insane" person would try to implement his principles; without an argument, Rousseau then appears as "the Homer of the losers," to borrow a marvelously patronizing epithet from Judith Shklar (see her "Jean-Jacques Rousseau and Equality," *Daedalus* CVII [1978]:24). Cf. Jean Fabre, "Réalité et utopie dans la pensée politique de Rousseau," *Annales Jean-Jacques Rousseau* XXXV (1959–62): 181–216.

53. *Mountain*, IX; *P* III, p. 881.
54. "Poland" [xi]; *P* III, p. 1005; *PW*, p. 227. *Mountain*, IX; *P* III, p. 881. *D'Alembert*; *D* I, pp. 395, 397; *LA*, pp. 126, 127. Rousseau is less distant from Montesquieu on this matter than is commonly supposed; cf. Montesquieu, *Spirit of the Laws*, bk. V, ch. 6: "True it is that when a democracy is founded on commerce, private people may acquire vast riches without a corruption of morals."
55. *Contract*, bk. I; *P* III, p. 351; *SC*, p. 46. Ibid., bk. I, ch. 8; *P* III, p. 364; *SC*, p. 56. *Emile*, bk. IV; *P* IV, p. 551; *EM*, p. 255.
56. *Contract*, bk. I; *P* III, p. 351; *SC*, p. 46.
57. *Mountain*, IX; *P* III, p. 895.
58. For more on the motif of rebirth, see Grimsley, *Religious Quest*, pp. 91–92.
59. André Breton, "Manifesto of Surrealism" (1924), in Breton, *Manifestoes of Surrealism*, trans. Richard Seaver and Helen R. Lane (Ann Arbor, 1969), p. 14. Cf. M. H. Abrams, *Natural Supernaturalism* (New York, 1971), esp. pp. 327–72, on "Revelation, Revolution, Imagination and Cognition."
60. *Emile*, bk. V; *P* IV, p. 859; *EM*, p. 474.

Chapter 5. *The Idea of Democracy*

1. For more on the relationship between democracy and the golden age, see above, ch. 2, and ch. 4.
2. To make matters worse, he also did not always employ the term *government* consistently, sometimes using it as a colloquial synonym for the state, sometimes as a technical term for administration as defined in the *Social Contract*.
3. See *Contract*, bk. III, ch. 4; *P* III, pp.404–06; *SC*, pp. 84–85. For what is "oddly strict" about Rousseau's administrative criterion, see the conventional republican criterion discussed below.
4. Ibid., bk. III, ch. 3; *P* III, p. 403; *SC*, p. 84. Ibid., bk. III, ch. 5; *P* III, p. 406; *SC*, p. 86.
5. All this is by way of explaining the paragraph in ibid., bk. III, ch. 4; *P* III, p.

404; *SC*, p. 84–85: "It is not good for him who makes the laws to execute them."

6. Ibid., bk. III, ch. 5; *P* III, p. 408; *SC*, p. 87. On diplomacy, see ibid., bk. III, ch. 5; *P* III, pp. 406–08; *SC*, pp. 86–87.

7. Cf. Vaughn, in *V* I, p. 36, who asserts that Rousseau endorses "nothing more nor less than Cabinet Government."

8. *Mountain*, VI; *P* III, p. 809. Virtually the same phrasing appears in *Writings on l'abbé de Saint-Pierre*, "Judgment on the Polysynodie"; *P* III, p. 645. Some months after completing the "Judgment," obviously after the publication of the *Social Contract*, Rousseau returned to this passage in his manuscript and added the following note: "I would bet that thousands of men will find right here a contradiction with the *Social Contract*. This proves that there are still more readers who ought to learn to read than there are authors who ought to learn to be logical" (*P* III, p. 645n.).

9. *Contract*, bk. III, ch. 11; *P* III, p. 424; *SC*, p. 99. See also ibid., bk. II, ch. 6; *P* III, p. 380 and n.; *SC*, p. 67 and n.

10. *D'Alembert*, *D* I, p. 385; *LA*, p. 115 (cf. *Contract*, bk. III, ch. 13; *P* III, p. 427; *SC*, p. 100: "The words *subject* and *sovereign* are identical correlatives, whose meaning is combined in the single word Citizen"). *Mountain*, VII; *P* III, p. 816. On rules of voting, cf. *Contract*, bk. IV, ch. 2; *P* III, p. 441; *SC*, p. 111: "Between unanimity and a tie there are several qualified majorities, at any of which the proportion can be be established, according to the condition and needs of the body politic."

From a practical point of view, it seems obvious in retrospect that Rousseau did not devote enough attention to distinguishing between fundamental laws that require unanimity; basic areas of interest, where a community might wish a rule of ⅔ or ¾ concurrence before a proposal could become law; and other areas, where simple majority rule would be generally agreeable. In this respect, however, Rousseau's assumptions merely reflect the conventional wisdom of the day. The very idea of "fundamental laws," as distinct from more narrow edicts, was one of the hardwon contributions of revolutionary American constitutionalism: see Gordon S. Wood, *The Creation of the American Republic* (New York, 1972), pp. 259–68.

About one thing, Rousseau was tolerably clear, although his clarity on the point suggests still another problem: when, on a given topic, an impersonal regard for the common good is lacking among the majority, "whatever side one takes, there is no longer any freedom," since any resulting laws would, by definition, be ill-considered as well as factitious. (See *Contract*, bk. IV, ch. 2; *P* III, p. 441; *SC*, p. 111.) This practical problem suggests the wisdom in establishing a "bill of rights" protecting the freedom of the individual, just in case such feckless majorities arise from time to time. Before warming to the theme of Rousseau as an incipient totalitarian, however, it is worth recalling that the American Federalists were no more astute on this point, at first arguing that a bill of rights was superfluous in any constitution founded on "popular sovereignty," and only relenting under pressure from the opposition: see Wood, *American Republic*, pp. 536–43.

236 NOTES TO PAGES 107–13

11. *Inequality*, dedication; *P* III, p. 112; *DS*, p. 79. *Mountain*, VII; *P* III, pp. 832, 834.
12. *Mountain*, VIII; *P* III, p. 862.
13. *Contract*, bk. I; *P* III, p. 351; *SC*, p. 46. Ibid., bk. I, ch. 8; *P* III, p. 364; *SC*, p. 56. Plato, *Crito*, 44d. For what may have been the views of Protagoras, see Plato, *Protagoras*, esp. 322c–324d, where the celebrated sophist, argues that *aretē* (or virtue) ought to be actively cultivated in all citizens, as is done through the practice of democracy at Athens.
14. *Contract*, bk. I, ch. 7; *P* III, p. 363; *SC*, p. 55. Ibid., bk. IV, ch. 8; *P* III, p. 464; *SC*, p. 128. For more on the end of alienation as the end of involuntary subjugation, see below, ch. 7. Marx developed the idea of "true democracy" in his *Critique of Hegel's "Philosophy of Right."* His dream of ontological communion—dissolving the duality of "existence and essence"—appears in his 1844 manuscripts.
15. *Mountain*, VI; *P* III, p. 811. *Contract*, bk. III, ch. 4; *P* III, p. 405; *SC*, p. 85. Ibid., bk. II, ch. 12; *P* III, pp. 393–94; *SC*, p. 76.
16. For more on the history of the word *democracy*, see Arne Naess, Jens A. Christophersen, and Kjell Kvalø, *Democracy, Ideology and Objectivity* (Oslo and Oxford, 1956), esp. pt. A, ch. 4, "An Historical Outlook on the Different Usages of the Term 'Demcracy,'" pp. 77–138. Democracy as a slogan and term of approval first gains modern currency in the French Revolution: see below, ch. 6 and also R. R. Palmer, "Notes on the use of the word 'democracy,' 1789–1799," *Political Science Quarterly* LXVIII (1953):203–26. But its lasting triumph only comes in the twentieth century; see below, epilogue, and also Ithiel de Sola Pool, with Harold Laswell, Daniel Lerner, et. al., *Symbols of Democracy* (Stanford, 1952); and Richard McKeon and Stein Rokkan, eds., *Democracy in a World of Tensions* (Paris, 1951).
17. Aristotle, *Politics*, 1279a26–28. (I have generally preferred Benjamin Jowett's translation.)
18. Montesquieu, *Spirit of the Laws*, bk. II, ch. 2. Cf. Plato, *Republic*, 557a. Aristotle, *Politics*, 1300a32–35, is less emphatic, allowing a mixture of elections and lot, so long as "all appoint all."
19. Plato, *Republic*, 557a. Aristotle, *Politics*, 1279b40–1280b3.
20. Plato, *Republic*, 561c–d, 561a, 560e. In *De Re Publica*, I, xliii–xliv, Cicero paraphrases part of Plato's account in the *Republic*, 562d–564d.
21. Plato, *Republic*, 569c (cf. 562b). Aristotle, *Politics*, 1301a28–30.
22. Cicero, *De Re Publica*, I, xxviii (I am following the English translation of George Holland and Stanley Barney Smith). For the epitome of democratic folly in Athenian defeat, see the remarks on Thucydides above, ch. 2, n. 64.
23. Polybius, *The Histories*, bk. VI, §4, 6–9 (I am following the English translation of W. R. Paton). On mixed government, see ibid., bk. VI, §10, 6–11. For Plato's cycle, see the *Republic*, bks. VIII and IX, 543a–576b; and cf. the *Statesman*, 302e–303b. For Cicero on the mixed regime, see *De Re Publica*, I, xxxv.
24. Aristotle, *Politics*, 1279a40–1279b2. Niccolò Machiavelli to Francesco Vettori, August 23, 1513; in Machiavelli, *The Chief Works and Others*, trans. Allan Gilbert (Durham, N.C., 1965), vol. III, p. 925. Machiavelli's model of disciplined ardor was the citizen army of Rome: see the *Discourses*, bk. III, ch. 36.
25. Aristotle, *Politics*, 1281b26–38.

26. Cicero, *De Legibus*, III, 38–39; quoted in Cumming, *Human Nature*, vol. I, p. 251. Machiavelli, *Discourses*, bk. I, ch. 4 (in all citations from Machiavelli, I am relying on the trans. of Gilbert). Montesquieu, *Spirit of the Laws*, bk. XI, ch. 6.

27. Aristotle, *Politics*, 1317b15–17; 1301a27–28. Machiavelli, *History of Florence*, bk. IV, ch. 1. Montesquieu, *Spirit of the Laws*, bk. VIII, ch. 2. Cicero, *De Re Publica*, I, xliv. For Polybius, see *Histories*, bk. VI, §57, 1–9.

28. Algernon Sidney, *Discourses Concerning Government* (Edinburgh, 1750), ch. 2, §19; vol. I, p. 268. Rousseau only refers to "the unfortunate Sidney" in *Mountain*, VI; *P* III, p. 812; cf. Dufour in *P* III, p. 1667. For Sidney's influence in America, see Bernard Bailyn, *The Ideological Origins of the American Revolution* (Cambridge, Mass., 1967), pp. 34–35.

29. Bailyn, *Ideological Origins*, p. 35, cites the historian Caroline Robbins calling Sidney's *Discourses* a "textbook of revolution." For more on the confusion over democracy in the American Revolution, see below, ch. 6.

30. Jean-Jacques Burlamaqui, *The Principles of Natural and Political Right*, trans. Nugent (London, 1763), vol. II, pp. 71–72 (*Droit politique*, pt. II, ch. 1, §10). (All citations have been checked against the French texts of *Principes du droit naturel* [Geneva, 1747] and *Principes du droit politique* [Geneva, 1751].) This passage parallels Samuel Pufendorf, *Of the Law of Nature and Nations*, bk. VII, ch. 5, §vii. Until his death in 1747, Burlamaqui taught at the University of Geneva. See Ray Forrest Harvey, *Jean-Jacques Burlamaqui* (Chapel Hill, 1937), esp. pp. 185–87.

31. Burlamaqui, *Principles of Right*, vol. II, p. 91 (*Droit politique*, pt. II, ch. 2, §25). Ibid., vol. II, p. 96 (*Droit politique*, pt. II, ch. 2, §44). These sentiments echo the decree of Geneva's constitution as an "aristo-democracy" in 1734. That is not surprising, since Burlamaqui himself served on the commission appointed by the Small Council that wrote this decree. See Spink, *Rousseau et Genève*, p. 22n. For Rousseau's relationship to Burlamaqui, see Derathé, *Rousseau et la science politique*, pp. 84–89; and below, ch. 7, n. 1.

32. See *Spirit of the Laws*, bk. III, ch. 3; vol. I, p. 20. Commotion was also caused by the corollary, "that Virtue is not the Principle of a Monarchical Government" (see ibid., bk. III, ch. 5; vol. I, p. 23). For more on the democratic elements in Montesquieu's thought, see Mark Hulliung, *Montesquieu and the Old Regime* (Berkeley, 1976).

33. De Jaucourt, "Démocratie," in Diderot's *Encyclopedia*, vol. IV, pp. 816–18.

34. Ibid., vol. IV, p. 818.

35. *Contract*, bk. III, ch. 4; *P* III, p. 406; *SC*, p. 85.

36. Ibid., bk. III, ch. 10; *P* III, p. 421; *SC*, pp. 96–97.

37. Pufendorf, *Of the Law*, bk. VII, ch. 5, §iv (cited from the English trans. of Kennett [Oxford, 1703], vol. II, p. 174). (Rousseau possessed a copy of Pufendorf's treatise by 1729: see *Confessions*, bk. III; *P* I, p. 110; *CO*, p. 110.)

38. *Inequality*, pt. II; *P* III, p. 186; *DS*, p. 171. For the democratic government at the origins of Geneva, see above, ch. 4.

39. *Contract*, bk. III, ch. 17; *P* III, pp. 433–34; *SC*, p. 105 (emphasis added).

40. "Corsica," foreword; *P* III, p. 901; *PW*, p. 277.

41. *Contract*, bk. III, ch. 1; *P* III, p. 397; *SC*, p. 80. Rousseau to Tronchin, November 26, 1758; *C* V, p. 242. *Contract*, bk. III, ch. 10; *P* III, p. 422; *SC*, pp. 97–98. I have followed roughly the parable of Swiss decline in "Corsica"; *P* III, pp. 914–17; *PW*, pp. 296–98. Cf. the account in *Mountain* discussed above, ch. 4, and the remarks on Geneva in *Héloïse*, pt. VI, v; *P* II, pp. 657–63. See finally *Inequality*, pt. II; *P* III, pp. 189–91; *DS*, pp. 175–78.

42. On the meaning of sovereignty in Rousseau's day, see Derathé, *Rousseau et la science politique*, pp. 382–84. Again, Montesquieu prepares the way for Rousseau: see *Spirit of the Laws*, bk. II, ch. 2, where he defines a democracy as a republic in which "le peuple en corps a la souveraine puissance." For Hobbes, see the Latin and English texts of *De Cive*, V, §11; and *Leviathan*, pt. II, ch. 17.

43. Pufendorf, *Of the Law*, bk. VII, ch. 7, §1; vol. II, p. 207; see also ibid., bk. VII, ch. 4; vol. II, pp. 165–73. Burlamaqui, *Principles of Right*, vol. I, p. 80 (*Droit naturel*, pt. I, ch. 8, §5); cf. ibid., vol. II, pp. 97–111 (Droit politique, pt. II, ch. 3).

44. Phillippe de Plessis-Mornay, *Vindiciae Contra Tyrannos*, trans. Julian Franklin, in Julian Franklin, ed., *Constitutionalism and Resistance in the Sixteenth Century* (New York, 1969), pp. 190–91. For medieval ideas on popular sovereignty, see Otto Gierke, *Political Theories of the Middle Age*, trans. Frederic William Maitland (Boston, 1958), pp. 37–61. For later developments, see Quentin Skinner, *The Foundations of Modern Political Thought* (Cambridge, 1978), esp. vol. II, pp. 318–48.

45. Jean Bodin, *Six Books of a Commonweal*, trans. Richard Knolles (Cambridge, Mass., 1962), p. 84 (bk. I, ch. 8); quoted in Skinner, *Modern Political Thought*, vol. II, p. 287. Proclamation of Louis XV, March 3, 1766, quoted by Cobban, *Aspects*, p. 140.

46. For Rousseau and the classical image of democracy, see above, ch. 2.

47. *Mountain*, VIII; *P* III, pp. 837–38. On the unobtrusive essence of the democratic constitution, see below, ch. 7, on the nature of an education in freedom. Cf. *Contract*, bk. II, ch. 12; *P* III, p. 394; *SC*, p. 77: "The true constitution of the State . . . substitutes the force of habit for that of authority."

(1764–1778) *The Reluctant Visionary*

1. Rousseau to Charles Pinot Duclos, July 28, 1763; *C* XVII, p. 98.

2. Rousseau to Lenieps, July 15, 1764; *C* XX, p. 280. See also Rousseau to Lieutenant Colonel Charles Pictet, March 1, 1764; *C* XIX, p. 190.

3. Rousseau to George Keith, Comte-Maréchal d'Ecosse, August 21, 1764; *C* XXI, p. 53. I am following the itinerary reconstructed in *P* I, p. 1581.

4. Rousseau to Lenieps, July 23, 1763; *C* XVII, p. 81.

5. *Confessions*, bk. XII; *P* I, p. 610; *CO*, p. 564.

6. I am here following the account in Guehenno, *Rousseau*, vol. II, p. 128.

7. *Mountain*, foreword; *P* III, p. 685.

8. Declaration of the Syndics and Small Council of Geneva, February 12, 1765; cited in *P* I, p. 1589. For the devastating impact of Rousseau's polemic on politics in the city, see the modern *Histoire de Genève*, p. 449.

9. For a more detailed account of the reaction in Geneva, see Spink, *Rousseau et Genève*, pp. 246–56; and, for a longer view, Palmer, *Democratic Revolution*, vol. I, pp. 133–38. For the sequel, see below, ch. 6.

10. *Confessions,* bk. XII; *P* I, pp. 623–24; *CO*, pp. 575–76.

11. See *P* I, p. 1590.

12. See Spink, *Rousseau et Genève*, pp. 277–78.

13. *Confessions*, bk. VI; *P* I, p. 216; *CO*, p. 207.

14. Rousseau to Moultou, February 18, 1765; *C* XXIV, p. 32.

15. Rousseau to Jean-André and Guillaume-Antoine De Luc, February 24, 1765; *C* XXIV, p. 87.

16. *Rousseau, Judge,* I; *P* I, p. 717n. For details on this affair, see *P* I, pp. 1646–47. For an example of the pose as peacemaker, see Rousseau to Moultou, March 7, 1768; in *Correspondance Générale de J.-J. Rousseau,* ed. Théophile Dufour (Paris, 1932), vol. XVIII, p. 149.

17. *Reveries*, I; *P* I, p. 995; *RS*, p. 31. For Rousseau's declining interest in politics, see Daniel Roche and Michel Launay, "Vers une analyse historique de la correspondance do Jean-Jacques Rousseau," in Launay, ed., *Rousseau et son temps*, pp. 217–37.

18. "Poland" [v]; *P* III, pp. 970, 971; *PW*, pp. 181, 183. Rousseau also thought a federation of European nations a possible solution to war. See his "Extract from the Project for Perpetual Peace by l'abbé de Saint-Pierre" and his "Judgment on the Perpetual Peace"; *P* III, pp. 563–600.

19. *Contract*, bk. III, ch. 13; *P* III, p. 427; *SC*, p. 101.

20. "Poland" [v]; *P* III, p. 971; *PW*, p. 183. Ibid., [vi]; *P* III, p. 973; *PW*, p. 185.

21. Ibid., [vi]; *P* III, p. 973; *PW*, p. 185. On rotation and instruction of representatives, see ibid., [vii]; *P* III, p. 979; *PW*, pp. 192–93.

22. *Contract*, bk. II, ch. 10; *P* III, p. 391; *SC*, p. 75. "Corsica"; *P* III, pp. 906, 907–08; *PW*, pp. 285–86, 287.

23. "Poland" [vii]; *P* III, pp. 981, 988, 1769; *PW*, pp. 195, 205, 204. On the manuscript variants, see *P* III, p. 1769, and *V* II, 459n.

24. *Contract*, bk. II, ch. 11; *P* III, p. 392; *SC*, p. 75. "Corsica," foreword; *P* III, p. 901; *PW*, p. 277.

25. "Corsica," foreword; *P* III, p. 901; *PW*, p. 277. *Inequality*, pt. II; *P* III, pp. 181, 190, 187; *DS*, pp. 162–63, 175, 172. *Contract*, bk. II, ch. 7; *P* III, p. 381; *SC*, p. 68.

26. Rousseau to d'Ivernois, January 31, 1767; *C* XXXII, p. 89.

27. Rousseau to George Keith, December 8, 1764; *C* XXII, p. 184. "Poland" [xv]; *P* III, p. 1041; *PW*, p. 273.

28. *Contract*, bk. III, ch. 12; *P* III, p. 425; *SC*, p. 99.

Chapter 6. *The Oracle and the Revolution*

1. Maximilien Robespierre, "Report on Religious and Moral Ideas and on the National Festivals," May 7, 1794; *ROC* X, pp. 443–44.

2. McDonald, *Rousseau and the Revolution*, pp. 172, 148; see also ibid., p. 37. Cf. R. A. Leigh's review article on McDonald's book in *The Historical Journal*

XII(1969):549–65. McDonald's work has proved invaluable for the present study, if only because many of the pamphlets cited by her have proved difficult to obtain in this country.

3. See Daniel Mornet, "Les enseignements des bibliothèques privées, 1750–1780," *Revue de l'histoire littéraire de la France* XVII(1910):449–95.

4. See Trenard, "Diffusion du *Contrat social*," in *ECS*, p. 432.

5. For the most recent inventory of different editions of the *Contract*, see Jean Sénelier, *Bibliographie générale des oeuvres de J.-J. Rousseau* (Paris, 1950).

6. On counterfeit editions of the *Contract*, see the remarks by Leigh in his review article on McDonald's book, p. 561.

7. I am here following the research of Robert Darnton, whose study of the publication and diffusion of Diderot's *Encyclopedia* gives an especially vivid and well-documented picture of Enlightenment book publishing. See Darnton, *The Business of Enlightenment* (Cambridge, Mass., 1979), pp. 273–79.

8. See Robert Darnton, "Reading, Writing, and Publishing in Eighteenth-Century France: a Case Study in the Sociology of Literature," in Felix Gilbert and Stephen Graubard, eds., *Historical Studies Today* (New York, 1972), pp. 250–52. On *cabinets littéraires*, see Darnton, *Business of Enlightenment*, pp. 298–99.

9. See Guehenno, *Rousseau*, vol. I, p. 286; and Robert Darnton, "In search of the Enlightenment: Recent attempts to create a social history of ideas," *Journal of Modern History* XLIII(1971):124–26. Cf. Peter Burke, *Popular Culture in Early Modern Europe* (New York, 1978), pp. 72–73, 118–21.

10. Darnton, *Business of Enlightenment*, p. 528.

11. See Lionello Sozzi, "Interprétations de Rousseau pendant la révolution," *Studies on Voltaire and the Eighteenth Century* LXIV(1968)191–92 and n.; and Sénelier, *Bibliographie générale*, pp. 195–200.

12. See Wilson, *Diderot*, p. 705.

13. A reproduction of the engraving appears in *S* III, p. 570.

14. See McNeil, "Cult of Rousseau," pp. 199–201.

15. On Robespierre and Rousseau, see George Rudé, *Robespierre: Portrait of a Revolutionary Democrat* (New York, 1975), p. 16. On Babeuf and Marat, see Claude Mazauric, "Le Rousseauisme de Babeuf," *Annals historiques de la révolution française* XXXIV(1962):454. On Marat and Rousseau, see Louis R. Gottschalk, *Jean Paul Marat: A Study in Radicalism* (New York, 1927), pp. 16–18, 21. See also McNeil, "Cult of Rousseau," p. 200.

16. *Reveries*, I; *P* I, p. 995; *RS*, p. 1. See also McDonald, *Rousseau and the Revolution*, p. 166.

17. Starobinski, *La transparence*, p. 314.

18. *Héloïse*, pt. III, xviii; *P* II, p. 364; *NH*, pp. 255–56. *Emile*, bk. III; *P* IV, p. 468; *EM*, p. 194.

19. See Jean Starobinski, *1789, les emblèmes de la raison* (Paris, 1979), p. 179, and McNeil, "Cult of Rousseau," pp. 204–05.

20. Along with Tom Paine and, later, the abbé Sièyes, Rousseau deserves to be counted among those who opened the language of politics to popular enthusiasm and broad public debate. For Paine, see Eric Foner, *Tom Paine and Revolutionary America* (New York, 1976), esp. pp. 74–87.

21. A. M. d'Eymar, "Motion relative to J. J. Rousseau," speech to the National Assembly, December 29, 1790; P. L. Ginguené, "Petition to the National Assembly containing demands to transfer the cinders of J. J. Rousseau to the French Pantheon," 1791; Collot d'Herbois, in *Journal des Jacobins* CVIII(1791); all quoted in McDonald, *Rousseau and the Revolution*, pp. 159–60.

22. See Avocat Morisse, *Essai sur la nature et l'exercice de l'authorité du Peuple dans un Etat* (1789), and Jean-Baptiste Salaville, *De l'organisation d'un état monarchique, ou considérations sur les vices de la monarchie française et sur la nécessité de lui donner une Constitution* (1789)—essentially a paraphrase of the *Social Contract*.

23. Le Père Guillaume-François Berthier, *Observations sur la Contrat social de J.-J. Rousseau* (Paris, 1789), pp. 49–50, 105, 106.

24. Achille Nicolas Isnard, *Observations sur le principe qui a produit les révolutions de France, de Genève et d'Amérique dans le dix-huitième siècle* Evereux, 1789, pp. 4–5; see also pp. 10ff. (on Cicero), p. 20 (on Montesquieu), and pp. 39f. (on the possible tyranny of a majority in Rousseau's system).

25. In America, Rousseau was cited in pamphlets of the revolutionary period by the likes of James Otis and Josiah Quincy, Jr., both of whom cheerfully lumped him together with Locke, Grotius, Pufendorf, and Montesquieu. The *Social Contract* and Rousseau's constitutional plan for Poland were both studied by John Adams, who possessed no less than four copies of the *Contract* in his personal library. But for most of the early American political theorists, Rousseau was at best merely one modern authority among many, at worst an idle dreamer, devoted to projects as "preposterous" as they were "impotent," to borrow the derisive adjectives of James Madison. See Bailyn, *Ideological Origins*, pp. 22–54; Wood, *American Republic*, pp. 3–45; Paul Merrill Spurlin, *Rousseau in America 1760–1809* (University, Alabama, 1969), p. 101; and, for a slightly different emphasis, Palmer, *Democratic Revolution*, vol. I, pp. 223–24. Madison's dismissal occurs in a 1792 article entitled "Is Universal Peace Possible?"; see Madison, *The Forging of American Federalism*, ed. Padover (New York, 1953), p. 261.

26. See Palmer, *Democratic Revolution*, vol. I, pp. 135–37; and the modern *Histoire de Genève*, pp. 449–52.

27. See Palmer, *Democratic Revolution*, vol. I, pp. 358–60; and *Histoire de Genève*, pp. 469–75. For more on the traditional division between Citizens and Natives in Geneva, see above, p. 14; for Rousseau's views, see above, ch. 4, n. 17.

28. The official of Berne is quoted in Palmer, *Democratic Revolution*, vol. I, p. 359. For the comments of the foreign ministers, see Jacques Godechot, *The Taking of the Bastille*, trans. Stewart (New York, 1970), p. 31.

29. Mme Roland is quoted in ibid., p. 32. For other figures linking Geneva with the French Revolution, see Leigh's review article on McDonald, p. 503.

30. See François d'Ivernois, *Tableau historique et politique des dernières révolutions à Genève* (London, 1789); an earlier edition of this partisan work, taking the story up till 1768, had appeared in Geneva in 1782. On Humbert, see Godechot, *Bastille*, p. 225, and pp. 277–86.

31. Cf. David Williams, "The influence of Rousseau on political opinion, 1760–1795," *The English Historical Review*, XLVIII(1933):425.

32. See McDonald, *Rousseau and the Revolution*, pp. 76–80.

33. *Révolutions de Paris*, November 21–28, 1789, XX, p. 17 (on sovereignty and representation). Idem, November 7–14, 1789, XVIII, p. 2 (on the need for a "democratic or popular" Commune). Idem, October 31–November 7, 1789, XVII, p. 2 (on mores).

34. See Darnton, *Business of Enlightenment*, p. 542. The rhythm of publication for the *Social Contract* is like a road map to modern revolutions: see Palmer, *Democratic Revolution*, vol. I, pp. 119–20. The Bible-size edition for soldiers "defending *la patrie*" is mentioned in McNeil, "Cult of Rousseau," p. 206.

35. See Albert Soboul, "Audience des lumières: classes populaires et rousseauisme sous la révolution," *Annales historiques de la révolution française* XXXIV(1962):429–34.

36. See ibid., pp. 433, 434; and Gundula Gobel and Albert Soboul, "Audience et pragmatisme du rousseauisme: les almanachs de la révolution (1788–1795)," *Annales historiques de la révolution française*, L(1978):608–40. In one collection of revolutionary hymns, twenty-one *titles* make reference to Rousseau by name (the closest competitor, Voltaire, is mentioned eleven times): see D. Higgins, "The Terrorists' Favourite Authors: Some Statistics from Revolutionary Literature," *The Modern Language Review* LIV(1959):403. For the hymn about the "free French," see McNeil, "Cult of Rousseau," p. 206. Cf. Albert Soboul, *Les Sans-culottes parisiens en l'an II* (Paris, 1958), pp. 670–73.

37. See McNeil, "Cult of Rousseau," p. 204; McDonald, *Rousseau and the Revolution*, p. 156.

38. "The genius of Rousseau enlightens the National Assembly," an engraving published by Chapuy, Paris, 1789; reproduced in Norman Hampson, *The First European Revolution, 1776–1815* (New York, 1969), p. 93.

39. See McNeil, "Cult of Rousseau," p. 207; and Trenard, "Diffusion du *Contrat social*," in *ECS*, pp. 447, 445. The playing card appears in *S* II, p. 579.

40. See *Prosopopée de J. J. Rousseau, ou sentiments de reconnaissance des amis de l'Institution d'Emile à l'Assemblée National . . . à l'occasion de son décret de 21 Décembre 1790*, published in 1790. I am following the account of this pamphlet in McDonald, *Rousseau and the Revolution*, pp. 167–68.

41. Rousseau's classical imagery fitted well with the revolutionary "cult of antiquity," particularly in the crucial period between September, 1792, and October, 1793. See Harold Parker, *The Cult of Antiquity and the French Revolution* (Chicago, 1937), pp. 25, 119–38.

42. Cf. the comments by Ernst Cassirer in *The Question of Jean-Jacques Rousseau*, trans. Peter Gay (Bloomington, 1963), pp. 69–71, with the discussion of Alexis de Tocqueville in *The Old Régime and the French Revolution*, trans. Gilbert (Garden City, 1955), pp. 10–13.

43. J. J. O. Meude-Monpas, *Eloge de J.-J. Rousseau* (Paris, 1790), pp. 5–6; quoted in Sozzi, "Interprétations de Rousseau," p. 197. Contemporary students of Rousseau will be familiar with this line of interpretation: in its emphasis, it strongly resembles the reading of Leo Strauss and his school. Cf., e.g., the conclusion of Masters, *Philosophy of Rousseau*, pp. 418–43.

44. See Charles François Lenormant, *J.-J. Rousseau, aristocrate* (Paris, 1790). I am relying on the discussion of this work in Gordon McNeil, "The Anti-Revolutionary Rousseau," *The American Historical Review* LVIII(1953):812; see ibid., p. 817, for other antidemocratic uses of the *Contract* by conservatives. The strain in Rousseau's work indebted to Montesquieu fueled readings that were almost Burkean in tone; a key text from this perspective became "Considerations on the Government of Poland." See Sozzi, "Interprétations de Rousseau," p. 207; see ibid., p. 205, for the conservative argument that the *Contract* is "only a utopia."

45. See Fauchet's inaugural lecture, printed in *Bouche de Fer* XI(1790):167–68; I am here quoting from McDonald, *Rousseau and the Revolution*, pp. 77–80, and relying on her discussion.

46. J. P. Brissot, *Discours sur les conventions* (Paris, 1791), p. 17; quoted in McDonald, *Rousseau and the Revolution*, p. 109. See also Eloise Ellery, *Brissot de Warville* (Boston, 1915), pp. 41–44. For a description of the Girondin almanac, see Gobel and Soboul, "Almanachs de la-révolution," p. 627.

47. For the use of the term *democracy* in 1789, see the article in *Révolutions de Paris*, cited above, n. 33. For Brissot's quote, see Palmer, "Use of the Word 'Democracy'," p. 213.

48. For the causes and structure of popular uprisings during the French Revolution, see, in addition to Soboul's work, Godechot's *Taking of the Bastille*; George Rudé, *The Crowd in the French Revolution* (Oxford, 1959); Richard Cobb, *The Police and the People: French Popular Protest 1789–1820* (Oxford, 1970); and, more generally, Barrington Moore, Jr., *Injustice: the Social Bases of Obedience and Revolt* (White Plains, N.Y., 1978) and Charles, Louise, and Richard Tilly, *The Rebellious Century 1830–1930* (Cambridge, Mass., 1975).

49. On the Constitution of 1791, see Palmer, *Democratic Revolution*, vol. I, pp. 522–28. For the constitutional issues, see ibid., vol. II, pp. 36–44, and J. M. Thompson, *The French Revolution* (Oxford, 1943), pp. 338–66. The device of an extralegal convention was of American provenance; see Wood, *American Republic*, pp. 306–43.

50. See Palmer, *Democratic Revolution*, vol. II, pp. 44–65.

51. See Rudé, *Robespierre*, p. 97; Gerard Walter, *Robespierre* (Paris, 1946), pp. 22–24, 565–66; and J. M. Thompson, *Robespierre* (Oxford, 1935), vol. I, pp. 180–81, vol. II, pp. 47, 280.

52. J. M. Thompson, *Robespierre and the French Revolution* (New York, 1962), pp. 9–10. Mirabeau's comment is quoted in Rudé, *Robespierre*, p. 22. For the highly condensed account that follows, I am heavily indebted to the two brilliant essays by Cobban in *Aspects*, pp. 137–91: "The Fundamental Ideas of Robespierre" and "The Political Ideas of Maximilien Robespierre During the Period of the Convention."

53. Robespierre, "On the Constitution," May 10, 1793; *ROC* IX, p. 497.

54. Idem, "On the Principles of Political Morality Which should guide the National Convention in the Internal Administration of the Republic," February 5, 1794; *ROC* X, pp. 352, 353. Idem, from a debate on the plan of the constitution of the Clergy, June 9, 1789, reported in *Le Point du Jour* X(1789):453; *ROC* VI, p.

400 (where Robespierre is already saying that "it is up to the people, and only them, to name ... public officers, it is up to those wherein sovereignty resides. ..."). Idem, "Observations on the Moral Causes of our Current Situation," in *Le Défenseur de la Constitution*, No. 4, c. June 7, 1792; *RPC* IV, pp. 115–16. Idem, "Letter to MM. Vergniaud, Gensonné, Brissot and Guadet, on the Sovereignty of the People," in *Lettres à ses commettans*, 2nd. series, c. January 5, 1793; *ROC* V, p. 191. Cf. Rousseau's views on the people in *Emile*, bk. IV; *P* IV, pp. 509–10; *EM*, pp. 225–26: "The people show themselves such as they are. ..."

55. Robespierre, "Dedication to Jean-Jacques Rousseau"; *ROC* I, pp. 211–12. According to Walter, *Robespierre*, p. 23, this document dates from 1789. Cobban lists five other instances of *public* eulogies to Rousseau by Robespierre: see *Aspects*, p. 293 (ch. 8, n. 110).

56. For Rousseau on the virtues of eloquence, see "Origin of Languages," ch. 20; *D* II, pp. 384–85; *OL*, pp. 72–73.

57. The account that follows is based on Albert Soboul's *Les Sans-culottes parisiens en l'an II*, partially trans. by Gwynne Lewis as *The Parisian Sans-Culottes and the French Revolution* (Oxford, 1964).

58. Indicative of the politicized autodidact and his experience is the education that Gracchus Babeuf gave himself. He seems to have become aware of Rousseau's ideas through secondhand sources: Marat's *Chains of Slavery* and, later, Girardin's *Discourse on the Necessity of the Ratification of the Law by the General Will*, a work based on talks given in 1791. Like Rousseau, Babeuf defended the value of chimerical thinking: "This passion for the public welfare," he wrote in 1791, "can only sustain itself on illusions." See R. B. Rose, *Gracchus Babeuf* (Stanford, 1978), pp. 29, 32, 35, 98, 106–07; and Mazauric, "Rousseauisme de Babeuf." On the literacy of the sans-culottes generally, see Rudé, *The Crowd*, p. 211.

59. Guiraut, speaking in the summer of 1793; quoted in Soboul, *Les Sans-culottes parisiens*, p. 509. Needless to say, Rousseau himself would scarcely have been thrilled by such sentiments.

60. Leclerc, *L'Ami du peuple*, August 21, 1793; quoted in Soboul, *Les Sans-culottes parisiens*, p. 518.

61. See Soboul, "Classes populaires et rousseauisme," pp. 424–25.

62. See Michael L. Kennedy, *The Jacobin Club of Marseilles, 1790–1794* (Ithaca, 1973), esp. pp. 114–18, 217–18.

63. Robespierre, "On the Constitution"; *ROC* IX, pp. 495–96, 498.

64. Ibid., *ROC* IX, pp. 500 (on devices limiting the power of magistrates), 501–02 (on the sovereignty of primary assemblies).

65. Ibid., *ROC* IX, pp. 502–03. Cf. Gordon McNeil, "Robespierre, Rousseau, and Representation," in Richard Herr and Harold T. Parker, eds., *Ideas in History* (Durham, N.C., 1965), pp. 135–56.

66. Robespierre, "On the Constitution"; *ROC* IX, pp. 500, 504–05.

67. See Gottschalk, *Marat*, pp. 157–66; and Soboul, *Les Sans-culottes parisiens*, pp. 39–40, 672–73.

68. Hérault-Séchelles, "Report, in the name of the Committee on Public Safety, on the Project of a Constitution for the French People." *Archives parlementaires de 1787 à 1860*, 1st series (1867–   ), vol. LXVI, pp. 257–59. Cf. Thompson,

French Revolution, pp. 392–97. For Condorcet's original draft of the Constitution, see his speech of February 15–16, 1793, in *Archives parlementaires*, vol. LVIII, pp. 583–624. Besides the discourse of May 10, 1793, Robespierre's major speech to the Convention on the Constitution was given on April 24, 1793; see *ROC* IX, pp. 459–70, esp. p. 461.

69. For the text of the 1793 Constitution, see *Archives parlementaires*, vol. LXVII, pp. 143–50. An English translation appears in Philippe Buonarroti, *Babeuf's Conspiracy for Equality*, trans. Bronterre O'Brien (London, 1836), pp. 279–92. The Constitution of 1793 became one lodestar of Babouvism: see Rose, *Babeuf*, pp. 235–39.

70. See Soboul, *Les Sans-culottes parisiens*, pp. 508–09, 633.

71. See ibid., pp. 151–75, 530–42. The revolutionary calendar was instituted on November 24, 1793, dated retroactively to September 22, 1792—the day the first French Republic was declared and the beginning of year I.

72. Robespierre, "Report on the Principles of Revolutionary Government," December 25, 1793; *ROC* X, p. 274. Idem, "On the Crimes of Kings Coalesced against France," May 26, 1794; *ROC* X, pp. 476–77.

73. Idem, "Principles of Political Morality"; *ROC* X, pp. 355 (on the danger of "aristocratic prejudices" leading to an inevitable loss of freedom, as government declines "from democracy to aristocracy to monarchy"), 357 (on virtue and terror).

74. Ibid., *ROC* X, pp. 352 (on combatting egotism, keeping the promises of philosophy, and democracy), 352–53 (the false and true definitions of democracy), 364 (on the government as "the master [*le maître*]"—a term, in this context, with pedagogical overtones), 353 ("freedom against tyranny").

75. See Albert Soboul, "Robespierre and the Popular Movement of 1793–4," *Past and Present*, V(1954):54–70.

76. For "democracy" as the great symbolic innovation of the revolution, see Furet, *Interpreting the French Revolution*, esp. pp. 24–32. The most comprehensive general account remains Palmer's *The Age of the Democratic Revolution*.

77. James Wilson, "Lectures on Law," quoted in Wood, *American Republic*, p. 603. For the origins of the English word *democrat*, see the *Oxford English Dictionary*. On early American usage, see Richard Buel, Jr., "Democracy and the American Revolution: a Frame of Reference," *The William and Mary Quarterly*, 3d ser. XXI(1964):165–90; and Bailyn, *Ideological Origins*, pp. 282–83. See also the sources cited above, ch. 5, n. 16. For an overview of the French impact on conceptions of self-rule in America, see Palmer, *Democratic Revolution*, vol. II, pp. 509–45; for a closer look, see the comments on the "democratic clubs" formed in America in the 1790s in imitation of the French, in Richard Buel, Jr., *Securing the Revolution* (Ithaca, 1972), pp. 97–105, 124–35.

78. Benjamin Rush, "Defects of the Confederation," quoted in Wood, *American Republic*, p. 374.

79. For representation in early America, see J. R. Pole, *Political Representation in England and the Origins of the American Republic* (Berkeley, 1971), esp. pp. 541–42; and Wood, *American Republic*, pp. 409–13, 562. Cf. Louis Hartz, *The Liberal Tradition in America* (New York, 1955), pp. 89–90.

80. Alexander Hamilton, James Madison, John Jay, *The Federalist Papers*, §14 (Madison, "a government wholly popular"); §63 (probably Madison, "exclusion of the people"); §28 (Hamilton, "the whole power of the government"). Madison to Thomas Jefferson, October 24, 1787, in Madison, *American Federalism*, pp. 42, 40 ("divide et impera" contra "simple democracy"); cf. the more discrete formulations of Madison in *Federalist* §10.

81. Bailyn, *Ideological Origins*, p. 198.

82. Tocqueville, *The Old Régime*, pp. 12–13.

83. McDonald, *Rousseau and the Revolution*, p. 161. Cf. Pierre Trahard, *La Sensibilité révolutionnaire* (Paris, 1936), esp. pp. 39–40.

84. For the causes of rebellion in revolutionary France, see the sources cited above, n. 48.

85. Theodore Zeldin, *France 1848–1945: Politics and Anger* (Oxford, 1979), p. 68.

86. McDonald, *Rousseau and the Revolution*, p. 172. A parallel error is made by Richard Cobb in *The Police and the People*, p. 206, where he flatly asserts that "Rousseau is . . . irrelevant to an understanding of the *sans-culottes*." His claim is based on the observation, doubtless accurate as far as it goes, that the sans-culottes invoked Rousseau's name and phrases as an act of ritualized rhetoric: "They were not political theorists." Granted. But since when is ceremonial language and ritual piety so utterly irrelevant to comprehending commonplace hopes and fears? Cf. Soboul, "Classes populaires et rousseauisme," esp. p. 438.

87. Condorcet, "Letter to a Theologian," in *Oeuvres de Condorcet*, ed. O'Connor and Arago (Paris, 1847), vol. V, pp. 306–07. I encountered this passage thanks to Williams, "The Influence of Rousseau," p. 417. Kant also spoke of Rousseau's "magic power of eloquence," although, characteristically enough, he tried to resist it. "I must read Rousseau," he once wrote, "until his beauty of expression no longer distracts me at all, and only then can I survey him with reason." See *Fragments*, ed. Hartenstein, vol. V, pp. 618, 624; quoted in Ernst Cassirer, *Rousseau, Kant and Goethe*, trans. Gutmann, Kristeller, and Randall (Princeton, 1945), pp. 6, 7.

88. *Qui est-ce donc qui gagne à la Révolution* (Paris, 1790), p. 19; quoted in Williams, "Influence of Rousseau," p. 424.

89. *Rousseau, Judge*, III; *P* I, p. 935. "Political Fragments"; *P* III, p. 539.

90. Moultou to Rousseau, December 23, 1764; *C* XXII, p. 278. For the festivities in Geneva, see Trenard, "Diffusion du *Contrat social*," in *ECS*, p. 448.

91. Report of Lakanal to the Convention, September 15, 1794; quoted in Starobinski, *1789*, p. 179.

92. I am following the description given in McNeil, "Cult of Rousseau," p. 209.

93. See Trenard, "Diffusion du *Contrat social*," in *ECS*, p. 447.

94. See McNeil, "Cult of Rousseau," p. 209.

Chapter 7. *The Forms of Freedom*

1. Derathé, *Rousseau et la science politique*, p. 377. For Rousseau's modern emphasis on freedom, see above, chs. 2, 3, and 4. What is radical in Rousseau's emphasis on freedom appears most clearly when he is compared with more conventional

republicans. We have already observed Burlamaqui, the celebrated Genevan professor of law, linking sovereignty with a "society of inequality" (see above, ch. 5). Elsewhere, Burlamaqui drew the obvious conclusions regarding the fate of free will in society:

> In fact, a being *independent* of all others has no other rule to pursue but the counsels of his own reason; and in consequence of this independence, he is liberated from all subjection to the will of others: in a word, he is absolute master of himself and of his actions. But the case is not the same with a being that we suppose dependent on another, as on his superior and master. . . . It is obvious that these remarks are in a particular manner appropriate to man: so that as soon as he acknowledges a superior, to whose power and authority he is naturally subject, in consequence of this state he must acknowledge likewise the will of this superior to be the *rule* of his actions. This is the *right* we call LAW.

(See Burlamaqui, *Principles of Right*, vol. I, p. 77 [*Droit naturel*, pt. I, ch. 8, §2]). Burlamaqui's conception of law helps explain the charges leveled by the Small Council against the *Social Contract*: "Such extreme Freedom is the Deity of the Author."

2. Plato, *Republic*, 562b–c. Of course, Rousseau doesn't endorse freedom understood in terms of limitless desire (the specific form of freedom Socrates proceeds to find blameworthy in a democracy). In speaking of an interest in perfecting the human being, I have in mind the Greek concept of a *paideia* (or education) in *aretē* (excellence or virtue). In general, see Werner Jaeger, *Paideia*, trans. Highet (Oxford, 1939–44). Rousseau absorbed this concern through his reading of Plato's *Republic*. See *Emile*, bk. I; *P* IV, p. 250; *EM*, p. 40.

3. G. W. F. Hegel, *Werke* (Frankfurt, 1971), vol. XX, pp. 307–08 (*Lectures on the History of Philosophy*, vol. III, pt. III, sec. I, ch. 2, §C, 3C). In this context, however—and given a common tendency to lump together Rousseau and Hegel when discussing freedom—it should be emphasized that Hegel, in his own philosophy, takes issue with much that is crucial to Rousseau's understanding of freedom: for example, the sentiment of being able to do as one wants. Symptomatic in this regard are Hegel's remarks about education:

> With regard to one side of education, namely discipline, the boy should not be allowed to follow his own inclination; he must obey in order that he may learn to command. Obedience is the beginning of all wisdom. . . . To allow children to do as they please, to be so foolish as to provide them into the bargain with reasons for their whims, is to fall into the worst of all educational practices. . . . Self-will and evil soon make their appearance in the child. This self-will, this germ of evil, must be broken and destroyed by discipline.

(See Hegel, *Philosophy of Mind*, trans. William Wallace and A. V. Miller [Oxford, 1971], p. 60 [Supplement to Encyclopedia, §396].) For Hegel, freedom has more to do with rational command than with spontaneous motion: from the outset, it is implicated in hierarchical relations of domination and discipline. From this standpoint, the question of individual assent to political institutions is of strictly subordinate significance. The quite undemocratic implications of these views are fully developed in Hegel's *Philosophy of Right*.

4. See Isaiah Berlin, *Four Essays on Liberty* (Oxford, 1969), pp. 123, 162–63. Cf. Maurice Cranston, *Freedom* (New York, 1967), pp. 6, 21.

5. *Contract*, bk. I, ch. 4; *P* III, p. 356; *SC*, p. 50. Hegel cites this passage in his discussion of Rousseau in the *History of Philosophy*.

6. *Contract*, bk. I, ch. 8; *P* III, p. 365; *SC*, p. 56.

7. Geneva Ms., bk. I, ch. 4; *P* III, p. 296; *SC*, p. 168.

8. Ibid., bk. IV; *P* IV, p. 586; *EM*, p. 280. *Inequality*, pt. I; *P* III, p. 142; *DS*, p. 114.

9. *Emile*, bk. IV; *P* IV, p. 574; *EM*, p. 272.

10. Ibid., bk. IV; *P* IV, p. 575; *EM*, p. 273. *Contract*, bk. III, ch. 1; *P* III, p. 395; *SC*, p. 78. For Rousseau's metaphysical dualism, see Masters *Philosophy of Rousseau*, pp. 66–74.

11. *Emile*, bk. IV; *P* IV, p. 576; *EM*, p. 274. Geneva Ms., bk. I, ch. 4; *P* III, p. 296; *SC*, p. 168.

12. On imagination, see above, ch. 1. On judgment, see *Emile*, bk. IV; *P* IV, p. 571; *EM*, p. 270. Cf. Masters, *Philosophy of Rousseau*, pp. 61–62.

13. Kant, *Critique of Pure Reason*, A448/B476. "Emile and Sophie," I; *P* IV, p. 905. The ability to begin anew is the disturbingly creative, as well as the redemptive, aspect of the capacity for spontaneous motion. See, e.g., *Inequality*, pt. I; *P* III, p. 141; *DS*, p. 114: "The will still speaks when Nature falls silent."

14. *Rousseau, Judge*, II; *P* I, p. 855. For more on the conservative uses of the will in Rousseau, see Shklar, *Men and Citizens*, pp. 70–74, 184–97; Shklar, however, lays insufficient emphasis on the derivative character of the will's constancy.

15. Evidence for this position in Rousseau can be found in his emphasis on learning by doing; see below. Also note the importance he attaches to preserving the possibility for change.

16. *Inequality*, pt. I; *P* III, pp. 141–42; *DS*, p. 114. *Mountain*, VIII; *P* III, p. 842. For spontaneous motion in animals, see *Emile*, bk. IV; *P* IV, p. 574; *EM*, p. 272. At first glance, "perfectibility" appears to supplant free will as the distinctively human trait in the *Second Discourse*: see *Inequality* pt. I; *P* III, p. 142; *DS*, p. 115. But the appearance is misleading, in part because perfectibility only becomes possible through imagination—and the spontaneous motion of imagination, we now learn, is grounded in free will. Perfectibility, in other words, is merely one particularly tangible and typically human manifestation of the "consciousness of freedom" engendered by free will. Cf. the remarks in Masters, *Philosophy of Rousseau*, pp. 69–72. For perfectibility and imagination, see above, ch. 1, n. 26.

17. *Emile*, bk. IV; *P* IV, p. 586; *EM*, p. 280.

18. Ibid., bk. IV; *P* IV, pp. 586, 594–95; *EM*, pp. 280, 286. Rousseau plays on the dual meaning of the French term *conscience*; for him, it signifies both a prereflective and unselfconscious immediacy of existential awareness (as in the natural

man's "consciousness of this freedom"), and a rationally elucidated and quite self-conscious sense of personal convictions (as in the Vicar's conscience).

19. "Discourse on this Question: *What is the Virtue most necessary to Heroes, and What are the Heroes in Whom this Virtue is Lacking?*"; *P* II, p. 1274: "In a word, all the other virtues have been lacking in some great men; but, without strength of soul, there would never be Heroes." *Contract*, bk. I, ch. 4; *P* III, p. 356; *SC*, p. 50 ("to renounce one's freedom"). Cf. ibid., bk. I, ch. 2; *P* III, p. 353; *SC*, p. 48: "Slaves . . . love their servitude."

20. *Emile*, bk. IV; *P* IV, p. 603; *EM*, p. 292.

21. Ibid., bk. IV; *P* IV, pp. 588, 604, 605; *EM*, pp. 282, 293, 294. Cf. *Inequality*, pt. I; *P* III, p. 141; *DS*, p. 113.

22. *Emile*, bk. IV; *P* IV, p. 586; *EM*, p. 280. *Contract*, bk. II, ch. 1; *P* III, p. 369; *SC*, p. 59. Geneva Ms., bk. I, ch. 4; *P* III, p. 295; *SC*, p. 167. *Emile*, bk. IV; *P* IV, p. 491; *EM*, p. 213.

   In saying that Rousseau defines the good in terms of pleasure, we need not take him to be some kind of typically modern hedonist (though this aspect of his thought is often underemphasized): for Rousseau's position also seems close, in many respects, to Plato's. See, e.g., Plato, *Laws*, 732c–733a; cf. Descartes, *Meditations on First Philosophy*, IV; in *Philosophical Works*, vol. I, pp. 175–76; and Locke, *Essay Concerning Human Understanding*, bk. II, ch. 21, §§41–43.

23. "History of Geneva"; *S* III, p. 393. *Emile*, bk. IV; *P* IV, pp. 535, 586; *EM*, pp. 243, 280.

24. Plato, *Protagoras*, 345d. Cf. Plato, *Laws*, 731c, 860d. See also W. K. C. Guthrie, *Socrates* (Cambridge, 1971), pp. 130–42. For Locke, see *Human Understanding*, bk. II, ch. 21, §§41–43. For Rousseau's skepticism, see above, ch. 1.

25. Virtue for Rousseau is but another name for the unusually strong free will: see below. Cf. *Inequality*, pt. I; P III, pp. 156–57; *DS*, p. 133: "Although it may behoove Socrates and Minds of his stamp to acquire virtue through reason, the human Species would have ceased to exist long ago, if its conservation had depended only on the reasonings of those who comprise it."

26. For what is "Lockean" in Rousseau's Protestant recourse to conscience, consider the role accorded free will in elucidating it, discussed below.

27. *Emile*, bk. II; *P* IV, p. 322; *EM*, p. 92. For Rousseau's influence on German idealism, see Kelly, *Idealism, Politics and History*.

28. *Inequality*, pt. I; *P* III, pp. 143; *DS*, p. 115. *Emile*, bk. II; *P* IV, p. 360; *EM*, p. 118. *Inequality*, pt. I; *P* III, pp. 147, 143; *DS*, pp. 121, 116.

29. *Inequality*, pt. I; *P* III, p. 144; *DS*, p. 117.

30. Ibid., pt. I; *P* III, pp. 138, 135, 136; *DS*, pp. 110, 105, 107. Ibid., pt. II; *P* III, p. 181; *DS*, p. 164.

31. *Contract*, bk. I, ch. 8; *P* III, p. 365; *SC*, p. 56. *Emile*, bk. II; *P* IV, pp. 304, 309; *EM*, pp. 80, 84.

32. Geneva Ms., bk. I, ch. 2; *P* III, p. 283; *SC*, p. 159. Not all of this idyllic imagery is original with Rousseau; sources for some of it can be found not only in Buffon and Pufendorf, but also in Lucretius: cf. esp. *De rerum natura*, bk. V, 989–93.

33. *Emile*, bk. III; *P* IV, p. 467; *EM*, p. 193. Cf. *Inequality*, pt. II; *P* III, p. 178; *DS*, p. 160.

34. *Héloïse*, pt. V, viii; *P* II, p. 612; *NH*, p. 361.

35. *Reveries*, VI; *P* I, p. 1059; *RS*, p. 132.

36. "Political Economy"; *P* III, p. 248; *SC*, p. 214.

37. *Inequality*, pt. II; *P* III, p. 181; *DS*, p. 164. *Emile*, bk. II; *P* III, p. 309; *EM*, p. 84.

38. *Reveries*, V; *P* I, p. 1040; *RS*, p. 103. Cf. "Moral Letters," 6; *P* IV, p. 1112: "Let us begin by becoming ourselves again, by focusing ourselves, by circumscribing our soul within the same limits that nature has given to our being. . . ." On the "necessity" of pain and the "need" for pleasure, see *Emile*, bk. II; *P* IV, p. 316n.; *EM*, p. 89n.

39. *Emile*, bk. III, *P* IV, p. 455; *EM*, pp. 184–85.

40. Cf. ibid., bk. II; *P* IV, p. 316; *EM*, p. 89. On the incoherence of absolute independence, see *Mountain* VIII; *P* III, pp. 841–42: "Freedom consists less in acting at will (*à faire sa volonté*) than in not being subjugated to the will of another; it also consists in not subjugating the will of another to our own."

41. *Emile*, bk. II; *P* IV, p. 311; *EM*, p. 85.

42. Ibid., bk. I; *P* IV, p. 252; *EM*, p. 42. Ibid., bk. III; *P* IV, p. 430; *EM*, p. 168. On labor and learning to reason, see ibid., bk. III; *P* IV, pp. 480–81; *EM*, p. 203.

43. Ibid., bk. II; *P* IV, p. 362; *EM*, p. 120. The will is indeed "made captive," as Bloom's translation of *captiver* would have it—but only by being "captivated" and "bewitched."

44. *Emile*, bk. II; *P* IV, pp. 421, 407; *EM*, pp. 160, 151. Cf. ibid., bk. III; *P* IV, p. 483; *EM*, p. 205; and ibid., bk. I; *P* IV, p. 253; *EM*, p. 42. These concerns obviously mark the limit of blind habit in the groundwork of free will: see ibid., bk. II; *P* IV, p. 421n.; *EM*, p. 160n.

45. Emile's "spontaneous reason" is developed through labor; the conditions of primitive existence force a similar "spontaneous reasoning" on the savage: see ibid., bk. II; *P* IV, p. 360; *EM*, p. 118. On educating a child of the rich, see ibid., bk. I; *P* IV, p. 267; *EM*, p. 52: "I will not be sorry if Emile is highborn. In any event, he will be one victim uprooted from prejudice."

46. Ibid., bk. III; *P* IV, pp. 481, 487; *EM*, pp. 203, 208.

47. Ibid., bk. IV; *P* IV, p. 492; *EM*, p. 213.

48. Ibid., bk. IV; *P* IV, pp. 658, 491; *EM*, pp. 330, 213. On fashion clouding judgment, see ibid., bk. IV; *P* IV, p. 672; *EM*, p. 341.

49. Ibid., bk. IV; *P* IV, p. 651; *EM*, p. 325. Rousseau uses the analogy with Ulysses himself: see ibid., bk. IV; *P* IV, p. 490; *EM*, p. 212.

50. Ibid., bk. V; *P* IV, p. 835; *EM*, p. 457. For images of perfection, see ibid., bk. IV; *P* IV, p. 656; *EM*, p. 329. For ideas about right, see *Emile*, bk. V; *P* IV, pp. 833–49; *EM*, pp. 457–67, where Emile learns about the principles of the *Social Contract*. On edifying histories, see ibid., bk. IV; *P* IV, pp. 526–31; *EM*, pp. 237–40.

51. *Rousseau, Judge*, III; *P* I, p. 936 (cf. above, ch. 3, n. 11). *Emile*, bk. IV; *P* IV, pp. 522–23; *EM*, p. 235.

52. Geneva Ms., bk. I, ch. 2; *P* III, p. 287; *SC*, p. 161. *Emile*, bk. IV; *P* IV, pp. 600–01, 522–23; *EM*, pp. 290, 235. Cf. ibid., bk. I; *P* IV, p. 288; *EM*, p. 67. On Emile

using free will to elucidate conscience on his own, see ibid., bk. IV; *P* IV, p. 521; *EM*, p. 234: "The heart receives laws only from itself." Cf. Locke, *Human Understanding*, bk. I, ch. 2, §8, n. from the *Marginalia Lockiana*, cited in Alexander C. Fraser's edition [reprint New York, 1959], vol. I, p. 71n: "Conscience is not the law of nature, but judging by that which is . . . taken to be the law."

53. *Emile*, bk. IV; *P* IV, p. 691; *EM*, p. 354. *Contract*, bk. I, ch. 8; *P* III, p. 365; *SC*, p. 56. *Emile*, bk. V; *P* IV, p. 819; *EM*, p. 445.

54. *Emile*, bk. V; *P* IV, p. 817; *EM*, p. 444.

55. Ibid., bk. V; *P* IV, pp. 817–18; *EM*, p. 444.

56. *Sciences and Arts*, pt. II; *P* III, p. 30; *DS*, p. 64. *Emile*, bk. III; *P* IV, p. 426; *EM*, p. 165. Ibid., bk. V; *P* IV, p. 818; *EM*, pp. 444–45.

57. *Emile*, bk. V; *P* IV, p. 818; *EM*, p. 445.

58. Ibid., bk. V; *P* IV, p. 835; *EM*, p. 457.

59. *Contract*, bk. I, ch. 2; *P* III, p. 352; *SC*, p. 47.

60. *Mountain*, VI; *P* III, p. 807; see also ibid., VIII; *P* III, p. 842. On the difference between "natural law" and "natural right," see above, ch. 3, n. 11, and below n. 63.

61. "Political Economy"; *P* III, p. 248; *SC*, p. 214. *Contract*, bk. II, ch. 6; *P* III, p. 379; *SC*, p. 66. Cf. Geneva Ms., bk. II, ch. 4; *P* III, p. 327; *SC*, p. 189.

62. *Contract*, bk. I, ch. 8; *P* III, p. 365; *SC*, p. 56. Ibid., bk. I, ch. 6; *P* III, p. 361; *SC*, p. 53. For more on the general will, see above, ch. 3.

63. "First Sketch and Fragments of the Article 'Political Economy'"; *S* II, p. 296. Some controversy still surrounds the assertion that free will, though it may be enchained, repressed, and even "renounced," nevertheless remains an inalienable innate capacity for Rousseau. In the *Contract*, bk. I, ch. 6; *P* III, pp. 360–61; *SC*, p. 53, Rousseau himself speaks of the social compact as "an alienation made without reservations." But what he mentions each person giving up are "all his rights" (*tous ses droits*)—*not* those attributes that are his by "the natural law that commands us all" (see above, ch. 3, n. 11). "Power can perfectly well be transferred, but not will" (*Contract*, bk. II, ch. 1; *P* III, p. 368; *SC*, p. 59). Free will is not a conventional "right," it is a natural gift, possessed by all men equally. As such, it is inalienable, although, of course, a mutual *respect* for freedom—a civilized sense of *justice*—is, to Rousseau's mind, among the greatest fruits of association. Cf. *Inequality*, pt. II; *P* III, p. 184; *DS*, p. 168: "The right of property is only conventional. . . . But it is not the same for the essential gifts of nature, such as life and freedom, which everyone is permitted to enjoy, and of which it is at least doubtful that one has the right to divest himself. . . ."

It is because free will is inalienable that sovereignty—the general will—is considered by Rousseau also to be inalienable. On this point, Louis Althusser manages, as usual, to confuse things hopelessly, declaring with much fanfare that "Discrepancy I" in the *Social Contract* is the proposition that "*Total alienation*," including the alienation of freedom ("there can be no ambiguity") "*is the solution to the state of total alienation*." One step forward, two steps back? See Althusser, *Politics and History: Montesquieu, Rousseau, Hegel and Marx*, trans. Brewster (London, 1972), p. 127.

64. Geneva Ms., bk. I, ch. 7; *P* III, p. 310; *SC*, p. 178.

65. *Emile*, bk. V; *P* IV, p. 841; *EM*, p. 461 (emphasis added; cf. *Contract*, bk. I, ch. 6; *P* III, p. 360; *SC*, p. 53). *Rousseau, Judge*, II; *P* I, p. 813. On the increase in power through association, see *Contract*, bk. I, ch. 6; *P* III, p. 360; *SC*, pp. 52–53.

66. *Contract*, bk. I, ch. 7; *P* III, p. 364; *SC*, p. 55. The idea of a "true self" has been sharply criticized by Isaiah Berlin: see *Four Essays*, pp. 131–34 and passim.

67. *Contract*, bk. II, ch. 1; *P* III, pp. 368–69; *SC*, p. 59. Geneva Ms., bk. I, ch. 4; *P* III, p. 296; *SC*, p. 168. On tacit consent, see *Contract*, bk. II, ch. 1; *P* III, p. 369; *SC*, p. 59.

68. *Contract*, bk. I, ch. 7; *P* III, pp. 363–64; *SC*, p. 55. Cf. Geneva Ms., bk. I, ch. 2; *P* III, p. 287; *SC*, p. 161: "Will he listen to the inner voice?"

69. *Contract*, bk. I, ch. 7; *P* III, p. 364; *SC*, p. 55. "Fragments of 'Political Economy'"; *S* II, p. 296.

70. Plato, *Protagoras*, 323c, 323d–e, 324b. (As portrayed by Plato, Protagoras lacks Rousseau's clear grounds for his democratic claims: the essential equality of each man, thanks to the universal gift of free will). "Political Economy"; *P* III, p. 248; *SC*, p. 214 (it may be noted that if the free will wants only the good, it is a simple tautology, in the event of wrongdoing, to declare that a person has done what he did not "want"). *Contract*, bk. II, ch. 5; *P* III, p. 377; *SC*, p. 65. Cf. ibid., bk. IV, ch. 2; *P* III, p. 440n.; *SC*, p. 110n.: "It is only wrongdoers of all classes who prevent the Citizen from being free. In a country where all such men were in Galleys, the most perfect freedom would be enjoyed." See also John Plamenatz, "'Ce qui ne signifie autre chose sinon qu'on le forcera d'être libre,'" in Maurice Cranston and R. S. Peters, eds., *Hobbes and Rousseau* (Garden City, 1972), pp. 318–32.

71. "Political Economy"; *P* III, p. 249; *SC*, p. 215. Cf. *Contract*, bk. II, ch. 5; *P* III, p. 377; *SC*, p. 65: "Frequent corporal punishment is always a sign of weakness or laziness in the Government."

72. Remembering the image of Geneva helps to illuminate Rousseau's other notorious remark on freedom in the *Social Contract*:

> The constant will of all the members of the State is the general will; it is by it that they are citizens and free. When one proposes a law in the assembly of the People, what one asks them is not precisely whether they approve or reject the proposal, but whether it conforms or not to the general will that is theirs; each one, by voting, expresses his opinion of this, and by weighing the voices himself obtains the declaration of the general will (*du calcul des voix se tire la déclaration de la volonté générale*). When the opinion contrary to mine then prevails, that proves nothing except that I was deceiving myself, and that what I reckoned to be the general will was not. If my individual opinion had prevailed, I would have done something other than what I wanted (*que j'avois voulu*) [namely, to act in harmony with the wishes of others for the common good], it is then that I would not have been free.

(See *Contract*, bk. IV, ch. 2; *P* III, pp. 440–41; *SC*, pp. 110–11.) The customary translations of this passage, by making it sound as if a simple counting of votes were involved, renders the paradox needlessly unpalatable. Here, as elsewhere,

Rousseau imagines a process of mutual persuasion and thoughtful *deliberation*, not mindless balloting. See ibid., bk. IV, ch. 2; *P* III, p. 439; *SC*, p. 110: "When the citizens, fallen into servitude, no longer have freedom or will. . . . fear and flattery turn voting into acclamations; one no longer deliberates, one adores or curses." Cf. Rousseau's advice to Geneva on assembling itself to renew its constitution, discussed above, ch. 4.

73. Frithjof Bergmann, *On Being Free* (Notre Dame, 1977), p. 37. On free will and spontaneous motion, see above, and *Emile*, bk. IV; *P* IV, p. 574; *EM*, p. 272. See also ibid., bk. IV; *P* IV, p. 586; *EM*, p. 280, where the Vicar states that "my freedom consists in this, that I can will what is suitable to me or what I deem to be such, without anything alien to me determining me (*sans que rien d'étranger à moi me détermine*)." One wants to know, then, just what this *moi* considers *étranger*.

74. Bergmann, *Being Free*, p. 37.

75. For more on freedom and choice, see ibid., pp. 55–78.

76. Friedrich Nietzsche, *The Will to Power*, §603. Cf. Bergmann, *Being Free*, pp. 41–53.

77. Maurice Merleau-Ponty, *Phenomenology of Perception*, trans. Colin Smith (London, 1962), p. 395. For a discussion of the sociological evidence, see Berlin, *Four Essays*, pp. x–xiii, xxi–xxiii.

78. Aristotle, *Nicomachean Ethics*, 1113b. For Rousseau's explicit admission of the possibility of doing wrong with deliberation and choice, see *Emile*, bk. IV; *P* IV, p. 605; *EM*, p. 294.

79. If we may assume that people generally like being reassured that they are innocent and naturally good, their shortcomings the corrigible product of bad institutions, we may also guess why Rousseau's rhetoric could be so appealing to a generation of French revolutionaries.

80. *Emile*, bk. V; *P* IV, p. 856; *EM*, p. 472.

81. *Reveries*, VI; *P* I, pp. 1051, 1059, 1054; *RS*, pp. 120, 132, 125.

82. *Emile*, bk. IV; *P* IV, p. 575; *EM*, p. 273 ("scattered and dead matter"). *Rousseau, Judge*, II; *P* I, p. 849 ("temperament determined by necessity"). *Reveries*, VI; *P* I, p. 1059; *RS*, pp. 132–33 ("Je ne fais pas non plus ma volonté même, parce que je suis foible"). Cf. Starobinski, *La transparence*, p. 291.

83. Søren Kierkegaard, *The Journals of Søren Kierkegaard*, ed. A. Dru (London, 1938), §§1204, 1204, p. 436 (both notes date from 1841). I was led to this material by Grimsley, *Religious Quest*, pp. 141–42.

84. *Reveries*, VI; *P* I, pp. 1052–53; *RS*, pp. 122–23.

85. *Confessions*, bk. IV; *P* I, p. 162; *CO*, p. 158. *Rousseau, Judge*, II; *P* I, p. 857.

86. *Emile*, bk. II; *P* IV, p. 362; *EM*, p. 120.

87. "Political Economy"; *P* III, p. 250; *SC*, p. 215. *Contract*, bk. II, ch. 12; *P* III, p. 394; *SC*, p. 77. *Emile*, bk. II; *P* IV, p. 362; *EM*, p. 120.

88. For a brilliant study of Rousseau's "images of authority," see Shklar, *Men and Citizens*, pp. 127–64. In the *Confessions*, bk. I; *P* I, p. 15; *CO*, p. 26, Rousseau tells of how a spanking aroused his affection for the woman who spanked him and gave him such intense pleasure that he felt a constant urge therafter to beg

for a repeat performance: "Who would have thought that this punishment of the child, received at the age of eight at the hands of a woman of thirty, would determine my tastes, my desires, my passion, and my self for the rest of my life?" A similarly submissive sensibility emerges in Saint-Preux's relation to Wolmar in *La Nouvelle Héloïse*.

89. *Emile*, bk. V; *P* IV, p. 833; *EM*, p. 455. Cf. *Contract*, bk. I, ch. 2; *P* III, p. 352; *SC*, p. 47. On the great Legislator, see ibid., bk. II, ch. 6; *P* III, p. 380; *SC*, p. 67.

90. "Poland" [vi]; *P* III, p. 974; *PW*, pp. 186, 187. On the value of docility, see *Contract*, bk. II, ch. 10, *P* III, p. 391; *SC*, p. 74.

91. *Reveries*, VI; *P* I, pp. 1052–53; *RS*, p. 122 (this is about as close to the mood of Kant's thought as Rousseau ever gets). The two supplementary criteria just introduced considerably narrow the scope of what we may call being free, particularly in comparison with Bergmann's definition. However, to hold that a person, in order to preserve his feeling of freedom in society, needs to be *able* to deliberate with reasons and to take responsibility for acting is *not* to say that "being free always involves choosing and acting responsibly." Such an assertion seems false, for reasons develped by Bergmann.

92. *Reveries*, VI; *P* I, p. 1053; *RS*, p. 122.

93. *P* IV, p. 1442.

94. "Poland" [vi]; *P* III, p. 974; *PW*, p. 186.

95. For the image of natural freedom, see the passages discussed above, p. 173.

96. *Emile*, bk. IV; *P* IV, p. 587; *EM*, p. 281. Ibid., bk. II; *P* IV, p. 311; *EM*, p. 85 (cited below, p. 196). See also *Inequality*, pt. II; *P* III, p. 192; *DS*, p. 179, where, speaking of the natural man, Rousseau writes that he "breathes only repose and freedom"—apparently in a single breath. "He wants only to live and remain idle; and even the perfect quietude of the Stoic does not approach his profound indifference for all other objects." The hope of making virtue an inclination evidently lies behind Rousseau's uncompleted project for a "Morality of the Senses," or "The Materialism of the Wise." On a "physical basis," Rousseau had planned to show how "an external organization" could be "varied according to circumstances" in order to "maintain the soul in the state most favorable to virtue. From what errors one could save reason, what vices one could prevent from being born, if one knew how to force the animal economy to promote the moral order that it troubles so often!" See *Confessions*, bk. IX; *P* I, p. 409; *CO*, p. 381.

97. *Reveries*, V; *P* I, pp. 1046–48; *RS*, pp. 113–15. *Inequality*, pt. I; *P* III, p. 136; *DS*, p. 107.

98. *Reveries*, VI, *P* I, p. 1057; *RS*, p. 129. See Jean-Paul Sartre, *Being and Nothingness*, trans. Hazel E. Barnes (New York, 1956), pp. 93, 615, 620.

99. "Origin of Languages," ch. 9; *D* II, p. 361; *OL*, p. 45. *Sciences and Arts*, pt. I; *P* III, p. 12; *DS*, p. 43.

100. *Confessions*, bk. I; *P* I, p. 43; *CO*, p. 50. *Emile*, bk. I; *P* IV, p. 249; *EM*, p. 39.

101. *Emile*, bk. II; *P* IV, p. 311; *EM*, p. 85. Also see the passage from the *Confessions* cited above, n. 96.

102. On the hidden God, see *Emile*, bk. IV; *P* IV, p. 581; *EM*, p. 277: "This Being

which wills and has power, this Being active in itself, this Being, finally, whatever it may be, which moves the universe and orders all things, I call God. . . . He is hidden (*se dérobe*) equally from my senses and my understanding; the more I think about it, the more I am confused." On the public eye as a surrogate for God, see Rousseau's epigraph for some of the letters written late in his life: "Unfortunate blind men that we are! / Heaven, unmask imposters / And force their barbaric hearts / To open themselves to the gaze of men." (See *Correspondance générale*, vol. XIX, passim: almost all the letters written in 1770 are prefaced with this curious form of salutation.) Rousseau's suspicion of the abundance freedom can make possible—his fear that it will undermine happiness—marks his great distance from Kant and Hegel, both of whom welcomed, in freedom, the propsect of "infinite progress," the concept of man "himself as infinite"—a Promethean perspective that Karl Marx later made his own.

103. *Mountain*, IX; *P* III, p. 894.

104. *D'Alembert*, *D* I, p. 398; *LA*, p. 128. "Poland" [xii]; *P* III, p. 1019; *PW*, p. 244. *Sciences and Arts*, pt. I; *P* III, p. 8; *DS*, p. 37. The image of the good man as an "Athlete" indicates not only the power of the tacit will-as-muscle metaphor in Rousseau; it also suggests why the Spartan archetype was so appealing to him. If the will was something like a muscle, it needed strength, discipline, tone. Sparta offered an image of all three. Our comments here on the "public eye" may be related to Rousseau's desire for transparency, exhaustively discussed in Starobinski's unsurpassed study, *La transparence et l'obstacle*. Rousseau's thinking in this regard approaches the kind of "disciplinary society"—"a design of subtle coercion"—defined by Michel Foucault in *Discipline and Punish*, trans. Sheridan (New York, 1977), esp. pp. 209, 221–24.

105. Rousseau to M. [de Sartine, Lieutenant-Général de Police], January 15, 1772; *Correspondance génrale*, vol. XX, p. 124. On the significance of Rousseau's psychotic episodes and the ways in which they may be used to illuminate his characteristic convictions, see Starobinski, *La transparence*, p. 243.

106. His longing for lasting fulfillment is linked, in Rousseau's own existence, with his preoccupation with death. The most striking example of his obsession is perhaps a letter written in 1770: "Sir, I have lived; I no longer see anything, even in the array of possibilities, that could still give me a moment of true pleasure on earth. Were someone to offer me here below the choice of being what I want (*veux*) to be, I would reply: *dead*." (See Rousseau to M. de Saint-Germain, February 26, 1770; *Correspondance générale*, vol. XIX, p. 82.) Cf. *Emile*, bk. IV; *P* IV, pp. 604–05; *EM*, p. 293, where the Vicar, spurning worldly pleasures, speaks of the ultimate happiness he awaits: "I aspire to the moment, when, after being delivered from the shackles of the body, I shall be *me* (*moi*) without contradiction or division, and shall have need only of myself (*moi*) in order to be happy."

107. Speculation on the freedom that may characterize the immortal soul and an infinitely perfect God need not detain us here; but it is worth noting that the idea of peace as the *telos* of freedom seems to be of Christian provenance. See St. Paul's epistle to the *Romans*, ch. 8 (cf. ch. 12); cf. the comments of T. H.

Green in his essay "On the Different Senses of 'Freedom' as Applied to Will and to the Moral Progress of Man," esp. §§1–2, in Green, *Lectures on the Principles of Political Obligation* (Ann Arbor, 1967), pp. 2–5. On eschatological Parousia in Rousseau, see also Derrida, *Grammatology*, esp. pp. 246, 262. For an account of the ambivalence of other thinkers confronting the contingency of will, see Hannah Arendt, *The Life of the Mind* (New York, 1978), vol. II (*Willing*), esp. pp. 28–34.

108. *Héloïse*, pt. VI, viii; *P* II, p. 693. *Reveries*, V; *P* I, pp. 1047–48; *RS*, p. 115. *Emile*, bk. V; *P* IV, p. 821; *EM*, p. 447. Julie also voices dissatisfaction with an ironclad spartan discipline: see *Héloïse*, pt. III, xviii; *P* II, p. 364; *NH*, p. 255. For more on the temporality and nature of fulfillment in Rousseau, see Georges Poulet, *Studies in Human Time*, trans. Coleman (Baltimore, 1956), esp. pp. 167–72.

109. *Inequality*, pt. II; *P* III, p. 181; *DS*, p. 164. *Contract*, bk. III, ch. 9; *P* III, p. 420n.; *SC*, p. 96n.

110. *Contract*, bk. III, ch. 4; *P* III, p. 405; *SC*, p. 85. *Mountain*, VII; *P* III, p. 827. "Poland" [i]; *P* III, pp. 954–55; *PW*, p. 161.

111. Geneva Ms., bk. I, ch. 7; *P* III, p. 310; *SC*, p. 178.

112. *Contract*, bk. III, ch. 14; *P* III, pp. 427–28; *SC*, p. 101. Ibid., bk. II, ch. 4; *P* III, p. 375; *SC*, p. 63.

113. *Mountain* VIII; *P* III, p. 846. *Contract*, bk. II, ch. 1; *P* III, pp. 368–69; *SC*, p. 59.

114. *Contract*, bk. II, ch. 1; *P* III, p. 369; *SC*, p. 59. Ibid., bk. III, ch. 10; *P* III, pp. 422–23; *SC*, p. 98. Ibid., bk. III, ch. 15; *P* III, pp. 431, 429; *SC*, pp. 103, 102.

115. Rousseau's efforts are necessarily incomplete for two reasons: the "unprovable" enigma of the cipher 'free will' and the necessity for "inspired" readers to complete his text (see above, ch. 3).

Epilogue: *Democracy After Rousseau*

1. Cited in J. Christopher Herold, ed. and trans., *The Mind of Napoleon* (New York, 1955), p. 67.

2. See McKeon and Rokkan, eds., *Democracy in a World of Tensions*, p. 527 (Appendix III).

3. *Mountain*, VIII; *P* III, p. 838.

4. In French radical thought, the link between patriarchy and the idea of personal autonomy runs from Rousseau through Proudhon to Georges Sorel. It is an important strain in socialist thought that needs to be studied in more detail.

5. For a survey of conservative critics of Rousseau, see Cobban, *Rousseau and the Modern State*, pp. 22–31. The sourcebook for much postwar conservative criticism has been J. L. Talmon, *The Origins of Totalitarian Democracy* (New York, 1960 [first published, 1951]); for Rousseau, see pp. 38–49. For the position of Marxists, see, e.g., the remarks by Lucio Colletti in *From Rousseau to Lenin*, trans. John Merrington and Judith White (London, 1972), p. 157: "Rousseau did not even remotely perceive this problem of development. . . . In fact, Rousseau's program . . . foresees a *regression* from a developed market economy to the economic self-sufficiency of small tenant farming." Cf. Iring Fetscher,

"Rousseau's Concepts of Freedom in the Light of his Philosophy of History," in Carl Friedrich, ed., *Nomos IV* (New York, 1962), p. 56; Althusser, *Politics and History*, p. 159; and Soboul, "Robespierre and the Popular Movement," p. 67.

6. Leszek Kolakowski, *Main Currents of Marxism*, trans. Falla (Oxford, 1978), vol. I, pp. 2–3.

7. See Thomas Paine, *The Rights of Man*, pt. II, ch. 3 ("Of the Old and New Systems of Government"). Paine was the first important source through which French democratic ideas influenced the British popular movement: see Foner, *Tom Paine*, pp. 219–33. Paine identified his idea of democracy with the limited government of the American constitution: a fateful link originally intended to make his defense of the French Revolution against Burke's criticisms seem more attractive. For Robespierre, see above, ch. 6.

8. In my earlier discussion of Rousseau's constitutional plan for Poland, I emphasized his hostility to centralized power and his interest in federalism. Other commentators have given greater emphasis to the nationalist strain in his argument. His aversion to cosmopolitanism points in a similar direction; in effect, Rousseau's concern for customs and mores presages the preoccupation, in the nineteenth century, with defining a distinctively national culture. See Cobban, *Rousseau and the Modern State*, esp. pp. 99–125.

9. In my earlier discussion, I stressed that Rousseau's great Legislator is expected to prove his wisdom by leaving the society for which he has crafted laws: see above, ch. 3. For a contrasting interpretation that stresses the sinister aspects of the legislator and points out the links between Rousseau's lawgiver and the idea of dictatorship, see Talmon, *Origins of Totalitarian Democracy*. Rousseau himself discussed dictatorship in the *Social Contract*, in the course of surveying Roman institutions. In ancient Rome, recourse to one-man rule was considered legitimate at times of military emergency: "In such a case, the general will is not in doubt." A dictatorship was nonetheless a temporary expedient, by Roman law limited to six months' duration. "The suspension of legislative authority does not abolish it." The sovereignty of the people either remains intact, or a legitimate dictatorship becomes an illegitimate tyranny. "The magistrate who silences [the legislative authority of the people] cannot make it speak; he dominates it, without being able to represent it. He can do anything, except make laws." (See *Contract*, bk. IV, ch. 6; *P* III, p. 456; *SC*, pp. 121–22.)

10. The present work is in part an attempt to collect the evidence linking Rousseau with the modern tradition of direct democratic action. In this regard, however, it should be stressed that the sans-culottes of year II also held decidedly mixed feelings about federalism. In principle, they supported the idea, since it would empower their own neighborhood assemblies; in practice, however, they feared that their own aspirations might be jeopardized by the conservativism of provincials. This was a contradiction played out within many subsequent democratic movements.

11. Benjamin Constant, *De l'esprit de conquête et de l'usurpation*, in *Cours de politique constitutionnelle* (Paris, 1861 [first published, 1818–20]), vol. II, p. 210; quoted in Jens A. Christophersen, *The Meaning of "Democracy"* (Oslo, 1966), p. 52.

12. For Bentham, James Mill, and democracy, see Elie Halévy, *The Growth of Philo-*

sophic Radicalism, trans. Mary Morris (Boston, 1955), pp. 251–64, 412–17. The evolution of Bentham's ideas in an avowedly democratic direction is traced by Halévy to his friendship with Francis Place, which began in 1812. Place, a veteran of the radical societies of 1792, was, like many members of these societies, influenced by Tom Paine in his favorable outlook on democracy as a form of government. See also Christophersen, *Meaning of "Democracy"*, pp. 93–100. For the status of the word *democracy* in America at this time, see ch. 6, n. 77; and Charles Beard, *The Republic: Conversations on Fundamentals* (New York, 1943), pp. 30–33.

13. Alexis de Tocqueville, *Democracy in America*, trans. George Lawrence (Garden City, 1969), pp. xiv (author's preface to the 12th edn. [of 1848]), 13 (vol. I, author's introduction), 740 ("Report given before the Academy of Moral and Political Sciences on January 15, 1848, on the subject of M. Cherbuliez's book entitled *On Democracy in Switzerland* [reprinted as Appendix II in the 13th ed., the last published under Tocqueville's supervision]). On the idiosyncrasies of Tocqueville's use of the term *democracy*, see Jack Lively, *The Social and Political Thought of Alexis de Tocqueville* (Oxford, 1965), pp. 49–50. For John Stuart Mill and Tocqueville, see J. S. Mill, "M. de Tocqueville on Democracy in America," in *Mill's Ethical Writings*, ed. J. B. Schneewind (New York, 1965), pp. 107, 109. Mill himself was wracked with doubts about democracy, fearing that a witless majority might lord it over the rest for the benefit of their own selfish interest as "operative classes," thus spoiling society for those with moral virtue, refined taste, and a superior education; hence his hostility to any form of radical democracy, such as the binding instruction of elected representatives. See Mill, *Representative Government*, ch. 12.

14. In associating liberal democracy and imperialism, I have in mind the covergence of reform and militarism in the careers of politicians like Joseph Chamberlain and Theodore Roosevelt. In his ideas about *Führerdemokratie*, Max Weber made this convergence explicit in theory. See Weber, *Economy and Society*, ed. Guenther Roth and Claus Wittich (Berkeley, 1978), pp. 268–69, 984–85, 1132–33.

15. For the details of Babeuf's program, see Buonarroti, *Babeuf's Conspiracy*, pp. 161–62n., 166–67, 171, 183, 188. Dictatorship, in the classical sense of extraordinary rule by one man, was actually rejected by Babeuf, who insisted that any such temporary power be exercised by a group. The holders of "extraordinary authority" were "to be charged with the double function of *proposing to the people a plan of legislation simple, and suited to ensure to it equality, and the real exercise of its sovereignty; and to dictate provisionally the preparatory measures necessary to dispose the nation to receive it.*" (See ibid., p. 105.)

16. On Buonarroti and Blanqui, see George Lichtheim, *The Origins of Socialism* (New York, 1969), pp. 21–25. It might be thought that Karl Marx belongs in this tradition. For a discussion of why he does not, see Hal Draper, "Marx on Democratic Forms of Government," in Miliband and Saville, eds., *The Socialist Register 1974* (London, 1974); and, for a thoroughly documented demonstration, Richard N. Hunt, *The Political Ideas of Marx and Engels* (Pittsburgh, 1974), vol. I ("Marxism and Totalitarian Democracy, 1818–1850"). Also see below, n.

18. Lenin's indebtedness to Blanqui is another question entirely. Although convinced that "'broad democracy' in party organization," was, under the circumstances of czarist rule, "nothing more than a useless and harmful toy," Lenin also believed that the self-governing soviets, first formed by workers and soldiers in Saint Petersburg during the abortive revolution of 1905, pointed the way toward what he called "the revolutionary-democratic dictatorship of the proletariat and peasantry." This dictatorship, organized under the leadership of Lenin's own Bolshevik party, was to subordinate the soviets as instruments for realizing social democracy. Lenin, like Babeuf, expected the dictatorship to be temporary. The aim, no longer moral regeneration, became industrial modernization; once a dynamic economy was set in place, the state was to "wither away." For a compact survey of different usages of the word *democracy* by Bolshevik authors, see Christophersen, *Meaning of "Democracy"*, pp. 252–70. For a useful comparison of Bolshevik theory with the actual fate of the soviets in 1905 and 1917, see Oskar Anweiler, *The Soviets*, trans. Ruth Hein (New York, 1974); and, more recently, Alexander Rabinowitch, *The Bolsheviks Come to Power* (New York, 1976).

17. The impression has sometimes been left that these efforts at direct democracy constitute a fortuitous tradition, with similar institutional devices being generated spontaneously in quite different situations; this is Hannah Arendt's thesis in *On Revolution* (New York, 1965), p. 266. In fact, we face a more complex and structured pattern, characterized in almost all instances by a more or less conscious recourse to differing national traditions of popular militancy and political discourse, resulting, in different countries, in popular democratic movements pursuing notably different aims. For example, the members of the Russian soviets of 1905 wanted the right to elect delegates to a representative constituent assembly—in the Russian context, a revolutionary demand, but nevertheless a plan worth distinguishing from the more radically democratic arrangements pursued by the Parisian sans-culottes in year II. For the national tradition of political protest emerging from the French Revolution, see Cobb, *The Police and the People*, esp. pp. 169–71, 210–11. Cobb discusses the ways in which militant dispositions were passed on within sans-culottes families, despite the discontinuities otherwise separating the movement of year II from the revolutionary agitation of the 1830s. An adequate comparative history of direct democratic movements in modern Europe has yet to be written.

18. Arendt, *On Revolution*, p. 267. Besides Marx, who will be discussed in a moment, socialists who have devoted thought to the problem of direct democracy include G. D. H. Cole, the British Guild Socialist influenced by Rousseau; the council communists of the twenties; and the contemporary group of Yugoslavian theoreticians interested in expanding their country's experiment in self-management to include the government as well as industry. For Cole, see particularly *Social Theory* (London, 1920), which lays out his Rousseauist principles; and *Guild Socialism Re-Stated* (London, 1920), an attempt to detail what these principles might look like in practice, if applied in the setting of a modern industrial nation. For a good selection of essays reflecting the Yugoslav perspective, see *Self-Governing Socialism*, Branko Horvat, Mihailo Marković, and

Rudi Supek, eds., (White Plains, N.Y., 1975). In this context, see also Carole
Pateman, *Participation and Democratic Theory* (Cambridge, 1970).

Marx's attitude toward democracy is complex. In his early writings, he praised
"true democracy" for allowing "the constitution" of a state to appear transparently as "the free product of men," thus forming "the first true unity of the
universal and the particular." By "true democracy," he meant an egalitarian
community in which the laws represented the self-conscious "self-determination
of the people"—a form in which the state would disappear as an alien power
dominating the associated individuals. (See Marx, *Critique of Hegel's "Philosophy
of Right,"* in Marx and Engels, *Works*, vol. III, p. 30.) But Marx soon became
convinced that demands for democracy might be misunderstood. The real
problem was not simply political, but also social. Mere legal reforms would
leave untouched the material constitution of domination—the social contract
of capitalism, daily renewed in the exploitative relations between capital and
labor.

Absorbing the idea of popular sovereignty into his own hopes for a classless
society, Marx came to base his outlook not on the realization of democracy, but
rather on a transitional rule of the proletariat, that distinctively modern class
"with *radical chains*" whose drive to "redeem itself," he conjectured, would spell
the "*total redemption of humanity*," through the dissolution of all class relations.
The aim of self-rule could no longer be properly called "political" at all: "Where
its organizing activity begins, where its *own aim* and *spirit* emerge, there socialism throws its *political* hull away." (See Marx, "Toward the Critique of Hegel's
Philosophy of Right: Introduction"; and idem, "Critical Marginal Notes on the
Article 'The King of Prussia and Social Reform'"; both in Marx and Engels,
Works, vol. III, pp. 186, 206.)

Politics of a sort nevertheless remained essential for Marx, if only as the
vehicle through which the proletariat could organize itself for the class struggle.
On this score, Marx, when confronted with the Paris Commune of 1871, felt
an instinctive affinity not for the elitism of the Blanquists, but rather for the
simple democratic program of the heirs to Rousseau (in this case, a strange
mélange of Jacobins and Proudhonists). In the Commune, he claimed to see a
strategically viable vessel for his hopes, a government of municipal councilmen
"chosen by the suffrage of all citizens, responsible and revocable in short terms,"
with a majority that "would naturally consist of workmen or acknowledged
representatives of the working class." While Marx thus expected that the French
proletariat would naturally follow a democratic path to communism, he also
insisted that the coming upheaval would ultimately be "a Revolution against
the State," whether its form be "legitimate, constitutional, republican or Impe-
rialist." (See Marx, First Draft of *The Civil War in France*, in Marx and Engels,
Writings on the Paris Commune, ed. Hal Draper [New York, 1971], pp. 154, 150.)

Unfortunately, Marx was wrong about the Parisian events he chronicled: the
insurgents of 1871 were remarkably like the Parisian insurgents of 1792, 1830,
and 1848: artisans, journeymen, apprentices, independent producers, professionals, and only a few laborers in the new factory industries. Though the
Commune of 1871 may be regarded as the last efflorescence of the French

NOTES TO PAGE 208

popular culture of politics Rousseau helped to define three generations before, it is far more difficult, particularly in the light of modern historiography, to find in it a harbinger of an international proletarian revolution. (Cf. Stewart Edwards, *The Paris Commune: 1871* [New York, 1971], p. 360.)

Moreover, where proletarians formed no "natural majority" of society, the strategic value of the Commune model seemed questionable. Thus Lenin, while in theory admiring the 1871 Commune (see *The State and Revolution*), in practice felt compelled to postpone self-rule, turning instead to a dictatorship that has long outlasted its original justifications. In truth, there is no living legacy like the one Marx projected: there is no communist society that might redeem the bloody defeat suffered by the Communards and all those radical democrats who have come after.

19. For the fate of socialist democracy under Stalin and his successors, see Roy A. Medvedev, *Let History Judge*, trans. Coleen Taylor (New York, 1971), pp. 534–37; and, more generally, his *On Socialist Democracy*, trans. Ellen de Kadt (New York, 1975). For contemporary fears in the West of an "excess of democracy," see Michel Crozier, Samuel Huntington, Jr., and Joji Watanuki, *The Crisis of Democracy* (New York, 1975), esp. pp. 113–15.

20. Walter Benjamin, *Illuminations*, trans. Zohn (New York, 1968), p. 255 ("Theses on the Philosophy of History").

Index

Abundance: and freedom, 103; and decay, 118; Rousseau suspicious of, 197, 255*n.102*. *See also* Luxury

Acton, Lord, 1–2

Agents: vs. representatives, 71, 80; in French Revolution, 151, 154

Alembert, Jean Le Rond d', 14–15, 55, 57, 79

Alienation, end of; and democracy, 4, 108–09, 202; in Alpine city, 36, 44; and sovereignty, 64; and French Revolution, 145, 160; and freedom, 196–98, 209; and death, 255*n.106*

Althusser, Louis, 251*n.63*

American Revolution: political theories in, 114, 140, 159–60, 205, 235*n.10*; and Rousseau, 140, 241*n.25*; mentioned, 4

Anarchism, 208

Ancient constitution: in Alpine city, 40; in Geneva, 88, 92–93, 96, 97, 101; in political theory, 94

Arendt, Hannah, 208, 259*n.17*

Aristocracy: in Geneva, 15–18, 67, 68–69; in republican tradition, 110, 112–13, 115, 222*n.64*; in French Revolution, 143, 157, 158

—in Rousseau: as form of government, 65, 67, 83, 105–07, 109, 118; as best government, 79, 83, 88, 106–07, 129; as form of sovereignty, 88, 107

"Aristo-democracy," 17, 73, 115, 237*n.31*

Aristotle: on politics, 41, 110–11, 112, 113, 222*n.64*; on wrongdoing, 188

Artisans: in Geneva, 15, 51, 57, 102; in French Revolution, 135, 143, 150, 162, 260*n.18*

—and Rousseau: in early life, 18, 57, 137;

on virtues of, 31, 118, 225*n.26*; as hero to, 51, 162

Assemblies: in ancient Athens, 42, 90; in French Revolution, 150–51, 152, 155, 156, 157–58; and direct democracy, 205–06, 207–08, 257*n.10*

—in Rousseau: in Alpine city, 37–38; in the *Social Contract*, 71, 131; as subversive of Genevan constitution, 81, 92; in Geneva, 89, 90, 92, 107, 231*n.3*; in federations, 128. *See also* General council

Athens: classical democracy in, 4, 41, 111, 222*n.64*; Rousseau and, 18, 42, 90, 121, 203; Plato and, 41–42; in Genevan political debates, 86, 90; Tom Paine on, 205

Authority: Rousseau's view of, 2, 90, 109; in Alpine City, 38; in a democracy, 91, 109; Robespierre on, 158; in education, 176, 191; concealment of, 191, 192

Autonomy. *See* Freedom; Independence

Babeuf, François Noel (Graccus), 137, 207, 244*n.58*, 258*n.15*

Bad. *See* Wrongdoing

Barbeyrac, Jean, 119

Barrillot, Jacques, 20

Bastille: fall of, 138, 142, 147

Beaumont, Christophe de, 84

Benjamin, Walter, 208

Bentham, Jeremy, 206, 257–58*n.12*

Bergmann, Frithjof, 185–86

Berlin, Isaiah, 166

Berne, 82, 83, 107, 126, 194

Berthier, G. F., 139–40

Blanqui, Louis-Auguste, 207, 258–59*n.16*

Bodin, Jean, 120

Body: and free will, 73, 168